Beyond Marx and Market

Outcomes of a Century of Economic Experimentation

Klaus Nürnberger

Cluster Publications
Pietermaritzburg

Zed Books Ltd
London & New York

1998

First published in Africa
in 1998 by
Cluster Publications,
P O Box 2400,
Pietermaritzburg, 3200
South Africa.

ISBN 1 875053-10-7

Published in the rest of the world by Zed Books Ltd, 7 Cynthia Street,
London NI 9JF UK, and Room 400, 175 Fifth Ave, New York, NY, USA in 1998.

Distributed in the USA exclusively by St Martin's Press, Inc., 175 Fifth Ave, New
York, NY 10010, USA.

The right of Klaus Nürnberger to be identified as the author of this work has been
asserted by him in accordance with the Copyright, Designs and Patents Act, 1988.

A catalogue record of this book is available from the British Library.

ISBN 1 85649 647 3 cased
1 85649 648 1 limp

Cover and diagrams: Klaus Nürnberger
Editing: Jacquie Withers
Design and typesetting by ARTWORKS,
Layout by Shakila Chetty and Gaylene Jablonkay

Printed and bound by
The Natal Witness,
Printing and Publishing Company,
P O Box 362,
Pietermaritzburg, 3200
South Africa.

The financial assistance of the Centre for Science Development towards the
publication of this work is gratefully acknowledged. Opinions expressed in this
publication, and conclusions arrived at, are those of the author and are not to be
attributed to the Centre for Science Development.

Contents

Preface   ii

Chapter 1
Introduction: The economic problem in a nutshell   1

Chapter 2
The liberal model - free enterprise capitalism   28

Chapter 3
The egalitarian model - socialism   52

Chapter 4
Radical socialism - Marxism-Leninism   68

Chapter 5
The two compromises - social democracy and
democratic socialism   108

Chapter 6
Two Third World models - Tanzania and Taiwan   131

Chapter 7
Value assumptions of liberalism and socialism   158

Chapter 8
Directions for the future   186

Epilogue - Faith and Economics   223

Annotated bibliography   242

Index and glossary   260

Preface

The chapters of this book evolved from my lectures during the heyday of ideological conflict. There was a need at the time for simple and factual information as a basis for serious discussion. When it came to capitalism and socialism, most students thought they knew which of the two ideologies came straight from the devil, and which was the panacea for all social problems! "Capitalism" and "communism" were simply curse words on alternate sides of the ideological divide. Slogans, prejudices and rationalisations bedevilled the discussion. After the course their arguments had *gained both in depth and competence*. It is this experience which gave me the confidence to offer the work to a wider public.

Recent opinion surveys in South Africa have revealed the wildest ideas about what the words capitalism and socialism actually mean. And South Africa simply reflects the international scene. For many people economic concepts have come to *express emotional needs,* rather than precise ideological content. In a situation of vast economic discrepancies, the affluent need reassurance that they are entitled to their privileged position. The disadvantaged need reassurance that their claim to a greater share in the economic pie is legitimate. Decades of Cold War propaganda have added to the confusion.

But people have to make sense of the situation. They even have to vote for or against parties which stand for "free enterprise" or which call themselves "socialist" or "communist". As one author has put it, "'the 'truth' is often buried beneath mountains of information" (Glaeser 1987:270). My aim is to survey the field and point out the directions. I want to lead the discussion beyond sterile confrontations of the past and towards the needs of the future. After wading through masses of impressive research, the question remains: Where do we actually want to go? What is the ultimate goal of organising a national economy?

This book deals specifically with *economic systems and ideologies.* They have to be seen against the background of the emergence and growth of some of the most intractable problems with which humanity is currently confronted, such as overdevelopment and underdevelopment, marginalisation and poverty, the depletion of resources and the destruction of the biosphere, the development of ever more sophisticated armaments and the rise of conflict potential. Chapter 1 offers a brief summary of these phenomena. It is only meant to place the subject matter of this book in its overall context. In a companion volume, *Prosperity, Poverty and Pollution* (Pietermaritzburg: Cluster Publications, 1998), I shall deal more profoundly with the economic structures, mechanisms and mindsets which give rise to these problems. The two texts complement each other.

Some of the chapters in this book are updated versions of previous publications, notably Klaus Nürnberger: *Socio-economic ideologies in a Christian perspective.* Durban: Lutheran Publishing House, 1979, and James Leatt, Theo Kneiffel and Klaus Nürnberger (eds): *Contending ideologies in South Africa.* Cape Town: David Philip, 1986.

I owe gratitude to the University of Natal both for a furlough and a research grant to complete this work. My wife was willing to do without me for a considerable length of time. The following persons have rendered assistance in various ways and at various stages: Megan Walker, Portia Derby, Prof Norman Bromberger, Peter Langerman, Hermann Knothe, Dr Marylee James, Jacquie Withers, Belinda Yiangou of Y Press, Shakila Chetty and Gaylene Jablonkay of Artworks - and of course my students who contributed with their pithy comments, challenging questions and engaged debates.

Klaus Nürnberger
Pietermaritzburg, January 1998

CHAPTER 1

Introduction: The economic problem in a nutshell

The aim of the book as a whole

The world changes rapidly. Not so long ago most people either feared, or looked forward to, a communist takeover. With the collapse of Marxism-Leninism in Eastern Europe most people seem to believe that the debate between capitalism and socialism is over. But the problems which gave rise to the debate have intensified rather than diminished. And so the debate will take on new forms, but it cannot be over.

What are these problems? We are witnessing *explosive growth* in all directions: growth in productive capacity among the rich; population growth among the poor; wasteful opulence and grinding misery; meteoric success stories and mass marginalisation; globalised competition for markets and rapid depletion of fossil fuels; increasing erosion and environmental pollution; growing conflict over diminishing resources and the proliferation of increasingly lethal weaponry. Of late all these historical processes seem to be accelerating.

The debate on these issues has become more urgent than ever. But a repetition of the old slogans will take us nowhere. To gain *freedom* for the future we must shake off the shackles of the past. To gain *directions* for the future we must understand how we got to where we are. We need to know what has worked and what has failed. We have to decide what we want to achieve and what we want to avoid. Deeper still, we need to reflect on what humankind is *supposed* to strive for, if it is to retain its humanity.

If there is one lesson to be learnt from the past, it is that economic policies can make or break a nation. Now that the East-West conflict seems to be over, at least for the time being, the clash between rich and poor again demands centre stage. And this again must be viewed in the context of humankind's total dependence on its natural environment. *Which insights can be gained from a century of struggle between the two economic giants,* capitalism and socialism? Radical socialism has failed. But socialism was merely a response to the persistant failure of capitalism. With capitalism in full control of the global economy, are we simply going to stagger along without thought and orientation, minding nothing but our petty interests of power, privilege and gain?

This book offers an *analysis* of the ideologies and systems of capitalism and socialism and their various adaptations. It also looks at the actual *perfor-*

mance of each. The failure of Marxism-Leninism, the greatest experiment in social reconstruction in human history, receives particular attention. Lessons are drawn from the contrasting experiences of two *Third World countries* of roughly comparable size and history, Tanzania and Taiwan. *Value assumptions* underlying the great social alternatives are subjected to critique. And on the basis of this stock-taking exercise a way *into the future* is mapped out.

My aim was to use a simple non-technical language, which should be accessible to any educated person. If you encounter unfamiliar concepts, please look up their meaning in the Index at the end of the book, which also serves as a glossary.

The aim of this chapter

The present chapter is an introduction to the economic problem as a whole. It serves to sketch the background against which the discussion of capitalism and socialism has to be seen. Section I gives reasons for the *persistence* of the "great economic debate" after the end of the Cold War. Section II offers an analysis of the economic contradictions and imbalances which sustain the debate. It also spells out causes and possible remedies. These reflections form the criteria for assessing the truth of the ideological arguments and the actual performance of the systems in question. They also offer suggestions for constructing the future. Section III contains a *survey* of the analyses of capitalism, socialism and its variations which will be found in the rest of the book.

Section I - The end of the "great economic debate"?

Humankind has experimented with different variations of two basic economic systems, capitalism and socialism, for more than a century. What has been the outcome? The last two decades have seen the gradual decline and the ultimate collapse of Marxism-Leninism in Eastern Europe, while its great rival, capitalist liberalism, has gone from strength to strength. After the fall of the Berlin Wall a *triumphant mood* took hold in Western liberal circles. Communism had proved a failure; the "free market" and "free enterprise" approach had been vindicated.[1] There were analysts who predicted that the 20th century will one day be known as the period in which two great totalitarian systems — fascism and communism — came and went.[2] Capitalism would continue, they said, though it would be a system undergoing major crises and adaptations.[3]

Even the *appeal of moderate socialism* declined sharply. The neo-liberal approach of authors such as Friedrich von Hayek and Milton Friedman found political expression in what was called *Reaganomics* in the United States and *Thatcherism* in the United Kingdom. President Clinton has given up the moderate welfare stance of the Democratic Party.[4] In former bastions of social democracy, such as Sweden and West Germany, conservative parties came to power. Communist regimes in Africa collapsed or changed course. African Socialism was abandoned.[5]

A few smaller South East Asian countries, adopting an aggressive, state-directed, export-oriented, capitalist approach, emerged from backwardness and began their spectacular ascent towards the status of industrial nations. Taking their clues from these successes, the World Bank and the International Monetary Fund imposed structural adjustment programmes on bankrupt Third World economies and forced their governments to abandon their welfare policies. Socialists, whether they had believed in Marxism-Leninism or not, were pushed into the defensive and forced to rethink their positions.[6] In fact, the very concept of socialism is in disarray.[7] The title of a 1992 article summarises the situation rather well: "What's left of what's left? Or: what does it mean to be a socialist today?"[8]

On the strength of these spectacular developments many economists and politicians have come to believe that the contest was over. Some spoke of the end of ideology, even of the end of history: free enterprise and a market economy had triumphed and would be the system of the future.[9] But there are a number of considerations which suggest that the debate on economic systems and ideologies will continue, albeit in new forms:

First, capitalist liberalism did not offer a solution

Marxism-Leninism as a social system has indeed proved to be a failure. But Marxism was a response to a problem, namely the failure of capitalism. Granted, it was an inadequate, even a deceptive response. Yet the problems posed by the failure of capitalism have not disappeared. On the contrary; despite all adaptations of the system to changing situations, the urgency to find a more appropriate response has increased, rather than diminished.[10]

I am not referring to the fact that the end of capitalism has been predicted again and again by economists and philosophers ever since Karl Marx's famous analysis.[11] The real failure lies in the fact that capitalism has not succeeded in eradicating *mass poverty*, reducing the *vast discrepancies* in income and wealth and preserving *the natural habitat* of humanity. It has not even tried. In fact, there are powerful indications that it was, and still is, primarily responsible for generating these problems.[12]

Most arguments raised against this thesis can easily be dismissed. It is true, for instance, that *the economy can grow* and that, if the pie grows bigger, the share of everybody also becomes bigger. But growth does not automatically lead to greater equity. In fact, although the share of everybody may grow, the shares of the rich grow faster and bigger than the shares of the poor.[13] This advantage can again be used by the rich to further improve their relative positions. Moreover, recently the phenomenon of jobless growth, combined with the marginalisation of the work force, has begun to rear its head. Only deliberate correctives can balance out these discrepancies.

It is true that some of the richer economies have mellowed the impact of capitalism through *welfare policies*. They have largely overcome poverty and secured a standard of living unheard-of in past history for the average man and woman on their streets. But the impression that capitalism levels out incomes is misleading. In the first place it is socialist correctives which have led to greater balance in these countries. In the second place rich countries can afford to distribute their wealth more evenly *within* their own societies, while discrepancies between rich and poor nations continue to rise. In the third place these correctives are now under heavy attack in various social democracies.

Many economists believe that the *newly industrialising nations* in South East Asia have shown the way forward for the Third World with their export-led growth policies. But in the first place these policies do not follow classical capitalist patterns. In the second place there are indications that the historical conditions of their rapid growth have been unique.[14] Their achievements cannot simply be replicated by the bulk of the Third World, or by the former Marxist-Leninist countries for that matter.[15] We shall return to these observations in chapter 6.

Even if greater prosperity and greater equity could be achieved through capitalist growth, where should the resources come from and what would the costs be to the *environment?* The entire industrial economy, including its highly productive agricultural sector, is built on strictly limited reserves of fossil fuels. Over time, these are bound to become scarce and, ultimately, unaffordable for poorer societies. So far there are no cheap and safe replacements in sight. Unless the whole character of our agricultural and industrial economy changes, growth in economic output means growth in the depletion of resources and the pollution of nature. Should the masses in India and China indeed reach the levels of consumption presently enjoyed in the United States, Europe and Japan — would the natural fabric of our biosphere be able to bear the pressure?

There is no doubt that the world capitalist economy is undergoing *fundamental changes*. There are those who maintain that capitalism no longer exists because Western countries have mixed economies.[16] Some believe that we are entering a new phase of history altogether: "That the new society will be both a non-socialist and a post-capitalist society is practically certain".[17] But will this "brave new world" simply be a new, amplified version of the old, with its horrendous economic discrepancies and its reckless destruction of the biosphere? Indications are that indeed it will be.

Meanwhile left-wing activism has <u>changed from Marxist macro-economics,</u>

which has fallen to pieces, to small scale community activities. *Ideology has made way for romanticism* about the symbolic universe of the marginalised or, alternatively, about a few isolated environmental issues. This is simply not good enough. While the emphasis on community empowerment at grass roots level is certainly important, and while we do not want elephants and rhinos to die out, it is the macro-economic structure which constitutes the overpowering context of grass roots development and an ecologically sustainable future. The urgency of justice and balance in the system has not subsided but increased and will have to be placed, once again, very forcefully on the agenda.

At present these are mere questions and hypotheses which must still be argued. All we are saying at this stage is that the answers to our economic problems have not as yet been found. Of course, we can point to a whole series of such failures in economic history. Feudalism and mercantilism are cases in point. But that is no comfort. We have to understand where we are and how we got there. We need to decide where we want to go and how to get there. And we have to scrutinise our ends and our means against the background of basic human values.[18]

It is for this reason that we deal with socialism, and especially with Marxism-Leninism, quite extensively. We cannot afford to lose the *insights to be learnt* from this giant experiment in social engineering, its achievements, its problems and its demise.

Second, the power of past history

Even if we had all the answers, we could not simply *climb out of our history*. The past determines the present and leads us into the future. For a long time to come, the consequences of Marxism-Leninism will determine Eastern European countries, just as the consequences of apartheid will determine Southern Africa.

This is also true for the *power of tradition*. The theory of an economic ideology may become obsolete. But the grievances are still there; the emotions still seek expression; the old arguments can still be heard; the leaders still find the rhetoric convenient; the literature is still available. A tradition has power in society and it is not prudent to overlook it.

Third, the power of collective interests

Ideologies do not represent basic, irreducible truths which convince people merely on the strength of empirical evidence or indisputable logic. Research has shown that attitudes towards capitalism and socialism *change as people move up or down the social ladder.*[19] Such shifts from one ideology to another also occur with the rising prosperity or economic decline of whole countries or regions. They also occur over time. It is likely that after the current swing to the right, there will be a swing to the left.

The power of ideologies lies in the fact that *they legitimate collective interests* with sets of rationalisations. There are people whose needs are fulfilled, and people whose needs are not. Those who suffer tend to believe that they have become the victims of injustice. They call for socialist reforms because it is in their interest to do so. Those who benefit tend to believe that they have achieved their superior situation by their own effort. They defend "free enterprise" because it is in their interest to do so. Collective interests also determine power politics. There are people who believe that another Cold War may be in the offing with China as the emerging new superpower.[20] What kind of ideology will inform Chinese politics in the future?

There is also a "spiritual" dimension to collective interest. Some people have *identified* with a particular cause, party and ideology. They have invested their lives, happiness, careers, status, and dignity in it. They have willingly suffered enmity, ostracism, and persecution for it. It is not easy to concede error and accept defeat. At the moment it is the "left" which is in this unenviable situation. It has lost its foundations and its self-confidence.[21] Recently erstwhile supporters of apartheid have been thrown into a similar situation. Believers in liberal capitalism may also face the moment of truth not too far into the future. The point is that you want to cling to a past which, for a long time, has given meaning, legitimacy and authority to your life.

Fourth, the role of values in society

There are those who are fed up with opportunism. They want to get rid of ideology, look at the facts in economics and be pragmatic in politics. These are brave sentiments, with which we wholeheartedly agree. But *objectivity and pragmatism alone cannot do the trick*. Imperialism, slavery, even genocide, have been based on hard-nosed analysis and pursued with singular efficiency. The question is what we want to see when being objective, what we want to achieve when being pragmatic. As responsible human beings we cannot avoid asking some very fundamental questions concerning the purpose and meaning of human life, whether in the science of economics or in the practice of economic politics.[22]

Responsibility is guided by values. We must not only know what we want to achieve, but also *what we are supposed to want to achieve* and for what reasons. We cannot simply drift into the future guided by personal desires and collective interest. At a time when, through science and technology, humankind has acquired powers unheard-of in past history, this has become far too dangerous. It is also not worthy of the human being and a mature society. We are meant to be in control of our lives and our worlds.

The basic values which are widely accepted today by different groups in society include freedom, power and prosperity; economic sufficiency and equity; long term sustainability of the economy and respect for nature. Such values will *seek to entrench* themselves in social systems and their variations. But they are also contradictory — thus containing the potential for conflict. It is for good reasons that Western economies have become mixed economies and that the right mix has become the issue.

The value assumptions of the author

So we cannot do without ethics. We shall base the argument in this book on a set of ethical assumptions which need to be made explicit before we continue. Economics is not, and can never be, a "value free science". While it is important for any academic discipline to be as factual and objective as possible, it must account for its presuppositions, its goals and its procedures.

As I see it, economics should have the following agenda: (a) ways must be found to *protect the natural habitat* on which not only human life but all life on earth depends; (b) ways to secure the material prerequisites of the *life, health and a modest level of prosperity* for all human beings, (c) ways to ascertain that the wealth generated by human creativity, and the sacrifices necessary for its production, are *distributed fairly*, (d) ways to care for those who are *unable to make a contribution*, even under conditions of equal opportunity, and (e) ways to *balance out* the satisfaction of the various kinds of human need. Material needs, for instance, should not be allowed to crowd out cultural or spiritual needs and vice versa.

At the root of these goals are fundamental requirements for a healthy communal life: to overcome suffering, to make space for initiative and creativity, and to normalise disturbed social relationships. If economics is meant to serve humanity, this should be the broad agenda both of economic policies and of economics as an academic discipline. Obviously economics and economic policies currently have a very different kind of agenda, otherwise it would not have been necessary to write this book.[23]

Our tasks in this book

Our first task is to *obtain clarity* on the concepts we use. What precisely do we mean when we speak of liberalism, socialism or Marxism? There is widespread confusion in the population about these concepts. Then we have to *analyse* the economic systems concerned. How did they come about? How are they constructed? What causes discrepancies in productivity, income, wealth and power? What are the most likely remedies?

Then we have to evaluate the *past performance* of the systems that have been implemented.[24] Have they had the whole spectrum of human needs in view? Have they diagnosed the causes of economic problems correctly? Have they tried to address them in a balanced way? In what respects were they successful? What precisely went wrong and why? Can they be ethically justified, and on the basis of which criteria?

Then we have to look at *the way forward*. Can particular failures be overcome without abandoning underlying values? Can Marxism-Leninism, for instance, become truly democratic? Can capitalism become truly free? Can either of them become ecologically responsible? Alternatively, is it possible to design a *synthesis* which combines the advantages of both systems and avoids their disadvantages? Is there an approach where values translate into a sort of flexible pragmatism, rather than into a fixed ideology?[25]

Questions

Revision: What are the reasons for studying capitalism and communism after the end of the Cold War?

Application: Which groups in your country still hold powerful liberal and/or Marxist convictions? Can you assess their relative impact on society?

Critique: (a)"You seem to be one of those who will not accept that the free market system has been proved superior by history to all kinds of socialism."
(b) "The working classes will continue their struggle in spite of your bourgeois denigration of their cause." How would you react to these statements?

Section II - Economic realities which sustain the debate

So far we have argued that the debate on capitalism and socialism will continue to be high on the agenda, not least because the disturbing situation which sustains this debate will not simply go away. What is this situation? In this book we provide only a brief summary of detailed analyses offered in *Prosperity, Poverty and Pollution*.[26] The aim of this summary is to place the debate on capitalism and socialism in its actual social context.

Anybody can see that there are rich people and poor people around. There are also rich countries and poor countries. Often the discrepancies between affluent and poor are extreme. When asked why this should be the case, people offer *contradictory sets of reasons*. Some focus on personal virtues and vices such as industriousness and efficiency versus laziness and poor performance. Others believe that the problem is located in the exploitation of the poor by the rich. Some say that the level of technological development determines the level of affluence or poverty in a society. Others believe that there are conspiracies among ruling elites which keep the poor in their subservient position.

Academics join the fray: theologians and moralists tend to blame all miseries on the sinful or asocial behaviour of human beings. Political scientists are more interested in social structures which cause economic discrepancies, whatever the motivations of the people operating within these systems. Even econ-

8

omists and sociologists are not agreed on the roots of the problems.[27] If we are to find our way through this maze, we must engage in *serious analysis*. For our purposes a simple overview of the economic problem must suffice.

The economic process

The economic enterprise consists of five major stages: *extraction* of raw materials from the resource base, *processing* of these materials into usable commodities, the *distribution* of these commodities, their *consumption* and their ultimate dumping as *waste*. We can also add *services* to commodities. They are the result of the extraction and transformation of human energy and time into useful activities. If there is poverty, something has gone wrong within or between these stages:

- The *resource base* may be too small to cater for the needs and wants of the population — or the needs and wants of the population may be too high for their resource base. In other words, people live beyond their means.

- The technical processes of *extraction, processing and distribution* may be underdeveloped, inefficient, or unbalanced.

- It is possible that the *flow of the output* of the economic enterprise is distorted; some get more, and others get less than their share. Part of the population may actually crowded out of the process altogether. We call this marginalisation.

- There may also be problems in the patterns of *consumption*. A society may indulge in luxuries and waste resources, while basic social and ecological needs are not addressed.

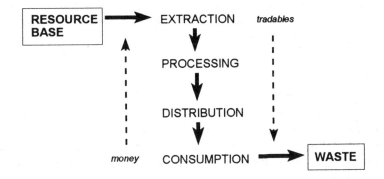

The use and abuse of power

These observations lead us to a much more fundamental problem. One of the most outstanding peculiarities of human beings as creatures is their ability to build up economic power. This can manifest itself in two ways: the growing ability to exploit nature more efficiently through advances in technology, and the accumulation of power by some human beings at the expense of others.

In the first case *nature is the victim.* When people were few on earth there was space for all and nature could absorb the impact. Nevertheless irreversible destruction of nature occurred even in antiquity. The denuded and rocky slopes of Greece were once covered by flourishing forests. They were chopped down by the Phoenicians, among others, to build their fleets. In recent times humanity has begun to multiply rapidly. At the same time it developed a rapidly expanding industrial economy. Both growth processes cannot but spell disaster for the natural environment. Disaster for the environment is tantamount to disaster for humanity, because humanity depends on biosphere for its survival and prosperity. Unlimited growth is not possible on a limited planet.

In the second case it is *people who are the victims.* As the power of some grows, the power of others becomes more confined. The losers may become totally disempowered. In other words, economic development is "asymmetrical", or unbalanced. There are centres of economic power, where productive potential and commercial activity develops very rapidly, and there are economic backwaters or peripheries, where economic development stagnates.

Curiously the *growth of population numbers* follows exactly the opposite pattern — at least for the time being. In economic centres population numbers remain constant, while in economic peripheries the population tends to grow rapidly. As a result we find growing discrepancies in power and prosperity between the two kinds of populations. Such discrepancies again lead to the rise in conflict potential, the build-up of armaments and war.

The growth of the industrial economy, the growth of the population, and the growth of destructive weaponry all have an impact on the natural environment. This, in a nutshell, is the structural problem of economic reality. Let us spell it out in some more detail.

Centre and periphery

As mentioned above, economic potency and activity tend to gravitate towards certain *geographical centres.* The area surrounding such a centre then becomes its *periphery.* Smaller centres belong to the periphery of larger centres. This pattern is found in the world as a whole, in a continent such as Europe, in a region such as Southern Africa, in a country such as Swaziland, in a city such as Johannesburg, even in a farming area where the local shop and police station form the centre for that environment.

Economic potency also tends to gravitate towards certain *population groups*. Income statistics show that in most societies we find a tiny minority with very high incomes, a majority with fairly low incomes and a gradual transition between these extremes. Applying the core-periphery paradigm to this phenomenon we can speak of the economic elite of a country as the centre population, and the less privileged majority as the peripheral population.

It can also be shown that, particularly in Third World countries, there is a tendency for *the centre population to remain stable in number while its economic potency grows.* By contrast, there is a tendency for *the peripheral population to grow in numbers while its economic potential remains constant or declines.* This phenomenon is partly concealed by the fact that impoverished rural populations flock to urban centres. Urban centres tend to grow demographically while rural areas are depopulated. But it is the peripheral population, not the centre population, which grows in urban centres.

When we take into account not only the income but also the *needs* of the respective population groups, we find that in the centre the income is higher than the need, while in the periphery the need is higher than the income. So there is an *affluence gap* in the centre and a *poverty gap* in the periphery. Since the need tends to grow in the periphery while the income tends to grow in the centre both the affluence gap and the poverty gap also tend to grow.[28]

Causes of economic discrepancies

What are the causes of this universal and disconcerting phenomenon? Depending on their need for legitimation, some people believe the main cause to be the greed of the rich, while others maintain that it is the lack of diligence or development on the side of the poor. But such simplistic answers will not do. Reality is characterised by a *complex network of causes* of which we can distinguish at least the following dimensions.

The first thing to remember is that the present situation is *the outcome of a historical process.* Part of this history is Western colonialism and imperialism. But exploitation as such has not lead the exploiters to self-sustained growth of productive capacity.[29] The robust and dynamic economy witnessed today in industrialised countries is based on the scientific-technological approach to reality, the industrial mode of production and sophisticated means of communication, all of which have emerged in the West over long periods of time. Once set in motion, technological progress tends to accelerate.

The rate of change during the 20th century has become breathtaking. And those who are in first gear are likely to be left behind by those who are in fourth gear. Other cultures have also witnessed changes in their respective histories, but in other directions and at a much slower pace. They have also been disturbed profoundly by the impact of Western cultural domination. *To catch up* with accelerating technological developments and to compete with highly efficient modes of production is a formidable task, particularly when the prevalent cultural assumptions and social institutions are not geared to the demands of the industrial age and when the owners of the latter have no intention of giving others a chance to adapt and become competitive.

Within this broad historical framework we can categorise the following types of factors:

- There are factors which enhance the growth of economic potency in the *centre* (C factors), factors which inhibit the growth of economic potency in the *periphery* (P factors) and factors which are due to the unbalanced or asymmetrical *interaction* between centre and periphery and which benefit the centre rather than the periphery (C/P factors).

- All three types of factors must again be divided into *structural mechanisms*, which function automatically once a system is in place, and the deliberate use of power. There is a dialectical relation between social structures and collective consciousness, which determines the way power is used.

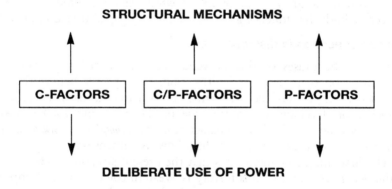

The structural sphere consists of *institutions*. There are institutions which enhance economic flow and others which obstruct it. This depends both on the underlying rationale of an institution and on its efficiency. The precision of the drill of a king's guard of honour produces no economic benefits; the efficiency of the computer system of a multinational corporation does.

The sphere of deliberate use of power is characterised by *motivations*. Institutions are kept in place by mindsets, that is, by internalised sets of assumptions, values, norms and procedures. They are formed by childhood socialisation, education, training and interactive learning. Mindsets have an almost determinative impact on behaviour because they contain implicit or explicit incentive systems: you are rewarded if you satisfy the respective requirements and punished if you do not.

Depending on the nature of these requirements, they can lead either to progress or stagnation; they can be either obsolete or state-of-the-art; they can be geared either to frugality and aestheticism or to consumption maximisation; they can promise either honour and glory or profit and growth; they can demand either humility and obedience or self-assertion and self-realisation; they can lead either to stability and harmony or to revolutionary change and competition.

An example of *structural* mechanisms inherent in the *centre* is the cumulative growth of technological sophistication and investment capital (C factor). In the *periphery* there is very little expertise and capital and what is not there can also not grow (P factor). An example of a structural mechanism located in the *relation* between centre and periphery is the fact that the centre offers greater opportunities to gifted people than the periphery, thus draining the periphery of the cream of its population (C/P factor). A more serious structural mechanism is the marginalisation of the peripheral economy through unbalanced market interaction.[30]

On the side of motivations one finds the deliberate *use of power to further one's interests.* The centre population generates power and quite naturally uses it to its advantage and at the expense of others. In traditional societies the use of potential for private gain is viewed as a crime and severely punished. In liberal societies the development of initiative and potential for private gain is not only allowed, but strongly encouraged. It is assumed that if you cannot compete you have only yourself to blame.

If traditionalism *begins to interact* with modernity, the latter will quite naturally out-manoeuvre the former. The whole modernist frame of mind is geared to the competitive struggle, while that of traditionalism is geared to upholding the stability and harmony of the social system. People have not learnt to defend themselves against the onslaught of the competitive spirit. Once the more competitive get an edge over their rivals, they can actively dismantle the remaining competitiveness of the latter.

Abuse of power and structural mechanisms reinforce each other and lead to ever widening discrepancies. There may be statutory controls to reduce the overt abuse of power in the capitalist system. If the elite has managed to *monopolise the powers of the state*, however, it can abuse its power without democratic checks and balances. The same is true in a situation of anarchy. This is what tends to happen at the international level because there is no world government which could check the abuse of economic clout.

As mentioned above, a powerful cause of discrepancies between centre and periphery is the *rapid advance of technology*. It is both a C factor and a C/P factor. Because of more highly developed techniques the products of the centre outcompete the products of the periphery. As a result, demand in the periphery switches to centre products and peripheral producers lose their markets. Without production the peripheral population loses its income. Those who have no income are "dispensable" as far as the economy is concerned, because they form neither part of the supply (production) nor of the demand (consumption) on the market.

In order to survive, the periphery population *sells its factors of production*, notably labour and raw materials, to the centre instead of using them for its own production. But due to technological developments the centre no longer needs a lot of unskilled labour for its production. As a result a growing part of the peripheral population drifts out of the formal economic process. This is called *marginalisation*.[32]

Marginalised people the world over have *large families*. It seems to be a general biological rule that threatened organisms respond to danger by multiplying rapidly. In social terms the absence of old age security seems to make large families a necessity. But large families find it even more difficult to make ends meet. And for the population as a whole the relation between needs and resources further deteriorates. It is a vicious circle.

All these factors are underpinned by processes which happen in our minds. In a system of feedback loops, the structures of a society shape the collective consciousness of the people concerned, while these structures are again shaped by the collective consciousnessof the people.

Liberal economists tend to emphasise the structural factors inherent in the centre and the periphery, while radicals (or neo-Marxists) tend to emphasise the unbalanced structural relation between the two.[33] Liberals also have a tendency to emphasise mental factors, while Marxists emphasise structural factors. The model of causation presented in this text attempts to integrate all relevant factors in a balanced way.[34]

Consequences and possible remedies

The consequences of these developments are highly undesirable. *Grinding mass poverty* is, of course, the most serious of them. *Excessive wealth* is not very wholesome for the elite either; *great discrepancies* in standards of living within a society lead to envy, resentment and frustration on the side of the poor and to arrogance and fear on the side of the rich. *Conflict potential* grows and may explode into a cycle of rebellion and repression, even escalate into civil war. Or it may find expression in crime. Competing nations struggle to secure dwindling resources and invest valuable resources in armaments. We have mentioned the impact of overpopulation, industrial overdevelopment and armed conflict on the *natural environment*. All these factors together lead to *massive suffering*. So if we want to be responsible we cannot afford to be complacent about these developments.[35]

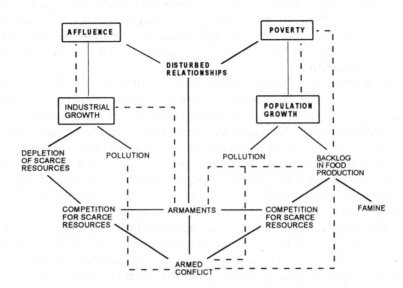

How can we come to grips with a problem of such complexity? To find preliminary answers to this question we need to follow up the causes we have analysed. *Abuse of power* can only be curtailed by legal institutions and law-enforcement agencies. It is not the freedom to take economic or technological initiatives that must be controlled, but the abuse of power which such initiative generates. Only the state - or a system of legally binding treaties between states and supervised by an International Court of Economic Justice - can do that. Equality of opportunity must become firmly entrenched as a political principle and a legal norm.

The interaction between unequal partners must be balanced out in two ways. First, *captive economies must be liberated*. Captive economies are peripheral economies which have become heavily dependent on centre economies. Their production may have collapsed, so that they are forced to sell their factors of production to the centre; or they have accumulated vast debts; or they can be held to ransom by the buyers of a single export product; or they are tied into crippling agreements such as military treaties. Heavily indebted Third World countries on which the IMF has imposed structural adjustment programmes are good examples.

The second way to balance out the interaction between unequal partners follows from this: Where discrepancies escalate, due to structural mechanisms, *countervailing processes must be institutionalised.* At the national level some of the economic power of the centre must be channelled into the infrastructure needed by the periphery for its development. Progressive taxation, used to pay for free and universal education, is a good example. The state can also decide to grant tax relief for employment generation rather than labour saving technology. When fuel prices are raised, animal traction may again become competitive.

At the international level, untenable debts must be written off to give poor economies a chance to develop and conserve their natural resources. Tariffs and trade agreements between states must balance out the superiority of highly developed economies. All this presupposes a new mind-set. We must learn to develop solidarity with the disadvantaged and those who are not yet born.

The *centre* has to change from large scale wastage of resources to minimal utilisation and recycling; from profit maximisation to the creation of meaningful employment; from luxury consumption to balanced need satisfaction; from greed to responsibility; from short term to long term concerns; from quantitative growth of industrial production and consumption to growth in the quality of the products and the environmental quality of life. Procedures can be made more efficient and less material-intensive. Products must again be characterised by quality and longevity. Energy must be made more expensive through taxation, so that labour and alternative sources of energy become more competitive and the environment suffers less harm![36]

In the *periphery* the quantitative growth of the population must make way for the growth of quality of life. Rather have two well-fed and well-educated children than ten street urchins without a future.

Experience has shown that the peripheral population must actively take over the responsibility for its own social and economic upliftment - nobody can do it for them. Development is based on interactive learning processes, the emergence of incentive systems and the evolution of efficient institutions. What the centre, the state or development agencies can do is to create *free space* for the initiatives of local communities to flourish and the *infrastructure* necessary to make development possible. The establishment of transport facilities and communication networks is a good example.

The first priority of the periphery must be to become self-sufficient in providing the *basic prerequisites of life* for its own population and only in the second place to develop into a more powerful trading partner which can interact on more equal terms with the centre. The constant flux of comparative advantages on world markets must be keenly observed and fully exploited.

A different problem is how to change obsessive and obstructive *beliefs, per-*

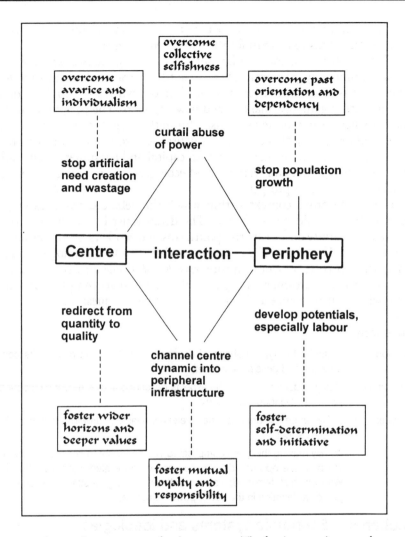

ceptions, values and norms among both partners. The basic questions are how traditional societies can add free initiative to communal responsibility (that is, how they can overcome traditions which obstruct progress), and how modernist societies can add responsibility to free initiative (that is, how they can overcome mindsets which are obsessed by self-interest).

In both cases the *horizons must widen* from the narrow concerns of communities (in the case of traditionalists) and the narrow concerns of interest groups (in the case of modernists) to include concern for the society as a whole at a national level and the whole of humankind at an international level. Horizons must also widen in terms of time from short term satisfaction to concern for generations to come, thus to concern for the natural environment.

These goals may sound utopian but *they make profound economic sense.* They are also immensely practical. There is nothing irrational or impossible in these goals as such. The centre will not lose out when the periphery develops, but rather gain new markets and new suppliers. The periphery will not lose out when its population stabilises, but rather begin to share some of the power and prosperity of the centre. Equalisation also reduces conflict potential; so resources can be channelled into capital and consumer goods, rather than arms production and warfare. And ecological sensitivity is the presupposition of long term prosperity.

This is the broad context within which the debate between capitalism and socialism should be conducted. The detail must be worked out by an interdisciplinary team of experts, politicians and workers on the ground in various fields. The point to be made here is that economic ideologies and systems, whether past, present or future, *must be able to give account* of their policies and their performances against this particular complex of needs. Otherwise their relevance and legitimacy are open to question.[37]

Questions

Revision: Describe the typical shape of economic structures, its causes, its consequences and possible remedies.

Application: Can you detect some of the aspects described above in your own country? And in a neighbouring country?

Critique: (a)"When people are poor, they are either unable or unwilling to work, it is as simple as that."

(b) "By making things so complicated you only want to conceal the fact that the poor are oppressed, exploited and discriminated against by the rich." With which statement do you sympathise? Could your stance be due to your particular location in the social power structure?

Section III - Economic systems and ideologies

The previous section was devoted to the *economic problem in general*. After sketching deficiencies of the global economy we offered afew broad suggestions on how to overcome them. When looking at the current predicament we may want to ask: could it be the overall organisation of the economy which is wrong? More profoundly, could a deceptive ideology underlie this organisation? Rather than tampering with the existing order, should we not rather ask: *which kind of system* causes such problems and will continue to do so, no matter how much we try to correct it? And which type of system could possibly yield the desired results? That is the question addressed in this book.

The attempt to dismantle the existing system and *construct a new one*, rather than trying to patch it up, has been characteristic for revolutionaries throughout the ages. It has sparked off a debate and a struggle in our century that has cost countless lives and which, in view of the weaponry at the disposal of the warring factions in the 20th Century, could have spelt the end of humankind. It is of incredible importance for the future that these issues be clarified and that a common way forward be found.

Rather than designing a theoretical blueprint on the drawing board, which may prove to be unworkable in practice, it seems prudent to look at the theory and the performance of *actual systems* which have been in operation for some time in various parts of the world and draw our conclusions from there. This is what we intend to do in the following chapters. Before we enter into these detailed discussions, it may be useful to give a brief survey of the argument as a whole.

During the long history of humankind a great variety of social, economic and political structures have emerged. Just glance through a few books on anthropology and you will get an impression of the great variety of systems that existed in the Third World alone before the advent of Western colonialism.[38] Concerning *economic* systems, it is convenient to distinguish the following in historical order:[39]

- Traditional *communalism* based on subsistence agriculture, as found, for instance, in sub-Saharan Africa.
- Societies based on *slavery*, as found, for instance, in the ancient Roman Empire.
- *Feudalism*, as found in mediaeval Europe.
- *Pre-industrial capitalism*, based on trade and colonial exploitation.
- *Industrial capitalism*, based on the industrial revolution.
- *Modern Western capitalism*, based on technological progress, in particular on the advance of information technology.
- *Marxism-Leninism*, a revolutionary response to capitalism which concentrates all power, including economic power, in the hands of a one-party state.
- *Social democracy*, which combines capitalist development with social securities.
- *Democratic socialism*, a Marxist system which moves in the direction of greater freedom and a market economy.
- *Third World socialism*, for instance African Socialism in Tanzania, which attempts to utilise African traditions to institute a modern socialist order.[40]

Capitalist liberalism and Marxist-Leninist socialism

In the world of the 20th Century the *dominant alternatives* have been free enterprise capitalism and Marxist-Leninist socialism. Because the latter is an extreme form of socialism, we found it prudent to devote a chapter to socialism in general before dealing with Marxism-Leninism in this book.

Capitalism has evolved in conjunction with a liberal spirit in which the freedom, rights and obligations of individual citizen against the state and other authorities have become the paramount consideration. The rights of the individual include the right to own property. "Free enterprise" is the right to take economic initiatives, compete or contract with others on the open market, and accumulate economic potentials for private gain.[41]

This principle has unleashed an economic dynamic of *efficiency and productivity* unheard of in previous history. But it has also led to incredible *discrepancies* in income and wealth. The reason is simply that people are not equally competitive and advantages in competitiveness can be used to undermine the competitiveness of others further.

Marxism-Leninism was a radical response to capitalism. It attempted to mobilise the collective power of the disadvantaged majority (the proletariat) to overthrow the capitalist elite (the bourgeoisie) in a revolutionary struggle, to install what it calls the "dictatorship of the proletariat", led by the communist party, to eradicate all vestiges of the capitalist structure and mentality, and then hopefully to usher in what it termed the "classless society", where no human would dominate any other human.

In fact, the opposite has happened. The Marxist programme has led, once again, to a massive *concentration of power* in the hands of a small elite. In as far as the leadership was sincere, this power could be used to attain a considerable measure of equality within the population. That this has not necessarily been the case is common knowledge. Moreover, the command system, the totalitarian philosophy, and the pervasive control of a clumsy and corrupt bureaucracy over all dimensions of life have had the effect of stifling the economy.[42]

Social democracy and democratic socialism

It is understandable that these contradictions have spurred the respective societies to try and compute a system which retains the advantages of both systems and avoids their respective pitfalls. Since the positive aspects of the one system are virtually identical with the negative aspects of the other, this can only mean that *some sort of compromise* had to be found. Note that a compromise between two alternatives is not a third alternative. Two such compromise systems have actually emerged over the last couple of decades: social democracy and democratic socialism.[43]

Social democracy (also called welfare capitalism or a social market economy) is a capitalist, free-enterprise system that has been modified considerably in the direction of egalitarian principles, such as equality of opportunity, social securities, and participation in decision making. The system has proved to be highly successful. Sweden, the prototype of a social democracy, is one of the richest countries in the world.[44] As stated earlier, however, the pendulum has again swung to the right in social democratic countries.[45]

Democratic socialism was the mirror image of social democracy. It was a Marxist system which had been modified considerably in the direction of entrepreneurial initiative and a free market, without sacrificing the concepts of state control and equal distribution of income. For quite some time the only operative democratic-socialist state was Yugoslavia. Other attempts in Eastern Europe and Latin America have been crushed before they could prove their worth. The Yugoslavian system was reasonably successful under the leadership of Marshall Tito. Then it began to show signs of severe economic strain and finally disintegrated in ethnic violence.

With the spectacular *collapse of Marxism-Leninism* in the Soviet Union and Eastern Europe in 1989, a new situation emerged. Some formerly communist states, such as the Soviet Union, tried to move in the direction of democratic socialism.[46] But when the iron grip of the Marxist system loosened, the economy went into a tailspin. The Soviet empire itself disintegrated and its constituent parts followed their own lines.

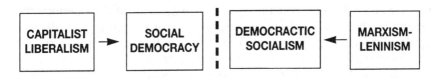

The Chinese leadership clung to power by letting the spirit of free enterprise out of the bottle under tight political control. Marxist-Leninist regimes in Africa and elsewhere in the Third World quietly changed course or went out of business. The communist regimes in Cuba and North Korea, and a few parties like the Shining Path in Peru and the Khmer Rouge in Cambodia, try to survive but their appeal has dissipated.

Pent-up desires for the glittering affluence seen on Western television programmes made capitalism, for the bulk of Eastern European populations, the dream for a better future. But *disillusionment* soon had to set in. A workable free market system cannot be instituted overnight. While the majority of these states do not seem to want to go back to Marxism-Leninism, their course of action has become uncertain.

The four systems we have mentioned have determined the debate during the 20th Century. We need to remind ourselves, however, that they *do not exhaust the possibilities*. Nor can it be assumed that they are applicable to conditions obtaining in non-industrialised or semi-industrialised countries. We shall analyse two further systems, therefore, that emerged in the Third World.

The first, *African Socialism in Tanzania*, tried to utilise African traditions and build on the principle of self-reliance. Though its underlying philosophy was widely acclaimed, the system could not survive and had to be abandoned. The second is the *Taiwanese system*. It pursued the goal of becoming integrated into the capitalist world economy through export-oriented industrialisation. It was highly successful both in terms of economic growth and equity. As stated above, however, it is not clear that this approach can be made applicable to other Third World countries.[47]

Underlying these systems we find deep-rooted *value alternatives*. Capitalism is built on the value of freedom, socialism on the value of equality. Both these values are important. Both become self-defeating when pushed to extremes. A situation must be created, therefore, where an optimum of freedom is combined with an optimum of equality. So far social democracy has been most successful in approaching this ideal. But much is left to be done, especially on the international level.

With this bird's eye view of the entire argument we are ready to go into detailed analyses and assessments. We shall begin with a survey of the *classical types*, a critique of their theory and an assessment of their performance. Because we need to combine responsibility with feasibility the failures of socialism merit our particular attention. This will take us through the next five chapters. In chapter 7 we shall try to sort out the underlying *values*, especially the dialectics between freedom and equality. In the final chapter we shall suggest some *directions for policy decisions*. An epilogue will deal with the important relation between *faith and economics*.

Questions

Revision: Describe four socio-economic systems and say, with reasons, which of them you think is most acceptable both in terms of ideology, practical performance and human values.

Application: Which of the types does the system in your country resemble most closely? Substantiate your answer carefully, weighing all the evidence.

Critique: (a) "You speak like a typical Western bourgeois who believes his own exploitative system to be the best and who is not in solidarity with the suffering masses of the Third World."

               (b) "If you still believe in the merits of socialism after its collapse in Eastern Europe you must be blind." Comment.

Let us summarise

The dramatic collapse of the Soviet Union at the end of the 1980s brought an end to the Cold War. The giant Marxist-Leninist experiment of social reconstruction had proved to be a failure. In the West, even moderate socialism has come under pressure for some time now, while neo-classical capitalism found expression in "Reaganomics" and "Thatcherism". So for many the "great economic debate" was over.

We have seen, though, that *this verdict is premature*. Capitalism fails to solve the problems of mass poverty, vast discrepancies in wealth and ecological destruction. The social constructs of the past continue to determine the present and bedevil our way into the future. Collective interests seek legitimation and utilise old arguments. Contradictory values inform and fuel the debate. All this makes it imperative that we have another close look at what has happened and what we can learn from it.

It is impossible to bypass *ethical* questions. We drew up five priorities on the economic agenda: ecological sustainability, material sufficiency for all, equity in the distribution of sacrifices and benefits, provision for the weak and vulnerable, and balance in the satisfaction of the whole spectrum of needs. To put them into practice we must obtain clarity on our concepts, analyse the economic factors which gave rise to the present problems, evaluate the past performance of current systems in relation to these problems, and seek a responsible and workable way forward.

This book is meant to subject current systems and ideologies to scrutiny. To see this task in context, we sketched the *main phases of the economic process*, namely extraction, processing, distribution and consumption, which operate between the resource base on the one hand and the rubbish dump on the other. We saw that economic imbalances can be caused either by inefficiencies anywhere along this line, or by powerful population groups who overexploit nature or crowd others out of the system.

To give an idea of how this happens we introduced the *centre-periphery model*: in the economic centres of the world productive capacity grows with constant population numbers, while in the economic peripheries the population grows faster and productivity stagnates. The *consequences* are misery, conflict and ecological destruction.

The *causes* of this phenomenon include both structural mechanisms and the use of power. The use of power again depends on the particular mind-set of the actors concerned. Some of these factors are located in the centres, others in the peripheries, and yet others in the asymmetrical interaction between centres and peripheries.

Remedies include curtailing the abuse of power through legal institutions, switching centre production and consumption from quantity to quality, boosting the productive capacity of the periphery, arresting population growth, and institutionalising processes which counteract the effects of asymmetrical interaction.

The failure of current arrangements, however, raises the more fundamental question whether we should not simply demolish the existing order and construct a new one, rather than patching up a system that fails to deliver the goods. This question led us to the debate and the struggle over *alternative economic systems.*

We discussed two basic modern systems, *free enterprise capitalism and Marxist-Leninist socialism.* The strength of the former is its emphasis on economic freedom, while its weakness is that it causes rampant economic discrepancies. The strength of the latter is its emphasis on equality, its weakness is its authoritarianism. Freedom enhances productivity, authoritarianism stifles it.

To get out of this impasse, two compromises have emerged in the 20th Century. *Social democracy* is a free enterprise system modified in the direction of socialism; while *democratic socialism* was a Marxist system modified in the direction of free enterprise. From the many systems applied in the Third World we chose two of particular relevance: self-reliant socialism in *Tanzania*, which failed, and export-oriented capitalism in *Taiwan*, which succeeded. The indispensable but contradictory values underlying these systems are freedom and equality.

Notes

1   See Bertoud in Sachs 1992:70ff

2   "At the end of the twentieth century, Hitler and Stalin aprear to be bypaths of history that led to dead ends, rather than real alternatives for human social organization" (Fukuyama 1992:127).

3   Drucker 1993 goes so far as to speak of a "post-capitalist" society.

4   Martin Walter in *Mail & Guardian* Aug 30, 1996.

5   In 1986 Barry Munslo could still write a book about "Africa: problems in the transition to socialism." In 1993 Arnold Hughes' book "Marxism's retreat from Africa" is more pertinent.

6   Hain 1996; Cleaver in Sachs 1992:234ff; Kenworthy 1990; note that Peter Moll 1991 speaks of a "radical's guide" in his title while what he presents is simple social democracy. For European socialists see Michael Elliot in *Newsweek* Oct 10, 1994, 12ff; and Newsweek , Oct 10, 1994.

7   Scott Arnold in Paul et al 1992:3ff.

8   Streeten, P in The Review of Black Political Economy 21/1992, 5-18.

9   Most prominent among these, perhaps, F Fukuyama 1992.

10   Cf Preston 1983 46f.

11   The great American theologian and social philosopher, R Niebuhr, for instance, believed in 1932 that the end of capitalism had arrived and the inevitable victory of socialism was at hand. Harries 1986:159, 168,173, 178 etc.

12   It is revealing to look at the critique of Marxism by a liberal classic: Rostow 1990:145ff. Rostow pinpoints some of the flaws in Marxist philosophy and policy, yet he shares some of these flaws, for instance, the certainty that technological achievement and economic growth will place humanity as a whole beyond scarcity within a few decades from now. "But on one point Marx was right ... the adventure of seeing what man can and will do when the pressure of sacracity is substantially lifted from him" (page 166).

13   Say the pie grows from a 1000 to 2000 and the shares between the rich and the poor remain constant at 90% and 10% respectively. Then the share of the rich grows by 900 from 900 to 1800, while the share of the poor grows by 100 from 100 to 200.

14   See for instance the nine points quoted by Vogel in Reynolds 1988:1ff. Cf Fontaine in Fontaine, Jean-Marc (ed) 1992: Foreign trade reforms and development strategy. London/NY: Routledge, page 5 and his reference to Cline.

15   "The lesson ... is that it will be extremely difficult to turn Eastern Europe into a region of market economies ... Briefly, the performance of poor capitalist countries since their reform has been terrible." Diane Flaherty (Center for Popular Economics, Amherst, MA) in an undated, unpublished paper on Can markets work in Eastern Europe? See also Bardhan & Roemer 1992:103.

16   "Has there really been a high-noon showdown in which pure capitalism outperformed *pure* socialism? Or was the triumph a triumph of the mixed economy over bumbling bureaucracies? Were Mises and Hayek right that such bumbling is *generic* not singular?" P A Samuelson in: Basu, K, Majumdar, M & Mitra, T (eds): *Capital, investment and development*. Oxford: Blackwell, pp 255.

17   Drucker, P F 1992: The post-capitalism world. *Public Interest* 109/1992, 89-100, p 92.

18   Chang 1992:1.

19   See for example my book Power and beliefs in South Africa, part II.

20   *Newsweek* April 1, 1996 (special report) pp 10ff.

21 They argue, for instance, that it is Stalinism which has proved unworkable, not Marxism-Leninism. Cf Cleaver in Sachs 1992:236, 242ff. Or they claim that the Soviets have made a mess of a valid and precious programme which, given a chance, could very well succeed. See e.g. Bottomore 1990. As we shall see in chapters 4 and 5, the facts do not seem to bear out this contention.

22 The theory of science has long established that complete objectivity is impossible. Even the natural sciences have realised that experiments depart from basic assumptions which must be accounted for and that pragmatism has to be guided by responsibility. This insight became inescapable when scientists had developed nuclear weapons which were capable of destroying all life on earth.

23 One of the most recent text books on macroeconomics states that there is consensus on the following goals of macroeconomic policy: acceptable levels of inflation, employment and economic growth. It is taken for granted that employment depends on growth (Richard T Froyen 1996: *Macroeconomics: Theories and Policies.* Upper Saddle River NJ: Prentice Hall, fifth edition, p 438.)

24 See e.g. Amuzegar 1981.

25 See Chang 1992:xvf, 135f.

26 Pietermaritzburg: Cluster Publications, 1998. See also Nürnberger 1988.

27 See Hurst 1995 for a good overview.

28 Suggested reading: Nürnberger 1988, chapters 2-4. Smith 1979 (browse through relevant passages).

29 Portugal exploited its huge colonial empire and is poor today. Sweden never had any colonies and is rich today.

30 For the relations between the USA and the Third World, for instance, see Klay 1986 183-186.

31 This is the situation we have had in South Africa under apartheid. For over a century the white economic elite has used the powers of the state to render the black majority economically uncompetitive on all levels. But apartheid South Africa was only a left-over of the colonial system which dominated the global economy until very recently. The great European empires competed with powerful weapons for control over land, resources and people. Today the physical occupation of colonies is no longer necessary because the use of power has become much more subtle and effective. It is based on productivity, information systems, trade networks, and so on.

32 See Nürnberger 1988, part I (or 1990:13ff for a concise description of the mechanism). Also read portions of Jones 1982.

33 Hunt 1981 ch 41.

34 Suggested reading: Nürnberger 1988, chapter 5. Cosmao 1984 ch 3. Kubalkova 1981 (selected portions). This is a book for the serious student. Look at the superb illustrations on pp 22, 26, 80, 128, 220 for various approaches to the problem.

35 Suggested reading: Nürnberger 1988 ch 5 and 10. Rasmussen 1981 ch 6. Cosmao ch 2. Hunt 1981 ch 41.

36 See Von Weizsäcker, Ernst U & Jesinghaus, Jochen 1992: *Ecological tax reform: A policy proposal for sustainable development.* Atlantic Highlands NJ: Humanities International / London: Zed Books.

37 Suggested reading: Nürnberger 1988 chapter 11. Wilson and Ramphele 1989, chapters 13-16. Wogaman 1986 pp 58ff, 68ff and 115ff. Brand 1980, selected portions, Herrera 1976, selected portions.

38 See for instance W D Hammond-Tooke: The Bantu-speaking peoples of Southern Africa. London: Routledge & Kegan Paul, 1974, chapters 5 and 8.

39 Hunt 1981, ch 1 - 8, offers a radical view of this history.

40 Suggested reading: Rasmussen 1981 ch 5; Hunt 1986; Kenworthy 1990.

41 For an understanding of the capitalist argument read Friedman 1979 ch 1-2. Read selected portions of Galbraith 1967 to gain an understanding of the operation of the modern industrial system.

42 Suggested reading: Hunt 1981 ch 4-8, 13-14, 42-43. Leatt et al 1986 ch 1, 3, 12, 13. Wogaman 1977: ch 4 - 5. To get an impression of the fierce argument between radicals and liberals on the assumptions of the underlying ideologies read selected chapters from Friedman 1979 and Gross 1985. Berger first tried to be even-handed in 1974 but turned radically capitalist in later writings. Theologians are just as divided: McGovern 1981 and Hinkelammert 1985 attack capitalism, Novak 1982 defends it. Benne 1981 defends it but is more careful in his assessment. Preston and Wogaman weigh the arguments on both sides.

43 Suggested reading: Lichtheim 1975 (selected portions on the history of socialism).

44 Suggested reading: Leijon in Burton 1986 175ff. Hunt 1981 ch 10 offers a radical view of social democracy.

45 See W Burger in *Newsweek* Sept 19, 1994 pp 22f.

46 For this new thinking in the former Soviet Union read portions of Gorbachev 1987.

47 Suggested reading: Encyclop. Britannica 1986 vol 17, pp 934-941; Leatt 1987; Hunt 1986.

CHAPTER 2

The liberal model - free enterprise capitalism

What is the goal of this chapter?

Having spelt out the overall rationale of our study in the previous chapter, it is now time to enter into detailed analyses. The present chapter is an attempt to give an overview of the character of the "free enterprise" system.

Section I is descriptive. We begin with a short survey of the *historical evolution* of economic systems, leading first to capitalism and then to its radical counter-part, Marxist socialism. Then we look at the *basic assumptions* of the liberal world-view. Finally we discuss the *economic principles* according to which the capitalist system is constructed. Section II contains our appraisal of the system and its ideology. First we enumerate the *advantages* of the system, some of which are acknowledged by its most ardent critics. Then we summarise the *arguments against* capitalism. Finally, we note how liberals would respond to this critique.

Section I - Description

A historical survey

Modern capitalism is a fairly recent development in world history. Probably the oldest known economic system is the "subsistence economy" of traditional societies, often called *communalism*. Here a community produces as much food, shelter and clothing as it needs for its own daily consumption. Both the work needed for production and the consumption of the proceeds are shared by the community; so there is a considerable degree of equality in the system. For various reasons, however, such a system is not able to generate much progress and prosperity. This system is still in operation in large parts of the Third World, notably in rural Africa.

Then we find kingdoms and empires. *Imperialism* means that ambitious rulers progressively conquer other territories and force their populations to pay tribute and supply labour. The most extreme form of this exploitation of other people's strengths and resources is slavery. Kingdoms and empires were usually structured hierarchically — kings, nobles, artisans, peasants, serfs, and so on. This was the system known as *feudalism*.

It was within feudalism that *merchant capitalism* developed in Europe. Enterprising merchants (called the "middle class" because they were located between nobles and peasants) progressively acquired wealth and influence through expanding trade, while the position of both landlords and peasants deteriorated. The "Protestant Ethic" of frugality and diligence justified the acquisition of wealth as a sign of the benevolence of God (Max Weber).[1] The influx of precious metals led to price inflation, without a corresponding rise in wages, and the main beneficiaries of this imbalance were the merchants. Colonialism further helped to open up the world for these traders. Rulers, who became more and more dependent on the wealth of the emerging "capitalists", liberalised internal trade and imposed tariffs against external competitors, a policy called *mercantilism.* This policy enhanced the accumulation of wealth in the hands of the middle class.

The next stage came when important inventions brought about a change in emphasis from trade to manufacturing as a means of generating wealth. This stage we call *early industrial capitalism.* Its main feature was "the use of the excess of production over consumption to enlarge productive capacity rather than to invest in economically unproductive enterprises, such as pyramids and cathedrals.[2] Adam Smith provided the legitimating theory for this development in his famous work *The wealth of nations* (1776). *Laissez faire* became the battle cry. It means, literally, "allow (them) to do", meaning that the state should keep its hands off the economy. Manufacturing moved from households to factories, from peasants and artisans to workers. Great masses of people moved from rural areas to urban centres, where they lived in slums and worked for long hours in appalling conditions for a meagre wage. This was the situation at the height of the "industrial revolution" which Karl Marx so vehemently attacked in his writings.

Three developments in the West changed this system into *Twentieth Century capitalism:* First, the great depression of the 1930s led to large scale intervention of the state in the economy. The advice of J M Keynes, that the state should invest in labour-intensive projects during an economic slump to counteract unemployment and withdraw in times of boom, was followed. Second, the rapid development of science and technology revolutionised productive processes and led to increasing wealth. In recent decades the emphasis has fallen more and more on electronic means of analysis, design, communication and control of construction. Third, the emergence of powerful trade unions and socialist parties in states with democratic constitutions made it possible for the worker population to gain a greater share in the wealth generated by capitalist production, to insist on equality of opportunity for all and to achieve the introduction of social securities. This is a development moving in the direction of *social democracy.*

Meanwhile, colonialism and imperialism have led to the integration of much of the Third World into the capitalist system. *Marxism-Leninism* had established a socialist counter-system of lesser magnitude which has since collapsed. The growth of productive capacity has long passed from the initiative of some daring entrepreneurs to institutionalised processes, fired by breath-taking advances in technology, information and organisation. This stage is sometimes called *late or mature capitalism*. The result has been an immense concentration of economic power in a few advanced economic centres and the progressive marginalisation of peripheral population groups all over the world.[3]

The liberal world-view

Economic systems are composed of structures and processes. But they are also undergirded by convictions, legitimating arguments, values and norms. The most prominent characteristic of the liberal world-view is its insistence on the *freedom of individuals* to organise their own lives, either alone or in cooperation with others. Sacred traditions inherited from past generations, and present authorities not freely chosen by individuals, should have no power over human beings. Self-determination, self-realisation, and self-responsibility are the watch words.

Liberals have, for this reason, also supported socialist initiatives aimed at liberating the oppressed, empowering the workers and alleviating the plight of the poor. It is important to note that the formulation of *basic human rights* occurred in the context of the liberal world-view which is also the context in which capitalism evolved.[4] In this chapter, though, we focus on the specifically capitalist version of liberalism.[5]

If individuals have the right to develop their full potential, then the provision of education, information and training are very important. But these are only the prerequisites for individuals to take their lives into their hands. *To take bold initiatives, to employ all your gifts and to work hard,* are the greatest virtues in liberalism. The liberal concept of justice is not geared to need but to achievement: you are entitled to the fruit of your labour. Those who do not pull their weight should not benefit from the labours of those who do. Ironically, it is this argument which Marxists have turned against the owners of capital!

The status of human beings too should depend on their achievements. There should be no roles or positions in society which are inherited from past generations, or ascribed by some people to others on account of mere respect. Whether you are a capitalist or a worker, you have to battle for your place in the sun in competition with all others.[6] In a competitive environment you either move up on the social ladder or you drop down. This is called *vertical social mobility.* You can even end up at rock bottom, whether due to irresponsibility or misfortune. In a consistent kind of liberalism, which is not mitigated by humanitarian considerations, there is no social network to protect you against folly or fate.

In economic terms capitalist liberalism believes that people do not react to moral appeals but to material incentives. If entrepreneurs, experts, administrators and workers receive their pay according to the quantity and quality of their work, they will automatically try to be more productive. This is true for the owners of all the factors of production. People will invest their capital and their energy where there are profits to be made, or where they can hope for promotions and higher wages. They will also improve their qualifications if this enhances their economic prospects.

The second prominent aspect of liberalism is *human sovereignty over the natural world.* No part of reality is forbidden ground for human investigation and utilisation. There are no uncanny forces, magical powers, divine beings or eternal principles which human beings must fear, respect, or obey. Human beings are masters over the world. This we call *secularism.* Reality is discovered by means of investigation (empiricism), penetrated by means of logical thought (rationalism) and manipulated to yield desired results (technology). Self-interest is the guiding principle in dealing with the natural world. Consumers are entitled to maximise utility (utilitarianism) or pleasure (hedonism), while producers are entitled to maximise their profits.

Liberalism is based on *individualism.* The requirements of the society play a secondary role. Adam Smith, the father of capitalist liberalism, believed that if all people were allowed to work for their own interests, they would all work harder and become more efficient. Because they would create more wealth, the society would benefit. An "invisible hand" would coordinate the manifestations of individual selfishness for the common good. This view was radicalised in the utilitarianism of Bentham. However, the invisible hand also worked in another way: individuals were free to cooperate with other individuals to reach more benefits for all participants in a common venture. Unproductive organisations and institutions, by contrast, would disappear because they could not compete.

Characteristic of the liberal world-view is its *optimistic future orientation.* It only becomes conservative when its established norms are questioned, say by Marxism. It believes in progress through the growth of human insight, science and technology. It takes neither nature nor society for granted as it is, but maintains that they need to be changed to serve the interests of humankind better. It is convinced of a basic goodness in the human being, which only needs to be developed and purified. It has confidence in the ability of the human race to overcome imperfections, evil and suffering. Characteristic slogans are "forward and upward", "bigger and better", "efficiency and productivity".

Economic principles of capitalism

The most prominent principle of free enterprise is *private ownership of the factors of production*. Control over these factors should not reside in the state or in other public bodies. This is true of all factors of production: land, raw materials, capital, labour, technology, organisation, entrepreneurial initiative etc. Historically the ownership of non-human factors (land, raw materials, machinery, and so on) has been the main bone of contention. These factors presuppose financial resources and can, therefore, all be subsumed under the concept "capital". Hence the name "capitalism".

But why private ownership? Heilbroner identifies the "single most important element in capitalism" as "the driving need to extract wealth from the productive activities of society *in the form of capital*". This "wealth" is derived from the "surplus" production of society, that is, the "difference between the volume of production needed to maintain the work force and the volume of production the work force produces." However, in capitalism, amassing wealth is not an end in itself, as in pre-modern societies, but "a means for gathering more wealth" through investment. This is again motivated, according to Heilbroner, by a drive for prestige and power.[7]

Typically owners of non-human factors of production are individuals, but it is just as typical that such individuals hold limited interests (shares) in *corporate organisations* with appointed and remunerated managers. In other words, they sell their financial resources to the corporation, just as others sell their administrative skills, their technological expertise, or their labour. Obviously they claim a proportionate part of the proceeds of the firm in the form of dividends, just as the labourers claim their portion in the form of wages.

Between the interests of the shareholders and the interests of the labourers, usually represented by trade unions, there is a constant tug of war. These *industrial disputes* can be settled by negotiation but, if no agreement is reached, they may also lead to strikes (labourers withhold their labour) or lockouts and retrenchments (capital owners withhold their productive assets).

The concept "free enterprise" refers to the demand that private citizens should be allowed to conduct their business *without state intervention*. According to the original liberal creed the state should only be responsible for establishing optimal conditions for production: the supply of infrastructure, social order and peace.

Due to extreme oscillations of the economy between boom and recession and the economic havoc this created, however, the state acquired more and greater functions in modern times — not only in the form of monetary policy, balance of payments regulation and market control, but also in the form of large bureaucracies and state corporations. In many cases the state has become the greatest owner of capital. Therefore we distinguish between the "private" and the "public sectors" as the two major components of the economy.

Some authors argue that the government is actually managing the economy and should do so more purposefully.[8] Both the approaches of the *Keynesians* and the *Monetarists* led to involvement of the state in the economy, the first to cushion the effects of depression and inflation, the second to regulate the flow of money in the economy.[9] This was followed by a *neo-liberal* backlash which tried to reduce the role of the state. Let us briefly discuss these historical stages in the debate on state intervention.

a) During the Great Depression in the 1930s, "not only had banks and stock markets collapsed through lack of confidence, but wheat was in fact being burnt and cocoa and sugar crops destroyed for lack of a market, while millions were unemployed and starving".[10] The most celebrated economist of the time, *J M Keynes*, realised that at regular intervals market demand fell short of the capacity to produce, causing a downward spiral. Keynes proposed that in times of crisis the state should invest in job creating and community serving projects, and withdraw from the productive economy in times of boom. This led to widespread acceptance of state intervention. Sweden was the first country to apply such a policy. The "New Deal", introduced in 1933 by President Roosevelt in the US, is the most well known case. Keynes was also instrumental in the establishment of international financial organisations such as the World Bank, the International Monetary Fund (IMF) and the General Agreement on Tariffs and Trade (GATT).[11]

b) The recipe seemed to work well after World War II, when the global economy enjoyed three decades of boom. But this was also due to the demand created by post war reconstruction, the extension of mass consumption from the United States to Europe and Japan, the continuous overspending of the US government, paid by US gold reserves, and the opening markets of the Third World. After this phase had worked itself out, a new crisis set in which could not be explained by the Keynesian model, namely a combination of economic stagnation and inflation, sometimes called "stagflation". A new school, the *Monetarists,* ascribed the problem to excessive and unproductive government spending and too great a supply of money. Their recipe was to privatise state enterprises, cut down on government expenditure and raise interest rates.

c) In the mean time a renaissance of the liberal theory of Adam Smith occurred. This *neo-classical school*, led by economists such as Friedman and von Hayek, proclaimed the virtues of total freedom for private enterprise: the state would get out of the way, unproductive enterprises would go out of business, trade union power would be broken and the foundations would be laid for a more efficient and competitive economy. This recipe found its classical expression in "Thatcherism" and "Reaganomics".[12]

d) This approach only created *new difficulties*. By this time capital had begun to float around freely on international financial markets without any commitment to local development; unemployment grew in spite of economic growth; the governments of some industrial countries, notably the United States, indulged in massive budget deficits; many Third World economies were paralysed by the crushing burden of high interests on massive debts; structural adjustment programmes, prescribed by the International Monetary Fund and the World Bank, led to drastic reductions in spending for education, health and social securities; free trade benefited the economically dynamic and powerful, while exposing the poor and vulnerable to reckless competition. The *ecological impact* of rampant economic growth has perhaps become the most daunting factor.

e) Because of these problems, the mood recently began to move towards a more controlled economy, at least in some circles (*neo-Keynsianism*).

The private sector operates according to the principle of *competition*. Private firms compete for a share in the market; workers compete with each other for jobs; labour as a factor of production competes with machines, and so on. Competition is not the same as confrontation or conflict. Competition means that people try to outwit and outperform each other within the limits of set rules. The world of sport provides us with an ideal example! It is believed that if people compete with each other they will reduce their costs, cut out inefficiency and become more productive, and that all this will enhance the overall performance of the economy.

The allocation of funds and functions to various factors of production, say labour and machines, depends on their *relative productivity*. Those factors of production whose contribution to output is greatest per unit of input, receive the greatest share of investment and the greatest share of the profit. The extra output generated by an additional unit of input is called marginal productivity. If an extra R 1000 invested in machines leads to higher output than an extra R 1000 in labour, labour is replaced by machines until the ratio swings in favour of labour. It is clear that the output of a firm (its profitability) is the prime consideration, not the need of labourers to earn their living.

The principle of relative productivity also leads to the assumption that specialisation is beneficial. Individuals, enterprises and whole countries should do what they can do best and trade among themselves on that basis. Large firms can farm out specialised phases in the production chain to smaller firms. Some countries are endowed with raw materials, others with abundant labour, others with technological sophistication. This phenomenon is called *comparative advantage*. According to this philosophy, Japan should not produce rice but computer chips, Argentina beef and Zanzibar cloves. Comparative advantage is in constant flux, however, and those who are keen in recognising market gaps as they emerge (socalled niche markets) and are versatile enough to exploit them, reap the greatest benefits.

The most important facet of this system is the so-called *market mechanism*. On a free market the supply of, and the demand for any resource, commodity or service balance out. If the price of a commodity is high, sellers want to sell more (supply rises), but buyers want to buy less (demand falls). Of course, you cannot sell what others do not want to buy; so either the quantity sold will be less or the price has to go down. If prices are low, demand rises and supply drops. Again you cannot buy what others do not want to sell; so either less can be bought or the price has to go up. Ultimately the price and the quantity are determined by the point where supply and demand meet.[13]

Thus if there is a high demand for potatoes, their price will rise, and farmers will plant more. Similarly, where there are many unskilled labourers and firms have no use for them, wages for unskilled labour will remain low. If at the same time there is a great need for skilled labour, it will be paid high wages. The growing discrepancy between the wages of skilled and unskilled labour will challenge labourers to improve their qualifications. In the end it is the marginal productivity of a factor of production (that is the rise in production gained by the last unit of that factor allocated to the production process), which determines whether the allocation of this factor of production is increased or decreased relative to others.[14]

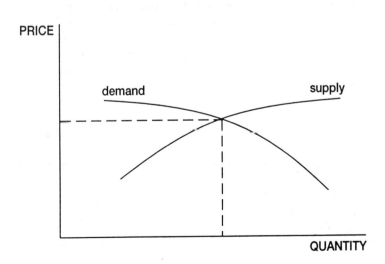

From these assumptions follows the belief in the *sovereignty of the consumer*. The argument is that, in a free society, nobody can force consumers to buy things they do not want. Producers depend on consumer demand for the type, the quantity and the quality of what they can produce. They will naturally produce what they think they can sell. But this cuts both ways: neither can you force people to produce what they do not want to produce. While consumers want to maximise the utility and satisfaction they get out of the money they spend, producers want to maximise the profit they get out of the money they invest. They will normally not produce anything unless they can make a profit on it. And naturally they will try to stimulate, even create, a demand for their product through sophisticated advertising techniques.

So you could just as well speak of the sovereignty of the producer. In fact, it is the interplay between these contrasting interests which determines what is produced and consumed. And in this interplay it is the relative *market power* of the two parties which decides the direction in which the production process moves. Economic power is purchasing power on the side of the consumer and investment power on the side of the producer. In modern times, it can be argued, producers have accumulated sufficient powers to manipulate markets in the form of aggressive marketing; control over markets and outlets; monopolistic concentrations of productive potential, or oligopolistic arrangements between firms.[15]

Finally, liberalism believes that all people have not only the freedom, but also *the responsibility to look after themselves*. It would be unjust if the state maintained loafers by taxing the income of those who work hard. People who are too careless to think of the future have only themselves to blame if they suffer in times of sickness or old age. It is also socially harmful to give to people what they have not worked for, because it creates a dependent mentality and easy-going attitudes. People who do not realise what it costs to make commodities and services available become wasteful in their use. If medical care, for instance, is free, people go to the doctor and swallow pills for trivial ailments, instead of allowing the body to recover on its own.

Questions

Revision: Describe the most important beliefs, values and principles of capitalist liberalism.

Application: Can organised crime be described as a variation of free enterprise? If not, what is the difference?

Critique: (a) "Your enthusiastic description of capitalist beliefs, values and principles betrays that this is where your heart beats."
(b) "What a distorted and simplistic portrayal you give of one of the greatest achievements of humankind!" How would you react to these two statements?

Section II - Evaluation

Advantages of the free enterprise system

Experience has shown that private property, personal freedom and self-responsibility indeed create *strong motivations* to improve your performance and cut down costs. Tenants do not look after gardens, owners do. Private cars last longer than vehicles belonging to the state. Employees are willing to work overtime for a good reward. It is claimed that Soviet peasants produced more on the little private gardens around their houses than on the great collective farms. But individuals can also co-operate and reach common goals through teamwork. Since the latter is goal-directed, it will be pragmatic and unsentimental, thus more efficient.

All this should not simply be ascribed to greed and selfishness. Karl Marx, whom we quote because he was the most radical critic of the capitalist system, recognised that *creativity* is a fundamental characteristic of human nature. In fact, he defined the human being as a worker. But *mastery* is an equally powerful motivation. To do one's own thing and be proud of it; to have new insights and devise new methods; to be crowned with success even with small initiatives; to be in charge of one's own domain — all these are powerful sources of satisfaction.

More fundamentally, humans need *recognition*, that is, the affirmation of their right of existence, or their dignity, or their worth for society. *Passion* and *ambition* must also find outlets which are constructive, rather than harmful. Instead of wasting their lives in violent adventures and striving for vain forms of glory, as countless "heroes" have done in the past, the gifted, passionate and ambitious can channel their energies into entrepreneurship, or research, or public service, where they create wealth and prosperity rather than devastation.[16]

Psychologically, self-reliance leads to maturity. An *enhanced self-image* depends on accomplishment. To be free, creative and sovereign belongs to the dignity of the human being. It overcomes a mentality of dependence on others, which is so detrimental to the development of creativity and responsibility. By contrast, if you are forced to do what others tell you to do, or if you are nothing but a cog in a great impersonal mechanism, you become frustrated, listless and bitter.

Freedom to develop one's *own initiative* has been the driving force of the capitalist system from its earliest history. An enterprising spirit is ready to sacrifice for envisaged rewards: dangerous journeys, painstaking research, risky investments, imaginative new approaches, the development and perfection of one's special gifts in years of probing and practice. To discover strange new lands, to find antidotes for diseases, to hunt for precious resources, to develop sophisticated machines, to overcome all sorts of obstacles — for these kinds of challenges people have placed their lives, health and happiness at risk.

The accelerating development of *science and technology* since the 17th Century has been the direct result of this spirit. Not only entrepreneurs, but also workers developed greater initiative. It is not by accident that the Marxist-Leninist command system was not able to keep pace with technological developments in capitalist countries. There is reason to believe that the productivity of labour has risen dramatically over the last century because of opportunities to improve your income through higher training and greater dedication. Enlightened managers give as much free play to the ingenuity of their workers as possible and reap the benefits.

Another benefit of the system is *structural freedom*. Instead of establishing artificial social structures, designed on the drawing board by ideologically motivated bureaucrats, thus forcing social reality into institutional straitjackets, the liberal system has allowed social forces to arrange themselves in the most suitable relationships under given circumstances. The rise of the trade union movement is a good example. Institutions which do not prove to be viable in the economic power play simply disintegrate. Many theorists argue that capitalism and democracy are twins because they are both based on individual freedom of choice.[17]

Capitalism also led, as its name implies, to a rapid and accelerating *accumulation of productive capital*. As we have seen, capital enhances the capacity of human beings to produce. If less is consumed than productive capacity would allow, the surplus capacity is utilised to produce more capital goods, and this leads to even higher levels of production. Karl Marx, the most radical critic of capitalism, believed that socialism can only be meaningfully applied after capitalism had built up these resources. You can distribute wealth, he said, you cannot distribute poverty. You must fatten the cow before you can milk her.

Paradoxically, the first Marxist state was established in an economically backward country, namely the Russian empire. To make up for this deficiency, the Soviets systematically "exploited" their workers by paying low wages and cutting back on consumer goods so as to build up productive capital. That is why the Soviet system was sometimes referred to as *state capitalism*.

The commanding goal of the capitalist system in the productive process is *efficiency*. You cut down costs to a minimum, and raise output to a maximum. This principle necessitates great care in the allocation of resources, time and energy. It also leads to the development and deployment of technology. Capitalist managers are ever on the look-out for more effective methods and streamlined procedures. In successful capitalist enterprises you will not find unoccupied people sitting in offices reading their newspapers.

All these factors have led to a *level of output* which is not found in alternative systems, either ancient or modern. Not only the capital owners but also the workers and the average persons on the street have been beneficiaries.[18] Countries which are wealthy today owe their wealth largely to the capitalist system — unless they have scarce resources to offer for which capitalist economies are prepared to pay, such as crude oil. This was freely acknowledged by Marx and Engels in their *Communist Manifesto*. If we have the desire to eradicate poverty this is certainly a consideration we should not overlook.[19]

Arguments against capitalism

Alas, this is only one side of the coin. Capitalism also has grave disadvantages and dangers. The most fundamental critique of the capitalist system is that it grants *human selfishness* free reign. The capitalist view of human nature implies a lack of moral rigour. Capitalist liberalism accepts that, given the opportunity, consumers will maximise their satisfaction and producers will maximise their profits. And they are entitled to do so, because the pursuit of self-interst is nothing but natural. Moral precepts, community concerns and personal loyalties are "irrational", unless they lead to greater material benefits.

We agree that selfishness and greed are characteristic of human nature and occur under any set of circumstances. Yet capitalism is unique in that it allows indulgence and acquisitiveness to operate without restrictions and inhibitions. More than that, it actually makes a *virtue* of them! By doing so, it destroys the equally natural sense of responsibility for others, for society, for the natural world and thus for coming generations. It is a kind of convenient fatalism when capitalist liberals believe that base human instincts cannot be moulded, controlled or transformed. The truth is that humans are able to suffer and even die for their peers, their convictions or their ideals. Capitalist liberalism treats the market as a law of nature, in which you can interfere only at the peril of economic progress. The truth is that it is a human institution among others which can be structured and guided according to particular sets of values.[20]

One of the reasons for this fundamental failure is a *deficient concept of freedom*. As we have seen, liberals have a positive and optimistic view of human nature and tend to overlook human sinfulness. They assume too readily that, if everybody was free, everybody would also be responsible. That is blatantly not the case. In fact, if freedom does not grow together with responsibility, a new kind of slavery is the result: human desires begin to rule. Commodities, which should serve, turn into idols, which determine people's lives. And sophisticated advertising systematically props up such idols. You seem to be missing fulfilment in life when denied the enjoyment of a luxury car, a television set, or a Coke!

Because *money* grants access to the desired goods, money itself turns into a slave-master. Marx called it a "fetish". In the struggle for money people trample on others, families break up, whole population groups are relegated to poverty, and the natural world is destroyed. Obviously various religions had warned against the consequences of covetousness long before Karl Marx. Building on Jewish insights, the New Testament, for instance, saw that "Mammon" was an idol which challenged God's sovereignty in the lives of people[21] and caused problems for its owners.[22]

But the quest for uncontrolled freedom also backfires at the social structural level. Those who acquire an advantage over others, either by virtue of greater gifts, opportunities and diligence, or by deceit and graft, see their wealth and power increase beyond all proportions. The rest of the population finds itself increasingly deprived of its freedom. The spirit of capitalism does not only strive to outcompete others, it also seeks to *undermine the competitiveness of others*. Deprived of their economic independence, the losers have nothing but their labour to sell - the one factor of production which is attached to their bodies and cannot be transferred to others. Freedom, because it is not controlled, destroys itself. Marxists say that the freedom of the capitalist system is like the freedom of a free fox in a free fowl-run: he is at liberty to have the fowl for breakfast.

The liberal ideology, so frequently used as a basis for economics in textbooks, assumes an ideal state of affairs in which there is "perfect competition" and a "balanced economy". Ideally, nobody should possess a monopoly; that means, no person or group should be in a position where they could dominate and dictate. If that was indeed the case, free enterprise would be a wonderful system. In fact, precisely the opposite happens. Capitalists and workers do not operate on the same level of influence, nor do producers, merchants and consumers.[23] The capitalist economy even takes over tasks and powers traditionally ascribed to the political order.[24] There are also huge *concentrations of power* in economic centres and gross impotence and dependency in the economic peripheries. This is also true for the international scene.[25] The discrepancies have become so severe that whole states are at the mercy not only of political and military superpowers but also of large multinational corporations.[26]

Production and distribution are today largely controlled by these *giant corporations*. They are under the management not of capital owners, who are thousands of individual shareholders, but of a small elite of paid executives which perpetuates itself. Already by 1980 the 300 largest corporations in the world controlled three quarters of the world's manufacturing assets. In

South Africa the four largest corporations controlled 76.5% of total assets registered on the Johannesburg Stock Exchange in 1994, with the largest among them, Anglo American, controlling 43.3%.[27] Within these corporations there is often very little freedom to develop your gifts. Where conveyer belt methods are in operation, workers are nothing but cogs in huge mechanised processes which they do not understand. Corporate administrations are big bureaucracies which differ little from state bureaucracies.

Moreover, because the rich possess financial means, they are also able to influence the *political scene* to their own advantage. Economic strength leads to political power. Some critics maintain that in capitalist societies the state is, to a large extent, the instrument of the rich to further their own interests, in spite of all the formal trappings of democracy. We just need to look at how money is allocated in public budgets to see that this allegation is not without substance. And in the US only the very rich can afford to stage a presidential campaign. Some critics go so far as to allege that international tensions are fostered deliberately to further the armaments industry which has become such an indispensable part of production in industrial countries. Governments certainly cannot afford to overlook economic power blocs.

Of course, capitalism as an economic system is anything but democratic. "It is an elemental proposition of democracy that every voting citizen has the right to cast but one vote, whereas it is an equally elemental proposition of capitalism that every market participant may rightly cast as many votes as his or her wealth permits."[28] So is freedom *nothing but a myth* in the "free enterprise" system? Is the science of economics nothing but an ideological smokescreen which covers up the stark reality of domination and enslavement?[29] Surely this would be an exaggeration. There is indeed much more freedom in liberal capitalist states than in Marxist socialist states. But the allegation is not entirely without truth.[30]

The emergence of the centre-periphery structure of the global economy, with its vast discrepancies of wealth and income, is largely due to the operation of the capitalist system. In terms of *production*, capitalism is a system which favours the powerful at the expense of the less powerful. The asymmetrical interaction between centre and periphery forces local producers in the periphery out of business. The same is true of smaller competitors in the centre. Of course, capitalism is not explicitly designed to favour the rich. These tendencies are also in operation in socialist systems. The difference is that capitalist liberalism allows both the structural mechanisms and the abuse of power to operate freely.

In terms of *consumption* it is a system which favours the rich at the expense of the poor. The cravings of affluent consumers for luxuries, artificially created by advertising and aggressive marketing, determine what is produced because they have the purchasing power. The needs of the poor are not met because they cannot pay. Due to these mechanisms, both the poverty gap and the affluence gap are growing — and thus also the discrepancies in income between rich and poor. Within the global capitalist system growing unemployment is unavoidable. Many people at the bottom of the pile are *marginalised* both in terms of production (their unskilled labour is not required) and in terms of consumption (they cannot afford to buy the commodities offered). Capitalism is perhaps not *designed* to favour the rich, but it provides for no mechanisms which could counteract the inevitable development of these imbalances.

As we have seen capitalist liberalism allows the economy to be determined by consumer demand on the one hand, and the profit motive on the other. Both consumer demand and the profit motive are irrational, short-sighted and selfish. They encourage consumption of luxuries and satisfy personal cravings, but *neglect public necessities.* As stated above, consumer demand is also bolstered and manipulated through advertising. It can follow directions which are harmful to the individual, the family and the society. Alcohol, tobacco and drugs, the compulsion to consume increasing quantities of sugar, fat and red meat, and the deliberate dismantling of sexual inhibitions and the horror of violence in the entertainment industry are cases in point. Moreover, the unpredictable ups and downs of consumer demand are partially responsible for boom and recession.

Another problem is the capitalist obsession with *economic growth.* The cycle of boom and recession shows that a capitalist economy must grow or decline. To ensure growth after the market has reached saturation point, artificial needs have to be created and resources are wasted. Economists argue that human wants are limitless. If that were the case, though, there would be no point in spending billions each year on advertising and marketing. Factual information on available products would be all that was needed. In fact, the limits of time, space and capacity to consume make it unavoidable that we discard one article to be able to consume another. The rationale of advertising and aggressive marketing is to create dissatisfaction with what we have acquired and raise ever new needs. It is not simply human avarice which lie at the root of the problem, but rather the goal of private enterprise to achieve a more rapid "throughput" of material and commodities.

This wastage leads to the unnecessary depletion of resources and to *ecological destruction.* Non-renewable resources, such as crude oil, are depleted faster than alternatives can be found; renewable resources, such as forests, are utilised faster than they can regenerate themselves, and garbage, waste and toxins accumulate faster than the rate at which natural "sinks" can absorb them. All this leads to biological devastation and pollution.

Moreover, to grow, the capitalist economy has to penetrate new markets. On the one hand, this leads to the *"commodification" of life.*[31] Everything, whether education, health care, recreation or sexual relations, becomes a commodity which is sold at a price. On the other hand capitalism is never far from *imperialist tendencies.*[32] It also grants credit to those who cannot pay, causing unmanageable debt problems in poor societies - whether in families or whole nations. The great discrepancies between rich and poor and the growing competition of everybody with everybody else again leads to the buildup of conflict potential, the arms race and a constant threat of war.[33]

As long as high demand levels can be maintained, production increases and the economy grows. The surplus profit is again invested in further productive capacity. We call that a *boom.* Once productive capacity outstrips market demand, a boom turns into a *recession.* More is produced than can be sold on the market. The capacities run idle, workers are laid off, unemployment is the result. But the regular cycle of boom and recession is not the only problem. There is a long term trend in which production makes use of more and more capital at the expense of labour. Though certain industries may create jobs, the economy as a whole sheds jobs and the scourge of global unemployment becomes ever more severe.[34] Of course, governments in capitalist countries have introduced various measures to control the cycle of boom and recession, as well as the related phenomena of inflation and stagflation. These measures have been successful at least to some extent. But on the whole they deal with symptoms rather than causes.

A liberal economy also has detrimental *socio-psychological effects.* The economy is geared to the achievement norm. The gifted are rewarded with affluence and prestige on top of their gifts, the handicapped are punished with poverty and contempt on top of their handicap. Competition creates perpetual fear, restlessness and anguish, lest you lose out. Moreover, in a system based on competition everybody compares him/herself with those higher up, not with those lower down. This leads to the development of chronic inferiority complexes. You can never relax because you have never achieved enough. On the other hand your attitude towards those below is one of contempt and lack of concern. After all, they have only themselves to blame for their fate.[35] Competition is particularly severe between capitalists themselves, because their asset — money — constantly flows and they have to ensure that inflow remains higher than outflow. This makes capitalists prone to the motive of self-preservation (in addition to the motives of power and prestige) which is "by popular repute the most intense and unrestrained of all instinctual responses."[36]

Where discrepancies in wealth and income coincide with ethnic or racial groups, another dynamic enters the picture. Many blacks in South Africa, for instance, have become very bitter towards capitalism because they equated capitalism with *racist oppression.* Liberals vehemently protest against the insinuation that capitalism is responsible for, or even compatible with, apartheid. They say that liberalism believes in the dignity and freedom of each individual and has no time for ethnic and racial prejudices. More than that, discrimination and oppression destroy the free operation of the market mechanism and are, therefore, economically counter-productive. So liberals maintain that they cannot possibly have anything to do with racist oppression.

While it is true that liberals have long been at the forefront of the struggle against apartheid, the black critique is not without foundation. Capitalism allows selfishness free reign. Selfishness is not restricted to the individual. On the contrary; group solidarity is a powerful weapon for defending your collective interests at the expense of other groups. *Collective selfishness* can easily manifest itself in the form of ethnic or racial nationalism. South African racial policies were not the only example, but certainly one of the most glaring examples of this general phenomenon. In fact the latter has a long history. Capitalism has grown together with colonialism and imperialism. Imperialism has always been accompanied by feelings of ethnic and racial superiority. Institutionalised racism in South Africa was just a continuation of the colonialist age within one country.

Finally, liberal economics is, in many respects, a deceptive ideology. In its negative meaning, an ideology is a set of arguments designed to cover up or legitimate the pursuit of self-interest at the expense of the interests of others.[37] Often the character of economics is exposed not by what it says, but by what it fails to say. For example, liberal economics ignores the fundamental problem of *human need and the means of its satisfaction;* rather, it concentrates on market demand and supply. At best it is assumed that demand reflects need. But the main factor in market demand is purchasing power, not need. And the main factor in supply is profit, not need satisfaction. Both concentrate on the interests of those who have economic power - whether purchasing power or productive power.[38]

Similarly liberal economics fails to recognise and analyse the mechanisms which lead to *growing discrepancies* between the rich and the poor - as if all this were of no consequence.[39] It works with the concept of the gross domestic product per capita (GDP) — which conceals all differences between individuals and groups — and neglects the distribution of this product within the population. It concentrates on the economies of single countries and fails to see economic processes in their global operation. It maintains that to create jobs we need economic growth and that for economic growth we need capital investment. In fact, capital competes with jobs, economic growth is not necessarily linked with employment growth and investments often destroy jobs - if not at home then elsewhere in the system.

Liberal economics says that the *tax burden* is carried by a handful of people and that it must be spread more equally over the population - for instance by shifting public revenue from income tax to sales tax - and fails to say that this handful of people also earns most of the money and that income also needs to be spread more equally. We could continue with such examples. The point is that far from being the objective scientific discipline it claims to be, liberal economics is heavily biased in favour of elite interests.

In fact, it is the self-expression of a class which take its world-view for granted without question because it unconsciously operates on the assumption that it is the "embodiment of the spirit and mission of the society that in fact it dominates".[40]

Finally, it is simply not true that free enterprise necessarily leads to initiative, productivity and efficiency, while socialism does not. In the first place many outstanding achievements of humankind have been motivated by the desire to know, to be creative, or to serve, rather than by simple greed. Numerous scientists, explorers, monks, soldiers or missionaries have suffered and died for their cause and gained no material benefits. By contrast, self-interest has often led to economically *counterproductive pursuits*; the extreme case is organised crime. In the second place there are many examples in recent times where tight state control has led to outstanding economic results, for instance in Taiwan and South Korea. There are also examples where free enterprise has led to confusion and inefficiency, for instance in the American railroad system, whereas the state run transport and postal systems in Europe are highly efficient.[41]

The response of liberals to the critique

The debate over capitalism rages on. Those who are convinced of the system defend its merits on the following grounds. Their most powerful weapon is a comparison with other alternatives, particularly Marxist-Leninist socialism. Even if capitalism produces enslaving structures, it is said, they are child's play compared to the *massive oppression* found in communist countries. Although there is a concentration of power in capitalism, you still have the counter power of free trade unions; the democratic process in which the less privileged have the advantage of their numbers and can enforce social policies; the division of power in legislative, executive and judiciary functions; freedom of speech, freedom of the press, freedom to organise and make your point or gain collective power in opposition to the ruling elite, and so on. In communist countries all power — military, political, economic, technological, propagandistic, judicial — is concentrated in the same hands, no opposition is tolerated, everybody has to keep quiet and follow the orders dictated from above.

It is conceded that there are large *discrepancies* in wealth but because the general prosperity of the capitalist world has grown steadily, the standard of living of ordinary workers is higher, and the discrepancies between rich and poor are less severe, than in non-capitalist countries. Moreover, discrepancies are deemed to have a positive effect on human motivation; they makes people develop their full potential. Also, capitalist enterprises invest increasing resources in worker benefits, ecological concerns, education and training, research, cultural achievements, sports, and other public responsibilities. Great firms form markets for a great number of smaller firms which supply tools, specialised services, or intermediate stages in production.

Liberals do not believe that *greater justice* is done in socialism. The efficient and diligent are taxed to subsidise the inefficient and lethargic. This is patently unjust. They maintain that the socialist critique is an "economics of envy and resentment". People should pull up their socks and use their gifts rather than blaming others and waiting for handouts! Liberals also point out the proverbial lack of productivity in systems depending on inefficient and unmotivated bureaucracies, rather than enterprising private concerns.

Further, *selfishness* is not due to the free enterprise system but to human nature. It makes itself felt in socialism in the form of massive corruption and carelessness. It is also preferable to raise productivity by motivating people through their greed and ambition, than through state coercion.

While socialism is rigid and dogmatic, capitalism is a *flexible system* which continuously adjusts to changing circumstances and accommodates new needs and new social constellations. The trade union movement and social securities are examples. Another is the informal sector where poor people carve out a living for themselves. Liberals would acknowledge the responsibility of the state in cases where people cannot help themselves, for instance in the case of unemployment, sickness or old age. In fact, the state has gained in importance as capitalism has developed. But it should supplement, not take the place of the initiative of the people.

Liberals say that much of the critique is not a critique against free enterprise but against *modern civilisation* as such, that is, against rationality, empiricism, science and technology. Socialist systems have shown themselves to be no better in coping with the problems of factory labour, urban congestion, pollution and ecological destruction. On the contrary; in Eastern Europe they have produced an ecological nightmare of the first order. Similarly, the centre-periphery phenomenon is not absent in socialist countries.

Concerning the lack of freedom, liberals maintain that this is not due to the liberal creed but due to the *failure to apply its principles* consistently. The blame should be laid before governments which do not control power concentrations with anti-monopolistic legislation. Moreover, large corporations have not prevented small businesses from mushrooming. In fact, small and medium enterprises form the greater part of a capitalist economy and supply most of the jobs. If this development was encouraged, the balance would be restored.

Liberal economists say that the culture of envy, resentment and suspicion against international capital has cost *Third World countries dearly*. The South East Asian "tigers" have welcomed international capital and the exploitation of their workers and, as a result, their economies have flourished: their own capital stock has grown; their workers, entrepreneurs and administrators have been trained; full employment has been achieved; wages have risen, and the means to pay attention to ecological cleaning up operations have now mean generated. In Latin America, India and Africa, by contrast, governments and citizens have been resentful of the wealthy, suspicious of foreign capital, indignant about exploitation and dependency, rigid in their pursuit of equality and self-reliance - and become the poorer.

Liberals say that the socalled side-effects of capitalist growth, such as pollution and slum formation, are the *consequence of mismanagement* rather than the implication of liberal principles. Countries like Switzerland and Singapore are clean and green and safe. There is nothing in capitalism which prevents other countries from emulating them. In Eastern European countries, by contrast, pollution and ecological deterioration have spun completely out of control under socialist rule.

Finally, liberals maintain that there is no substitute for the *freedom of the individual*, for personal dignity and human rights. While capitalism is not perfect, there has never been a system in history which has guaranteed more freedom, more rights and more dignity to the individual. Individuals can again agree to cooperate in groups, and even build up huge collective ventures, according to their own choice and the demands of productivity. They can consume or save their assets. They can expose themselves to the mass media or switch them off. They are also free to take public responsibility upon themselves. Social services are increasingly being expected from private enterprises. Moreover, in capitalist countries you find a great proliferation of voluntary initiatives and non-governmental organisations (NGOs) in which concern for the wellbeing of the society, the local community and the natural world is free to develop its own specific goals and channels. So what is there to gain from a socialist system?

Questions

Revision: Summarise the most important arguments for and against the capitalist system.

Application: Who do you think would be more easily convinced of the merits of capitalism — the privileged or the poor? Why should this be the case?

Critique: (a) "After the dramatic collapse of socialism the free enterprise system has been vindicated as the sole solution to the economic problems of humankind. Your negative attitude will not alter its victorious march through history."

               (b) "How can you belittle the incredible ravages brought upon the majority of humankind by this inhuman system of institutionalised greed and brutality!" Could you comment on the probable motives leading to these two statements?

Let us summarise

We began with a short survey of the *historical evolution* of Western economic systems, beginning with traditional communalism, through the slave economy, feudalism, merchant capitalism and mercantilism, early industrial capitalism and modern fully developed capitalism.

Then we looked at the general *ideological presuppositions* of liberalism which underpin the capitalist system. Its most cherished value is the freedom of the individual. Freedom is the prerequisite for the development of potentials and initiative. Material incentives enhance the productivity of people and the entire economic process. It is also assumed that human beings are to be masters of the natural world and that the latter should be utilised for human benefit. It is believed that the human race can attain ever greater insight and wellbeing through science and technology.

The *economic principles* of the free enterprise system include private ownership of all factors of production, a minimum of state intervention in the economy, free competition, the allocation of resources according to their relative productivity, the determination of the quantity and price of any resource, commodity or service through the balancing out of supply and demand in the market, the sovereignty of the consumer, and self-responsibility for your economic security.

Among the *advantages* of this system we enumerated individual freedom, the powerful generation of human motivations, the enhancement of efficiency, the principle that institutions prove their viability or perish, the accumulation of productive capital, and, as the overall result, greater levels of prosperity than attained in any other system in human history so far.

Critics point out that capitalist liberalism allows human selfishness free reign and undercuts public responsibility; that uncontrolled freedom leads to the concentration of wealth and power — which again destroy freedom; the manipulation of the state by the rich; the bias of production, distribution and consumption towards the wealthy; the irrationality of the profit motive and consumerist attitudes; the dangerous and misleading obsession with economic growth; the psychological effects of competition; the formation of ethnic or racial interest groups, and the failure of liberal economics to reveal the truth and tackle the problems generated by this system.

Finally, we saw how liberals would *respond* to this critique. They would point out, especially, that in the alternative system, namely Marxist socialism, power is much more concentrated; that it is much more oppressive; that bureaucratic planning smothers initiative and leads to a lack of efficiency and productivity; that it is inflexible; that the development of the modern urban-industrial system must be accepted, and that there is no substitute for individual freedom, human rights and personal dignity — all of which are central to the liberal creed. So let us now look at the socialist alternative.

Notes

1   For a short summary of Weber's thesis see Davies, C 1992: The Protestant ethic and the comic spirit of capitalism. Brit Journ of Sociol. 43/1992 421-42.

2   Encyclopaedia Britannica, vol 2, 1986, p 831.

3   Suggested reading: Encyclopaedia Brittanica 1986, vol 18, pp 730ff, 752ff, 777ff, 805ff; Armstrong 1991.

4   For more detail on liberalism consult: Encyclopaedia Britannica 1986 vol 27 pp 471ff; on the genesis of modern ideologies in general see Ingersol 1991.

5   For a description of liberalism see Bellamy in Eatwell 1993, pp 23ff.

6   Heilbroner 1985:63.

7   Heilbroner 1985:33ff.

8   For instance Robinson 1991.

9   Hunt 1981:522ff.

10 Barratt Brown 1984:57.

11 For a lucid description of the Keynesian argument see Barratt Brown 1984:57-70. Cf Hunt 1981:429ff.

12 For a lucid description and critique of the Monetarist model see Barratt Brown 1984:71-83; cf also Hoover 1989 and Henry 1990.

13 If you have difficulties with the graph consult any conventional text book on economics.

14 For a critical description and assessment of the market mechanism see Hunt 1981:209ff and Berthoud in Sachs 1992:70ff.

15 For more detail see Galbraith 1958; Tawney 1948; Heilbroner 1985:63f; Hay 1987.

16 This point has been highlighted by Fukuyama 1992:315ff.

17 See Heilbroner 1985:125f. The latter quotes Friedman as an exponent of the theory, and argues that there are no explanations for this theory, because capitalism has often been combined with oppressive systems or authoritarianism. Yet it is true that political freedom in the modern sense of the word has only appeared in capitalist states. For a deeper reflection on this problem see Fukuyama 1992.

18 According to Drucker the cost of Ford's Model T was equivalent to a worker's salary of 3 - 4 years, while a year's wages and benefits of a worker today is the equivalent of the 8 times the cost of a cheap new car in the US (1993:35).

19 Suggested Reading: Berger 1986; cf Hirschmann 1977.

20 For a critical account see Berthoud in Sass 1992:74ff.

21 Mt 6:24.

22 1 Tim 5:6ff.

23 Heilbroner 1985:65ff.

24 Heilbroner 1985:95ff.

25 "Goods moved to where the richest markets were; capital and labour followed them. Development took place in the already developed economies and in the most developed parts of them." Barratt Brown 1984:65.

26 For a very radical view see Gross 1985.

27 Turp 1994:54.

28 Heilbroner 1985:129.

29 "... economics is patently the instantiation of the very illusions of autonomy enjoyed by the economic process itself." Heilbroner 1988:32.

30 Holland 1987, for instance, argues that, while small national firms continue to survive, multinational corporations have conquered more than 50 % of the national and international markets and can manipulate or bypass government policy.

31 Heilbroner 1985:59ff.

32 For more detail on imperialism see Hampe P 1986; the classical Marxist-Leninist theory was formulated on the basis of earlier writers such as Hobson and Hilferding by Lenin (Imperialism: The highest stage of capitalism); the theme was picked up by Nkrumah 1965 and others in the Third World.

33 For a critical discussion of competition as an economic concept see Lutz & Lux 1979:103ff.

34 Cf Offe 1985.

35 Cf Newman 1988.

36 Heilbroner 1985:56.

37 Apart from Marxist critics this has been shown time and again by Western critics, including economists, such as Heilbroner 1985:107ff and 1988:187ff, Galbraith, Tawney, and others.

38 Cf Hirschmann 1977.

39 For a contrary view see Williamson 1980 and 1985.

40 Heilbroner 1985:130.

41 Suggested reading: Barratt Brown 1984; Berthoud in Sachs 1992:70ff; Arnold 1990; Hoover 1989; Baird 1989.

CHAPTER 3

The egalitarian model - Socialism

What is the task of this chapter?

In the introduction we gave an impression of the glaring discrepancies between rich and poor sections of the population and their impact on nature. Economic systems are supposed to address this set of problems. In chapter 2 we discussed the liberal capitalist model. Basically it maintains that we should not reduce the productivity of the nation by forced redistribution; we should rather concentrate our efforts and resources on enlarging the cake, then everybody's slice would grow with it.

In this chapter we shall discuss the opposite argument, as advanced by the egalitarian or socialist school of thought. While growth, achievement and performance are not unimportant for socialists, *equality*, or at least equity, is their decisive consideration. As in the previous chapter, section I is descriptive. It offers a *short historical survey* of socialist ideas and systems and a survey of the *basic assumptions and principles* of socialism. In section II we deal with the *critique* of the socialist approach, including its advantages and disadvantages, and close with the *response* of socialists to this critique.

Section I - Description

A historical survey

Whatever its causes, the contrast between wealth and misery, existing side by side in the same society, has always been a sting which *poisoned social relationships*. It arouses the resentment of the disadvantaged and troubles the conscience of the privileged. It produces ever new accusations, rationalisations and self-justifications and on either side. Throughout history there have been attempts to prevent it, to castigate it, to rebel against it, to establish a counter-culture based on equality, or to eradicate it from society altogether.

In *subsistence cultures,* for instance those found in traditional African societies, we find a rigorous social system which is designed to nip in the bud any emergence of economic discrepancies. Both production and consumption are communal concerns and the development of individual initiative for private gain is a severe offence.

Great *thinkers and moralists,* such as ancient Greek philosophers (Plato), Old Testament prophets (Amos), Jesus and his early followers, founders of world religions (Buddha), and many others have expressed concern about the accumulation of wealth in the midst of poverty. In the history of the church, religious orders established communities which lived out the ideal of frugality and equality. *Religious movements* such as the Waldensians, the Hussites, the Anabaptists and the Moravians had egalitarian ideals. Beginning with the famous *Utopia* (Greek for "no place") written by Thomas More in 1516, a series of *philosophers* attempted to design an ideal social system. During both the English and French revolutions, which were directed against the economic privilege and political power of the nobility, strong *egalitarian movements* such as the Levellers in England and the Babeuf in France, became politically significant but did not reach their goals. The battle cry of the French Revolution (liberty, equality and fraternity) did not materialise.[1]

Social conditions had to become ripe for socialism to emerge as a real force in society. This happened in Europe during the 19th Century as a result of the industrial revolution. Huge economic discrepancies evolved between wealthy factory owners and impoverished workers. The collapse of the feudal system removed the humble social securities which the poor had previously enjoyed, and, according to the reigning doctrine of liberalism, the state was not supposed to interfere. In the face of injustice and misery, creative thinkers took up the challenge and socialist movements gained momentum. Eclipsing more moderate authors, *Karl Marx* and *Friedrich Engels*, fathers of a radical type of socialism, became the most influential socialist theorists. Rejecting socialist reforms, they believed in the overthrow of the existing order and the creation of a new society.

Early socialist revolts, notably the uprising of 1848 in Germany, were unsuccessful. But social pressures continued to build up. Some governments saw the dangers of an explosive situation, and began to institute *democratic reforms*. Others, among them the leaders of the vast Russian Empire, failed to heed the signs of the times.

A watershed was reached when, under the leadership of Lenin, the communists in Russia turned a popular revolution to their favour and assumed power in 1917. For decades the *Soviet Union* remained the only example of a successful Marxist revolution. This fact led to a shift in communist policy from the ultimate goal of world revolution to achieving "socialism in one country", that is, entrenching the regime in Moscow and securing its leadership over the international communist movement.

Gradually Marxism-Leninism gained momentum and spread all over the world, particularly in poorer countries. World War II made it possible for the Soviets to occupy *Eastern Europe* and impose communist regimes there. Successful revolutions in South East Asia followed, notably in *China, Korea and Vietnam*. Inroads were made into *Latin America* with the Cuban revolution, followed by the short-lived regime of Allende in Chile, and the Sandinista revolution in Nicaragua. For a time the revolutionary mood against military dictatorships characterised large parts of that continent. A number of *African* governments and liberation movements opted for Marxism-Leninism.[2] By 1989 more than a third of humanity was ruled by communist regimes. Since then the system has undergone a dramatic decline. In the Soviet Union, its mother country, and in Eastern Europe, it collapsed completely. We shall return to these developments in chapter 4.

In the West, Marxism played a leading role in the formation of socialist parties. For a number of reasons, however, Marxism was outflanked and ultimately ousted by more *moderate socialist trends*. Here are some of the reasons:

- When Marxism was first formulated, it was not believed that the existing capitalist system could be reformed. However, Western states increasingly yielded to pressures for a democratic system. The attainment of *democratic rights* seemed to make it possible for the worker population to gain power "by the ballot, not the bullet" and to transform the economic system from within. In this way the disruptions and totalitarian tendencies of the Marxist revolution would be avoided. Even Marx and Engels had contemplated this possibility in their time. By 1912 the Social Democratic Party, which believed that social conditions could be changed through democratic, rather than revolutionary means, had become the largest single party in the German parliament (Reichstag). Its success encouraged the spread of social democracy throughout Western Europe.

- In this development, *moderate socialist ideas and movements* had their impact. The Chartists and the Christian Socialists are examples of such movements in the 19th century. The Fabian society in Britain, which rejected both liberal capitalism and Marxist radicalism in favour of an evolutionary approach, gained considerable influence. In Germany Edouard Bernstein and others had called for a revision of Marxist assumptions (that is why moderate Marxism was called *revisionism*). For some decades a heavy conflict raged between orthodox Marxism and the growing social democratic movement. Gradually it became clear that the two could not be reconciled. Only a minority remained committed to the radical Marxist version of socialism.

- During the first half of the 20th Century the political climate was such that it favoured the *rise of totalitarianism* in Europe. In Central and Western Europe fascist regimes emerged, notably in Germany, Italy, Spain and Portugal. In the East, the Soviet Union entered its Stalinist era. This was followed by Maoism in China. Whether fascist or communist, totalitarian regimes displayed incredible ruthlessness. All vestiges of freedom and respect for human dignity disappeared. Millions of people perished. These traumatic experiences led to a powerful reaction among those who stood for human rights and social justice. World War II led to the demise of totalitarian systems in Germany, Italy and Japan, and the mood swung back from totalitarianism to democracy. As a result Marxism-Leninism became extremely unpopular in the West. The fact that the Soviets crushed one revolt after the other in their Eastern European satellites did not enhance the confidence of Western populations in the communist system.

- A blend of free enterprise with socialist principles led to *rising living standards* among poorer sections of the population in Western Europe. Workers began to enjoy a level of prosperity unheard-of in previous history. Great discrepancies became visible between Eastern and Western Europe, not only in terms of political freedom but also in terms of the wealth of the avarage citizens. The workers, who were supposed to lead the revolution against the capitalist system according to the Marxist creed, had more to lose than to gain from a communist takeover and became hostile to the student revolutionary movement in the late 1960s.

As mentioned above, the relation between communists and social democrats was never a very happy one. In 1924 the Soviet communist leadership abandoned its united front policy and declared social democrats to be their enemies. The result was the isolation of communist parties in Europe. In 1935 the communists again tried to form common fronts with socialists, reformists and liberals against fascism. But Stalin's pact with Hitler in 1939 exposed the opportunististic motives of the Soviet leadership.

The *final break* came when the Soviet army crushed popular uprisings against imposed Marxist regimes in Eastern Europe (East Germany, Hungary, Czechoslovakia, Poland). Then came Afghanistan. The abhorrence of Soviet oppression became so intense in Western countries that social democrats could only maintain their credibility among voters by forswearing Marxism and communist policy objectives. Even communist parties could not survive in the West without adapting to democratic principles. Marxist theory remained a source of inspiration for radical intellectuals but then mainly in "revisionist" or "Neo-Marxist" forms, rather than in the form of Marxist-Leninist orthodoxy.

The history of socialism in Europe and elsewhere seems to show that radical versions of socialism flourish in *situations of extreme deprivation* and become unpopular once the situation of the poor improves. People crave social justice, but they also crave freedom. Above all they crave economic prosperity. When equity is achieved at the expense of prosperity, the pendulum begins to swing towards prosperity. And if people have been persuaded to accept a lack of freedom for the sake of prosperity, they feel betrayed when the system does not deliver the goods. It is the mix of these three needs — equity, freedom and prosperity — which is decisive, not ideology.

This observation also goes a long way towards explaining the situation in the Third World. After World War II *decolonisation* gathered momentum. Communist countries were ready to support liberation movements with weapons and propaganda against recalcitrant colonial powers. Many of the leaders of emergent Third World countries opted for socialism — in some cases not out of conviction but to link up with popular sentiments and to maintain strategic alliances forged during the struggle for independence.

After liberation other factors came into play: large scale poverty; inflated expectations; indignation over income discrepancies; state planning to achieve economic development; the desire to shake off Western cultural domination and return to indigenous social traditions, and the desire of the new leadership to wrest control over their countries from Western economic interests. Even elites who were not willing to forgo the privileges which capitalism provided, had little choice but to pay lip service to socialist principles.

There were essentially two kinds of approach in the Third World. One attempted to build a new society on *traditional social patterns* (African Socialism, Arab Socialism and so on). The best known of these is *Ujamaa* in Tanzania.[3] This is an indication that the newly liberated societies were not in the mood of wanting to exchange Western imperialism with Eastern imperialism. By and large, however, this approach was unable to generate a dynamic modern economy which could pull underdeveloped countries out of their economic plight. Where peasant communities lost their cattle and their land to collective villages, the socialist approach was also not particularly popular. We shall come back to this in chapter 6.

In countries which did not apply egalitarian principles, large income discrepancies developed between elites and ordinary citizens. This prepared the ground for *Marxism-Leninism,* the more radical and more modern form of socialism, to take root. African countries with regimes that professed Marxist-Leninist convictions included Congo-Brazzaville, Somalia, Benin, Madagascar, Ethiopia, Mozambique, Angola and Zimbabwe. This does not mean that Soviet type policies were actually implemented in all these cases. When the demise of the Soviet system unfolded, Marxism-Leninism was quietly abandoned in most of the Third World. Some formerly communist parties changed their policies in the direction of free enterprise and multiparty democracy, while others were simply ousted.

It is difficult to apply socialism in a poor country. The national economy simply does not have the resources necessary for large scale social securities and services. A welfare mentality does not enhance economic initiative and efficiency. Socialist governments tend to reinforce the popular view that the society owes its members a good life. If the population begins to *live beyond its means*, however, economic deterioration gathers momentum. This can become a problem even in richer countries, where budget deficits have become the order of the day, but then such countries can afford extravagance.

Of course poverty is not simply due to socialism as such. Whether African countries, for instance, would have been better off had they adopted a capitalist system after independence is a moot point. Kenya, the classical show-case of capitalism in Africa, has not been a story of unmitigated success. Perhaps there are just too many factors in poor countries which militate against rapid economic progress. The point to be made is that socialism did not necessarily improve the situation.[4]

The socialist world-view

The most fundamental principle of capitalist liberalism is achievement. To achieve, individuals must be free to develop their gifts. If this freedom is granted, however, some will surge forward and *outstrip others* in the competition for economic power and income. They can also use their power to undermine the competitiveness of others further. That is why economic discrepancies grow rapidly in capitalist societies where no countervailing policies have been adopted.

Modern socialism is a response to this phenomenon. Its ultimate goal is *economic equality*. Its radical vision is a classless society. Because equality cannot be reached when economic mechanisms are allowed free play, socialists expect the political leadership of a society to take over control of the economy and consciously direct it towards greater equality.

Equality presupposes a definite system of meaning, values and norms. It is humanistic, but in a communal rather than individualistic sense of the word. Equality implies that all people are of *equal dignity*. Nobody has a right to dominate others. Nobody deserves greater privileges than others. All people have basic needs which must be fulfilled. Luxuries should only be allowed as far as everybody can afford them.

This presupposes *solidarity*. Those with gifts have an obligation to serve those with handicaps. The interests of the community are more important than the interests of the individual. Private gain at the expense of others is immoral. You work for the community, not for your own profit or satisfaction.

Economic equality can refer either to production or to consumption. If it refers to reward for production the slogan is: *To each person according to his/her work!* This may seem to be in line with liberal-capitalist thinking. For socialists, however, the slogan has two implications. First, there must be *equality of opportunity* to raise an income. Everybody who can work is entitled to a job. Access to training for various jobs must be freely available. Second, there should be no possibility to derive an income from *sources other than work*, such as dividends, interests or rent. For that reason all forms of capital should be owned by the community or the state. Those who cannot work should be supported by the community.

If economic equality refers to consumption the slogan is: *To each person according to his/her needs!* If we combine production and consumption, it reads: *From each person according to his/her ability; to each person according to his/her needs!* Smaller communities of committed people may be able to operate on this basis more or less successfully. To cast it into economically viable institutional arrangements for the society as a whole, however, is much more difficult. Yet to socialists it provides a vision which indicates the direction in which humanity ought to move.

Marxists believe that the two approaches would follow each other in two distinct historical stages. The first they called *socialism.* In this stage it was believed necessary to pay people according to their contribution to the wealth of the society. But ultimately, when economic abundance had been reached and the classless society had materialised, distribution would take place according to need, not according to achievement. This stage they called *communism.* No Marxist-Leninist countries ever claimed to have reached the stage of communism. It is a utopian ideal.

Economic principles of socialism

The most fundamental principle of socialism is the *use of the powers of the state to achieve economic equality.* State control can be centralised or decentralised. In its most decentralised form the state may provide nothing but a framework in which workers or communities can build up their own management structures. There are various degrees in the application of this principle, both in terms of production and in terms of distribution. In terms of production state intervention can aim at one of the following:

- *Complete nationalisation* of all factors of production. This means that the state becomes the owner of all land, resources and capital. It is responsible for the provision of initiative; planning; allocation of capital and labour; management; technological development, and training. In radical cases it also determines where workers have to invest their energies.
- *Socialisation* of the factors of production. In this case it is not the state that takes over the economy; local communities are given autonomy to run their local enterprises collectively. Examples are the worker-owned cooperative and the factory managed by worker committees. Socialisation means, how-

ever, that there is no private ownership of the means of production.

- *Selective nationalisation* of key industries and private ownership of other industries, but under the control of the state, thus a "mixed economy".
- A market economy with private ownership but directed by *state planners* within a socialist framework.

In terms of distribution socialism aims at:

- *Guaranteed employment* for all able-bodied people during their economically active life.
- *Equality of opportunity* in terms of education, training and employment.
- A fair and *adequate income* for all citizens, covering at least basic needs of housing, food and clothing.
- *Social securities,* such as medical care and pension schemes.
- Free access to *education* and the enjoyment of *cultural assets.*
- *Levelling of status differences* in the society as far as possible. This implies equal political rights for all citizens.[5]

Questions

Revision: Give a brief account of the historical evolution and the basic principles of socialism.

Application: Because the South African state under apartheid intervened heavily in the economy, some people argue that it was a socialist rather than a capitalist state. How would you react to such a view?

Critique: (a) "You make much of the totalitarianism of communism, conveniently confusing Stalinism with genuine Marxist socialism. In fact, communism offers the only true form of democracy because it transfers power to the workers and peasants."

(b "You sing the praises of socialism under the guise of objectivity. Why don't you concede openly that you are a socialist at heart?" Can you find evidence to support one of these statements in section I?

Section II - Evaluation

Advantages of socialism

The advantages of socialism are a mirror image of the disadvantages of capitalism as discussed in the previous chapter. Let us mention the following arguments in favour of socialism:

- *Absolute poverty is alleviated or eradicated.* Apart from the intense suffering caused by physical, social and psychological deprivation, poverty makes people dependent on the goodwill of others. This is incompatible with human dignity. That some people live in affluence, while others lack basic means of subsistence, is a scandal to which humankind should never get accustomed. Human dignity presupposes a quality of life which is out of reach for the poor.

- *Communal responsibility is institutionalised.* Those who are advantaged either by nature or by history are obliged by the social structure to assist those who are less gifted or less fortunate. By implication this means that every human being is of equal worth. Those who suffer the greatest need, receive the greatest attention and care. This is how it should be in an enlightened human society. Only the state has the power to institutionalise this principle against opposition from sectional interests.

- *The reduction of discrepancies in living standards.* This is an important structural prerequisite for improved communication and social interaction. Affluent and destitute people are unable to communicate and interact naturally. Vertical relationship tend to be relationships of dominance and dependency. Socio-economic discrepancies also heighten the conflict potential in society, leading to crime, social unrest, and increasing investments in security rather than social upliftment. A socialist system is capable of overcoming these problems to an appreciable degree.

- *The democratic ideal is enhanced.* Human dignity demands self-determination. Democracy grants all individuals a share in collective self-determination. Capitalism as an economic system is undemocratic in the sense that large parts of the economy are run by a small group of people without the mandate and control of all the stakeholders. Socialism is democratic in the sense that economic decision making lies in the hands of representatives of those who are involved in the economy. These can be worker representatives on the boards of enterprises, or the organs of the state which act on behalf of the population as a whole. In contrast to Marxist orthodoxy, most socialists believe that true democracy only obtains where the government is given a mandate by secret ballot in regular elections.

- *Rational planning of the economy.* The economy is run not by the irrational whims and desires of market demand or a supply determined by the profit motive, but by the application of human reason for the benefit of the society as a whole. In the 20th Century it does not seem to make sense that scientific planning is applied everywhere except in the running of the economy. In fact, all modern economies need at least some planning.

Arguments against socialism

Unfortunately these lofty ideals have often proved to be elusive. The degree of benefit derived or harm done depends on how radically the ideas have been applied. Those convinced of the merits of a free market economy have raised the following objections against socialism in general:

- *Lack of motivation and efficiency.* Formulated in negative terms, human self-ishness is a fact. It cannot be eradicated by moral appeals, propaganda or force. People only develop their potential for attractive rewards. Formulated in positive terms, humans, as opposed to animals, long for creativity and mastery. Building up your own enterprise and to improv-ing the prosperity of your family are sources of inspiration and satisfac-tion. Initiative, risk-taking, efficiency, careful allocation of resources, maintenance of capital assets, and dedication to your task will normally not be forthcoming unless people have a personal stake in the operation. Increases in income and status are powerful incentives. By contrast, peo-ple's motivations are crippled when they are expected to exert their ener-gies for that great impersonal monster, the state, particularly when it makes no difference to their income whether they work hard or not.

- *Lack of responsibility.* Responsibility is a personal attitude. If you *institu-tionalise* responsibility, the level of *personal* responsibility declines. People expect the state to be responsible for everything. In capitalism, dissatisfied workers go on strike. After their grievances have been addressed, they con-tinue to apply themselves. In socialism, especially where strike action is prohibited, they fall into a kind of permanent, and largely unconcious, go-slow strike. Radically socialist states are characterised by incessant propa-ganda which appeals to group loyalty. But whether this actually motivates people to do their best is questionable. To improve performance the state then resorts to social, psychological and even physical coercion. Given human nature, is it not preferable to motivate people by granting them the freedom to pursue their self-interest?

- *Corruption.* Human selfishness can get out of hand in any society. In a sys-tem where it has no other outlet, it leads to lethargy on the one hand, to corruption on the other. In a socialist state officialdom has a great deal of power because the entire economy depends on the bureaucracy. If avenues to make more money through private initiative are blocked, enterprising people will try to climb up the bureaucratic hierarchy. The more power they gain, the more they will use this power to better their income and status. If they cannot do this openly, they do it underhandedly. It is easy for them to insist on bribes because people have no alternative avenues of achieving their goals. It is also easy for bureaucrats to manipulate the flow of finances, goods and services in their own favour. They can also cooperate and cover up their operation. In really bad cases corruption per-meates the entire bureaucracy. There is no will among the authorities to eradicate corruption within their own ranks because they all stand to lose by doing so. Leaders who stand up against corruption are quickly eliminated. The exploited are scared of the revenge of the powerful and cannot report or resist blatant cases without harming themselves. Corruption has been a major scourge in all state-run societies.

- *Welfare mentality.* Social securities tend to generate a mentality in the population which assumes that the society owes everybody a living. If all medical expenses are paid for by the state, why should you bother to look after your own health or to cure little ills on your own? If you can live comfortably from an unemployment grant, why should you try to make yourself useful or find a new job as soon as possible? Where the state acts as a parent, citizens never grow up.

- *Punishment of talents and initiative.* Egalitarian principles tend to militate against the development of the gifts of talented and enterprising people. The implicit assumption of egalitarianism is that it is immoral to be more successful than others. Elitism is a curse word. If in a school class hardworking and intelligent children are constantly required to mark time until their poorest class mates catch up, they will get bored, listless and discouraged. They gain the impression that it does not pay to exert themselves. To put it bluntly, socialism taxes diligence and intelligence while it subsidises lethargy and inefficiency. This is not only morally unfair but also socially counterproductive. A society which suppresses its most important assets - creativity, diligence and intelligence - should not be surprised if its economic performance is poor.

- *Lack of freedom.* Human beings were made to be creative. State or community control implies that roles are ascribed and actions are prescribed. For some the opportunity to avoid responsibility and leave major decisions to some authority above is comforting or convenient. For others it is highly frustrating. But ultimately it is the society that suffers when personal initiative and responsibility are stifled. People tend to become like sheep guided and protected by the "good shepherd" of the state or the party. Originality and creativity can only thrive in an atmosphere of freedom.

- *Bureaucracy.* In contrast to the private sector, state-run institutions are notoriously inefficient. Public enterprises do not have to fear bankruptcy; public servants do not have to fear retrenchment. The red tape and the lack of productivity found in the public sector have become proverbial all over the world. Even in the Soviet Union the struggle against bureaucracy was one of the perpetual preoccupations of the leadership. But you cannot have your cake and eat it. Radical socialism means that the economy is run by the state and that means by the bureaucracy.

Inevitably, every call for the state to intervene implies another block of offices populated by civil servants whose prime occupation seems to be to fill in forms, hold meetings, read their newspapers and drink their tea. They come late and leave early. "Bureaucratic drag" is a phenomenon were economic processes are stifled by the carelessness and inefficiency of those on whom these processes depend but who have no stake in their operation. Files are simply not processed. Mail never reaches its destination. Urgent matters are not addressed. Government computers are not looked after. A car belonging to the state belongs to everybody and to nobody - so why bother! Studies have shown that bureaucracies can survive without public notice long after their actual usefulness has vanished. An example is the continued existence of bloated defence bureaucracies after the war is over. Excessive administration consumes valuable resources without adding to the productive capacity of a nation. In a free enterprise system state bureaucracy is also a problem, but at least it is subject to critique. It must compete with the private sector for capital, experts and skilled labour. The bureaucracy which emerges in large corporations is not more acceptable than in the state, but at least it is trimmed by the dictates of competition on world markets.

- *Faulty allocation of resources.* To plan the entire economy of a nation is an enormous task. How do you know whether the population needs more stoves and fewer bicycles? There is no market mechanism to guide you. If you blunder with the allocation of resources in the free enterprise system, you feel the pinch because you cannot sell your goods. Enterprising firms sniff out market gaps because these provide opportunities for making profits. In a state-run economy faulty allocations are not easily discovered. Any command economy is characterised, on the one hand, by long queues of people waiting for items in short supply and huge stocks of items no one wants to buy on the other.

- *Deficient capital formation.* As we have seen, capital accumulation is one of the most important engines for rapid economic growth. To accumulate capital, a society must produce more than it consumes. Apart from a lack of motivation to produce in a socialist state, much of the surplus is also drained away by a large bureaucracy and the demands of the welfare system. In poorer countries this can have a crippling effect on development.

- *Does socialism not presuppose capitalism?* Karl Marx was the first to appreciate the enormous innovative and productive capacity of the capitalist system. He also realised that the wealth to be distributed must first exist; you cannot distribute poverty. So Marx believed that only an economy which has matured under capitalism is ripe for socialism. History has not honoured Marx's predictions that the contradictions generated by a mature capitalist system would lead to its revolutionary transformation. Communist revolutionaries only scored successes in relatively underdeveloped regions in the East and the South. But the truth of the matter is that social democracy only flourished in highly developed countries.

- *Is socialism nothing but state capitalism?* Whether socialism presupposes capitalism has since become a bone of contention among Marxists. What happened in practice? When the communists took over Russia in 1917, they inherited a fairly backward country. So they forced their way through the capitalist stage. The population had to work long hours for meagre wages to produce a social surplus. This capital was then invested in heavy industry. In this way the Soviet Union was able to become a modern industrial state in a relatively short period of time. This approach is sometimes called "state capitalism". Communist states which did not follow the recipe of state capitalism produced no such economic miracles. Liberals ask: could this accumulation of capital not have been achieved much more efficiently, much more humanely, and in a more balanced way, under the free enterprise system? If workers have to be exploited so that capital can be created, what difference does it make whether they are exploited by private business or by state officials?

- *Alienation.* Marxists say that in capitalist societies workers are alienated from their product because capitalist enterprises use them like cogs in their machines. If that is true, why make that alienating monster a thousand times larger by concentrating all economic activity in a giant state apparatus? Public control is even more impersonal, faceless and alienating than private control. In a radically socialist state nobody is granted the opportunity to own the means of production. Nobody is allowed to develop initiatives. Artisans lose their workshops, peasants their cattle and fields. They all become employees with nothing but their labour to sell. The argument that it is "the people" who own the wealth of the nation, when the state owns the wealth of the nation, is nothing but a propaganda ploy. In fact, everybody is alienated and this alienation is complete.

- *Selfishness and service.* Customer service is important for a vibrant economy. In capitalism service is induced by the need to compete and perform. Paradoxically the profit motive does not lead to a service of inferior quality. Nor does a socialist system generate a service of high quality. It has often been observed, for instance, that people serving in shops in socialist countries are unfriendly and uncooperative, while their counterparts in capitalist countries are friendly and patient. Arrogant and unfriendly attitudes can also be found among government servants in Western countries. Where there is competition you have to do your best and win over your clients or you lose them.

The response of socialists to the critique

The debate between capitalists and socialists continues. Committed socialists defend their system with the following arguments:

- Liberals want *freedom*. But where is freedom in a society dominated by giant multinational corporations? What sort of freedom do workers enjoy who have to sell their labour or perish? Capitalist freedom is the freedom of a free fox among a bunch of free fowls; a predator is free to exploit the defenceless at will.

- Liberals want *human rights* and personal dignity. But what is the use of human rights when you starve? What kind of dignity do you have when being reduced to a beggar? The advantages of capitalism are advantages for the rich and powerful. It is an ideological gimmick to interpret such advantages as advantages for the whole population.

- Liberals complain about *corruption*. But is a system based on cut-throat competition, in which less powerful competitors are at the mercy of their more powerful counterparts, more acceptable? True, human beings are selfish, whether in socialism or in capitalism. But in socialism greed is, at least, a vice, while in capitalism it is a virtue.

- Capitalists complain about *bureaucracy*. However, the giant multinational corporations, which dominate capitalist societies, are so big that they function like states, and the problem of bureaucracy and red tape is found there as well. These corporations are also not subject to democratic controls.

- Capitalists complain about the *welfare mentality*. But they conveniently forget to mention the capitalist playboys who live in wealth and boredom, wasting the nation's resources on a much grander scale than those exploiting the dole.

- Capitalists accuse socialist societies of *living beyond their means*. But it is not only socialist governments that have misled their peoples to live beyond their means. In capitalist societies ruthless marketing techniques and easy credit facilities induce irresponsible spending among the poor. Capitalist governments also overspend. The United States, the richest and most powerful economy the world has ever seen, has the greatest public debt in the world.

- Capitalists complain about *faulty and wasteful allocation of resources*. But is the wastage caused by luxury consumption - rather than catering for the real needs of the poorer sections of the population - really better? Is the emphasis on "throughput" at all costs a more responsible allocation of scarce resources?

- Capitalists complain about *productivity*. But Sweden and West Germany, who have adopted moderate socialist policies, belong to the richest nations of the world. The USSR emerged as a superpower within half a century. Maoist China emerged from misery within a quarter of a century, while income discrepancies were lower than anywhere else in the world.

- What about all the others advantages of socialism, such as employment for all, *greater contentment* of the less privileged classes, greater *solidarity* within the society, a sense of *security* for the disabled and vulnerable, mutual *respect* accorded to each person irrespective of education, income and position? Human beings do not have only material needs, but also social and psychological needs. To make everything dependent on profit and material gratification dehumanises people.

Questions

Revision: Summarise the strong and the weak points of socialism as they have come to light in the debate.

Application: Which groups do you think would opt for socialist policies in a country with great discrepancies of income such as South Africa or Brazil?

Critique: (a) "Your critique of socialism betrays your bias against the spirit of communal responsibility. As an intellectual you can afford to be a selfish individualist, but it is the labour of the poor which pays for your privileges."

(b) "Socialism has been an unmitigated disaster and belongs to the scrap yard of history. If you give these obsolete arguments a platform you simply keep alive a myth which has cost humanity dearly." How would you react to these statements?

Let us summarise

Chapter 3 on socialism is a mirror image of chapter 2 on capitalism. Again we began with a short *historical survey*. We followed the evolution of socialist ideas from traditional communalism through ancient thinkers, religious communities, early socialist parties, the emergence of Marxism, to social democracy in Western countries and socialist leanings in the Third World. We paid particular attention to the historic relation between Marxism-Leninism and social democracy.

Then we turned to the convictions and principles of socialism. Among these the *equality* of status, dignity and income among all members of the society is paramount. According to socialists, income equality is the key to social equality. You should not derive an income except from your own honest labours. Those who cannot work should be looked after by society. Capital should be owned collectively or controlled by the state. To achieve equality the *state must intervene* in the economy or, more radically, it must plan and run the economy itself. Socialism is, in various degrees, a command system.

Among the *advantages* of socialism we enumerated the eradication of poverty, the alleviation of income and status discrepancies, the institutionalisation of public responsibility, the extension of the democratic ideal to the economic sphere of life, and the greater utilisation of human reason in the determination of the economy.

Critics of socialism have pointed out the lack of motivation and efficiency, corruption, welfare mentality, lack of freedom, discouragement of talent and initiative, bureaucratic drag, faulty allocation of resources, deficient capital formation, worker alienation, and so on. To all these charges socialists have advanced counter-arguments.

Notes

1   For an overview of egalitarianism see Phelps Brown 1988.
2   For more detail see Albright 1980.
3   For a first introduction see Moll 1991:25ff.
4   For an historical overview read Lichtheim 1975.
5   Suggested reading: Encyclopaedia Britannica 1986 vol 27, pp 442-451. Cleaver in Sachs 1992:233ff.

CHAPTER 4

Radical socialism - Marxism-Leninism

What is the task of this chapter?

Marxism is a *radical version of socialism* which derives its inspiration from the seminal thought of Karl Marx, a 19th Century German-Jewish philosopher and social scientist. When we talk of Marxism, however, the first thing to note is that Marxism is not a static and uniform ideology. There are as many different versions of Marxism as there are of Christianity or Islam. To do justice to Marxism we have to distinguish at least the following versions:

- The thoughts of the early, and the later Karl Marx.
- The Marxism of Friedrich Engels.
- The Marxism of Lenin, and of Marxist-Leninist orthodoxy.
- Stalinism.
- Maoism.
- Third World Marxism, for instance in Africa.
- Democratic Socialism, which we shall discuss in the next chapter.
- Western Euro-Communism.
- Revisionist Marxism or neo-Marxism.
- Marxist tools of analysis used by Western social scientists and radical theologians without any intention of adopting the Marxist metaphysic.
- Floating Marxist slogans which make sense to disaffected population groups the world over.[1]

In this chapter *we shall focus on Marxist-Leninist orthodoxy* as it found its classical expression in the former Soviet Union before Gorbachev. Why do we spend all this time on what now seems to be a dead system? Future generations may remember the 20th Century for the emergence and disappearance of two types of totalitarian regime on opposite sides of the spectrum: fascism and communism. Fascism, the monster of the thirties and forties, is almost forgotten half a century later. Communism may be forgotten within decades from now.

However, as we argued in chapter 1, *history is unpredictable*. Marxism may "reinvent itself", or produce new, more viable versions.[2] New kinds of fascism may also appear. There are still some people who believe that the Soviets have corrupted the Marxist system; if applied correctly, it would certainly be capable of solving the world's problems. Moreover, the next few decades may witness a fundamental crisis of the world capitalist system. In such a cases people tend to fall back on ideas which the scrap heap of history has left behind. It is also important to understand why this great experiment of humanity to achieve social justice by totalitarian means has failed. The least we can do is to learn from the past, so that we do not repeat old mistakes.

In section I, we offer a short historical survey of the *origin* of Marxism. In section II we examine *Marxist philosophy,* the Marxist view of history, some basic concepts such as bourgeoisie and proletariat, and Marxist ethics. Section III sketches its further development under *Lenin, Stalin and Mao Zedong.* In section IV we *critique* Marxism's fundamental assumptions. In section V we indicate some of the *reasons for its demise* and consider its possible future.

Section I - The origins of Marxism

Western society has been troubled by a *basic contradiction* throughout its long history: its faith and philosophy have declared all humans to be equal, but its socio-economic system has divided them into masters and servants, rich and poor. The attempts which have been made over the centuries to resolve this issue had virtually no impact on the situation of the poorer sections of the population. By the middle of the 19th Century, the rift between the haves and the have-nots in Europe had reached alarming proportions. This was due to early capitalism and the industrial revolution.

During the 19th Century the old order was still legitimated and upheld by established religious and political authorities. But the English (1642-60), the French (1789-99) and the American Revolutions (1775-83) had already aroused an enormous socio-political ferment. Various social theorists had proposed alternative systems and some attempts were made to put them into practice. Spectacular scientific and technological advances fuelled belief in progress towards a better world. An optimistic mood prevailed concerning the ability of the human race to overcome both physical deprivation and social evils. It was in this *context of social unrest, glowing expectations and high ideals* that Marxism was born. Marxism must be seen, therefore, as a true child of the spirit which dominated the West ever since the Enlightenment — a spirit which attempts to subdue the world and emancipate humanity from the fetters of imposed religious and social authorities.

Karl Marx (1818-1883) was a German Jew with a long rabbinic ancestry and an excellent education. His father was a wealthy lawyer and the family converted to liberal Protestantism when he was six. Marx married the daughter of an aristocrat and was a loving husband and father. He was a deep and flexible thinker, a witty journalist and a shrewd political activist. Yet he never worked in a factory, nor did he ever join revolutionaries on the barricades. As far as his circumstances permitted, he led a cultured bourgeois life. After the failure of the 1848 revolution he was forced to emigrate. He spent most of his later life as an exile in London under conditions of poverty, illness and family problems, supported financially by his friend Friedrich Engels (1820-95). He spent his time in the British museum, ardently studying and writing. He died in his arm-chair.

The following factors helped to shape Marx's thought:

- *His enlightened Jewish-Christian upbringing.* We can conjecture that his childhood impressions instilled in him a sense of belonging to a cosmopolitan community, which transcended the narrow nationalism prevalent in Europe at the time, a strong urge for social justice and a messianic expectation for a better world.

- *His studies in law and philosophy.* Like many young academics at the time Marx was engaged in an intensive intellectual exercise under the celebrated leader of *German historic idealism*, G W F Hegel (1770-1831). This philosopher believed that reality as a whole evolved through a historical process in which the "spirit" (that is, the sphere of ideas) increasingly becomes conscious of its own potential by positing itself as a *thesis,* extrapolating its own opposite as *antithesis* and reconciling itself with the latter in a synthesis - which then forms the next thesis. This logical movement, in which seemingly opposite statements are reconciled with each other, thus leading to a dynamic evolution of insight, is called *dialectics.* Hegel believed that this historical process had reached its climax, intellectually in his own philosophy and socially in the Prussian state of his time. Nothing greater could be expected. A conservative attitude was the result.

- Marx retained Hegel's historical dialectic. However, he applied it not to the world of ideas but to the changing *material conditions* of society. He also denied that the culmination of the historical process had been reached. According to him the final social order was still to come, and it would be achieved only through a revolutionary struggle. A dynamic world view, positing the evolution of social structures, was the result.

- Some of the radical disciples of Hegel became disillusioned with his philosophical speculations. *Ludwig Feuerbach* (1804-72), an erstwhile student of theology, led the way in turning Hegel's philosophy on its head. For him the sphere of ideas (including religion), was not the primary entity from which all reality emerged, but a set of abstractions from human nature (for instance the capacity to love) and a set of projections of unattainable human wishes (such as immortality). According to Feuerbach, humanity is called upon to reappropriate the potential of the human race which had been projected onto a distant God and to give up all cravings which cannot be fulfilled.

- Marx accepted Feuerbach's critique of religion and philosophy, but felt that it *did not go far enough*. According to Marx it was not sufficient to explain the world; we have to change it. An appeal to reason alone was bound to fail, because at the root of the confusion between ideas and material reality lay the social conditions of the people who cherished these ideas. Therefore *the critique of wrong consciousness must make way for the critique of the social structures which led to this wrong consciousness*. Religion was, for Marx, the cry of the oppressed, as well as the sedative administered to the poor to make their suffering tolerable. This "opiate" would disappear automatically as soon as oppression, exploitation and misery were overcome. What Marx did not recognise, however, was that his philosophy itself constituted a new secular religion whose vision of a perfect world would inspire millions in decades to come.[3]

- In Paris Marx came into contact with *French socialist thinkers*. His life long friend and supporter, Friedrich Engels — who was the wealthy son of a German manufacturer — opened his eyes to the plight of the workers, the functioning of the capitalist system and the position of Britain as the leading industrial power of the time.

- Encouraged by Engels, Marx made a deep study of *British classical economics:* Smith, Ricardo, Malthus and Mill. He came to the conclusion that all would-be economic "laws" were human products designed to legitimate and stabilise the structures of oppression and exploitation. As such they were subject to revolutionary change.

Marx was a deep philosophical thinker and his writings are not readily accessible to ordinary people. His thoughts were supplemented, developed, popularised and, to a certain extent, vulgarised by his close friend and co-worker, *Friedrich Engels* (1820-1895). Engels grew up in a rich bourgeois family with pietist convictions. But he soon adopted the materialist stance of Feuerbach and began to develop a communist philosophy of economics. He used his position as a leading businessman in Germany and England to support Marx and his family financially, to highlight the plight of the English worker and to exert political influence. Together with Marx he compiled the *Communist Manifesto* and became actively involved in the abortive 1848 revolution in Germany.

The greatest contribution of Engels was the attempt to *design a comprehensive Marxist world-view*. He drew up a Marxist dogmatics which includes all dimensions of reality. For this reason, Engels is considered to be the father of what Marxists call "scientific socialism". This world-view assumes that nature, society and human thought all follow the historical-dialectical principle: contradictions emerge continuously and their resolutions are followed by new contradictions on a higher plane. In this way history moves automatically towards ultimate fulfilment. His work became the bible of socialist intellectuals. It led to the naive deterministic assumptions found in vulgar Marxism and to a rigid orthodoxy in all academic disciplines.

Yet Engels himself was flexible enough to declare, just before his death, that his and Marx' early ideas of revolution were obsolete and that proletarian rule could probably be achieved through the institution of parliamentary democracy. This flexibility led to the "revisionism" of *Edouard Bernstein* and his followers, who began to rethink Marxist philosophy in terms of changing conditions, but whose works were rejected by orthodox Marxists.

Questions

Revision: Give a brief account of the historical background of Marxist thought.

Application: Do you think that dialectical thinking could be understood and appreciated by ordinary people in your environment?

Critique: (a) "Why bother about Western intellectual history; Marx showed us that there is a struggle to be won!"

(b) "Why do you give these godless and blasphemous destroyers of religion a platform?" What do these two sentiments have in common?

Section II - The theory of Marxism

Marxist philosophy

We need to interrupt the historical account at this juncture and give a brief overview of the thoughts of the two founding fathers of Marxism. In 1848, the year of the abortive German revolution, Marx and Engels together published the *Communist Manifesto*. This still constitutes the basis for an understanding of classical Marxism. This document needs to be seen, however, in relation to its basic motive and in the context of its philosophical assumptions.

The driving forces behind Marxism are an extreme *dissatisfaction* with the alienation of the human being and the injustices and contradictions of existing social arrangements, a radical *impatience* with traditional explanations and recipes and a radical *commitment* to substituting the status quo with an entirely new, rational and humane dispensation by determined collective effort. Marxism is the theory of revolutionary action which derives its inspiration from faith in the possibility, if not the inevitability, of a positive outcome of human social history.

At the roots of Marxist philosophy lies an *anthropological assumption:* humankind is its own creator. Humankind collectively harnesses nature to secure its subsistence. Then it creates further needs, as well as the means to satisfy these needs. In this process it creates social relationships, the state, the family, religion, philosophy, science, technology, the arts and so on. But differences in capability lead to a division of labour. As a result people no longer produce for the satisfaction of their own needs but for barter or trade. Things now acquire an importance of their own, apart from their capacity to satisfy immediate human needs. Marx calls this phenomenon "fetishism".

Through trade, therefore, a product acquires a market value which is different from both its labour value (the value of the effort invested to produce it) and its utility value (the value it has for the consumer). This value can be expressed in terms of money. Because people can buy anything and everything with money, people now produce for money, not for the satisfaction of their needs. In fact, money becomes the overriding consideration in all dimensions of life. Therefore money becomes the basic fetish, idol, god or slave master of humankind. As a result of this development *human beings become alienated* from their own product, from their fellow human beings, from the community, from nature, even from themselves — all for the sake of money or profit.

This historical process reaches its peak in the *capitalist stage* of history. Now those who were more successful in outcompeting or ousting others in the economic war of all against all, have appropriated the entire product of society to themselves and barely keep alive those who do the actual work in the processes of production. Such a system is unjust, irrational, not worthy of humankind, and — doomed to collapse under the force of its own contradictions.

Only a revolution can remedy the situation: the system of a division of labour into autonomous units, each fending for its own interests against all others, needs to be replaced by a system in which everybody is integrated into a *planned process of communal production* to satisfy the needs of the community as a whole. Once the human being is no longer forced to compete with others, because the community produces enough for everybody, once nobody strives for private gain and everybody works for the common good, all things fall into place: human beings are reconciled to themselves, their fellow human beings, their products and nature. When the structural roots of competition, greed, envy, hostility, aggression, wars and so on have been eliminated, you no longer need religious and political authorities to maintain justice and order. The state can be expected to "wither away".

From these statements it is apparent that Marxists have a *positive and optimistic image of human nature and human history*. It is not sinful human nature which leads to unjust social structures, but wrong social structures that lead to wrong attitudes and ideas, and from there to all vices, conflicts and miseries. But these structures can be overcome by collective effort and will be overcome in the course of human history. It is clear, therefore, that for Marxists socio-economic structures and processes determine everything else in life. Beliefs, philosophies and social institutions form a "superstructure" built on the economic "base".

The Marxist view of history

Like most modern philosophies Marxism perceives reality not in terms of a static ontology, but in terms of a *dynamic historical process.* Taking their cue from Hegel, Marxists assume that this process is determined by the principles of the historical dialectic discussed above: a thesis reconciles itself with its antithesis in a synthesis, which then forms a new thesis.

In socio-economic terms this dialectic takes the following form: (a) due to advances of science and technology the means of production continue to develop. (b) They begin to clash with outdated social relationships derived from the previous stage in history. (c) When the contradiction can no longer be contained, revolutionary change replaces the old social order with a new one. So the determining force of history is the clash between the *rapidly developing* technical means of production and the *lagging* social relationships prevalent in the current processes of production.

When the base moves, there is a time lag until the superstructure follows suit. This creates the *tensions* leading to revolutionary struggle.

This view is called *historical materialism* (histomat) or *dialectical materialism* (diamat). It is called "materialism" because economic processes and relationships are believed to be the foundation ("base") on which social and mental structures develop ("superstructure"). It is called "historical" because social reality evolves in human history, and "dialectical" because this process is due to interplay between contradictory social forces.

Concerning the present dispensation, Marxism is pessimistic. The current situation is doomed. The attempt to maintain or reform it, is futile. It is also counterproductive because it can only prolong the agony of the transition from the old order to a new order. However, *the advent of the transition itself is considered to be inevitable:* human ideas, actions and institutions can delay or expedite, but not prevent its coming. Concerning the future, therefore, the Marxist dialectic is optimistic. Because the economic dynamic is in operation anyway, nothing can stop the world from moving to a better future.

Let us explain the historical process further. The elite which enjoy power and privilege, uses existing institutions, especially the state and the economy, to *entrench its position.*[4] It also uses religion, philosophy and propaganda to legitimate both the existing system and its own privileged position. The attempt to cover up or legitimate privilege is called "ideology" in Marxist philosophy.

On the other hand, the underdog population group, which gets a rough deal, obviously wishes to change the system. It can only do so if it is able to muster sufficient power to *overthrow the elite*. When this takes place, a new elite emerges which creates new institutions and new ideological legitimations - and thus the dialectic continues.

Therefore the historical dialectic must be understood as a *series of class struggles*, each based on a fundamental clash of interests between ruling elite and subservient population groups. In Marxist thought the class struggle has had a historical origin, namely the primitive communalism of subsistence peasants. It also has a historical goal, namely the communism of the classless society. In the former there was no class struggle yet, in the latter there will no class struggle any longer. Between these two points the class struggle moves through various stages: a slave society such as the Roman Empire, then a feudal society such as found in mediaeval Europe, and finally the modern society of industrial capitalism.

The elite of capitalists in this stage of history is called the "bourgeoisie" and the underdog majority of industrial workers is called the "proletariat". When the proletariat overthrows the bourgeoisie, a situation is reached which Marxists call "socialism". This will eventually usher in the ultimate goal of history, namely "communism", or the classless society. No Marxist state has ever claimed to have reached this last stage as yet.

Bourgeoisie and proletariat

According to classical Marxism the *bourgeoisie* plays an indispensable role during the stage of capitalism. The bourgeoisie emerged from the underdog class of the previous stage of history, namely feudalism, by outwitting, outworking, out-manoeuvring and finally deposing the elite of the feudal age, namely the aristocracy.

Since then the bourgeoisie has gone from strength to strength. It is characterised by an incredible *revolutionary dynamic* which turned the entire social system upside down. The rapid development of science and technology, commerce and industry, colonisation and imperialism must all be attributed to the restlessness and growing efficiency of the bourgeoisie. The inherent dynamics of the capitalist system cannot help but continue to revolutionise all existing economic, social, political and mental structures.

So vast are the powers which the bourgeoisie has unleashed that advanced industrial societies have now reached a stage in which the bourgeoisie is no longer able to control them. In particular, it is unable to cope with the *contradiction* between the growing productive capacity of the industrial system and a gradual collapse of the market for these goods.

The market collapses because the majority of the population is systematically *exploited and impoverished*. This happens because the capitalists appropriate the "surplus value", that is, the difference between what the workers produce and the wages they are paid for their work.[5] These wages are kept on a level which merely allows them to "reproduce" themselves. Because of starvation wages the bulk of the population is unable to buy the products of the industrial system. So while the process becomes more productive, it loses its markets.

The resulting crisis manifests itself in the concentration of capital in fewer and fewer hands, in overproduction, depression, unemployment, famine, social unrest, international war, and so on. These conditions indicate that the time is ripe for the next jump in the historical dialectic, namely the *overthrow of the capitalist system* by the proletariat. In this phase of history the bourgeoisie begins to fear for its position and turns from a revolutionary, to a conservative frame of mind. It now uses all its resources to maintain the capitalist status quo.

The *proletariat* is the dialectical counterpart of the bourgeoisie. It is a class of disinherited and exploited industrial workers. The proletariat is a product of the historical dynamic set in motion by the bourgeoisie. During the agricultural and industrial revolutions masses of uprooted and impoverished people have streamed into the cities and slums with nothing but their labour to sell. They are forced to work for long hours under abhorrent factory conditions for a wage which barely keeps them alive. They are dehumanised as mere cogs in the industrial machine. While the bourgeoisie controls more and more of the resources the proletariat sinks deeper and deeper into misery.

But this class is a *sleeping giant*. It has nothing to lose; so it is not interested in maintaining the status quo. On the contrary; it can only gain from the overthrow of the capitalist system. And so it is the only agent fit to bring about the new stage in history. In spite of severe repression by the bourgeois state, it begins to organise itself.

Some far-sighted members of the bourgeoisie now defect from their own ranks, join the proletariat and, with their superior expertise and initiative, take over the leadership of the revolutionary movement. Marxists call this group the *avant garde*. Without doubt, Marx and Engels saw themselves as examples of this special group of people. Under the leadership of the avant garde the proletariat organises itself into the communist party which develops into a formidable revolutionary power,

As the crisis of the capitalist system deepens, the class struggle intensifies. Before long the revolutionaries overthrow the bourgeois elite and establish the *"dictatorship of the proletariat"* under the leadership of the communist party. Marxists consider the rather harsh regime which follows as unavoidable in the transition from the capitalist order to the classless society. The reason given is that the revolution is not complete when the Communist Party come to power. The might of the bourgeoisie is still entrenched, not only in all the other institutional structures of society, but also, and especially, in the collective consciousness of the population. It has to be broken down systematically before the new system can become effective. Marxists call this stage "socialism" because the means of production are now controlled by the state on behalf of the people. In this stage the motto is: *from all according to their capabilities and to all according to their contribution.*

The aim is, however, to arrive at a situation where the motto shall be: *from all according to their capabilities and to all according to their needs.* That is the vision of "communism" which communist regimes aspired to reach. When this goal has been achieved, Marxists believe, all discrepancies in status and income will have vanished. This presupposes (a) a level of production which is capable of covering all conceivable needs and (b) the *emergence of a classless society.* The high level of production is the result of ongoing technological advance. The classless society is the outcome of the liquidation of the bourgeoisie, the dismantling of the capitalist system and the eradication of the bourgeois mentality. When there is only one class left, the class struggle comes to its end. The means of production are controlled by the workers themselves. Complete equality, optimally organised communal labour and advanced technology lead to equality and general prosperity.

The ethics of Marxism

Once a completely egalitarian society has been achieved, the structural roots of competition, envy, hatred, conflict, war, economic crises, exploitation, crime and so on will have disappeared. And so *the state* — as an agency necessary to enforce law and order — will lose its function and begin to wither away. There will be no domination of human beings over human beings any longer and the domination of human beings over nature will have become complete. The last synthesis will have been reached and the historical dialectic will cease to operate. That the communist leadership could itself develop into a new oppressive class, against which the rest of the population would want to rebel, and that the class struggle could therefore enter into yet another stage, was not a possibility.

Marxists have a *dynamic philosophy and a teleological ethic* which are both based on this vision. Human beings are perceived to be the supreme agents of the historical dialectic and thus the creators of human destiny. This means: (a) There is no power higher than nature, humanity and the historical dialectic. All change happens in and through human beings. (b) It is action which counts, not "mental gymnastics". Marxist theory is the theory of practical political action. Theory is based on praxis and its task is to analyse praxis with the aim of clarifying praxis. There is no knowledge for the sake of knowledge. Marxism is, therefore, an immanentist, humanist, action-inspiring, goal-directed philosophy.

This stance also determines the Marxist perception of *good and evil.* Human beings cannot stop the historical process, but they can obstruct or enhance it. Those who consciously or unconsciously try to obstruct it, are reactionaries; those who enhance it are revolutionaries. Those who do nothing inadvertently reinforce the status quo by the dead weight of their passiveness — and therefore belong with the obstructers. You are either for the revolution or against it. There can be no third position and no impartiality.

Any step which has the effect of perpetuating, stabilising, condoning, or legitimating the status quo is counter-revolutionary, thus evil, even if it is designed to improve the lot of the poorer classes. Any step which contributes to the overthrow of the capitalist system and to establishing the new order is intrinsically good, even if it implies violence and totalitarian coercion. *The end justifies the means.*

Marxists believe that they provide empirically verifiable analyses of social realities. They also believe that the basis of this analysis, the dialectical principle, is entirely rational. Therefore they consider their approach to be *scientific and incontrovertible.* In fact, their "scientific socialism" is believed to be the only possible scientific approach to social reality. All alternatives to their view are believed to be based on either myth or speculation.[6]

Questions

Revision: Summarise the main teachings of Marx and Engels.

Application: Can you detect any similarities between Marxism and the apocalyptic expectations found in Judaism and the New Testament, for instance in the prophet Daniel or the Book of Revelation?

Critique: (a) "Your description of this cruel and godless philosophy is so positive that it is hard to believe that you are not a Marxist yourself."

         (b) "You will never be able to understand, let alone convey, the spirit of Marxism unless you have committed yourself to the revolutionary struggle." How would you assess these statements?

Section III - Further developments of Marxism

Lenin

For decades the Marxist movement had its ups and downs in Europe, and both founders died without seeing the fruit of their labours. The *revolution in the Russian Empire in 1917*, however, gave the communists their historic opportunity. They shrewdly outmanoeuvred the other parties in the emergent democratic order and founded the first Marxist state. At the helm of this development was the brilliant theorist and politician Vladimir Illyich Lenin (1870-1924). He came from a petit bourgeois Russian family and was a lawyer by profession. He was banned and exiled because of his communist activities and publications and only returned with the outbreak of the revolution.

Lenin accepted the ideas of Marx and Engels, but added important dimensions to both the theory and the praxis of the communist movement. Most important of these was the insight that backward peasants and factory workers with a "trade union mentality" could not be trusted. Workers are not automatically in favour of the revolution. They can easily be bought with higher wages and more comforts. It was necessary, therefore, to build up a small, centrally controlled, highly disciplined and ideologically educated party as the decisive agent of the revolution. Its members must be ready to fight, suffer and die for the revolution.

Philosophically Lenin developed an aggressive anti-religious materialism on the basis of the works of Engels. He also added the famous Leninist *theory of imperialism* as "the highest form of capitalism" to Marxist philosophy. This theory says that the crisis of the capitalist system forces the bourgeoisie to find new markets, investment opportunities and exploitable workers elsewhere in the world. The subjugated colonial peoples become, as it were, a great global proletariat. Therefore the revolution against imperialism will be conducted not from the highly developed European centres but from the economic peripheries, the colonies, which are the "weakest links" of the system.

Being a shrewd politician Lenin first utilised the idea of locally elected councils (called "soviets") which were beginning to be institutionalised by the popular revolution in Russian territories. He also granted minorities in the right to develop their own languages and culture, even to break away from the Soviet Union if they so wished. But as his party gained ground he progressively established, both in theory and in practice, the *Leninist party as the sole agent* of the "dictatorship of the proletariat". The soviets became organs of a party-controlled state. All other parties, all independent trade unions, even the beginnings of worker control over enterprises, were prohibited. Ethnic groups which had opted out of the Russian Empire after the 1917 revolution were forced back into the fold. Lenin believed that state repression was indispensable until the time was ripe for communism.

Lenin's thoughts became the accepted doctrine of the international communist movement, the so-called *Comintern* established in 1919. With his dictatorial approach he was able to consolidate the revolution in the Soviet Union and to defend it against the onslaught of Western powers. Although he became critical of developments in the Soviet Union and, just before his death, issued

a warning against Stalin, Lenin had laid the theoretical and political foundations for a totalitarian and repressive regime - including its atrocities.[7]

Stalin

Joseph Stalin (1879-1953), who ruled the Soviet Union with an iron fist for
more than 30 years, perfected the totalitarian dictatorship for which Soviet
communism has become known. After Lenin's death Stalin eliminated his
rivals, Leon Trotsky (1879-1940) and Nikolai Ivanovich Bukharin (1888-
1938), and established Stalinism as a *personal dictatorship*. The polit-buro of the
party became the centre of power. As instruments of the party the bureaucracy and the security system began to control and restructure all aspects of life.
All potential critics and opponents were eliminated. Half of the two thousand
delegates to the 17th Party Congress were executed for alleged counter-revolutionary tendencies. Millions of kulaks (more wealthy peasants) became casu-
alties of Stalin's ruthless policy of collectivisation in agriculture.

With his five-year plans, beginning in 1928, Stalin forced industrialisation upon an economically backward country. In spite of its severe human
costs, this policy was economically successful, at least in its initial stages.
The Soviet Union became a superpower within half a century, in spite of the
devastating war against Germany. The capital necessary for the growth of
heavy industry was extorted from the population - a policy sometimes called
state capitalism. Labour camps provided forced labour in remote places. Vast
population groups were resettled.

All these actions were legitimated by the Stalinist version of Marxist-
Leninist ideology. No deviation from the official doctrine was permitted and
dissidents were cruelly persecuted.

Since the world revolution did not materialise as expected, Stalin formulated the doctrine of "socialism in one country". The Soviet Union had to be established as the firm *basis for building up world socialism* and as a launching pad for
the revolution elsewhere in the world. As a result communist parties in other
countries were expected to subject themselves to the interests of the Soviet
Union. This amounted to a new kind of imperialism. The Comintern gradually became Stalin's foreign policy instrument until it was dissolved in 1943.

World War II (1939-45) gave Stalin the opportunity to follow his "salami
tactics" of adding slices of Eastern European territory to his sphere of influence. He annexed parts of German territory (Eastern Prussia), shifted Poland
geographically to the West into German territory and added the Eastern
parts of Poland to the Soviet Union. Millions of people had to be resettled.
The Baltic States were annexed as well. In other Eastern European countries
communist regimes were set up and protected by Soviet military might. As
a counter to the Marshall Plan, Stalin integrated the economies of Eastern

Europe with that of the Soviet Union in the "Council for Mutual Economic Assistance" (Comecon). The military capabilities of these "satellites" were integrated in the Warsaw Pact.

Although left-overs of the Stalinist approach persisted in various communist countries, Stalinism was disowned and condemned in the Soviet Union during the late 1980s. This development had begun under Nikita Khrushchev (1894-1971) and found its peak under Mikhail Gorbachev (1931-). During the transition Lenin was still considered to be the fundamental authority for the communist party, but shifts in both ideology and policy indicated that a *break with this history* had occurred. Soon the giant monuments of Lenin came tumbling down in one city after the other. We shall deal with these developments in the next chapter when we discuss democratic socialism.

Mao Zedong

In 1949, when Marxist-Leninist revolutionaries under Mao Zedong (1893-1976) gained the upper hand over Chiang Kai-shek in China, a quarter of humankind came to fall under direct communist rule. Under the somewhat different political, economic and cultural conditions existing in China, the genius of Mao forged an *Asian version of Marxism*, called Maoism. It began with Mao's development of the theory and praxis of guerrilla tactics during the "Long March" of the Red Army through China. After victory, he applied this approach to the social transformation of the country.

Mao was very suspicious of any entrenched power, including that of communist functionaries. He believed that the revolution *must be perpetual* and that the younger generation can only learn the praxis of revolution by turning against their own (Marxist) superiors. That was the rationale behind the "cultural revolution" of the "Red Guards" which at one stage turned the whole Marxist establishment upside down, brought the economy almost to a collapse and created incredible havoc and suffering, until the army was deployed to restore order.[8]

This exercise was symptomatic of a *general shift of emphasis* in Mao's approach — an emphasis from towns to rural areas, from the elite to the masses, from intellectuals to simple people in Mao's approach. Mao realised that the vast Chinese population, rather than capital and technology, was the greatest economic asset of the country. He emphasised agriculture and small scale, labour-intensive industries. He believed in the wisdom and creative power of simple peasants and workers and forced all administrators and intellectuals to do manual work at regular intervals. All luxuries were forbidden. Rather than building hospitals for the few, Mao sent thousands of "barefoot doctors" with a basic knowledge of nutrition, hygiene and simple cures into the villages. While all political, social and economic initiatives came from the peak of power, Mao himself, the local village was the basic unit for their implementation. Self-reliance of the local community took the place of an elaborate bureaucracy.

For such a policy to succeed in a nation of a billion people it was necessary to control their minds. Mao strongly believed in the *transformation of collective consciousness* through re-education. Structural change was not enough. Traditional religion was viciously attacked and could only survive in underground cells. To cure the "wrong consciousness" of the bourgeoisie, sociopsychological methods, called "brain-washing", were developed.

Mao added a strong *religious-moral zeal* to the movement so as to capture the enthusiasm and dedication of the masses for a life of service to "the people". Mao himself and his teaching assumed almost divine significance in the ordinary lives of all Chinese. The "Little Red Book", which contained a selection of his sayings, had to be read daily in a sort of communal devotion at the workplace.

Mao forced a conservative population to *turn away from the past and towards the future.* He attempted to generate motivation through propaganda, success stories, regular mass campaigns and fostering a heroic, self-effacing spirit. In the villages primary group control was perfected. Every community had to undergo spiritual exercises with public self-examination, self-accusation and self-purification. There were regular public trials and executions of the unrepentant. A person would be pilloried as a scapegoat for whatever went wrong in society and then handed over to public anger. In this way a frustrated population could let off steam.

When evaluating this version of Marxism, we have to say two things. On the one hand, while Mao's measures did not generate a wealthy country, they certainly succeeded in *eradicating absolute poverty* in this vast, once dismally poor population. They also reduced income discrepancies between the less and the more privileged to the lowest in the world (at one stage about 1:5). Mao seems to be a hero among poor rural communities, who do not benefit from the new economic dynamic in China, even today.[9] For one man to control a billion people without challenge until his death was an incredible achievement. Under his leadership a demoralised and technologically backward country regained its self-esteem and dynamic.

On the other hand, the *human costs* of his programme were staggering. Visitors to China got the impression of a people who were preprogrammed in all details of life, worked like ants, and could no longer laugh. There are an estimated 20 million prisoners in China even today. Maoist China also followed the Soviet example of subduing and oppressing other nations, Tibet (1959) being the most glaring example. The fact that Mao's economic policies proved not to be sustainable makes the human costs seem even more unacceptable.

After Maos's death in 1976, China went through a period of turmoil and Maoism was officially abrogated. Mao's widow and the "Gang of Four" assumed dictatorial powers until they were ousted. Under *Deng Xiaoping* a cautious policy of economic liberalisation and opening up to the outside world was introduced. The Chinese have grabbed the new opportunities enthusiastically. In 1989, however, when pro-democracy demonstrations had reached proportions which the regime considered to be dangerous, there was a massive and tragic crackdown — with the massacre on Tiananman Square as its most visible manifestation.

But the policy of change towards free enterprise and a market economy was not abandoned. As a result, China recently achieved *one of the highest growth rates in the world,* 10.2% in 1995, and measures against "overheating" of the economy had to be introduced.[10] By comparison the North Korean economy is reported to be contracting by an average of almost 5%.[11] Inevitably the differences in development between Chinese coastal cities and rural backwaters, and the discrepancies in income between elites and ordinary people, widened rapidly and led to massive migrations.[12] Ironically, although not unexpectedly, some of the higher placed communist cadres of yesteryear have become the most cunning private entrepreneurs. So much for ideological dedication! The same trend can be observed in Eastern Europe and the former Soviet Union.

Elsewhere in the Third World

After World War II Marxism-Leninism *gradually spread* to other countries of the Third World. In some countries, notably in Latin America and Indonesia, it was ruthlessly suppressed. In others it succeeded in taking control of the state: North Korea, Vietnam, Cambodia, Cuba, Nicaragua, the Congo (Brazzaville), Angola, Mozambique and Ethiopia are examples.

A mild form of "Euro-Communism", which discarded Soviet hegemony and accepted the principles of Western democracy, survived in Europe. Many Western social scientists have adopted the analytical approach of Karl Marx without committing themselves to orthodox Marxist metaphysics or its revolutionary ethics. They are called *revisionists* or neo-Marxists.

The rather sudden demise of communism in Eastern Europe caused a chain reaction elsewhere in the world: in one country after another communist regimes silently changed their policies, even their names, or they were ousted. We shall come back to that below.[13]

Questions

Revision: How was the original theory of Marx and Engels modified and applied in later history?

Application: Do the communists found in your country fall into any of the categories mentioned above or have they since changed to a kind of social democracy?

Critique: (a) "Your description confirms what I have always believed: the only good communist is a dead communist."

(b) "It is simply not fair to measure the great humanist ideals of Marxism against some of its historical aberrations. What would you say if Christianity was discarded because of its mediaeval abuses such as crusades, the burning of witches on the the stake and the inquisition?" Comment.

Section IV - Critique of Marxism-Leninism

Humans are neither angels nor devils. There are positive and negative aspects in every human endeavour. Before we begin with the problematic aspects of Marxism, it is only fair to acknowledge its *considerable achievements:*

- *Philosophically* Karl Marx helped to overcome an idealism which located the engine of history in the sphere of human thought, rather than economic forces and collective action. By identifying the material prerequisites of collective survival and prosperity as the most powerful motivators of history, he helped Western thought to acquire a sense of realism. In this respect it is important to state that Marx himself was an idealist of high standing, in the sense that he believed it possible to reach a just, prosperous and dignified future for all of humankind through concerted human effort.

- As a *social analyst* Marx was the first to recognise the basic mechanisms of the capitalist system. His social theory, though considerably modified, has become an integral part of Western thinking. He also recognised the important role which ideology played in society as a way of concealing or legitimating elite interests.

- With his *vision of a better world*, and the emphasis on the human agent to attain it, Marx helped to break open a conservative mentality which cannot imagine the demise of the status quo. He turned fatalism, lethargy and dependency into enthusiasm for liberation, equity and prosperity. Of course, in this respect he was a child of his time: many great thinkers of the 19th Century were enthusiastic about human progress, cultural evolution, science, technology, economic development and social reconstruction.

- Marx accorded the dignity, the needs and the rights of the oppressed and exploited masses top priority in policy making. Put differently, Marx *placed social justice onto the world agenda* more forcefully and uncompromisingly than anybody else at any time in history since the old Israelite prophets. He also enabled the poor and powerless to regain their self-esteem, self-confidence and initiative by designating to them the role of prime agents of history. Marxists turned these ideas not only into an elaborate theory but also into practical power politics.

- *Personally,* genuine Marxists are characterised by total and selfless dedication to the cause of social justice as they see it. Admittedly this can easily degenerate into destructive fanaticism. But to say, as Drucker does, that "Marxism, the creed, did not have a single saint" is blatant nonsense - apart from the fact that there are no perfect human beings.[14]

- The sheer size of the *social engineering*, that took place in the USSR and in China, is impressive both in its organisational power and in its results. As stated above, the USSR developed from an economic backwater to a superpower within half a century, while China emerged from abject misery within a quarter of a century. Although the standard of living is still very modest in China,[15] unemployment and destitution had largely been overcome. Income discrepancies had been levelled out to a considerable degree. Fertility has been reduced dramatically, albeit through unacceptably draconian means such as the one-child policy.[16] Many Third World societies would have liked to see such results in their countries.[17]

So much for the positive aspects of Marxism. Coming to the criticisms which can be levelled at both the ideology and the system, we have to reiterate that Marxism-Leninism is a radical form of socialism. So the whole debate about *advantages and disadvantages of socialism* discussed in the last chapter is applicable to Marxism-Leninism as well. We invite the reader to refer back to those pages. Our intention here is simply to add a few facets which are peculiar to the Marxist-Leninist approach as it found concrete expression in Marxist-Leninist countries. We begin with a few remarks on the basic assumptions of the Marxist-Leninist philosophy and then come to its structural manifestations.

Marxist anthropology

Let us begin with a list of flawed assumptions which will surface again in further discussions:

- that all revolutionary leaders have pure motivations;
- that the motivations of original leaders can be transferred to the second generation of leaders;
- that followers become pure in their motivations as soon as the structures change;

- that dictatorship leads to freedom;
- that private property is inhuman and state control of property is more human;
- that acting on behalf of the proletariat without their consent is democratic;
- that history follows a Hegelian dialectic;
- that the class struggle comes to an end with the advent of communism;
- that history moves towards a classless society;
- that the collapse of capitalism is inevitable.

The first anthropological assumption of Marxism is that *the human being is autonomous.* Humans are supposed to be sovereign creators of their destinies, masters of their world and subduers of nature. This idea Marx shared with secular humanism in general and we mentioned similar ideals when we characterised Western liberalism. It has since become apparent that while human mastery is not wrong, a one sided and exclusive emphasis on human autonomy is dangerous. Human *self-absolutisation* has led not only to the ruthless subjugation, exploitation and destruction of nature, but also to similar attitudes towards human beings. We shall come back to that below.

Paradoxically, the craving for absolute mastery *enslaves* humans rather than liberating them. People who believe themselves to be autonomous have no transcendent reference point from which they derive their right of existence and to which they are responsible. It comes as no surprise if they subjugate or sacrifice others. It also comes as no surprise if they allow themselves to be enslaved by rigid patterns of thought, or to be oppressed by their own social-structural creations. Marxism shares this weakness with its arch-enemy, capitalist liberalism. Indeed Marxism is an outstanding example of this phenomenon.

The old problem of *the relation between means and ends* is relevant here. Granted, Marxists have lofty ideals concerning the ultimate destiny of humankind: equity to the point of economic equality, sufficiency to the point of the satisfaction of all needs, freedom to the point of making the state obsolete, participation to the point of placing responsibility for the community above all self-interest. But how do Marxists intend getting there? The means in communist countries have been ruthless oppression and the denial of human rights. But is it appropriate that human life, dignity, freedom and wellbeing be sacrificed for the sake of an end, an idea, a system, an ambition? We believe it is not, quite apart from the fact that the Marxist recipe failed to deliver the goods.[18]

In practice the precise opposite of what was intended occurred. Could it not be argued that this was an accidental aberration of a worthy motive? No, it cannot, because orthodox Marxist theory itself *foresees and legitimates these means.* The underlying assumption is that humankind is a kind of "material" which can and should be moulded by means of social engineering. The theory explicitly states that the oppression applied by the "dictatorship of the proletariat" is necessary for the classless society to be achieved.

Of course, communist oppression did not usher in liberation. On the contrary; it stifled human freedom and inhibited human progress. Marxism claims to be the theory of a praxis. If that is true the praxis must be taken to reflect the quality of the theory. It is here, more than anywhere else, that Marxism has *lost its credibility* among those who would otherwise have been attracted by its message. One has to concede, of course, that this disillusionment is also true for much of Christianity and secular humanism with their great promises, which are not necessarily matched by their achievements.

The second anthropological assumption which Marxism shares with capitalist liberalism and secular humanism is that the human being is basically good. It is only the social structure, and the bourgeois mentality caused by the social structure, that is at fault. Both can be *rectified by social and psychological engineering.* In other words, the human mind is a neutral sort of material with positive potential which can be, and must be, reconstructed. The history of the Marxist-Leninist experience has, I believe, exposed the fallacy of this contention.

To make the point, let us compare Marxism with a related creed, Christianity. Christians cannot be surpassed in the positiveness of their statement that God, though opposed to sin, loves the sinners. You will notice, however, that this positive statement includes the negative statement that *human beings are sinners.* In Christianity it is God who sacrifices himself in Christ for the redemption of sinful human beings. For Marxists, by contrast, it is human beings who can be, and must be, sacrificed to redeem the social structure. Christian abuses of human rights are aberrations; Marxist abuses of human rights are derived from the core of their creed! plow

The human personality is not a neutral material to be moulded at will. It can be raped, but it cannot be reconstructed through brain-washing techniques. Self-determination and self-realisation are the most basic aspects of human dignity. Their repression is likely to inhibit the growth of *personal initiative.* Totalitarian coercion is not likely to generate initiative either! Initiative grows naturally, motivated by the urge for self-realisation. But it can only grow to the extent that freedom is granted. You cannot make a plant grow; you can only provide the space and the nutrients which allow it to grow.

The same is true for responsibility. The will to serve the community can emerge and grow through insight and persuasion, but it cannot be imposed by force. *To become responsible you need to be given responsibility.* Society must take the risk of allowing people to think for themselves and take their own decisions. A person who is required to take orders and nothing more will not develop responsibility. In the Soviet Union people were treated like children and, as a result, they acted like children. That is, they adopted an attitude of waiting for "big brother" to solve their problems.

You cannot overcome *selfishness* through force. In spite of decades of the severest totalitarian controls imaginable, which Mao imposed on the Chinese people, the slightest liberalisation immediately led to what communists considered to be "bourgeois" attitudes: profit and pleasure maximisation! Moreover, selfishness continued to be evident under communist rule in the form of listlessness, lack of responsibility and corruption. While Marxists must be commended for trying to generate initiative, responsibility and efficiency, evidence suggests that they tried to do so with the wrong means.

It is also highly unlikely that *democratic institutions* will emerge from totalitarian coercion. It is no use to call a system "democratic" in which an elite claims to act on behalf of "the people", while the latter are not consulted, not even given an opportunity to object. Democratic institutions grow together with collective experiences in actual processes of communal self-determination. Freedom, self-determination and responsibility can only be acquired where the space for the actual exercise of freedom, self-determination and responsibility is granted to the population at all levels of life. People must be allowed to debate pressing issues, discover the social implications of their attitudes and actions, and widen the horizons of their interests to include everybody concerned.

It goes to the credit of Gorbachev's reforms that at least some of the presuppositions of democracy had been rediscovered in what used to be the Soviet Union and its satellites. But you cannot have it both ways: the reform-minded Khrushchev had been ousted way back in 1964. Once space for participation in decision-making had been granted by *perestroika* under Gorbachev, the pent-up yearnings of the population exploded. Because Gorbachev had no intention of exposing the communist party to open elections, the Marxist-Leninist system was simply swept away. In China the leaders recognised this danger and oppressed the democratic spirit with brutal force.

Marxist atheism

Obviously our view of human nature is intimately linked to the question whether humans are accountable to an authority higher than their own. It also makes a difference whether this authority is deemed to be collective humanity (such as the "interests of the working classes" or "the historical dialectic" in Marxism), or whether it is a divine being who is believed to be the master and judge of both individual human attitudes and social history (as we find it in Judaism, Christianity and Islam). Because the *question of atheism* has been of great concern for followers of these religions, let me add a few reflections on this issue. I shall base the argument on my own faith, Christianity.[19]

- To begin with, it would be inappropriate for progressive Christians to downplay or simply ignore the atheism of Marxism-Leninism as accidental and ephemeral, which some exponents of liberation theology have done. Atheism is a *necessary component* of the Marxist-Leninist creed.

- But we are not concerned in this book with metaphysical or religious assumptions about ultimate reality; we are concerned with the adequacy of economic structures. How do faith and atheism affect this realm? On the one hand texts such as Psalm 10 correctly identify the roots of ruthlessness to be *human autonomy* and self-sufficiency. Whether autonomous humans intend to transform the world into heaven or into hell for their fellow humans, they can still step over corpses in the process, if they are entirely free to set up their own norms, follow them when it suits them, or dispense with norms altogether.

- You could also reasonably expect that people, who acknowledge a God of redemptive love as their supreme master and guide, do have a conscience which precludes inhuman and ruthless behaviour. That this is not necessarily the case belongs to the *failures of Christianity*, rather than to the essence of its conviction. For Christians the means must match the ends. A new world of justice and concern can only be built by a praxis of justice and concern. As mentioned above, in Marxist philosophy the end justifies the means, a principle which has characterised Marxist praxis not only under Stalin but in many revolutionary struggles and totalitarian regimes the world over.

- On the other hand it is *simply not true* that atheists are necessarily more ill-intentioned, irrational, naive or brutal in political terms than believers. There are high minded humanists, agnostics and atheists, including communists, who spend their lives in self-sacrificing service to their fellow humans. There are also mean, misguided, inhuman and incompetent believers. There are also no demonstrable differences in economic motivation and efficiency between believers and non-believers. It is also not true that there are necessarily more atheists among communists than among secularised Westerners.

So we should not be quick in jumping to conclusions. We should also not hide behind the *issue of atheism* to escape from Marxism's radical challenge to social justice. It is the believers who should take the beams out of their eyes instead of complaining about the splinters in the eyes of atheists and communists. Yet the basic philosophy of Marxism must be challenged at this point.

Totalitarianism and repression

Marxism-Leninism has operated as a totalitarian philosophy for most of its history. To be fair we have to concede that this was *not the intention of Karl Marx himself*. Marx did not offer a fully developed cosmology, logic, epistemology, psychology, or ethical theory. Concerns like individual freedom, human rights, the relation between theory and practice, or even life after death for that matter, were all not spelt out sufficiently, because they did not belong to his prime interests. Marx' philosophy was incomplete and open ended.

It was also *subject to major changes* between his early and his later life. His early emphasis lay on a particular vision of humanity. Later it shifted to a perceptive analysis of a particular socio-economic situation. These were Marx's lasting contributions. He also ventured into bold extrapolations of probable future developments - most of which did not materialise as predicted. But Marx himself was flexible and willing to adjust his ideas to evolving historical reality.

It was *Engels* who recast all of this into a comprehensive speculative system of thought. *Lenin* then absolutised this intellectual construct as a creed to be imposed on every communist. No debate and no deviation was allowed: dissidents who had discovered major theoretical flaws in the system were persecuted; "revisionist" Marxists were disowned as traitors and counter-revolutionaries. Marxist-Leninist ideology became *a metaphysical and ethical strait-jacket.*

This had an stifling effect not only on the development of human thought (philosophy, science, education), but also on the evolution of economic policy, democratic institutions, foreign relations, and so on. One can hardly overestimate the impact this inflexible doctrinal system has had on human performance in general and on economic achievement in particular.

It would seem, therefore, that *the built-in lack of flexibility* of this doctrine made it incapable of adjusting to changing realities. It was like a block of concrete, heavy and lifeless. Like any other orthodoxy or fundamentalism, classical Marxism-Leninism cannot claim to be "progressive", least of all in its Stalinist version. With a pinch of salt we could say that its philosophy takes us back to the 19th Century, and its political praxis to the Middle Ages. In its initial phases it may have offered a new framework for social and mental reconstruction, but in the long run a system must be able to adapt to historical flux — or it will die.[20]

There is also a *built-in tendency towards fanaticism* in Marxism-Leninism. Marxist-Leninists are prepared to sacrifice not only their own lives, freedom and prosperity for their lofty ideals, as we have stated above with great respect, but also those of others. It appears that a morally perfect but unrealistic goal can be as inhuman in its effects as a morally despicable goal - such as material greed at all costs in rampant capitalism, or the idolatry of absolute power in fascism. In economic terms Marxism-Leninism produced great and largely unnecessary social costs without the guarantee that they would produce dividends for society.

The argument that the totalitarian character of communist regimes is *an aberration* of Marxism-Leninism, which Marxists then call "Stalinism" or "personality cult", is not convincing because Marxist-Leninist ideology explicitly excludes democratic controls at the level of social structures and freedom of expression at the level of collective consciousness. It clearly envisages a "dictatorship" for an unspecified time.

Power and ideology

This brings us to the problem of power. As we have seen in previous chapters there is a formidable concentration of financial power in the capitalist elites of Western societies. But in Marxism-Leninism the concentration of power is *much worse.* The basic question is not who owns the capital (and other factors of production) but who controls them. In the West the concentration of capital power is offset at least to some extent by independent trade unions, consumer choice on an open market, competition between companies, competing political parties, regular elections, the division of powers into legislature, executive and judiciary, freedom of speech and communication, a lively public debate, and so on.

By contrast, Marxism-Leninism deliberately concentrated all power — political, economic, judiciary, military, educational, propagandistic — in the hands of *the same small elite* and its bureaucratic apparatus. The party leadership assumed that it knew best what was good for the rest of the population in all spheres of life — from what they should eat to what they should think! The people had no say and no choice. They simply had to adjust to the dictates from above.

Ironically, therefore, Marxism-Leninism acted as an *ideology in the Marxian sense of the word:* it concealed and legitimated the power interests of a ruling elite. The origins of this development can be clearly pinpointed. Contrary to Marx's expectations, Lenin soon discovered that the workers and peasants — in fact the masses of the population — could not be trusted to carry out the revolution. A small and disciplined task-force had to do that on behalf of the population. At the best of times the Party constituted only a small proportion of the people of the Soviet Union, some say about 5%. Only the Communist Party was believed to have the "right consciousness" because it had been drilled into Party members. The party ostensibly acted on behalf of and in the interest of the population. If the population objected, this simply proved that the people had not yet developed the right consciousness. In short, the population was treated like a bunch of minors by an ostensibly benevolent but authoritarian parent.[21]

But even the rank and file of the party had no say. They received their orders from above. So the "dictatorship of the proletariat" was in effect the *dictatorship of the polit-buro* of the party and its general secretary. All this can be understood on the basis of the communist creed. What the creed did not foresee, however, is that people who have obtained power and are not subjected to democratic controls, may get addicted to it and use it to their own advantage, rather than to the advantage of the population.

Marxist-Leninist ideology is also deceptive in other ways. While Western countries used their historic links as colonial powers and their economic muscle to gain influence in the Third World, the East had to compensate for that with ruthless propaganda. It suggested that *every conceivable evil on the globe was due to capitalism*, while its own brand of socialism would create unlimited prosperity, justice and peace. Obviously this was nothing but eye-wash.

Racism, ethnic nationalism and fascism, for example, were all treated as outgrowths of capitalism. In socialist countries there was peace and harmony. Similarly insights into the dangers of uninhibited industrial growth on our planet and the perils of the population explosion have been discredited by Marxist propaganda as nothing but a clever device of the capitalists to keep poor nations poor and their numbers small. Under communism, it was promised, all people would enjoy unlimited prosperity.

Even problems emerging *within* its own realm of control were ascribed either to left-overs of the bourgeois spirit in the population, or to the manipulations of international capitalism. For a long time Marxist-Leninist governments denied, for instance, that they had problems of overpopulation, unemployment, crime, alcoholism, drug addiction, ecological disasters, shortages, inflation and so on. These were all decried as capitalist evils from which socialist countries had been liberated.

Of course, such realities could not remain hidden for ever. Once the oppressive cover was removed, all these evils *exploded into the open* in Eastern European countries. The ecological mess covered up in formerly socialist countries is almost insurmountable. Even China, still under communist control, more and more ecological disasters come to light.[22] As nationalist violence in the former Soviet Union and Yugoslavia show, ethnic rivalries and conflicts had not been resolved, but simply concealed by oppression. Similarly, the problem of unemployment had been concealed, mainly by resorting to inefficient job creation. When state crutches fell away, unemployment figures soared. Organised crime too has become an almost insurmountable problem in Russia. By allowing open discussion, non-directed research, a free press and parliamentary opposition, democratic countries have been able to work fairly successfully through at least some of these problems.

In the functioning of this ideology, the utopian goal acted as *a palliative.* The suffering inflicted upon their people by communist leaders was justified as a necessary stage in the historical dialectic. But the envisaged future had been conceived in such unrealistic terms that it was highly unlikely that it would ever materialise. So it is something of an irony that, while Marxism-Leninism accused Christianity of producing a "pie in the sky when you die" sort of piety, it was in effect itself one of those convictions offering a never-never land.

Imperialism

Lenin was a profound analyst and critic of Western imperialism. But what about the Soviet Union itself? The Soviets had inherited the vast Russian empire with a long tradition of conquest and oppression.[23] Less than half of the Soviet population was composed of ethnic Russians. As mentioned above, ethnic groups which had opted out of the Russian Empire after the 1917 revolution were forced back into the fold. Millions died, further millions were deported to Siberia, other millions were resettled far from their original homes. We have already mentioned the Chinese occupation of Tibet in 1959. As in the Soviet case, the regime tries to integrate the territory into China by means of large scale population transfers.[24]

While the Spanish, Portuguese, Dutch, British and French empires all crumbled, the Soviet Union remained intact as *the last of the great European empires.* It has since broken up into numerous ethnically based independent states. This indicates that it had not been held together by the free choice of its population, but by military might. The Russian Federation is a composite state even today, and the brutal repression of the rebellion in Chechnia shows that imperialism in that country is far from over. The high percentage of ethnic Russians in non-Russian former Soviet republics makes Russian intervention a continuing temptation in these countries.[25] Yugoslavia too broke up in a devastating civil war when communism lost its grip over the population. China, too, keeps its many ethnic minorities under tight military control, including the Tibetans.

Marxist imperialism was also in evidence on the *international* scene. For a long time communist parties all over the world were supposed to follow Moscow's line. After World War II the whole of Eastern Europe was subjugated to communist rule and most popular uprisings or reform efforts, even by communists, were crushed by force of arms.

Clearly it was not only ideological zeal but also *simple power politics* that was behind the Soviet strategy. Some peripheral countries were able to distance themselves from the Soviet Union and were tolerated because they posed no threat and continued in the Marxist line. Yugoslavia left in 1948, Albania in 1962, and more ambiguously Romania from 1968 onwards.

But where power interests mattered, the *iron fist ruled*. Examples were the suppression of the East German uprising in 1953, the "Hungarian way to socialism" in 1956, the Czechoslovak "socialism with a human face" (the "Prague Spring") in 1968 and the reform movement in Poland. Significantly the domestic regime in Poland was left to sort out its crises in 1956, 1968, 1970, 1976, 1980/1, apparently because it was powerful enough to do so. "The simplest common formula is that the Soviet Union only intervened militarily when seeing geopolitical vital parts of the *glacis* as threatened."[26] It is only towards the end of the 1980s that this tightly held fortress has been forced open by economic necessities.

To be fair, we have to say that similar goals and means were employed by Jews, Christians, Muslims, liberals and those with other convictions long before Marxism came into the picture. Western imperialism and aggressive capitalism have also exacted staggering human costs, not to mention fascist regimes in Central and Western Europe. Both World Wars I and II were unleashed in the West.

The flaws and failures of Marxism-Leninism have also often been exploited by those who defend the capitalist or even a fascist system, as if these alternatives were more acceptable. Western *anti-communism* developed into a set of ideological arguments designed to *conceal or legitimate the abuse of power* to maintain systems of dominance, oppression, discrimination and exploitation in apartheid South Africa, in Nazi-Germany, Indonesia and many other countries. Western democratic powers have often used anti-communism as a smoke-screen for the most questionable designs, often propping up oppressive regimes, such as found in Zaire, or anti-communist parties, such as found in Angola and Mozambique.[27]

Communists hold *no monopoly* of ideological deception and political brutality. Before complaining about arbitrary detentions, the suppression of truth, mass removals of people and the denial of democratic rights in Marxist-Leninist countries, the West should put its own house in order.

Economic theory

Concerning *economic theory*, I once again refer you to the critique of socialism in chapter 3 which also applies to Marxism. It is common knowledge that most of the economic predictions of Marx did not materialise. Very early in the history of Marxism "revisionist" or "neo-Marxist" thinkers exposed flaws in the theory and suggested changes. Usually such voices were "liquidated", persecuted or marginalised. This indicates that the ideology is an artificial construct, not an analysis of fact as it claims to be.

We cannot go into further detail. It is sufficient to mention the centre piece of Marxian economics, the *labour theory of value.*[28] To assume that the value of goods and services is determined solely by the quality and quantity of the labour needed to bring it about, as Marxists do, is an interesting theoretical idea with noteworthy moral implications. But the theory does not present a practical key capable of unlocking the secrets of economic efficiency and productivity. To reach economic efficiency all the scarce factors of production - capital, labour, natural resources, initiative, technical expertise, and organisation - must be allocated to the production process in optimal combinations and rewarded accordingly. "The value of labor must be determined by the value of the product, not the value of the product by the value of labor."[29]

How do we find out what this optimal combination might be? Not by looking back at the amount of work spent on obtaining these resources, but by looking forward to the relative contribution these resources will make to the productive process. Each factor of production must be valued in terms of the relative *increment in production* which an increment in investment in that particular factor of production would generate in any given economic situation. This increment is called "marginal productivity". Failure to calculate the marginal productivity of the various factors of production and to remunerate them proportionately leads to inefficiencies.

The value of produced goods again depends on what the population is willing and able to buy, thus on *market demand.* Market demand for a commodity is entirely independent of the amount of labour its production might have involved. Whether a tree has been uprooted by a storm or chopped down by workers makes no difference to the value of the timber.

Questions

Revision: Mention the most important criticism's levelled against Marxism-Leninism.

Application: If Marxism-Leninism was to be applied in your country, do you think that some of the weaknesses and dangers mentioned above could be avoided? Be specific.

Critique: (a) "The glee with which you tear to pieces the heroic attempt of the working class to overcome the ravages of capitalism, is nauseating. You conveniently overlook the fact that it was capitalist ruthlessness which made it impossible for Marxism-Leninism to succeed."

(b) "If you are really opposed to communism, why don't you say that this is a satanic ideology, which we should shun like the pest, rather than apologetically pointing out a few mistakes?" How would you react to these statements?

Section V - The demise of Marxism-Leninism

The dramatic collapse of Marxism-Leninism in Eastern Europe seems to have demonstrated at least two things:

- the *economic failure* of Marxism-Leninism to compete with liberalism under current conditions on world markets, and
- the popular *resentment* of those who have lived under Marxist-Leninist rule against the system and its ideology.

Concerning the first factor, Soviet Marxism-Leninism began with building up heavy industry and then, on this basis, constructed a formidable and highly sophisticated armaments industry. These developments were forced upon the economy by all available means and with considerable success. For half a century the Soviet Union was considered to be a superpower, on a par with the United States, and rightly so. During the time of the first Sputniks the Soviet Union was the leader in the field of space exploration. But the price of this success was an *extremely uneven development.* Since the resources of the Soviet Union were limited, the economy lagged behind in many other respects, notably consumer goods and computer technology.

In spite of the fact that the Soviet Union covered the greatest land mass on earth, its agriculture *could not feed its population* and large quantities of grain had to be imported from its arch-rival, the United States. Obviously this must have been a cause of great embarrassment for a party which not so long ago had claimed that the Soviet Union would overtake Western economies within decades. The Soviet economy was also unable to keep pace with the new wave of electronic communications and control technology; the development of new materials; more efficient use of crude oil, and so on. In the end the Soviet Union was no longer able to maintain its colossal war machine.

The economies of other *Eastern European countries* were similarly prone to failure. Poland virtually went bankrupt. East Germany, for some time the economic flagship of the Eastern bloc, was sadly lagging behind its Western counterpart and its total collapse was only prevented by speedy reunification of Germany. Since then it has continued to ail, and even the powerful West German economy went into an economic recession under the burden of reconstruction. In Albania there was total economic chaos, not to mention the economic plight of former Marxist-Leninist Third World countries. Some of these — such as Ethiopia, Angola and Mozambique — have also been ravaged by decades of civil war. Admittedly the problems of the communists in the latter two countries were compounded by the support the apartheid regime in South Africa and the United States granted the insurgents.

Concerning the second factor, that of popular resentment against Marxist-Leninist rule, it must have been humiliating for a movement which had always claimed to represent the true interests of the masses, to be ousted by an *uprising of these masses* in one country after the other. In Poland, the party which claimed to represent the workers tried to suppress a popular trade union, only to be toppled by this union. In the first open election in East Germany the communists were relegated to oblivion. In some Marxist-Leninist countries, for instance Romania, communist parties conceded multiparty elections, sometimes after heavy fighting, and tried to survive by changing names and policies. Ion Iliesco, the communist leader in Romania, was defeated at the polls only in 1996.

Even Marxist-Leninist regimes in the *Third World* - such as Ethiopia, Mozambique and Mongolia - changed their policies, though partly under pressure from the International Monetary Fund (IMF). Zimbabwe never really became Marxist-Leninist, in spite of the communist convictions of its leader. The stance of the South African Communist Party has become social-democratic for all intents and purposes. In Nicaragua the Sandinistas were defeated in an election, though under considerable US pressure. In Afghanistan the Soviet Union had propped up the communist regime by force of arms against Muslim rebels at great cost and without success. Vietnam is poised to jump on the bandwaggon of the "Asian Tigers". In China popular uprisings were brutally suppressed, but the regime changed its economic policies radically in the direction of free enterprise and a free market. At the time of writing old style communists continue to cling to power in Cuba and North Korea, but the writing seems to be on the wall for them as well. There are also a number of die-hard revolutionary movements left, such as the Khmer Rouge in Cambodia and the Shining Path in Peru.[30] Often they have combined Marxist ideas with racial and ethnic nationalism, which is incompatible with the Marxist ideals of global proletarian solidarity.[31]

Within the space of a few years, then, Marxism-Leninism seems to have been *discredited beyond redemption by these occurrences.* The disillusionment of the populations of some of these countries after abolishing the system and adopting free enterprise capitalism may lead to temporary backlashes and romantic yearnings for the "good old days". But it is highly unlikely that the old system will ever be retrieved. Communists in China can, at best, stage a holding operation and gain time for finding a workable alternative. Not so long ago, Marxism-Leninism was seen by many people as the sparkling solution to the global economic problem; it seems clear that this is no longer the case.

Reasons for the demise of Marxism-Leninism

The collapse of an empire, a social system and an ideology is, obviously, a highly complex phenomenon in which numerous factors play a role. Just as in the case of the British Empire, the demise of the Soviet Union will excite the imagination of researchers for generations to come. At least the following factors seem to have played a role: [32]

- The system of *central planning* was successful in the first crude phases of industrial development, but could no longer handle the increasingly diversified and sophisticated development of modern technology and industrial organisation. There was insufficient flexibility at the top, and innovative initiatives lower down were stifled by the hierarchical structure of the system. The same handicap made itself felt in the inflexibility of the monetary system within the Eastern European economic bloc (CMEA).[33]

- The top leadership fell victim to its own *suppression of information within the system.* They were increasingly guided by an unrealistic picture of the economy. Moreover, economic decision making was in the hands of politicians who followed ideological dictates, rather than practical considerations. The experts, who were guided by more pragmatic criteria, were constantly overruled.

- Following a deficient pricing system, great blunders were committed in the *allocation of resources.* The full costs of maintaining economic assets and social benefits were not taken into consideration. For instance, new buildings were erected while the maintenance of old buildings was neglected. Budgets did not always take into account necessary replacements for wear and tear in the infrastructure, like railway lines, roads and telephone systems. Factories had to operate with outdated technology and worn out machinery, and so on.

- In line with socialist principles *social benefits were generous.* But the system had to pay the price. The state guaranteed everybody employment, but this led to thousands of artificial "jobs" that made no productive contribution to the economy. Transport and telecommunications were exceptionally cheap but they operated at a loss. Agricultural prices were kept at low levels. When market principles were introduced, food prices soared tenfold in some cases - proving that previously food had virtually been given away.

- The overall effect of the welfare state was, moreover, that the population was fooled into believing that stable jobs, cheap food, transport and housing, and other social benefits such as free education and medical care, were a guaranteed right and could be enjoyed without a corresponding investment in productive effort. Compared to the West, *the economic pace in the East was very relaxed.*

- Similarly state enterprises were not allowed to go bankrupt. Those which operated at a loss were *subsidised.* They drained away the resources of the nation, rather than contributing to its assets. Because state run enterprises are generally less productive than privately owned firms, inefficiency permeated the whole system. Modes of production were also allowed to become obsolete; in time they not only became inefficient but also produced massive ecological disasters.[34]

- One has to concede that, if assessed on its own terms, the achievements of the communist system may appear to be quite impressive. Many Third World countries could have congratulated themselves had they been able to produce such progress in such a short time. But the system *could not keep pace* with the accelerating development of technology in the West. When the Soviet Union as the prime market for Eastern Europe disintegrated, Eastern industries could not dispose of their products because nobody wanted them. It was then that the whole system spiralled downward. In East Germany, for instance, people had waited for their little Trabant cars for up to 10 years. But as soon as the borders opened up and second-hand Volkswagen Golfs became available from the West, within a single month over 1000 Trabants were simply abandoned on the streets of Berlin alone.

- Part of the problem was that the Eastern bloc had sealed itself off from international competition. As long as these countries traded mainly among themselves, the system worked reasonably well. But the *lack of innovative challenges* caused them to lag behind the US, Japan and Europe, particularly in electronic technology, crude oil utilisation and ecologically clean technology. Thus when the system began to open up to the outside world, the old enterprises were knocked out by competition and there was no way of replacing them overnight with new and competitive ones.

- The economic difficulties of Eastern Europe are also reflected in the increasing *debt burden*.[35] Although the Soviet Union produced its own oil, it suffered under the same crippling debt as countries such as Brazil or Mexico.

- The Soviet Union was also unable to keep up with the United States in the *arms race*. At some stage the US deliberately accelerated its armaments development programme to force the Soviet Union into allocating more and more resources to arms production. The aim was to bring the Soviet economy to its knees and the strategy succeeded remarkably well. In 1987 the West's North Atlantic Treaty Organisation (NATO) spent US $ 446.6 billion, and the East's Warsaw Pact US $ 364.5 billion on defence. Yet the former represented only 15% of the budget of central governments, while the latter represented 36.5%.[36] Armaments simply drained the Soviet economy.

- Why did the Soviets not simply ignore this challenge, when they knew that they already had sufficient nuclear weapons to blow up the West several times over? In the first place there was *genuine fear*; in the second place it was a matter of *prestige*. Arms were the one area in which the USSR had shown that it was equal to its Western counterparts. By the time Gorbachev realised their mistake, the downward spiral could no longer be contained.

- Due to faulty planning, the distribution of goods and services did not work properly. Long queues for *goods in short supply* and *great surpluses* of items which nobody wanted could be seen in all the shops. If people could not get their daily needs through normal channels, they had to operate through the "black market". You had to barter, say, bricks for rafters. Artisans who should have done repair work on behalf of their companies during working hours, preferred to do so at night for their private pockets. The result was that, apart from the malfunctioning of the economic system as a whole, the state lost billions in state revenue.

- The system *sapped the morale* of the population. Constant repression by the communist security system took its toll. There were no human rights. Marx's adage, that the ruling law is the law of the rulers, became true in Marxist countries. Initially the promise of vast improvements in social benefits and living standards may have galvanised the people into working hard. But time dragged on and the sacrifices called for by the leaders failed to produce improvements in standards of living. This generated popular disillusionment, listlessness and lethargy.

- To this we have to add the stifling effect of state control in all spheres of life. There was no freedom to develop individual ideas, initiatives, gifts and potentials. Peasants consistently produced more on the little plots around their homes than on the large state farms.[37] Meanwhile the people saw *the wealth and the freedom of the West* on their television screens - at least in countries close to the borders to Western Europe. When large scale corruption in the leadership was exposed — as well as the fact that these leaders had secretly lived on imported Western luxuries — people became very angry. When faith in the viability of the command system began to wane, morale broke down and the economy began a process of "imploding".[38]

The future

When Marxism-Leninism collapsed in Eastern Europe some people were jubilant, others devastated. But whatever our sentiments, we must not overlook the fact that it was one of the great attempts of humankind to find a way out of the economic impasses of the modern world. It is true that the ideology and the system were flawed to such an extent that they could not deliver the goods, not even survive. But there should be a *sense of tragedy* about it all.

The danger inherent in the demise of the Marxist-Leninist economy is that the *tragedy may get worse*.[39] The reformers wanted to achieve a rapid transition to a Western type economy. But it seems that it is not easy to switch overnight from a failing command economy to a highly efficient market economy. Former Soviet republics are losing ground economically across the board.[40] There are many reasons for this, some of which we have already mentioned. One is the resistance of people in leadership positions with entrenched interests in the old order. The imperial tradition of Russia is far from broken and a liberal democracy is not in sight.[41] The unwieldy bureaucracy cannot simply be dismantled. People and institutions who operated in radically socialist countries are not geared to survive in a climate of fierce competition on the open market. ·

Former Soviet leaders and citizens *have not experienced free enterprise for three generations*; so they do not know how to operate such a system.[42] Their collective mentality has been lulled by state control and welfare. "In the countryside, passivity is a way of life ... Private farms now make up about 5 percent of the local farm population, but account for about 30 percent of Vologda's output."[43] Soviet technology and organisational structures have lagged behind, especially in the crucial sphere of computer technology. In the mean time much of the former industrial capacity of the Soviet Union has fallen into rot. Many enterprises are simply not viable. The great markets of the Eastern bloc have disintegrated and alternative markets are nowhere in sight. Sudden freedom, without the development of an internalised set of norms of acceptable competitive behaviour, creates space for the worst in humanity to unfold. Organised mafia-type crime has soared in Russia.

It would come as no surprise, therefore, if for quite some time the economic situation in *Russia*, and in some of the former Soviet republics, would continue to be fairly dismal. But one wonders why the urban economy in *China* was able to enter into a process of fast growth on capitalist lines when given the opportunity to do so. There too the lack of experience with a free enterprise system led to massive problems, but this did not cripple developments.[44]

A Marxist sociologist in Hungary told me that, in his opinion, the real problem was *traditionalism*. Marxism was a giant attempt to modernise a traditionalist culture by force - and failed to so so. Eastern European countries who had been under Western influence for generations, such as the Hungary, the Czech Republic and Poland, find it much easier to change. Modern processes cannot be imposed on a culture which has not adapted to modernity. It may well be that under such conditions any system will fail.

On the other hand a modern mentality cannot operate successfully if fettered by the social structure. China shows that liberalisation can lead to rapid growth. Yet, liberalisation also implies inequality. At present the great majority of people in the rural areas of China do not benefit. In a country which under Mao had achieved the highest equality rate in modern times, vast discrepancies of income and wealth open up, and predictably the great trek to the Eastern seaboard in search of greener pastures has begun.

Perhaps again due to cultural reasons, prospects seem to be better in some of the *former satellites* of the Soviet Union, especially those on the fringes of the European Community. The East German economy is undergoing some trauma at present but the economic power of a united Germany is sufficient to keep it from sinking. The Poles, Czechs and Hungarians have a good chance of adjusting to the Western dynamic and to form the semi-periphery around the European Community. Some of the other countries, such as Romania and Albania, may have been marginalised to such an extent that they will become part of the Third World in economic terms.

Before we leave the subject two things must be stated once again. The first is that the historic failure of Marxism-Leninism *does not vindicate global capitalism.* Marxism was, after all, a reaction to the failure of capitalism. In Western industrial nations, social democracy has vastly improved the situation since Marx wrote his critique. But in global terms the situation has become much worse. The task of achieving a truly free and equitable system has become more urgent than ever. Nobody should bewail the collapse of a totalitarian system. But, as stated above, we should also sense the tragedy of the fact that a giant human attempt to eradicate social inequity has failed. Far from giving up on that score, we need to analyse the reasons for the failure and come up with something more realistic and workable.

Secondly it is inappropriate either to embrace or reject Marxism on the strength of its most inflexible version. Our historical survey has shown that Marxism is *not a static system of thought.* Sterile periods of dogmatisation and institutionalisation have occurred in most other convictions as well. Witness orthodox Judaism, Catholic Scholasticism, 17th century Protestant Orthodoxy, modern Christian fundamentalism, fundamentalist Islam, and so on! While almost everybody seems to agree that the static and enslaving aberration must be rejected, great ideals do not easily die and there is much in Marxism which will continue to exercise its fascination.[45]

The potential dynamic of Marxism is particularly evident in its "revisionist" or *Neo-Marxist versions.* At present even this school of thought is in disarray, but it is unlikely simply to disappear. It has infused the idea of the class struggle, the practical option for underdog population groups and the ideal of social justice into ever changing and ever more complex situations.

But it did not feel bound to the obsolete metaphysics, historical predictions, economic fallacies and authoritarian structures of classical Marxism-Leninism. Instead it developed the humanistic elements of Marx's philosophy in a non-doctrinal, open and creative way which has penetrated all Western social sciences. Lukacs, Bloch, Kolakowsky, Gramsci, Althusser, Horkheimer, Adorno, Marcuse and Habermas are some of the more prominent exponents of Neo-Marxism. The French existentialist Sartre also turned Marxist.[46] To reach their level, our critique must be much more profound.

For another reason Marxism may continue to have an impact. For a considerable time, Marxism had generated *hope and motivation* among the poor and oppressed. The collapse of the system seems to have thrown many of these people into despondency. Hopelessness is far more dangerous for the prosperity of a nation than a revolutionary spirit. But this atmosphere may not continue indefinitely. People need a vision to survive. Where must such a vision come from?

Apart from established parties and sophisticated schools of thought, *bits and pieces of Marxist insight* are readily absorbed and utilised by disillusioned and underprivileged population groups. Their Marxist origin may not be recognised, nor do people necessarily understand all the implications of the Marxist system. Marxist slogans simply make sense to the victims of a deteriorating social situation. And with growing misery in the poorer countries of the world, this is not likely to change very soon.

There are also people around who maintain that the Soviets have betrayed the ideals and principles of the system and that, given a chance, they would apply it correctly and succeed. The danger is that these people will fall prey to old delusions, try to reinvent the wheel and commit the same mistakes all over again. It seems prudent for us to listen to those who have actually experienced life under this system for a couple of decades, and to be skeptical. It does not make much sense to continue believing in a theoretical construct whose social reality has failed to back up its idealistic claims. Our task is, rather, to *find a pragmatic alternative* to both capitalism and communism, an alternative which tries to retrieve the strengths and to overcome the weaknesses of both systems as far as possible. The next chapter will look at two attempts going in this direction.

Questions

Revision: Summarise the causes of the demise of Marxism-Leninism in the Soviet Union and Eastern Europe and its future prospects.

Application: Do you know people in your environment who have had Marxist leanings? How do they interpret the demise of Marxism-Leninism in Eastern Europe?

Critique: (a) "The collapse of Marxism-Leninism was not due to weaknesses of the

system as such, but to its betrayal by unscrupulous stooges of capitalist powers, such as Gorbachev and Yeltsin."

(b) "Communism is dead and buried; why do you try to unearth it?"
Comment.

Let us summarise

We began with the reminder that Marxism is not a single social phenomenon but is split up in a *great variety of forms*. In this chapter we focused on
classical Marxism-Leninism as it had evolved during the first half of our century in the Soviet Union and its former satellites.

The *history of Marxism* can be traced back to the works of Karl Marx, a
19th Century Jewish-German social philosopher who analysed the glaring
discrepancies caused by the industrial revolution in England, and who predicted that they would be overcome by a proletarian revolution. He was
influenced by his Jewish-Christian upbringing, by the idealist philosophy of
Hegel and by classical English economists. His ideas were cast into a comprehensive world-view by Friedrich Engels.

Central to this philosophy is the concept of the *class struggle* as the determinative factor in history. It proceeds through various stages and finds its
culmination in the capitalist system. The capitalist bourgeoisie, the most
revolutionary and productive social force in history, also produces its own
adversary, the proletariat. Due to the inherent contradictions of the system
the proletariat will be able to overthrow the bourgeoisie, establish the "dictatorship of the proletariat" and eventually usher in the classless society. At
this stage all alienation will be overcome.

Marxism was first applied in 1917 in the *former Russian Empire* by a
shrewd strategist, Lenin. He was followed by a ruthless dictator, Stalin, who
forged the Soviet Union into an economic giant, imposed his will on the
world Marxist movement and established his hegemony over Eastern Europe
and some Asian countries. In China Mao established an Asian version of
Marxism-Leninism with its own peculiarities, called Maoism. Probably due
to internal rigidities and inefficiencies the Soviet system began to show signs
of economic strain during the late 1980s and then collapsed dramatically.

In our critique we began with the *achievements* of Marxism. The most
important of these was that it placed social justice firmly onto the global
economic agenda and inspired many people to dedicate their lives to its real-
isation. Apart from the disadvantages of socialism in general, the *dangers of
Marxism* are that it absolutises human autonomy; defines not only nature but
also society as material for social engineering; tends towards fanaticism;
places the human mind into a totalitarian strait-jacket; smothers human creativity and economic initiative; obstructs the evolution of democratic insti-

tutions; concentrates all power in the same small elite; covers up the interests of this elite with an ideological smoke-screen, and develops imperialist tendencies towards world domination. We also cast doubt on the feasibility of the economic assumptions of Marxism, notably the labour theory of value.

Coming to the *future of Marxism*, it seems that the orthodox version of Marxism-Leninism has been discredited beyond repair by its economic failure and the resentment in the populations who were subjected to the system and its ideology. We enumerated the reasons given for its collapse in its former bastion, the Soviet Union, and in Eastern Europe. But this does not exclude the continuing impact of Marxist thought on the struggle for a viable, sustainable and equitable system. Nor does Marxism's failure vindicate the equally devastating failure of classical capitalism. The most important message for those who believe in social justice is that this approach is unworkable and must be superseded by something more viable. This brings us to the next chapter.

Notes

1 For greater detail see Lichtheim 1982; Kolakowski 1978.

2 The term is taken from *Newsweek*, October 23, 1989 cover title. Slovo 1990 is an example of such an attempt.

3 "The religious promise of Marxism, far more than its convoluted ideology and its increasingly unrealistic economics constituted its tremendous appeal, especially to intellectuals ... For them... the most powerful appeal ... was Marxism's promise of an earthly paradise, that is, Marxism as a secular religion." Drucker 1993:10. For detail see my essay "The eschatology of Marxism". Missionalia 15/1987 105-109.

4 Cf Heilbroner 1985:78ff.

5 For detail of this idea, already found in Smith and Ricardo, see Heilbroner 1985:65ff, especially 72f, 74f.

6 Suggested reading: Ingersol 1991; Lichtheim 1982; Millar 1981.

7 Lenin wrote "Hang (hang without fail, so the people see) no fewer than one hundred kulaks, rich men, bloodsuckers ... Do it in such a way that for hundreds of (kilometers) around, the people will see, tremble, know, shout: they are strangling and will strangle to death the bloodsucker kulaks" (quoted by G F Will in Newsweek Sept 16, 1996.

8 For a fuller historical picture see Barratt Brown 1984:147ff. and G Wehrfritz in *Newsweek* May 6, 1996, pp 16ff.

9 G Wehrfritz in *Newsweek* May 6, 1996, pp 16ff.

10 S Strasser in *Newsweek* Dec 19, 1994, pp 28ff.

11 Tony Emerson in *Newsweek* April 1996, p 30ff.

12 L H Sun in *Mail and Guardian*, Oct 28, 1994.

13 Suggested reading: Encyclopaedia Britannica 1986 vol 23, pp 573-585;Ogden 1989; Derbyshire 1987; Chang 1988.

14 Drucker 1993:11.

15 While China has 21.3% of the world's population it only has 1.9% of the world GNP. Feinberg 1990:5.

16 C Bogert & G Wehrfritz in Newsweek Jan 22, 1996, 20ff; P Tyler in *Mail and Guardian*, July 14, 1995, p 21f; Tom Post in Newsweek Nov 28, pp 30ff.

17 Suggested reading: Moll 1991:14ff.

18 "... the long lesson of history is that the ends actually achieved are largely a function of the means used to pursue them." Rostow 1990:162.

19 Other religions will have to work out their own responses.

20 Cf Myers 1987:96ff.

21 For a good summary of political illegitimacy and economic ills in the German Democratic Republic see: Keithly 1992:59ff.

22 E.g. G Wehrfritz in *Newsweek* Oct 7, 1996.

23 For a history of the rise of the Russian empire before the revolution see Pipes 1995.

24 In the 7th and 8th Century Tibet was a powerful empire, which waged successful wars againts China. In the 18th Century the Chinese imposed a Dalai Lama of their own choice and declared Tibet a "protectorate". In 1912 the Tibetans shook off Chinese authority; in 1918-1920 they defended themselves successfully against a Chinese attempt to conquer the country. Mao occupied the country in 1950. A treaty was signed in 1951 leaving the Tibetans with internal autonomy. The Chinese responded to a Tibetan rebellion in 1959 with brutal terror; 80 000 Tibetans fled the country, including the Dalai Lama. "Over 1,2 million Tibetans are reported to have died through torture, starvation or suicide" (according to a report by Guy Lieberman of the Dewachen Tibetan Cultural Centre in the Natal Witness 23.12.1996).

25 D Elliott in *Newsweek* June 27, 1994.

26 Wiberg 1991:337.

27 See for instance Haas 1991 in connection with US policies in Cambodia. There are many similar examples in Latin America.

28 For a synpathetic treatment see Heilbroner 1988:120ff.

29 W S Jevons, quoted by Heilbroner 1988115f.

30 For the Khmer Rouge see W Shawcross in *Newsweek* Sept 5, 1994 pp 26ff.

31 According to Drucker, the Shining Path is a revolt of the decendents of the Incas to undo the Spanish conquest and re-establish their ancient identity (1993:195). The Khmer Rouge has similar motivations.

32 For an earlier critique from a left-wing perspective see Barratt Brown 1984:129ff.

33 For detail see Csaba 1990.

34 Alcamo 1992.

35 According to Csaba 1990:374 the debt of the Soviet Union soared from $ 26.5 million in 1981 to $ 128.6 million in 1987, that of Poland from $ 25.4 billion to $ 37.6 billion during the same period.

36 World Bank 1990:17.

37 See A Nagorski in *Newsweek* Oct 16, 1995, pp 40ff.

38 Suggested reading: Moll 1991:19ff; Dembinski 1991; Feinberg 1990; see also Brand, H 1992: Why the Soviet economy failed: consequences of dictatorship and dogma. Dissent 39/1992 232-44. Bottomore 1990.

39 See Clark 1995 for the following.

40 Newsweek Jan 16, 1995, p 3.

41 See Clark 1995:81ff, 97ff, 118ff.

42 See Clark 1995:66ff.

43 A Nagorski in *Newsweek* Febr 20, 1995, p 18ff.

44 D Elliott in *Newsweek* Aug 12, 1996.

45 For an attempt to explore the compatibility of Marxism with liberalism and democracy see Paul et al 1986.

46 For an account of Neo-Marxism in the country most opposed to its thought see Buhle 1987:221ff.

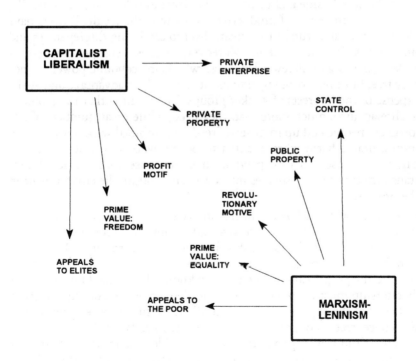

BM & M — H

CHAPTER 5

The two compromises - social democracy and democratic socialism

What is the task of this chapter?

We have discussed two extreme approaches to the problem of how the political economy should be organised: free enterprise capitalism and Marxist-Leninist socialism. Each of them has *advantages*, which continue to tempt policy makers and whole population groups, but each also has *disadvantages* which make them quite unacceptable. Let us once again summarise the position.

- *Free enterprise capitalism* grants freedom in economic terms. Initiative and achievement are rewarded, slack and failure are punished. The market mechanism regulates the allocation of resources according to profitability on the supply side and utility on the demand side. A highly versatile, innovative, efficient and productive economy is the result. But we have also seen that structural mechanisms lead to escalating discrepancies and imbalances in the system. Moreover, because competitiveness is acclaimed and gain is rewarded, those who gain economic power are not only free, but even encouraged to use it to their best advantage and at the expense of the interests of weaker groups. The result is that the economic elite acquires much more than they need, while great numbers of less fortunate people end up in misery. Freedom combined with power can do immeasurable harm when granted to people who are ruthlessly selfish. The system also has to expand its markets, raise consumption levels, transform ever more resources into waste and pollute the environment in the process.

- *Marxist-Leninist socialism* is a mirror image of capitalism. It is committed to the liquidation of the oppressive and exploitative economic elite, the bourgeoisie, and to the establishment of a "classless society". The transition has to be brought about by a "dictatorship of the proletariat". Because the people cannot be trusted to know what is good for them, this dictatorship must be executed by the leadership of the Communist Party on behalf of the population. Paradoxically the result is, once again, a massive concentration of power in a small elite. In as far as the leadership is sincere, it can use its power to attain a considerable measure of equality within the population. But the command system, the totalitarian philosophy and the pervasive control of a clumsy bureaucracy over all dimensions of life stifle the economy. Moreover, the lack of democratic institutions make the control of corruption virtually impossible. In short, equality is achieved at the expense not only of freedom and human rights, but also of efficiency and productivity.

Against this background the question arises whether it would not be possible to construct a new system which would retain the advantages of both systems and avoid their respective pitfalls. Since the positive aspects of one system are virtually identical to the negative aspects of the other, this can only mean that some sort of *compromise* must be found in which the respective trade-offs are carefully balanced against each other.

Two such systems have actually emerged over the last couple of decades: social democracy and democratic socialism. *Social democracy*, which is also called welfare capitalism or a social market economy, is a capitalist, free-enterprise system which has been modified considerably in the direction of egalitarian principles, such as the equality of opportunity, social securities and participation in economic decision making. *Democratic socialism* is a Marxist, state-controlled system which has been modified considerably in the direction of entrepreneurial initiative and a free market. In short, the first is modified capitalism, the second modified Marxism-Leninism.

In this chapter we shall discuss both these systems briefly and subject them to critique. In section I we look at the principes of social democracy, a classical example of which is Sweden, and then examine the system's achievements and problems. In section II we do the same for democratic socialism, with a close look at the former Yugoslavia as a classical example. Section III reviews other attempts to reform Marxism-Leninism which were conducted in the former Czeckoslovakia, the former Soviet Union and China.

Section I - Social democracy

Principles

There are a number of variations of this system in Western countries. The classical example is the Swedish economy. Here are a few principles which are generally applied:

- *Democracy*. Social democrats believe that it is not only possible, but also prudent for the disadvantaged majority to gain power through democratic means, and then subject the existing capitalist system to progressive reforms, rather than disrupting the economy by violent revolution and having to entrust a totalitarian regime with the task of constructing an entirely new system.

- *Free enterprise*. The principle of free enterprise is retained to encourage private initiative and achievement. But the state lays down basic parameters within which the economy is allowed to operate. The state also channels the economy in socially desirable directions. Specific responsibilities of the state include order and stability, equitable education and training for all, social securities, maintenance of economic growth and employment, control of inflation, a sound balance of payments, the provision of infrastructure, and so on. The general guideline is: *as much government intervention as necessary, as little government intervention as possible.*

- *Private ownership.* The means of production remain in private hands but the state has to guard against undue concentrations of economic power. The ideal is to break up monopolistic conglomerates and ensure free competition. The state may take over key industries to protect essential infrastructural services, such as transport, power, and water supplies, from disruption. It may also acquire substantial share holdings in private companies to gain experience on how the economy works and to influence the direction it takes.

- *The market mechanism.* The free market remains the basic mechanism regulating the allocation of resources and the distribution of goods and services. However, the state may fix minimum wages for certain job categories. It may also regulate the prices of essential commodities such as agricultural products to cut out excessive price fluctuations, or to aid disadvantaged sectors of the economy.

- *Equality of opportunity.* Social democrats are moderately committed to egalitarian principles in that they want incomes to level out without jeopardising economic achievement. Private initiative is encouraged but power advantages are neutralised as far as possible. Progressive taxation and heavy death duties are meant to cancel out undue accruals to the rich, while weaker sections of the population are helped to become more competitive through such measures as regional equalisation policies, subsidies, free and equal education for all, consumer protection, state run research and credit facilities and so on.

- *Social securities.* While competition is encouraged and achievement is rewarded, the less gifted or less fortunate are protected from falling into misery and disrepute. Unemployment insurance, compulsory pension schemes, old age homes, subsidised health services and compulsory medical schemes, life-insurance policies and the provision of sub-economic housing are some of the measures taken to prevent less successful or less fortunate citizens from destitution. Taxation is high, but so is the level of care.

- *Industrial peace.* The freedom of contract between employers and workers is retained, but free trade unions are encouraged to counterbalance the power of employers' organisations. Channels of communication and negotiation between major interest groups, as well as the legal instruments to settle industrial disputes, are institutionalised. Ideally the workers or their unions are represented on the boards of enterprises, so that they acquire information on the running and the financial situation of the firm and participate in the decision making process. Workers may also be encouraged to become shareholders in the companies which employ them, and the state encourages the spread of capital ownership in the wider population. Workers are protected by law from arbitrary dismissal or inhumane working conditions.

- *Technological advance.* Technological innovation is encouraged so that the national economy remains competitive on international markets. Workers are protected from losing their jobs when new technologies are applied, mainly by extensive retraining programmes and the provision of alternative jobs. At times when national competitiveness on world markets was at stake, social democrats have often abandoned extended welfare services, demanded wage restraints and allowed a greater degree of capital concentration. The rationale is: if more is produced, more can be shared out.

Thus one could argue that social democracy is an attempt to retain the efficiency, productivity and freedom of the capitalist mode of production while ensuring a large measure of social security and a greater degree of economic equality in the population.

Achievements and problems of social democracy

In countries of Western Europe where it has been implemented, social democracy has worked remarkably well. *Sweden*, the classical social-democratic country, counts among the richest nations of the world. The Swedish social-democratic party has ruled continuously for over forty years, which suggests a high degree of legitimacy of the system among the majority of the population. Industrial conflicts have been kept to a minimum. Often workers have been willing to tighten their belts to secure the competitiveness of their enterprises. As a result the standard of living has risen steadily.

German social democracy has also been highly successful. *West Germany* experienced relative industrial peace for decades and an "economic miracle" to boot. Although it had lost the war, it soon forged ahead of the victors, France and Britain, and became the most powerful economy in Europe. In contrast to Eastern European countries, where you find an ecological disaster of the first order, Germany now spends millions to clean up the impact of industrialisation on the environment.

Nowhere in social-democratic Western Europe have the workers ever attempted to stage a revolution. The results achieved by the system have clearly succeeded in convincing the less privileged that a steady rise in productivity leads to greater national wealth which, in a democracy, can then be shared out more equitably. The economic disruptions and the loss of freedom implied in a Marxist revolution were deemed unnecessary and counterproductive.

But after a time *strains appear* in any system. Social welfare reached levels which the economy could no longer afford. High labour costs threatened to render industries uncompetitive on world markets. Soaring welfare claims led to exorbitant budget deficits. Recently, then, the pendulum swung back from the welfare state in the direction of straight capitalism in European social democracies. This shows that the social democratic system is not without its flaws. In most instances these flaws constitute nothing more than failures to overcome the problems of the other two systems completely. Since social democracy is a compromise between capitalism and socialism, it is reasonable to expect that it will encounter the problems of both, though to a much lesser degree.

Concerning its *capitalist* nature, social democracy is still saddled with substantial income discrepancies, though they have been reduced to a point where further reductions might be counterproductive. It still battles with the oscillation between boom and recession, though there are fiscal instruments to reduce the amplitude. The effects of technological innovation on employment as well as the ecological effects of industrial growth continue to cause headaches, though much less so than in some other countries. The basic motive of producers and consumers is still the maximisation of profit and utility respectively, though social and ecological responsibility is accepted as a crucial concern.

Its negative *socialist* heritage becomes visible in a widespread welfare mentality. There is considerable meddling of the bureaucracy in the economy, and this is not always very popular amongst members of the innovative elite. Recently too there has been a marked swing towards the right among ordinary voters. A serious problem is that the growth of the welfare apparatus went out of control. In Sweden direct and indirect taxes were 50% of gross domestic product in 1994. A society cannot consume more than it produces without creating problems for itself. This is particularly true for the ageing population in European countries, where birth rates are low and people live longer.[1]

One has to state, however, that the problems associated with the welfare state are not intrinsic to social democracy. They are due, rather, to a flawed organisation of the system. Just as in the case of the economy as a whole, *the state should facilitate, rather than run the social securities system.* The state should not take over welfare, play Father Christmas and dish out gifts which have not been earned by the productive arm of the economy. It should also not yield to powerful lobbies demanding special privileges.[2] Budgets should begin with available income and then prioritise needs in such a way that expenditure falls within these limits, rather than drawing up a list of needs (which can be extended endlessly) and then borrowing the money to cover the shortfall.

While the state can act as an insurance agency, and impose the obligation to welfare measures, social securities should not normally constitute a claim against the state. Social securities should remain part of the responsibilities of enterprises and be financed by the output of the factors of production. From the recipients' point of view, securities represent deferred and potential consumption, which *must be part of the total salary package*. If social securities go up, the rest of the salary package must go down. The nation simply has to learn to live within its means.

It should not be too difficult, therefore, to overcome this weakness. Social democracy is, in principle, an *open, flexible system* in which the chosen representatives of the people are free from rigid ideology, able to gain new insights and willing to adapt to changing circumstances. While the system is not perfect, we are not likely to find a better one under current conditions. We should also not be confused by the popularity of the trend towards the right in social-democratic countries in recent times. It is typical of Western democracies that they oscillate from left to right, because once the disadvantages of one direction make themselves felt, people move in the opposite direction.

However, the two greatest problems with social democracy have not yet been mentioned. The first is that egalitarian principles and social securities demand *a high level of economic output*. So far social democracy has achieved greater equity and security mainly within nation states that belong to the global economic centre. As we have seen, it is only possible to share out what is produced; living above your means is a sure recipe for financial disaster. This is true for families and for whole nations. If even rich nations have burnt their fingers by offering too many benefits to their populations, and demanded too little productivity in return, it stands to reason that poor nations, which apply welfare principles too lavishly, find themselves in serious difficulties. Rampant inflation and economic deterioration have been typical for such cases.

The question then is whether a weak economy *can actually afford* extensive social benefits like institutionalised pension schemes, unemployment insurance, free education and health services, food subsidies, subsidised housing and so on. I would argue that the answer to this question is twofold:

- *Inefficiency and corruption.* In many cases the problem lies in the fact that the economy is not run as efficiently as it could, that the bureaucracy is careless and corrupt, that members of the ruling elites take more than their share, live luxuriously or transfer state funds to their private accounts in Swiss banks. If all this money was available it would go a long way towards making life more secure for the poorest of the poor.

- *Prioritising social securities.* The security afforded by the extended family in traditional societies should be maintained as far as possible. Poor countries should make a beginning with social policies in areas which are essential for rapid development. Free education and training, for instance, are prerequisites for economic progress. Where traditional family structures are breaking down, pension schemes are essential to contain population growth. Some other benefits, such as housing, are important but not equally urgent, because people will always construct homes for themselves as best they can. The important thing is to keep expenditure within the limits of what the economy can yield and to make increases in social services subject to growth in national productivity.

The second problem with social democracy is that it *cannot be applied at the international level.* A centre state will normally work for economic justice only within its own borders. On international markets it continues to pursue its own interests at the expense of weaker competitors. Equity within a state does not automatically imply justice between states, except in the case of regional conglommerations, such as the European Union. Loving families can be very selfish towards outsiders! Social democracy has, so far, led to gains for the less privileged in centre nations, but at the expense of the less privileged in poorer nations.

The application of social democracy *on a world scale* would presuppose a powerful world government, great sacrifices on the side of rich nations and vastly increased output on the side of poor nations. None of these prerequisites are likely to materialise in the foreseeable future. The attempt to integrate a mere 16 million relatively well trained former East Germans into the thriving West German economy of over 60 million led to massive financial and economic problems. One can hardly imagine, therefore, that it would be possible for the industrial economies to grant social securities to billions of people in the Third World within a global state.

On the other hand, the nation state is no longer the only organisational power in the modern world.[3] More and more international agencies are emerging, whether statutory bodies, multinational corporations, non-governmental organisations, or religious formations. The task of the future will be to direct this multipolar network towards global responsibility and solidarity.

Questions

Revision: Describe the principles of social democracy.

Application: Which parties in your country propagate social democracy and how strong is their following?

Critique: · (a) "This is nothing but a defence of capitalism with some palliatives."
(b) "Socialism has proved to be detrimental in practice and wrong in theory. Even in Sweden social democracy has recently come under fire. Why do you continue to defend an outdated system?" Comment.

Section II - Democratic socialism

Since the establishment and spread of Marxism-Leninism outside the Soviet Union, quite a number of attempts have been made to liberalise and modernise the system, usually without much success. We have already noted that similar attempts to gain political and economic liberalisation in *East Germany, Hungary and Czechoslovakia* were put down with an iron hand by the Soviets and their allies. But more moderate reforms continued.[4] Another abortive attempt to establish a liberal kind of Marxism was undertaken in *Chile* under Salvador Allende. It was also crushed, this time by the army aided by the United States. Up to the mid-1980s there was only one working example of democratic socialism in the Marxist world, namely that developed in the former *Yugoslavia* by Marshall Tito (1892-1980). It has since disintegrated.

In *China* Mao Zedong put his own typically Chinese stamp on Marxism-Leninism, but this was not a more liberal or democratic system than its Soviet counterpart. More recently a calculated experiment was undertaken under the leadership of Deng Xiaoping to allow a limited liberalisation of the system.[5] After decades of severe oppression the Chinese have responded with enthusiasm. When thousands of students gathered in Tiananmen Square to demand democratic freedoms in 1989, the popular movement became too dangerous for the regime and a massive crackdown put an end to the flirtation with political freedom. On the economic front, however, the trend towards free enterprise and a market economy has continued and China has witnessed phenomenal economic growth rates.[6] But Chinese experimentation with a free market economy is not typical for democratic socialism because Marxist economic principles have, for all intents and purposes, been abandoned.

The most ambitious and far-reaching reform yet undertaken in a Marxist-Leninist country was *perestroika* in the Soviet Union. But this attempt has led to the demise not only of the Marxist-Leninist system but also of the Soviet Union as such. Communist parties in the former Soviet republics and in Eastern Europe have changed their colours and their policies to such an extent that they are no longer comparable to the classical system of Marxism-Leninism.

The classical example: Yugoslavia

To understand the principles of democratic socialism, let us take a look at the example of *Yugoslavia*.

- *One party state.* Democratic socialism is an adaptation of Marxism-Leninism. The control of the Communist Party over national affairs is retained. However, communist leaders are committed to democratisation and the decentralisation of power. The ideal is "participatory democracy". This means that those who are affected by decisions should also be the decision makers. There is much less repression and much more freedom of expression, initiative, movement and organisation than in classical Marxism-Leninism. The devolution of power into small local entities is, of course, also a way of retaining overall control in a society which is riddled with cultural, historical and regional divisions.

- *Worker self-management.* This principle is implied by participatory democracy. It says that the employees of an enterprise should be in charge of its management. In all non-agricultural firms which employ more than five people, workers' councils are established. If there are more than thirty employees, these become representative councils. Such councils are chosen and can be dismissed by the workers. The councils again choose, and can dismiss, the managers of the enterprises. This type of participatory democracy is also practised in services such as hospitals, schools, courts, research institutions and cultural organisations.

- *State ownership.* The socialist principle that capital is a social asset and should be owned by the state is retained. All enterprises above a certain size - thus excluding small workshops and family farms - belong to the state. Workers run them and benefit from them, but they do not own them. When workers leave their firms, they cannot take their shares along.

- Relative degrees of *free enterprise* and the *market system.* The state lays down parameters within which all enterprises have to operate, and managers are controlled by the party, the banks and local authorities. But within those limits there is a degree of freedom unusual for a Marxist-Leninist state. Any person or group is allowed to establish a new firm. The managers and their councils, who are accountable to their employees, have to find gaps in the market, determine what the firm is to produce, and whether it should diversify. They have to obtain the raw materials and other resources, organise the productive process and establish marketing channels. They have to make profits - or face the consequences of low productivity. They also distribute the proceeds among the workers after certain deductions for the firm and the state have been made. In short, democratic socialism has combined the market system not with private enterprise but with employee enterprise.

- *Socialist distribution.* Firms have to make a profit or go bankrupt. This removes one of the great drains from a socialist economy, namely enterprises which run at a loss without being found out. From profits, deductions are made for national concerns, the welfare of the community in which the firm operates, and the capital needs of the company. The remaining surplus is distributed by the worker committee among its employees. Workers are paid mainly according to their contribution, but particular needs may also be taken into consideration. The criteria for evaluating the contribution of each worker are laid down. There is, however, a guaranteed minimum income in proportion to the time spent at work. Distribution also takes account of housing, recreation, creches and so on, and does not only take the form of wages. In contrast to capitalism, democratic socialism regards work as a value and not just as an economic resource which is to be paid a price as determined by the market.[7]

Achievements and problems of democratic socialism

As with social democracy, democratic socialism constitutes a *compromise* between the two extremes, but now with the emphasis on Marxism. As in the case of social democracy, democratic socialism can be expected to reveal both the strengths and the weaknesses of the two systems of capitalism and Marxism-Leninism, yet to a much lesser degree. We do not have to repeat them here.

Unfortunately Yugoslavia was also saddled with great problems which had *nothing to do with the system* it had chosen. The country was devastated during World War II. Because it did not toe Moscow's line it had to contend with the hostility of the Soviet Union and the Warsaw Pact. Because it was Marxist it was not accepted in the Western community of nations.

Under these circumstances it was no small achievement that Yugoslavia showed an average growth rate of 5% per annum between 1960 and 1980. It had reached a gross domestic product which equalled that of other semi-industrialised countries such as Brazil, Mexico and South Africa. But in contrast to these countries it had achieved a *much greater equality of income*. The equalisation policy between central and peripheral regions was, at least to some extent, successful. There had been more freedom and consultation than in other Marxist states.

After a time, however, Yugoslavia ran into *grave economic and political dif-*

ficulties. On the one hand productivity levels lagged behind those of Western countries. Inflation became rampant. Unemployment soared. The workers did not really feel that they were in charge. Poor discipline, bad work, cynicism and stealing increased.[8] To alleviate frustration, more efficient regions, industries and individuals were given at least some freedom to forge ahead. Those who expected equality from a socialist state were resentful because they felt that egalitarian principles had been compromised. The political system continued to be authoritarian.

But the most intractable problem of Yugoslavia was posed by the *composition of its population*. The nation was an artificial creation made up of groups with vastly different cultures, religions, national histories and levels of economic development. Long standing enmities were ingrained in the collective consciousness of opposing groups. War time atrocities were not forgotten. The predominance of the Serbs was resented by the other ethnic groups. Some ethnic groups (Slovenes and Croats) were economically more advanced and were loathe to subsidise the economic backwardness of others.[9]

To keep such a population together was difficult even for the authoritarian regime of Marshall Tito. After his death *centrifugal interests* slowly gained the upper hand. The economic crisis did the rest. Yugoslavian youth became disillusioned with the performance of the communist leaders.[10] Ethnic nationalism, particularly of the Serbian population, provided a catalyst for built-up tensions and exploded into full scale civil war. In the meantime the country has fallen to pieces.

Unfortunately, therefore, it is no longer possible to depict the Yugoslav experiment as a great success story. But does this mean that the principles of the economic system were wrong, or were the *political circumstances* so difficult that problems would have arisen irrespective of the economic system applied?

In at least one respect the economic system itself was to blame: similar to its Soviet counterpart, it was *not able to keep pace* with accelerating technological developments in the West. Of course, this is also true for many capitalist countries at the semi-periphery and the argument is not all that strong.

However that may be, we do well to look carefully at the theory, the practical policies and the concrete experiences of the Yugoslav system. The point is that Yugoslavia had demonstrated for decades that it was possible, during a particular stage of socialist development, to move away from orthodox Marxism-Leninism in the direction of democracy and freedom.

By the end of the 1980s it was no longer alone on this journey. Soviet *perestroika* has led to a massive movement in similar directions and this time reform triggered off an avalanche. But before we come to that, events in Czechoslovakia in 1968 are worth recording here, as they represent a remarkable, though unsuccessful earlier attempt to reform Marxism-Leninism.[11]

Questions

Revision: Describe the principles of democratic socialism and compare them with those of social democracy.

Application: What is more divisive in your country: economic discrepancies or ethnic tensions? Are these two factors interrelated?

Critique: (a) "The former Yugoslavia was an authoritarian one-party state. Why do you call it 'democratic' socialism?"

(b) "It is unfair to call an economic system a failure when it was shipwrecked by non-economic factors such as ethnic tensions or imperialist designs. Neither in Yugoslavia nor in Chile was democratic socialism given a chance to prove itself." Comment.

Section III - Other attempts to reform Marxism-Leninism

A. The Prague Spring

The so-called "Prague Spring" in Czechoslovakia was a typical revolution "from above" which was suppressed from "higher above". It all began when the conservative Novotny-regime did not join the anti-Stalinist trend during the Khrushchev era. Novotny's repressive rule made his regime extremely unpopular. The high-flung targets of its 5-year plan led to an economic disaster. In 1968 Alexander Dubcek began to criticise Novotny and was elected chairman of the Communist Party. He set out to establish *"socialism with a human face"*. Crucial cadres were replaced. Repressive practices and abuses of power were curtailed. Public opinion was allowed to express itself through freedom of information and assembly. Censorship was abolished and press freedom was granted. As a result the truth about abuses committed during the 1950s came to light and many bureaucrats lost their positions. This again strengthened the credibility of the Party for the population.

In the meantime, a neo-Stalinist direction under Breshnev had gained the upper hand in the USSR. The neo-Stalinist Parties in Eastern Europe perceived developments in Czechoslovakia as "counter-revolutionary" and "contagious". The regimes in Poland and East Germany were believed to be especially vulnerable to the Czech example. The cohesion of the Warsaw Pact seemed to be threatened. So the Soviet Union demanded the right to station Soviet troops in Czechoslovakia. When Dubcek refused, the USSR engineered a coup d'etat led by the police force — which failed. *The country was then invaded* by the armies of the Warsaw Pact and the reformist leaders, including Dubcek, were arrested. The entire country was occupied. The National Assembly defiantly declared the invasion to be illegal and the population staged a rebellion: hundreds of thousands of people took to the streets; clandestine radio stations and underground newspapers sprang up. For a time the Soviets tried to negotiate with Dubcek, but then moved their tanks against the demonstrators and imposed a dictatorial regime loyal to the Soviet Union. Old style Marxism-Leninism had triumphed once again.

B. Perestroika in the Soviet Union

All this changed when the situation in the USSR itself began to move. When Gorbachev came to power, the Soviet bloc was catapulted into the vortex of breathtaking change. The word *perestroika* means "restructuring". Gorbachev's policies involved new attitudes, new ideas, a new praxis, new institutions, new foreign relations. There is no question that perestroika was intended to move away from dictatorial rule. Stalinism was officially reject-ed. Gorbachev even called for a monument to be built for the victims of Stalinist rule.[12] Democratic participation, freedom of expression, and open critique became key concepts.

Gorbachev claimed that he had built his entire philosophy and praxis on Lenin. He also *defended the policies* of earlier Soviet leaders, such as the empha-sis on heavy industry, the collectivisation of agriculture, the build-up of a powerful armaments industry, the centralisation of decision making, and so on.[13] I would argue, however, that these assurances merely show that great leaders have to legitimate their innovative action in terms of the dominant tradition of their constituencies. In fact not only the ghost of Stalin but also the political theory of Lenin had been replaced by a new approach altogeth-er. We glean the following characteristics of the reform movement from Gorbachev's famous book on Perestroika (Gorbachev 1987):

- The necessity of reform was seen to be rooted in two threats: annihilation through *nuclear war* (11) and the *decline of the Soviet economy.* The former led to a new definition of the Soviet role in international politics. Concerning the latter the leadership recognised that during the seventies "the country began to lose momentum" (18ff) both economically and ide-ologically.

- Perestroika was understood to be a new attitude, a new theory, a new praxis and a new set of institutions - in short, a *total renewal.* This renew-al quite clearly attempted to overcome the disadvantages of the Marxist-Leninist approach in its entirety.

- In contrast to orthodox materialism, there was a new emphasis on the individual, on the *spiritual* dimension of life, on motivation, on moral strength.

- In contrast to the old command mentality there was a pervasive and pow-erful emphasis on *democratisation.* While Gorbachev did not foresee a multiparty state, he insisted on the participation of the population in decision making in all aspects of society (32).[14]

- Reform was not seen as a deviation from the socialist ideal but rather as an attempt to replace a distorted form of socialism with true socialism (36). *True socialism* was seen to be a dynamic and creative idea which evolved in history and constantly adapted to changing circumstances. Contrary to the beliefs of Western analysts that Gorbachev moved in the direction of free enterprise, capitalism was rejected as an option for the Soviet Union.

- Perestroika was, therefore, *seen as a revolution* (49ff) in which conservative and stagnant tendencies had to be overcome by a "jump forward in the development of socialism" (51). It was seen as a difficult process "accompanied by the struggle between old and new" (271). The old was characterised by "conservatism, inertia and dogmatism in thinking and acting" and by functionaries who "cannot, or do not want to, part with the command style of administration, who respond painfully to new developments" (272).

- At the same time perestroika was seen not as a mood or an unrealistic ideal but as a *carefully planned process* geared to the principle that politics was the "art of the possible", that it would be a difficult process, and that miracles were not to be expected.

- The leaders recognised that, while extensive *social securities* were a major achievement of the Marxist-Leninist system, the system also led to despondency, poor work, shirking, drinking, corruption, living on unearned incomes, and so on. So Perestroika introduced a great deal of healthy self-criticism into the Soviet culture.

- The Soviet leadership no longer claimed to have the key to the salvation of humankind, the only valid ideology, and the global system of the future. With that the commitment to the Marxist-Leninist doctrine had actually been abandoned in favour of pluralism and liberalism. It was conceded that each society had the *right to self-determination* (177ff). Ideological conflicts were to make way for pragmatism, confrontation for cooperation. Regional conflicts were to be resolved by political, rather than military means (279). Arms control and arms reduction were placed high on the agenda. The prevention of nuclear war was seen as the most pressing demand of the time. And for the first time this was no longer mere propaganda. An unbelieving world witnessed the first successful arms reduction talks between the US and the USSR. It was like a miracle.

- "More light!" In contrast to the secrecy and censorship of traditional communism, the people of the Soviet Union were now deliberately exposed to foreign ideas as well as to the unpleasant realities within their own country. *Glasnost* means "openness". The population was to get to know the truth, so that it could overcome what was bad and support what was good. Public debate and criticism of the authorities and their policies were encouraged. High-handedness and corruption were exposed and punished (75, 302ff).

- In the economic sphere, *profit and loss accounting* as well as the *market forces* of supply and demand as determinants of volume and price had to be rediscovered (47).

- The fact that *state ownership* of the factors of production *alienates* the property "from its true owner - the working man" was recognised. Again this is an insight quite incompatible with classical Marxism-Leninism. It was seen that there was a "lack of coordination between public interest and the personal interests of the working person" which demotivated people and acted as an economic brake (47). "Of prime importance ... is for the people to be the true master of production, rather than a master only in name. For without it, individual workers or collectives are not interested, nor can they be interested, in the final results of their work" (83). A "lack of inner stimuli for self-development" was recognised (85). Self-employment and grassroots initiatives are, therefore, encouraged (274). "Amazing things happen when people take responsibility for everything themselves. The results are quite different, and at times people are unrecognisable" (97). It is acknowledged that "attitudes of equalisation and dependence are still a serious handicap for intensive economic growth" (272). These pages read like passages from a text book on liberal economics!

- *This does not mean that the command economy was abandoned entirely,* but the central planning authority was relieved of the burden of prescribing all the detail. The detail could be worked out much better by the enterprises themselves (90). Whatever problems collectives and state farms, for instance, could solve independently were not to be subject to centralised command (274). This is a principle which comes remarkably close to the Catholic social-ethical principle of "subsidiarity" which says that whatever task a lower level of organisation can achieve successfully should not be taken over by a higher level.

- *World technological standards* were to be achieved by the Soviet economy and the latter was to become less dependent on foreign technology.

- *Bureaucracy* was acknowledged to be a real problem (291). The authoritarian attitudes of officialdom were to be overcome. The state apparatus was to be cut back and made less cumbersome, and the qualifications of civil servants were to be upgraded (272, 291).

- It was acknowledged that the command system, that is the centralised power of the Party and its agencies, pushed the Soviets (local councils chosen by the people) into the background after the 1917 revolution. The original *democratic idea of the Soviets*, which had emerged after the fall of the Czarist regime and before the communists took control of the country, were to be reactivated (110ff).

Critique of Gorbachev's reforms

What do we make of all of this? Surely perestroika was a brave vision. But it had some inherent weaknesses. In the first place perestroika was seen as a revolution from above, a revolution which was born within the Communist Party and which was to be implemented by the Party. But a *revolution from above*, which an established, dogmatic and inflexible regime is to conduct against itself, has its difficulties. Authoritarian leadership patterns are ingrained in the very fabric of society on every level of authority. Powerful interests are entrenched in the old structures. A people nurtured and manipulated for three generations by "big brother" does not necessarily know how to use its newly granted freedoms.[15]

Granted, Gorbachev wanted his revolution from above to merge with the ground swell of a grassroots movement which would take up the challenge of the leaders because it realised that this was in the long term interests of the working class. But all this smacked of old style paternalism. The Party claimed to do the people's thing. Given the chance, however, the people *wanted their freedom*, not a reform of authoritarian rule. Above all, they dreamt of the prosperity of the West which the Communist Party seemed to have withheld from them for all these years.

In the second place perestroika thought it was reforming the system; in fact it *dismantled its foundations*. Lenin would have turned in his grave if he could have learnt of this programme. Remember that from Lenin's time onwards communist rule had never been popular among the masses. Its survival had depended on dogged conviction; legitimation by a totalitarian ideology; comprehensive planning, and authoritarian rule — all of which imposed from above by force! Once these pillars of strength gave way, the system began to totter and there was nothing left which could prevent its fall. The promulgators of perestroika were no longer believers; their vision was no longer Marxism-Leninism. But with this they unconsciously abandoned the validity of their claim to rule the country. They had been in power on the strength of a totalitarian ideology; they had no popular mandate. Gorbachev himself had never been voted into power in an open election. Once the ideology had lost its credibility, the rulers had lost their legitimacy.

In the third place Perestroika *was not radical enough* in its implementation. The economy deteriorated rapidly and this called for decisive action. Gorbachev depended on the cooperation of the old guard. He could not afford to go too far without undermining his power base. For a time, Boris Yeltsin, the more radical reformer, was sidelined and Gorbachev was enveloped by the old guard. In the meantime the population had become restive and yearned for radical change. The dynamic unleashed by "openness" and "reform" soon went out of control and swept the old system away - together with its idealistic reformers. A short-lived conservative backlash, attempting two coups, only hastened its demise. Yeltsin, who had stood firm against the coup leaders, triumphed.

On the other hand, the Russian Federation *did not succeed* so far in putting a liberal democracy and a free enterprise system in place. This is hardly surprising. Western affluence, the dream of the East, is the outcome of a long development and cannot be achieved by simply switching to another principle. The old structures had been discredited, but there were none to take their place. The societies of Eastern Europe, which had been built on a totally different set of principles for decades, lacked the capital, the experience, the organisational structures, the markets and the values underlying the liberal system. Instead of achieving a prosperous market economy, the Russian economy went into a tail-spin.

This experience created a serious *vacuum between two unworkable recipes*, at least in the short term. The same can be said of other Eastern European countries, though to varying degrees. Systems built on the free initiative of individuals and groups take time to develop, particularly in a situation where the citizens had been under state tutelage for all their lives. The population of the former Soviet Union had not experienced multi-party democracy and free enterprise for at least three generations. Old structures do not simply fall apart. When they do, they tend to create chaos before a new organisation of the society becomes fully operational. Economic failure, unemployment, poverty, crime and corruption abound. While some get rich quickly, many Russians are now worse off than they were under communism. A backlash is almost inevitable under such circumstances and in 1996 Yeltsin almost lost his second term of office to a communist rival.[16]

C. Lessons from China?

At the end of the last chapter we raised the question why developments in China did not end up in a similarly dismal situation. Is there simply a different kind of spirit among the Chinese? Less alcohol, greater self-discipline, and harder work? Or is its greater economic success due to the structural aspects of the Chinese experiment?

Critical of the Soviet transformation from the outset, the Chinese leadership adopted a very different approach. On the one hand the Communist Party sensed that political freedom would spell the end of its regime and *retained complete control*. When things seemed to get out of hand, authoritarian rule was tightened. As a result the trauma of a sudden breakdown of the old system was avoided.

On the other hand the Chinese leadership gradually *opened the economy* to market forces. Certainly the Chinese confound Western attempts to categorise policies according to ideological alternatives. Realising that capitalism was good at creating growth while socialism was better at creating equitable distribution, they tried to *balance out* the two. As we have seen, that is the general approach of both social democracy and democratic socialism.

What is unique in the Chines case, however, is that the leadership initially opened up only *certain geographical areas* for capitalist development.[17] The result was that two systems began to operate within the same country. This allowed them to steer the overall economy either way - to stimulate the socialist economy, or to put on the brakes in the capitalist economy, depending on changing circumstances in the society.

Although the Chinese economy now shows signs of becoming increasingly unbalanced, especially between the Eastern urban-industrial areas and the rural hinterland, the option of the leadership for a *market economy* whose parameters are *controlled by the state* should be noted. As we shall see in chapter 6 this is an approach which has led to remarkable results in the case of the four "Asian tigers" and subsequently all along the Pacific Rim. It is unlikely that Marxist-Leninist or Maoist principles, even in the mellowed form of democratic socialism, will ever be applied in China again.

Conclusion

We have to end this chapter with the finding that, so far, democratic socialism has not proved to be viable in actual historical situations. Every attempt to run the economy along these lines has failed. As we have seen, the particular failures had a variety of different reasons and so one could argue that *the case is not yet closed*. At least the attempt to democratise and liberalise Marxist socialism should be given the credit it deserves. Dubcek and Gorbachev were certainly men of integrity, vision and courage. Whether a truly democratised and liberalised Marxism-Leninism would still have been Marxism-Leninism, is a moot point.

The more relevant question is, however, why we should think of reforming the Marxist-Leninist system after it has collapsed. In the end those who are committed to social equity may be left with only one choice, social democracy, though perhaps in a revised form. *Social democracy* has prospered beyond all expectation, at least in developed countries. In the end it is performance that counts, not ideology. So we may be forgiven if we take our clues for the future from social democracy rather than from democratic socialism, though we do this with an open and critical mind.[18]

Questions

Revision: What are the differences between perestroika and social democracy?

Application: What lessons can be learnt for your own country from the Soviet attempt to restructure the Marxist-Leninist system?

Critique: (a) "Why do you accord a system which has brought ruin upon millions of people so much honour? The sooner we simply write off and forget that evil past, the more attention we can give to the construction of a free society."
(b) "Your bias against Marxism-Leninism is intolerable. You confuse Stalinism, which has nothing to do with social responsibility, with Marxism-Leninism, which has never been applied correctly in the Soviet Union." Comment.

Let us summarise

We began with the observation that both of the two extremes, namely free enterprise capitalism and Marxist-Leninist socialism, are *unacceptable* because of their severe disadvantages. Historical development has been away from free enterprise capitalism to social democracy, and away from Marxism-Leninism to democratic socialism. Currently the ideological trend goes in the direction of a free market economy, but this may change again. We discussed these two intermediate systems in this chapter.

Social democracy is a free enterprise, market-oriented system which has been considerably modified in the socialist direction. Its main socialist characteristics are greater social equity and social security. While it has been remarkably successful where sensibly institutionalised, there is no pretence that it solves all problems. Its most formidable disadvantage is that its application seems to depend on a powerful and versatile economy. Its adoption by poor countries is at least problematic and its application on the international scene is, so far anyway, utopian.

Democratic socialism was a Marxist-Leninist system considerably modified in the direction of free enterprise and a market economy. For a long time it was operative only in Yugoslavia, although similar reforms were attempted in other places such as Czechoslovakia. In its initial stages democratic socialism was reasonably successful in Yugoslavia; subsequently it ran into intractable problems. These are partly due to the great discrepancies and diversities found in the country, and partly to economic failures.

Under the leadership of Gorbachev *perestroika* took root in the Soviet Union. This was a giant experiment in democratic socialism. We have briefly sketched its main characteristics. However, perestroika was swept away by the forces of change it had unleashed. The collapse of Marxism-Leninism in its former stronghold has had devastating consequences for Marxism all over the world, including democratic socialism.

The *goal of economic justice* is still as valid as ever, but the Marxist means to reach that goal have proved to be deceptive. This is also true for its mild form, democratic socialism. It is only a matter of time, however, before the failures of capitalism once again attract attention, and so the struggle for an acceptable alternative will continue.

But these developments have rendered old positions and animosities obsolete. The opportunity for dialogue has opened up. It is now the time to have another good look at the fundamentals involved. Before we deal with basic choices, priorities and trade-offs in chapter 7, however, we have to complete the picture by sketching experiences made in the Third World.

Notes

1 ·For an introduction to the problem see Philippe Wojazer in *Newsweek* Dec 11, 1995, 14ff.

2 According to Drucker this was the case until after World War II, when the state took over welfare functions (1993:111).

3 Drucker 1993:103ff.

4 See Boote 1991.

5 For detail see Cheung 1982; Bulletin of Concerned Asian Scholars 1983.

6 For more detail see Blejer et al 1991; the social consequences are equally staggering: Shanhai alone is reported to have gained 10 million migrants from rural areas, while rural Sichuan has lost 5.5 million people, mostly single men who send some of their income back home (Newsweek March 7,1994, 28ff).

7 Suggested reading: Feinberg et al. 1990; Dyker 1990; Lydall 1984; Prout 1985.

8 Lydall 1984:290.

9 In 1979, for instance, the GNP per capita in Macedonia was $ 67, in Serbia $ 97 and in Slovenia $ 197 (Lydall 1984:175).

10 Dyker 1990:171f.

11 Suggested reading: Bardhan & Roemer 1992.

12 Gorbachev 1987:268.]]

13 Gorbachev 1987:38ff, 46f.

14 According to Gorbachev democratisation meant that "every Soviet is fully entitled to choose the forms and methods of its work with due regard for local conditions. Nominations of several candidates, voting by secret ballot and electoral contests should be the rule ... limiting the time in elective offices ... to two consecutive terms, ... the listing of more candidates in the ballots than there are seats to be filled ... regular reports ... a real mechanism for their recall", the establish-

ment of the rule of law, "free dialogue, criticism, self-criticism, self-control and self-assessment within the Party and within society" (286), human rights such as to take part in government, to express one's views on any issue and to enjoy freedom of conscience, personal dignity etc. The different nationalities and republics were to be given greater equality and autonomy in a multinational state (297ff). The principle of bilingualism, that is the use of the mother tongue as well as the common medium of Russian, was reaffirmed (300). Ethnic diversity was to be taken seriously but chauvinism was to be overcome.

15 Cf Tsypko 1991.

16 *Newsweek* May 6, 1996, pp 11ff; June 10, 1996, pp 18ff; June 17, 1996, 11ff.

17 See Galtung in Glaeser 1987:32ff. Note that Galtung corrects his original analysis at the end.

18 See the section on reform in Eastern Europe in the bibliography.

Time to pause and reflect?

If you have read up to this point, you may long for a break. To help you catch your breath, we offer the following little exercise. If this is your private copy, you can write your answers in the spaces provided (if it belongs to a library, don't!).

1. Capitalists and socialists are divided on the relative weight given to two basic concerns. Can you describe them briefly?

2. On which of these two concerns would you personally place the greater emphasis?

3. Where would most of the members of your community place the greater emphasis?

4. Do you think that this could have something to do with your (or their) location in the social hierarchy - that is, whether you (they) belong to the elite, or to the middle class, or to underdog population groups?

5. The macro-economic experiments discussed so far have all been conducted in the so-called First World. Do you think that the insights gained there are also applicable to a Third World country such as South Africa or Brazil? What would be different here?

6. Do you think that African traditions could provide us with an alternative to capitalism and socialism, which would avoid the pitfalls on both sides?

7. Do you think that such a traditional African system could be adapted to work under the conditions of a modern industrial economy, which is part of the global economic system?

PTO

An exercise for small groups

Form a group of 6 - 8 people from various walks of life. Give a brief introduction to the problem. To help them express their views, hand out photocopies of this page and let them jot down their personal responses. Then open the discussion.

1. What is more fundamental for a prosperous national economy: the freedom to take initiatives, to which capitalists aspire, or the equality of dignity and income, which socialists strive for?

2. Which population groups would reap the benefits, and which would pay the costs of each alternative?

3. Is there any way in which both concerns could be accommodated?

4. Why have radical socialists changed their basic assumptions in the early 1990s?

5. Does the system of "free enterprise", as proposed by capitalist liberalism, really provide the freedom for all people to develop their full potential, regardless of their backgrounds? If not, what can be done about that?

6. Does the equality proposed by socialists really allow everybody to participate freely and fully in the decision making processes? If not, what can be done about that?

7. Do you think that free enterprise and free trade on a global scale will help us:
(a) overcome poverty and
(b) preserve the environment and save scarce resources for future generations?

8. What do you think would be necessary to achieve these goals?

CHAPTER 6

Two Third World models - Tanzania and Taiwan

What is the task of this chapter?

So far we have focussed on the two systems found in the industrialised world and their variations. But what about the *experiences of the Third World?* In this chapter we shall look at two Third World countries of comparable size, Tanzania and Taiwan. Half a century ago, the plight of these two countries was in many ways similar. Their aspirations too were similar in many ways. Yet the economy of one of them failed to get off the ground, while that of the other experienced spectacular economic success.[1]

We shall offer a brief history, the principles adopted, and the reasons for success or failure in each case. In section I we analyse and asses the Tanzanian experiment of socialist self-reliance, called Ujamaa. In section II we examine Taiwan's policy of capitalist export-orientation. In section III we compare the two systems and consider what lessons can be learnt from these experiences.

Section I - Socialist self-reliance in Tanzania[2]

Historical survey

Before European colonisation, East Africa had two different regions which, for a long time, had little contact with each other. The coast line had been part of Arab and Portuguese trade routes for centuries while the interior had been inhabited by African subsistence peasants. Tanganyika became a German colony in 1890 and a British protectorate after World War I. It gained its independence in 1961 without a protracted liberation struggle. In 1964 it united with the island of Zanzibar to form Tanzania.

In comparison with its neighbour, Kenya, the territory did not attract much development and European settlement, mainly due to the absence of lucrative natural resources. But Dar es Salaam was established as the capital, a regional administration was built up, railways were constructed and cash crops, especially sisal and coffee, were introduced.

Due to the extraordinary calibre of its first President, Julius Nyerere (1922-), and his particular policy of African Socialism, called *Ujamaa*, Tanzania attracted a lot of attention after independence from people interested in the economic development of Africa. Ujamaa certainly became one of the classical models of economic organisation in the Third World.

After initial successes, however, the Tanzanian experiment began to run into insurmountable difficulties and was gracefully abandoned by Nyerere's successor, Ali Hassan Mwiini (1925-). Severe financial constraints forced the country to seek assistance from the International Monetary Fund and the World Bank, who imposed their standard structural adjustment programme.[3] As a result the Ujamaa pattern was largely undone.

Principles of Ujamaa

The Kiswahili word *Ujamaa* refers to the spirit of the African *extended family* which Nyerere introduced as a model for the new state. His point of departure was not a Western idea of socialism, nor the metaphysics of Marxism, but the beliefs and customs of traditional Africa. It consciously harked back to the African past and claimed to be firmly grounded in the African soil.[4] In fact, Nyerere distanced Ujamaa clearly from "scientific socialism."[5]

Ujamaa centred upon concern for the human person. According to the African mind, a person could only be authentic *in community*. In South Africa the term *ubuntu* has become widely used for this worldview, expressed in the saying *umuntu ngumuntu ngabantu* (a person is a person through people). Service to the community, cooperation, and collective advancement were to cut out all acquisitiveness, profit making, exploitation, or power seeking. The existing wealth was meant to fulfil the people's needs and not to be used for selfish purposes. All people were to be regarded as equal. There should be no friends or enemies in society.

The spirit of harmony and cooperation in the extended family was to *embrace the nation*, the continent, and ultimately humankind as a whole. Though this vision could be compared with the Marxist ideal of the classless society, it was as incompatible with the socialist idea of a class struggle, as it was with racism, tribalism, religious intolerance, domination and discrimination. Building a new nation excluded the use of violence, except where there was no other way out. The revolution was to be achieved through evolution. Non-socialist features of the society were to be overcome gradually through the growth of Ujamaa. The latter again was to happen through a pragmatic step-by-step approach, based on the unfolding needs of the situation.

Nyerere's philosophy as the "teacher" (Kiswahili: *Mwalimu*) was formulated in the famous *Arusha Declaration* of 1967 which committed the country to a socialist creed. It was much more than a policy statement; it defined the morality of the nation. The most important ingredients of Ujamaa Socialism as a policy were the following:

- *A one-party state.* Nyerere was committed to freedom and democracy, but Tanzania shunned the conflict of a multiparty state. The country has a very heterogeneous population. Apart from a few Europeans, there are more than 100 different African tribes, as well as Arabs and Indians. There are Christians, Muslims and Animists. One of Nyerere's prime considerations was to unite the diverse population of the country under a single leadership with a single loyalty. As in other African countries at the time, it was believed that this could only be done in the form of a one-party state. In 1965 the ruling party, TANU (later called CCM),[6] became the only party allowed. Its model was the extended family where consensus was reached through discussion on the basis of common values.

- *Equality.* The Constitution of TANU commits itself to equality between all human beings. This equality is to be understood in social, economic and political terms.[7] While skill and performance can be rewarded, gross inequalities of income are deemed incompatible with equality. All people who can make a contribution should work for their living.

- *Nationalisation* or collectivisation of the "commanding heights" of the economy. The principle of equality seemingly implied that banks and larger enterprises had to be placed under national, collective or cooperative ownership to cut out exploitation.

- *Party control.* Going much further than other African countries, and in strange inconsistency with the ideal of retrieving the African cultural heritage, all traditional forms of authority, notably chiefs and elders, were abolished and replaced by TANU officials. Again the principle of equality ruled: there was to be no ascribed status; everybody could run for elections and everybody had the vote. But as in communist countries, the party dominated public life at all levels.

- *Villagisation.* Scattered homesteads were required to draw together in villages which would operate under the guidance of paid party officials with extensive political, legal and economic powers. The aims of this policy were to build up the cooperative potentials of the population, to render essential services such as clinics, schools, roads and local administration, and to gain political control over the peasants. A minimum acreage ploughed, attendance at meetings, and work performance were enforced. Family workshops and small scale industries were encouraged in the rural areas.

- *Self-reliance.* Abandoning post-independence reliance on foreign investment and aid, the Arusha Declaration changed development policy to self-reliance. Foreign assistance was not categorically excluded, but according to the First Five Year Plan (1969) the nation should mobilise its own resources rather than depending on overseas aid and investment. This was not only to be an economic policy, but also a frame of mind. Frugality, diligence and efficiency were to pull Tanzania out of poverty, even if it took longer than development initiated by world capitalism. The country was subjected to a strict austerity programme.

- *Self-reliance* was again a *communal*, rather than an individual principle. It had to move from the bottom up: the basis was the family, then the ward, the district, the region, and finally the nation. The goals were to achieve a healthy diet, adequate clothing, acceptable housing, access to basic education and health care for all Tanzanians, as opposed to grand projects. This philosophy greatly enhanced the self-respect and self-confidence of the Tanzanian people. Moreover, menial work was never despised and the arrogance of a new elite was avoided.

- *Agricultural development.* In an overwhelmingly agrarian society the population has to utilise the resources it has. Industrialisation can only be built on a firm agricultural base. Imported industries can only lead to dependency and failure. The emphasis of the state was, therefore, on the development of agricultural production. Agriculture, like everything else, was to build up its capacities gradually and from the bottom up. The ox-plough was to eliminate the hoe before the tractor could eliminate the ox-plough. The people had to become ready financially and technically for each new step.

- *Education and training.* Education was to be available for everybody. It was to foster the values and principles of Ujamaa and be geared to the needs of the nation. This principle was not to remain mere theory. Schools were expected to become community based and economically self-reliant. Illiterate peasants were drawn into Adult Education projects which included training in useful skills and cooperative methods. By 1980 illiteracy had fallen to 27% — a remarkable achievement under African conditions. Vocational training was emphasised, rather than purely academic education. Elitism was discouraged in favour of community service.

Reasons for failure

Again we have to begin with the *achievements*. "Tanzania has been hailed as one of the hopeful models of socially and politically responsible development in Africa."[8] Food production, literacy rates, life expectancy etc. compared favourably with those of many other Sub-Saharan countries. Repression was mild compared to countries such as Malawi or Uganda. There was political stability and maturity. In 1985 Nyerere handed over power voluntarily and constitutionally to his successor. Tanzanians were more equal than their neighbours in capitalist Kenya, or further afield in Zambia, where another form of African Socialism was ostensibly in force. The poor not only enjoyed respect, but built up self-respect. When they realised that current policies were not working, the authorities quietly and pragmatically changed course. These are no small achievements.

The Tanzanian economy made reasonable progress between 1967 and 1974. In 1974 it had reserves of $ 3 billion. But thereafter that the system ran into difficulties. The most serious of these was a severe negative *balance of payments* caused by a combination of unfortunate events:

- *The oil crisis.* In the early 1970s Tanzania, like all other non-oil producing countries, was hit by petroleum prices jumping to record levels. Fledgling industries, mechanised agriculture and the transport system depended on oil imports. They also depended on machinery and spare parts from industrialised nations, which became more expensive partly because of the oil crisis.

- *World recession.* A world recession was accompanied by a drop in coffee prices, Tanzania's main export product. The world sisal market also collapsed due to the rapid development of synthetic fibres.

- *Lack of foreign currency.* Socialist policies and the idea of self-reliance had cut the country off from international investment markets. The lack of foreign currency made essential imports difficult and the result was that Tanzanian industries operated at a fraction of their capacity.

- *The war against Uganda.* In 1978 the country was attacked by President Idi Amin of Uganda and the Tanzanian leadership decided to oust his regime. The war itself and the occupation of Uganda was a financial disaster which depleted Tanzania's resources.

- *Floods and droughts.* In 1979 there were floods. In 1973/4, 1980 and 1984 there were serious droughts. With so much of the economy dependent on agriculture these were crippling blows which greatly exacerbated a deteriorating situation.

- In recent times the *AIDS epidemic* has begun to threaten much of the countryside.

Apart from these unfortunate events, the system itself had serious flaws. The country is predominantly rural and the enhancement of agriculture would have been crucial for the initial stages of development. Rather than building a sound agricultural base, Ujamaa policies severely *disrupted agricultural production.* After 1978 food production fell short of population growth. By 1981 there was a food crisis and Tanzania, an overwhelmingly agrarian country, became a net importer of food. Even when good rains fell in 1985/6, 12% of the food needs had to be imported. There was a similar decline in cash crops because peasants switched back to subsistence farming. The World Bank, which had invested heavily in the villagisation programme, had to write it off as a failure. Villagisation worked well in the regions where villages had grown of their own accord. Elsewhere the policy was very unpopular. Let us see why this should have been the case.

- *Use of force.* Initially villagisation was to be voluntary.[9] But when progress was sluggish, force was applied. In 1973 Nyerere said that "to live in villages is an order".[10] Millions of peasants were resettled. Over-zealous party cadres even burnt down homesteads to force people into villages. In many cases the sites of the villages were not well chosen and their infrastructure was not in place. Party cadres were inefficient and arrogant.

- *Resistence to collective farming.* Initially fields were to be allocated to individual families. But there were not enough land surveyors around. African peasants are as attached to their land and livestock as peasants everywhere else in the world and they resented collective farming under party tutelage.

- *Artificially low food prices.* As in many other socialist countries food prices were kept artificially low. This helped the urban proletariat, the darling of socialism, but it frustrated the peasants. They were discouraged by low producer prices, late payments and poor administration. The marketing and distribution system did not work. The storage and transport facilities were inadequate.[11] Traditional subsistence farming made it possible for peasants to withdraw from state control to quite an extent. This again frustrated the development effort.[12]

- *Clash with African traditions.* At this stage it is in order to ask whether Ujamaa was really all that true to African traditions. African culture is based on the extended family. Unquestionable group solidarity constitutes an extended social safety net. There is also much cooperation between families. But cooperation between autonomous communities is not the same as collective farming. In African traditional society extended families own their own livestock and are in full control of their allocated fields. The replacement of traditional chiefs and elders by party officials is an indication that Eastern socialist thought had gained the upper hand over African communalist traditions.

- *Ideological aberration.* The fact that it was precisely the traditional peasantry which resented the villagisation programme reveals a great deal of alienation and exposes the policy as an ideological imposition from the top, rather than a home grown approach emanating from the African grass roots. Experiences in Zimbabwe, the only African country which achieved large grain surpluses merely through agricultural price policies, suggest that subsistence farmers respond favourably to a combination of price incentives and technical assistance. Perhaps the Tanzanian leadership should have had more confidence in peasants than in cadres.[13]

Consistent *nationalisation* of the means of production has not worked very well anywhere in the world. Even for highly developed countries state planning is a complex undertaking which demands great skills and commitment. In Tanzania skills and experience in organising and running such a system were badly lacking.

- *Bureaucratic mismanagement.* Analysts point out that there was a general lack of efficiency in the all powerful bureaucracy. The yields of privately owned estates plummeted when nationalised in 1976. In a report by RenÇ Dumont, requested by Nyerere, the state corporations were castigated as "inefficient, under-equipped, badly managed and extravagant spenders."[14]

- *Entrepreneurial proficiency destroyed.* When local banks, industries, plantations, eventually even smaller trading posts and workshops were taken over by the state, the existing pools of entrepreneurial initiative and technical efficiency were destroyed. The state was not able to cope with the problems of production and distribution and the economy was winding down. The population suffered shortages and was increasingly alienated. This led to resentment and frustration.

- *Inflation.* A growing and unproductive bureaucracy becomes a burden to any state. To meet its obligations the state borrowed from the national bank at levels which fuelled inflation.

As a result of all these developments there was a severe *lack of foreign exchange.* The transport system collapsed. The availability of spare parts, fertilisers and fuel resources declined. Tanzania had no choice but to borrow money abroad. Self-reliance turned into dependency. While it received generous "soft grants", a severe *debt crisis* could not be avoided. The debt crisis left the country no option but to agree to the structural adjustment programme of the IMF and the World Bank as a precondition for receiving financial assistance from these bodies.

These were the intrinsic deficiencies of Ujamaa which forced the system to its knees. There were a number of other factors which contributed to its failure:

- *Lack of capital formation.* The country failed to attract foreign capital after independence. It also failed to recognise and develop its export potential. The East African Community broke up in 1977, depriving the countries concerned of a more extended market. More seriously, the government believed that dependency on foreign capital was harmful and its economy became isolated from world capitalist markets. In Cold War terms, its natural allies were the non-alliant socialist countries of the Third World, notably Red China, which were all struggling to make ends meet, not the financially and technologically powerful industrialised nations of the West.

- *Compromises with capitalism.* There are left wing critics of Ujamaa who charged that the system failed because it compromised with capitalism. It is true that the dearth of foreign exchange and growing trade deficits forced the government to make concessions to capitalists. However, the actual impact of capitalism seems to have been much more subtle. There was quite some development on the Northern rim of the country, from Dar es Salaam via Arusha to Lake Victoria, while the rest of the country stagnated. This is an area of greater rainfall, fertile soils and the location of the game reserve tourist industry. But it is also the region closest to the influence of the Kenyan economy. The latter had inherited a higher level of development from colonial times and followed a capitalist route. Cross-border interaction had its effects on the population. It is particularly understandable that the affluence of the Kenyan elite stung the Tanzanian officialdom and professional classes. Resentment led to undercover operations, corruption and lethargy which undermined the system. It is a familiar socialist disease.

- *Lack of expatriate expertise.* In contrast to neighbouring Kenya or Zimbabwe, for instance, the absence of locally seasoned expatriates made itself felt. TANU had little economic experience and foreign experts seriously misjudged the situation. Strategic errors were made in the allocation of foreign exchange and large investments were made in uneconomical projects.

- *The failure of educational ideals.* One of the achievements of Ujamaa was the rapid development of education. But the ideal of the integration of education and village agriculture did not work. As elsewhere in the world, pupils with higher education tried to escape to the cities. As in many other African countries, higher education concentrated on non-technical subjects. The result was that key positions had to be given to expatriates, while educated locals had to be bribed with privileges or they left for greener pastures.

- *Cultural and religious factors.* The Tanzanian society is largely rural. Urbanisation, commercialisation and industrialisation are still in their infancies. Modern economic assumptions have not penetrated the lives of most of the population. The African traditional world-view is not geared to economic progress, competition and individual achievement, but to subsistence agriculture, social harmony and communal dependency.

Individual economic initiatives are viewed with suspicion. The perception is widespread that if one family does well, others must be losing out. Such cultural and religious factors may not be decisive on their own, but they certainly make a considerable contribution to stagnation if other factors are not powerful enough to override them.

- *Rapid population growth.* Tanzania was not able to arrest its population growth. Its population grew from 17,5 million in 1978 to over 23,1 million in 1988 — a rise of 32% over a decade or 3.2% per year. The rise in food production could not keep pace. The attempt to introduce family planning worked in the cities, but not in rural areas. The policy was perceived as having been designed by the Westernised elite in contradiction with indigenous cultures. Insufficient supplies of contraceptives and a lack of education worsened the situation.

After Ujamaa

The *Structural Adjustment Programme* did not bring relief.[15] To be fair, we have to concede that the IMF and the World Bank are usually called in by developing countries only by the time their economies are in ruins. In such a situation harsh prescriptions can hardly be avoided. Because the measures are unpopular, governments drag their feet until the situation demands drastic and sudden implementation, causing enormous shocks to the economy, instead of introducing measures gradually and allowing the economy to adjust.

In Tanzania the *prescriptions* included: devaluation of the currency; an obligation to service external debts; stepping up exports to earn foreign exchange; liberalisation of trade; dependence on the market mechanism rather than economic planning and price controls; drastic reductions in government expenditure, including employment generation, education and welfare; higher (that is, realistic) producer prices, and abolition of subsidies.

The *short term consequences* of this programme were devastating.[16] The shops filled up again with goods, which had not been available for a long time, but few people had the money to buy them. While a new breed of entrepreneurs made rapid progress, the pockets of the ordinary population emptied. Prices of foodstuffs and commodities soared. Wages did not match the inflation rate. People were forced to hunt for additional incomes and this exacerbated corruption. Health services and education plummeted to pathetic levels. In 1971/2, for instance, 17,3% of the budget was earmarked for education, in 1989/90 it had dropped to 6,4%.

The social safety net created by the Ujamaa villages disintegrated. The system, which had been run by the state, did not make way for a community based alternative, but left a *vacuum*. Under the old system the youth were expected to play their role in rural areas; they were not allowed to move to towns unless they had a job. Now they flocked to the cities in search of employment, money and excitement. The number of street children and homeless people multiplied. Countless hawkers tried to eke out a living by selling a few vegetables and imported plastic wares. Competition with established traders led to social conflict. The crime rate soared.

Whether *long term benefits* will justify this deterioration is far from clear. There are reasons to be skeptical. The attempt to "unleash market forces" presupposes that there is such a market. In fact, the internal market in very poor countries such as Tanzania is very limited. Most people are involved in the subsistence and barter economy. The external market is restricted by world recession and the drop in coffee and sisal prices. To compete with more developed countries in manufactured goods is virtually impossible.

The competence of the administrative, financial and commercial system is still very low. Foreign and local investors do not know what will happen next and invest their money elsewhere. The envisaged "trickle down effect" does not necessarily materialise because the affluent spend their money on imported luxuries or get it out of the country. Tanzania still has unutilised land, but agriculture is not a very powerful engine for development, and farming is unpopular among the youth. If people move away from home at all, they rather move to the cities rather than to virgin land.

Did Ujamaa really fail?

Some observers argue that Ujamaa did not really fail but that it was not given a chance to succeed. Because there were grave external reasons for its collapse, there may be some truth in this contention. However, there are also sufficient flaws in the system itself which prevented it from delivering the goods. *Agricultural* development would have been crucial. But the way the villagisation programme was implemented stifled progress, caused resentment and crippled initiative. Individuals, groups and communities were not allowed to become self-respecting and self-reliant masters of their lives. Where arrogant cadres tell people what to do and obstruct local initiatives, no development gets off the ground.

Urban-industrial development was also stifled. Making a success of nationalisation and a planned economy has proved to be difficult even in highly developed countries such as East Germany. Expecting the state to run the economy rather than creating the space for the people to develop their gifts is simply not the right approach. Moreover, the internal market was too small for industrialisation based on import substitution and the industrial export potential of the country was not developed sufficiently to build up bargaining power on international markets. Contrary to its philosophy of self-reliance, the country began to rely heavily on donations, international aid and debts.

Despite the attractive philosophy of an indigenous way of development, it is not clear that the dynamic needed for rapid economic progress can be generated on the basis of a traditionalist value system. Such a system is *geared to the ancestral past* and binds initiative into a network of family dependencies and loyalties. In a pre-industrial situation, governed by traditional African values, such a system may have appeared to be the best way forward immediately after decolonisation. But then the system should have adapted rapidly to changing circumstances. There are indications both in South Africa and Zimbabwe that African peasants are eager to produce for markets, once such markets promise attractive rewards.[17] As mentioned above, the question remains, therefore, whether Ujamaa was really all that traditionally African, or whether it was not simply an inflexible leftist ideology disguised as African culture.

In sum, while we can learn a great deal from both the achievements and failures of Ujamaa, the system *does not seem to offer a way forward*, whether for marginalised rural population groups or for a semi-industrialised Third World economy.

Questions

Revision: Summarise the strengths and the weaknesses of African Socialism as it was applied in Tanzania.

Application: Are there groups in your country who would go along with the principles of Ujamaa? Are there regions or sectors of the economy where some of these principles could be applied?

Critique: (a) "You have no right or competence as a white privileged person to pass judgment on African Socialism. It is for Africans themselves to find their way into the future."
(b) "Tanzanian socialists have resettled more than three times as many people by force as the apartheid state in South Africa. How can you give so much moral credit to such an inhuman system!" How would you react to these statements?

Section II - Capitalist export-orientation in Taiwan[18]

"Taiwan has a good claim to be ranked as the most successful of the developing countries."[19] Taiwan is one of the four "young tigers" or "young dragons" in South East Asia, which succeeded in forcing their way into the club of industrialised nations within a few decades starting from very modest beginnings. The other three are South Korea, Hong Kong and Singapore. In the mean time the dynamic has spread to other countries along the Pacific Rim.

My reasons for *picking out Taiwan* as a model are the following: two of the others are city states, whose circumstances are not very typical of other Third World countries; Taiwan was more successful than Korea in general, and Taiwan managed to combine the motive of growth with the motive of equity.

Severe handicaps

Taiwan's economic upswing began with severe economic handicaps. The island had gone through a *dramatic history of conflict and occupation*. From the 1400s Fujian Chinese had migrated to the island of Taiwan and driven the aborigines from the fertile plains into the mountains. From 1624 to 1661 Taiwan was part of the Dutch empire in East Asia. In 1682 the Manchu dynasty ousted the rule of the Ming dynasty on the island. In 1895 Taiwan was ceded by the Chinese to the victorious Japanese. After World War II the Chinese regained control. When the Maoists ousted the Kuomintang from the mainland of China in 1949, the latter fled to Taiwan and ruled the island with an iron fist.

Taiwan was a *poor agrarian country*; its per capita income was roughly $ 200 in 1950;[20] it had been neglected by China for centuries; it had been subject to Japanese colonial exploitation since the end of the 19th Century; its educational system had not been allowed to develop fully under colonial rule.[21] The country suffered heavy destruction and deterioration during World War II; with the withdrawal of Japan it lost its pre-war market and source of capital and entrepreneurship; it has no crude oil and few other natural resources. With Japan and Korea, Taiwan has the highest population density relative to fertile land in the world;[22] the average farm size is just under one hectare; the country has no good harbours; it is located far from the markets of the great industrialised nations; it does not have a vast domestic market; it lies on the borders of the tropics.

When the ruling party on the mainland, the Kuomintang, was defeated by the communists and fled to Taiwan in 1949, it brought in a huge and demoralised army and bureaucracy; there was an influx of about one and a half million refugees, pushing up the population by 25%. Thereafter, Taiwan had to endure the constant threat of invasion from mainland China and had to spend scarce resources on armaments, until the Korean War led to a neutralisation of the Taiwan Strait.[23] After Red China had been recognised as the sole representative of the Chinese people, Taiwan suffered international ostracism.

The country had an authoritarian government which was heavily involved in the economy; its workers had low incomes and few rights; by 1950 the Taiwanese currency was heavily overvalued and supported by complete import control. There was little export, virtually no investment, much excess capacity in manufacturing and inefficiency in production.

In short, half a century ago *nobody could have dreamt that* Taiwan's economic performance would be much different from that of all other poor countries. Yet in the 25 years after 1950 its per capita national income trebled, rising by 4.7% on average and reaching up to 9% on occasion.[25] Currently, there is not only full employment, but indeed a labour shortage! The inflation rate is low by any standards. It is a text book case of "from rags to riches".[24]

So why has Taiwan succeeded? There is much talk of a "miracle" or a "puzzle" among analysts when it comes to the "Asian tigers" in general and Taiwan in particular. To a large extent Taiwan simply confounds conventional wisdom, whether such wisdom is derived from liberalism, dependency theory, or Marxism.[26] It is indicative of the Taiwanese approach that we cannot continue our deliberations here by spelling out the principles of a model, as we did in previous cases. Most of the time the autocratic Taiwanese leadership followed a sort of trial and error pragmatism, rather than a full blown ideology. The few principles that were applied are best spelt out while telling the story.

The darker side

Before we continue, however, we need to remind ourselves that the situation in Taiwan is *far from perfect*. Has Taiwan really succeded — and what are the criteria of success? Certainly we cannot condone the domination, repression and persecution meted out by the minority mainlanders. Now that the system becomes more democratic it also becomes more confrontational. Some members of lower classes and minorities benefited only marginally from the economic miracle. The country is characterised by internal rigidities, contradictions and irrationalities. Its bureaucracy is far too big and cumbersome. There are large state-owned monopolies. Bureaucratic controls, especially in licencing and taxation, are so stifling that many businesses prefer to operate illegally.

One result is that Taiwan is probably much richer than reflected in official statistics.[27] There is also a substantial degree of dependency of the economy on outside technology and markets. There are high levels of pollution and the streets are congested. The housing shortage in Taipei is a nightmare. Self-interest has become aggressive both internally and internationally. The positive balance of trade is a headache. Financial capital is piling up in real-estate speculation and prices are skyrocketing.[28] The stock market is volatile.[29] There is uncertainty over whether the upward surge can continue beyond certain thresholds.

The question is, therefore, whether Taiwan is on its way to prosperity or to a particularly bad case of the spiritual, social and ecological jungles created by rapid industrialisation. All we are saying in our discussion here is that many developing countries have reason to *envy the achievements* of Taiwan and the other three "young tigers".

Reasons for success

Japanese *development of agriculture*.[30] During the first half of the century the Japanese had earmarked the colony of Taiwan to become a supplier of agricultural produce to the motherland. Traditional agriculture and transport were modernised. In spite of colonial exploitation, the standard of living of the islanders rose. During World War II the country's agricultural potential was largely destroyed, but the foundations for a modern economy had been laid. Subsequently a policy of "the development of dense networks of local organizations in their rural areas, and policies aimed at increasing rural incomes and developing domestic markets" was followed.[31]

A *flying start* after the war. The recovery of agriculture from a very low base to pre-war levels led to high growth rates of the economy.[32] It has often been observed that the necessity to rebuild and catch up after defeat and destruction gives great impetus to economic growth: witness Japan and Germany after 1945! In Taiwan, when agricultural development had reached its limits, it was used as a basis for small scale industrial development, which then continued the growth track record. Small scale entrepreneurship contributed greatly to flexibility and adaptability to changing conditions. It was also the foundation for growth to larger scale industrialisation.

Benevolent authoritarianism. We mentioned previously that, when the Red Army had defeated the Kuomintang on mainland China, the latter fled to the island of Taiwan and took over control there. The results were far-reaching:

- The vacuum left by the departing Japanese in terms of leadership and skills was filled with relatively competent elites from the mainland.

- The island received a government which was determined to withstand the pressures from the mainland and to prove its economic superiority over the communist alternative. This necessitated a strong, no-nonsense style of rule which led to long term political stability. Stability is one of the most fundamental prerequisites for economic growth.[33]

- For the same reasons the administration was technocratic, efficient and relatively free from corruption.[34] Government expenditure declined in relative terms and taxes remained low. Partly this was due to the fact that companies engaged in illegal operations to avoid bureaucratic strangleholds. Public buildings remained modest and money was not squandered on status symbols. There was tight monetary control. We see that imminent danger can keep a people alert, rather than having a paralysing effect.

- Because of its strength, the government was able to execute land reform, successive devaluations, influx of foreign capital and other unpopular measures. In spite of its authoritarian nature, the government enjoyed a degree of legitimacy, not only because of the threat of communism from the mainland, but also because of the combination of rising prosperity and considerable equity in the economy.

Equalisation policies. Early in its history the government executed a radical land reform programme, laying the foundations for deliberate equalisation policies.[35] While landlords lost out on the deal, the bulk of the peasant population benefited greatly. Though these plots were very small, the population eagerly utilised their potential and developed it to the full. There were further spin-offs of land reform:

- When small scale manufacturing began, peasants obtained nearby employment to supplement their incomes. As a result, industrial development was spread remarkably evenly across geographical space and no large scale migrations to urban-industrial conglomerations, with their inevitable social and cultural disruptions, took place.

- In later years the policy of equalisation was pursued further. Following the Japanese example, Taiwan committed high investments to education and training. The emphasis of traditional Chinese culture on the education of elites was changed in favour of wide spread vocational training and the development of blue-collar skills.[36] Thus the widening gap between the incomes of a few skilled people in protected labour markets and the marginalised bulk of the population, as found in other industrialising countries such as South Africa, was avoided.

- High and market related interest rates led to the world's highest savings ratio. This had the effect of spreading income more widely and generating numerous small and medium enterprises. These were efficient, flexible and labour intensive. In contrast, South Korea lowered interest rates "which gave cheap money to favoured borrowers who quickly grew into giant conglomerates."[37]

- Government intervention in Taiwan enabled free enterprise at grass roots level rather than smothering it. Equalisation was not based on nationalisation and collectivisation, but on spreading private property equally across the population. In 1950 most enterprises were still under government control, but they were gradually privatised.[38]

- Equalisation was also not based on welfare handouts but on making economic resources and opportunities available across the board, thus allowing family solidarity to retain its traditional welfare functions. As a result, the state was never overburdened with unwieldy welfare budgets.

The principle of free and equitable enterprise seems to be fundamental to healthy development.

Successful family planning. In 1952 Taiwan had a birth rate of 4,66%. Rampant population growth presented a considerable burden to the economy. Family planning programmes, supported by economic progress, achieved the drastic reduction of the birth rate to 1,56% in 1993.[39]

Export-oriented industrialisation. As in most developing countries, Taiwan's industrialisation began with an import substitution programme. But its leaders soon recognised that its population was too small to warrant large scale industrial production for the internal market. So Taiwan turned to exports.[40] Taiwan's business community took advantage of specific gaps in world markets. The exploitation of "niche markets" has since become an indispensible aspect of successful development. "The manufacturing capability of the newly industrializing nations was not mainly directed at satisfying the demands of their own markets but at invading the markets of other countries, including those of their own economic fatherlands".[41]

Utilising comparative advantages on world markets. Taiwan had no natural resources to build on. Her only asset was plenty of cheap labour with rising levels of education and training. The leaders built on this asset almost unscrupulously. Multinational corporations — the horror of many leaders in other developing countries — were welcome to exploit this resource. It seems as if the hardship caused by this ruthlessness paid out in the end.

Favourable conditions for investment. Labour was cheap because there were no wage regulations, no labour disputes, no restrictions on sacking. Unions were weak and strikes illegal. So Taiwan could compete very successfully with the expensive kind of labour found in industrialised nations. In addition, investments were guaranteed for 20 years against expropriation. As a result, overseas investors responded positively and the economy grew in leaps and bounds, pulling with it the standard of living of the population. It is interesting to note that, in marked contrast to Taiwan, South Korea's industrial growth was built on vast amounts of foreign loans, as well as local savings, while foreign investments were viewed with suspicion.[42]

Labour-intensive production.[43] Taiwan concentrated on light, labour-intensive industries, such as textiles and electronics, rather than on heavy capital-intensive industries. In this way, rapid progress could 'be achieved without great capital investment, and all benefits could be channelled into the labour force and capital accumulation. Interest rates were kept high, making capital investments expensive. Thus Taiwanese industries resisted the temptation of mechanisation, often used obsolete and second hand machinery, sustained long working hours and worked in multi-shifts.[44] In South Korea the same pattern was followed, but the authorities were open to capital-intensive production when the time became ripe.[45]

Balance of trade control. Although Taiwan was totally dependent on foreign exchange, the country never fell into the trap of foreign debts but saw to it that aid, exports and foreign investments balanced out imports. As mentioned above, South Korea generated explosive growth on the basis of huge international debts. The Korean economy generated capital of its own, due to a phenomenal savings rate[46]. The country could perhaps have done better without these debts. South Korea has been hit much more devastatingly by the recent crisis in S E Asia than its peers.

American involvement. For the United States, Taiwan was of great strategic importance. This led to a heavy influx of American aid, far above the average for developing nations. Naturally, US military hardware was shipped to the island. The agricultural recovery programme, especially, was conducted with American financial and technical assistance. The US market was also willing to absorb the supply of industrial commodities produced in Taiwan. In the initial phases half of the exports had been taken by Japan.

World economic boom. The economic dynamic of Taiwan picked up speed during a time of world economic expansion where it was not too difficult to find markets. The same was true for South Korea.

A conducive collective mentality. There is no regional conflict in Taiwan. The population consists almost entirely of Chinese people. There is no cultural and religious fragmentation, as found in many other developing countries, including Tanzania. In Taiwan great emphasis is placed on diligence, thrift and self-improvement. People work like bees, save a lot and further their education.[47] Merit-based mobility is not frowned upon. Family solidarity is important, but families are not ashamed of improving their financial assets. In fact, some say there is a ruthless materialism.

The collective mentality of the population is moulded, but not inhibited, by *Confucian and Taoist* traditions. Religious convictions are this-worldly and pragmatic and allow for material progress.[48] *Ancestor veneration and superstitions* are widespread, but the rituals do not seem to draw the attention of people backwards into the past, but provide self-confidence and legitimation in the competitive game. In South Korea too consensus building around Confucianism and patriotism is believed to have been pivotal for economic success.[49]

Pragmatism. Taiwan's leaders did not follow an economic ideology, but a policy of pragmatic and step by step adaptations to changing circumstances. This was also the case in South Korea, where the government guided the economy through successive stages of development.[50] At a time when development wisdom prescribed import substitution industrialisation, import control and disengagement from the capitalist system, Taiwan went in the opposite direction. Though the Chinese tradition was against free enterprise, initiative was allowed to flourish, first partially, then full-scale.[51] Though the economy is based on private enterprise, the state owns considerable assets inherited from the Japanese, including the banking system, the railways and a number of large corporations dealing with fertilisers, chemicals, petroleum products etc. Trade liberalisation is selective, and not based on free trade principles. Though there is state planning, plans usually underestimate rather than overestimate potential targets, are adaptable to changing circumstances, and enhance rather than obstruct private enterprise.[52] When the time was ripe, Taiwan began to move in the direction of more capital-intensive production.

Section III - Comparison and conclusions

Many development economists believe that the choice between the two alternatives found in Tanzania and Taiwan is obvious. The Taiwanese model has proved itself, while the Tanzanian model has not. Yet we should *not rush to conclusions*.

Tanzania's situation cannot be compared with Taiwan's. As we have seen, there are vast differences in history, culture, composition of the population, stages of development, international relations, and so on. It is quite possible that, given the circumstances of Tanzania at the time, Taiwan's approach would not have worked there either. The sorry performance of the economy in neighbouring Kenya, which was the darling of Western investors because of its pro-*capitalist* inclinations, shows that it is hazardous to generalise in the realm of economic policies.[53] This is also borne out by the fact that South Korea achieved success by following policies diametrically opposite to those of Taiwan in many respects. On the other hand, it must be conceded that it is equally unlikely that the Tanzanian approach would have brought Taiwan to its present position of strength.

The "four tigers" have been called the "four successful exceptions".[54] In the mean time the economic dynamic has begun to spread widely along the Pacific Rim. Yet, many analysts have warned that their extraordinary feat *cannot simply be replicated* because the historical and cultural conditions, which made their success possible, have been unique.[55] They also maintain that Taiwan owes much of its success simply to "good fortune".[56] If this is the case, surely Tanzania's lack of success can similarly be attributed to bad fortune?

We can mention three main structural reasons why the "tiger" model cannot easily be applied to the entire Third World. First, export-directed industrialisation presupposes *markets which can absorb* the increased output. Small countries like Taiwan and Singapore could squeeze into the great American, European and Japanese markets, but what would happen if giants like India and China were to attempt to follow the same route? Would they perhaps swamp the world economic system and bring about its collapse? And would the industrial countries allow such devastating competition to take place? Other analysts believe, though, that adequate markets will be generated by economic growth within these regions. As industrialised countries advance to higher levels on the ladder of sophistication and value added, other countries can occupy their place. It is argued that Japan should not produce rice, but expertise! But this consideration would still leave underdeveloped regions, which are fairly isolated from world markets, out in the cold.

Second, the *supply of energy* would pose a serious problem. Fossil fuels would soon be depleted, nuclear energy generation would create enormous hazards and its alternatives would be too expensive to be viable. Others argue that as conventional sources of energy become depleted, alternative sources of energy will be developed and become economically feasible through increases in scale and efficiency. But is this not an overoptimistic scenario?

Third, the full industrialisation of these giants would severely *overtax the ecosystem*. "The earth cannot afford another America." This is probably the most intractable problem.

Whether we agree with any of these sentiments or not depends more on our interests and on our degree of optimism or pessimism than on established facts. But even if the Taiwanese model cannot be replicated, this does not mean that we cannot learn from the two examples analysed above. Perhaps the most important lesson to be learnt is that it is time to get out of *ideological strait-jackets*.[57] The two Third World models discussed in this chapter do not follow text book patterns. Tanzanian Ujamaa differs fundamentally from both social democracy and Marxism-Leninism. Taiwan's capitalism is very different from Western liberal capitalism. In many ways the goals and methods of Tanzania and Taiwan were similar. But the respective outcomes were very different. Their similarities and differences can be summarised as follows:

- Both were *authoritarian one-party states* with a high level of legitimacy and stability, but Tanzania's government intervention was geared to a socialist policy of nationalisation and collectivisation, while Taiwan's government intervention was geared to a capitalist policy of private accumulation.

- Both governments were committed to *economic equity* but Tanzania forced people into collectives, subjected them to party tutelage and controlled prices, while Taiwan set people free economically, enabled them to develop their gifts and let the market determine prices.

- Both governments did not apply free trade principles and both tried to be *responsible and thrifty*, but Tanzania followed a policy of self-reliance and import substitution, while Taiwan followed a policy of export industrialisation and integration into the world economic system.

- Both systems had *strong cultural and religious bases* which emphasise family solidarity, but Tanzania built on African traditional communalism with its orientation to the past, while Taiwan encouraged the Confucian self-improvement ethic with its orientation towards the future.

- Both systems were forced to operate under *Cold War rivalries and pressures*, but Tanzania was drawn towards Red China, itself an isolated and struggling economy, while Taiwan was supported by the financially powerful United States, and integrated into the global capitalist system.

Lessons to be learnt

Following the example of Taiwan, a country should not build its economic system on any kind of orthodoxy but rather on *pragmatism*. Flexibility and the capacity to adapt rapidly to changing circumstances is one of the keys to survival and progress. It can be argued convincingly that Taiwan was not a shining example of the success of capitalism, but rather of the success of pragmatism. Similarly, Tanzania was not a proof of the failure of socialism, but of the failure of dogmatism.

In agrarian societies, the foundation of prosperity must be the development of a sound *agricultural base*. But there are limits to agricultural development. When the ceilings are reached, the peasant economy should be allowed to grow into homestead workshops serving the local community. Small industries can evolve on this basis and gradually grow in scale.

A country should then utilise its *comparative advantage* on world markets. If it has plenty of labour, this is what it should offer to the world economy. Its entrepreneurs should be alert enough to discover any niches in the global market. Through market related diversification, countries can get out of the trap of having only a single export product. It is important to note that comparative advantage is not static, but evolves in time and calls for a high degree of alertness and flexibility.[58]

Import substitution can be applied for a short time to allow local industries to get on their feet. The problems are the following: import substitution needs foreign capital and technology which may not be readily available; foreign capital also leads to dependency; the domestic market is too limited for large scale industrial development, and the protection of local industries beyond a certain point is counterproductive because protected industries never "grow up".

Export oriented industrialisation, by contrast, utilises foreign capital for domestic development, finds gaps in the global market and outcompetes other manufacturers. Leaders should be *alert enough to recognise the threshold* where import substitution industrialisation must make way for export-oriented industrialisation — and in which increments.[59] But again this insight should not become an inflexible dogma. As wealth is accumulated, internal markets too must be given a chance to develop.

It is essential that *trade liberalisation* be disciplined and selective and that the balance of payments remain sound at all times. Exposure to the ravages of free trade is not automatically in the interest of an emerging economy. Hostile attitudes towards international capital are counterproductive, but it is also necessary to be alert to the dangers caused by the volatility of globalised financial capital, the abuse of power by multinational corporations, and the harmful effects of foreign investments on the local economy. It must be realised that international capitalism is motivated not by local development but by profit maximisation. The financial crisis in S E Asia in 1997 provides ample proof for this.

Modesty exercised by government, workers and management is a strong recommendation. One of the chief prerequisites for success is to live within your means, to keep the country out of debt, and to keep its production competitive. There should be no extravagance in government spending, workers should be satisfied with a modest and gradually rising standard of living and employers should keep the legitimate interests of their workers in mind. Comparative advantages on world markets are lost to competitors with a lower cost structure if incomes rise too rapidly.

For the same reason there should be no *overinvestment* in machinery, transport and fancy infrastructure. Local energy, such as draught animals, should not be abandoned until the threshold is reached where their continued use inhibits progress, and where the economy can afford greater dependency on capital and oil imports.

Education and training are key factors in development. It is most curious that this obvious fact is so often overlooked by economic planners and political leaders. But again, the education and training offered must be non-ideological, relevant to the development process, and adaptable to changing situations.

One of the most important ingredients of economic progress is a *lean and clean administration.* Where there is a will, there are ways of overcoming corruption and building up efficient, conscientious and accountable structures.[60] This is also a way of keeping inflation under control - another important ingredient for development.

Taiwan has demonstrated that, contrary to popular belief, there is no inescapable trade-off between *equality and rapid growth*, or between equity and free enterprise.[61] On the contrary, equality builds up markets by spreading purchasing power; it gives more people access to the prerequisites of entrepreneurial initiative; it leads to a higher utilisation of human potential, and it reduces social conflict — all of which are most beneficial for economic progress.

A similar equalisation programme, including land reform and the breakup of great corporations, was instituted at the onset of Japan's post-war economic reconstruction, this time by American occupational forces — which one would have expected to be staunch capitalists. Makes one think, doesn't it! Deliberate equalisation policies led to a belief in equality, social solidarity and a high degree of legitimacy of the economy.[62] Sweden too prospered with equalisation policies. So the ideological excuse for inequality, namely that it is necessary to stimulate growth, must be debunked.

But then equality must be *based on production* rather than consumption, on the space granted for the development of free initiative, rather than on welfare handouts. The state should endeavour to equalise economic opportunity and productive potential, then equality of consumption will look after itself. If the economy allows for equitable participation in the processes of production, huge budget deficits to pay for welfare programmes — the Achilles heel of social democracies — are no longer inevitable.

In this connection we made a few rather surprising, and in some cases disconcerting discoveries. Under certain circumstances *equality is served*

- not by the training of a few to higher skills, but by training across the board;
- not by powerful unions, who push up their demands at the expense of other job seekers, but by equal access to the labour market;
- not by special labour protection, but by labour-intensive modes of production;
- not by concentrating on urban-industrial development, but by land reform and agricultural modernisation;
- not by legitimating patriarchal powers and privileges in the family but by the emancipation and greater participation of women in the economy.

All this shows that it is necessary to look at the total context before deciding on a particular measure.

It can also be argued that on a global scale equality is served when developing countries *capture markets* from industrialised countries. This forces down inflated incomes in the industrial nations to the benefit of incomes in the newly industrialising countries, as well as to the benefit of consumers world-wide. However, it does not narrow the gap between capital owners and workers, nor between newly industrialising countries and the poorest countries in the world. It also hits the workers and the marginalised in industrial countries hardest, rather than the capital owners.

Taiwan has also shown that it is quite possible to have an authoritarian government, which curtails democratic freedoms and trade union activities, but which is also *benevolent and free from corruption*. Such a government has the advantage of being able to maintain stability and impose unpopular but necessary reforms. Imposed measures are economically not harmful if they open up the free space for grassroots initiatives on an equitable basis, rather than dictating everything from above. In the long term, such a regime can build up its legitimacy by providing both equity and prosperity.

With this we certainly do not wish to recommend authoritarian rule, which is hazardous at the best of times, but call upon existing authoritarian governments to use their powers to liberate rather than oppress their people. There is no substitute for *democratic institutions*, a commitment to a social contract, a culture of negotiation and compromise. Fanaticism, ambition, pride and obstinacy of leaders and followers should at long last be recognised for what they are: the scourges of humankind.

Political stability is a fundamental ingredient for development. Any progress will come to grief through oppression, political instability, violent conflict, or war. Investors, developers, producers and markets all need security and social peace. How can a nation develop if endless streams of refugees have to leave their productive pursuits and become dependent on aid; if homes, farms, factories, shops, schools and natural resources are repeatedly destroyed; if financial and human potentials are squandered on armies and armaments; if the cream of its youth is drawn from educational or productive pursuits, maimed and killed; if motivations are turned to hatred and revenge rather than cooperation and development!

In the long run there is also no substitute for *economic motivation*, especially integrity, reliability, efficiency, diligence, frugality and the ambition to improve your qualifications. Without these virtues all reforms and plans emanating from high places will come to grief. Such attitudes cannot be imposed, but space can be provided for their development. Incentives do not need to be material; they can include communal rewards and religious affirmations. We should not underestimate the potential role of religious communities and educational institutions.

Questions

Revision: Can you summarise the similarities and differences between the Tanzanian and Taiwanese approaches to development? Which are the main reasons for the success of the latter?

Application: How could the combination of the principles of growth and equality be applied in a country such as South Africa where you find a highly developed commercial and industrial sector side by side with a badly underdeveloped traditional sector?

Critique: (a) "You can afford to paint Taiwan as a paradise because you do not live under that ruthless capitalist and oppressive regime!"

(b) "Taiwan has shown the infinite superiority of capitalist freedom over socialist slavery; any developing country which does not follow its example has only itself to blame for its misery." How would you react to these statements?

Let us summarise

In this chapter we compared two models which have been applied in the Third World. Despite its attractive philosophy, Tanzanian socialism proved to be a failure, while Taiwanese capitalism has been a success. We have seen that numerous factors contributed to these divergent outcomes and that not all of these factors can be attributed to the fact that the policies were either socialist or capitalist. There were cultural differences, political pressures, historical fortunes and misfortunes. To a very large extent, therefore, both these approaches *defy easy categorisation* in ideological terms.

Nyerere's philosophy of Ujamaa socialism has been hailed as one of the most enlightened programmes of social construction. Particularly appealing was its grounding in indigenous African traditions. But its practical application manifested *serious flaws*. Problematic aspects include enforced villagisation of agriculture; nationalisation of industries; industrialisation based on import substitution, and isolation from world markets. Perhaps the most serious mistake was to obstruct rather than liberate and support the initiatives of idividuals and communities on the ground. *Historical misfortunes*, such as droughts, the oil crisis, the drop in coffee and sisal prices, and the war against Idi Amin, led to a balance of payments crisis which precipitated its downfall.

The most remarkable feature of the Taiwanese approach was the combination of a deliberate policy of *equalisation* with a deliberate policy of *export oriented* industrialisation, implying selective economic integration into the world capitalist system. The country realised its comparative advantage in the area of low labour costs and emphasised labour-intensive production. Its policies were marked by a high degree of flexibility and pragmatism. *Historical advantages* included the Japanese modernisation of Taiwan's agriculture, the influx of a skilled elite, substantial American support in the early stages of development, and a world economic boom which secured foreign investment and overseas markets.

Because many of these factors were historically unique we must be cautious not to draw overhasty conclusions. Whether the Taiwanese approach could have worked in Tanzania, and whether it can be applied to other Third World situations, are moot points. Nevertheless there are *important lessons* to be learnt. One is that pragmatism is preferable to dogmatism. Another is that growth and equity are not necessarily at cross purposes, provided that equity is based on free access to economic activity, rather than on welfare grants. A third lesson is that authoritarian governments can either stifle or enhance individual and communal initiatives, and that we should beware of the growth of an inefficient bureaucracy. Finally, a culture of forward-looking self-improvement may be more conducive to economic development, than an orientation towards the ancestral past, even though both may be built on family solidarity.

Notes

1   A similar comparison could be made between Malaysia and Sri Lanka. World Bank 1991:138.

2   For an excellent historical survey see Uwechue 1991:1818ff.

3   Representatives of these organisations will say that their programme is neither standard nor imposed, because in each case it is the result of negotiations with the respective government. Yet policy directives have been fairly rigid and the pressure to follow them considerable.

4   Nyerere 1968:2.

5   Nyerere 1968:14-16.

6   TANU (= Tanganyika African National Union) was extended to the CCM (= Chama Cha Mapinduzi) in 1977.

7   Rwelamira 1988:14ff.

8   Rwelamira 1988:33.

9   I owe some of the following information to verbal communication by the former Tanzanian Minister of Finance, Mr A Jamal, at a conference.

10 Van Buren 1993:373.

11 A passionate and illuminating plea for the peasants is contained in Padre Athanasius OSB 1988: Justice for the peasants: The question of our time. Peramiho, Tanzania: Benedictine Publications Ndanda.

12 Cf Hyden (described by Kasfir 1986:336ff) argues that African peasants are motivated by a "peasant model of production" and an "economy of affection". Both these traditions make them self-sufficient enough to partially withdraw from the control of the state.

13 Herbst, J 1990: State and politics in Zimbabwe. Harare: Univ of Zimbabwe Publications, pp 85ff.

14 Van Buren 1993:372; O'Neil & Mustafa 1990:xii also list mismanagement as one of the crucial factors.

15 For a critical analysis of the crisis and the prescriptions of the Structural Adjustment Programmes of the IMF and the World Bank see Lensink 1996 as well as the contribution of Paul Mosley in Fontaine, Jean-Marc 1992:27ff.

16 For an overview of aspects to this problem see Semboja & Therkildsen 1995.]

17 Bundy 1988; Herbst 1990, chapter 5.

18 Suggested reading: Chang 1992.

19 Ian Little in Galenson 1979:448.

20 Little in Galenson 1979:452.

21 Little 1979:453.

22 Little 1979:450.

23 Chang 1992:32f.

24 Little 1979:448.

25 For a description see Chang 1992:32ff.

26 Chang 1992:2ff,7f,97ff.

27 "No one knows for sure, but some sources estimate that up to 40% of Taiwan's economy operates outside the law and therefore doesn't show up in official statistics." (Storey 1994:19).

28 Storey 1994:18.

29 Chang 1992:3f.

30 See Thorbecke 1979.

31 Korten 1990:54.

32 The same happened with the German and Japanese economies.

33 The same is true for South Korea which was under intense pressure from the North. The Park administration successfully elevated export-led growth to a national priority and a patriotic duty (Müller 1996:78-82).

34 A notable exception seems to be arms procurement, which is surrounded by secrecy because of pressure exerted by Red China on arms dealers not to supply to Taiwan (Newsweek, March 14, 1994, p 43).

35 Little 1979:498ff. Japan too began its modern industrial history with a land reform programme, as part of a programme of equalisation of the distribution of assets. Vestal 1993.

36 Schive 1996:41.

37 Schive 1996:35.

38 Schive 1996:35.

39 Schive 1996:41.

40 See Ranis 1979; cf Måller 1996 for Korea.

41 Heilbroner 1985:174.

42 Müller 1996:89f,91f.

43 Little 491ff.

44 Little 1979:478, 497.

45 Müller 1996:86f.

46 Müller 1996:91ff.

47 Little 1979:461ff.

48 Schive 1996:26.

49 Müller 1996:81f, 96f.

50 Müller 1996:78ff.

51 Little 1979:475; Schive 1996:31ff.

52 Little 1979:485ff.

53 Between 1982 and 1985 Kenya received more than $350 million in gross official development assistance from bilateral creditors. In 1979, foreign aid covered 35% of the state development budget, in 1990 this figure had risen to 90%. Between 1984 and 1992 Kenya's external debt to bilateral donors nearly doubled to $ 2.4 billion. Total external debt rose to 71.7% of GDP. Lehman 1993:122-124.

54 Keesing 1988

55 Reynolds 1988:1ff; Bardhan and Roemer 1992:103; and others.

56 Chang 1992:134f. The same has been said of Japan. Vestal 1993:154.

57 Chang & Clark extend this to conventional scientific models of explanation and propose "eclecticism beyond orthodoxy" 1992:xvf,135ff.

58 Chang 1992:6.

59 Fontaine summarises the liberal argument against import-substitution: "The global result is that, comfortably wrapped in the blanket of protectionism, import-substitution sectors never grow out of infancy. They fail to reach their optimal scale of production on the domestic market, where high costs and prices arsing from below-capacity operation discrourage demand. Furthermore, they fail to break into the world market, because of anti-export bias. If, in addition, imports of inpouts rise faster than imports of finished products fall, the economy turns globally more dependent on imports. And export-sectors are increasingly relied upon to provide the foreign-exchange need to supply industrial sectors with spare-parts, inputs and machinery. The inward-orientation becomes a spiralling self-aggravating feature, industry becomes more and more dependent on export sectors and is threatened with collapse when export prices or volume fall." But this argument is against protectionism, not import substitution (Fontaine 1992:7). Cf also Nash p 47, and Yentürk-Coban 274ff in the same volume.

60 See Klitgaard, Robert 1988: Controlling corruption. Berkeley et al: University of California Press.

61 See also Fields 1980:122ff. There seems to be no correlation between inequality and growth.

62 Vestal 1993:15ff.

CHAPTER 7

Value assumptions of liberalism and socialism

What is the task of this chapter?

Let us recap. We began this book with a brief analysis of the facts, consequences and causes of *growing discrepancies* between affluent and poor sections of the population — both on the social-structural level and on the level of collective consciousness. We also alluded to the need to preserve the biosphere, which is the natural habitat of humankind. We have tried to indicate the direction in which we may have to think and act if these imbalances are to be contained or overcome.

The main body of the book has been devoted to an analysis of traditional economic wisdom as it manifests itself in socio-economic *systems and ideologies*. The insights we have at present is the result of a hit and miss experiment through which the human race has proceeded. The great store of collective experience now available should give us some clues for the way ahead.

We saw that neither of the *two extremes*, capitalist liberalism and Marxist-Leninist socialism, is very helpful. The *two compromises*, social democracy and democratic socialism, seemed to be more promising. Because of the ill-fated history of democratic socialism, social democracy seemed to be the only viable option left at present. Fortunately social democracy is a flexible and versatile system which can be adapted to local situations, ongoing developments and widening horizons.

Then we looked at *two models from the Third World*. Again a model based pragmatic flexibility proved to be superior to a model based on ideological imposition. What was particularly intriguing was the fact that the Taiwanese model was able to combine a capitalist economy with a powerful concern for equity, without sacrificing economic performance. State intervention seemingly does not have to stifle the development of free initiative; it can also facilitate and empower it.

But pragmatic flexibility in the choice of means still presupposes that we know what we want to achieve. Past experiences alone are not sufficient to guide us into an unpredictable future. If we do not want to blunder along, we need a sense of direction. Apart from an *analytical* mind, which takes the needs of a given situation into consideration, apart from a pragmatic mind which seeks to find the most workable procedures, we also need a *ethical* mind which gives account of the goals we try to achieve and the values underlying these goals.

Before we formulate a few policy directives, therefore, we need to reflect on fundamentals. What are the basic *value assumptions* which inform liberals and socialists? Are they equally valid? Are they mutually exclusive, or is a dialectical combination more appropriate? How can they be translated into policies and structures? Because we are ploughing through the same alternatives again and again from differing perspectives there will be some repetition in this chapter and the reader is requested to be patient.

Let us redraw the battle lines

Human beings are neither angels nor devils. They are also not infallible. Wherever we go in the world, we find good and bad, insight and error. If this is true, we can expect distortions to occur *in both ideologies* which must be exposed. We should also expect elements of truth in both, which should be retrieved. Likewise we should expect dehumanising structures in both systems which have to be overcome, as well as positive developments which should be reinforced.

It is, therefore, not very helpful to jump on one of the ideological bandwagons. *The battle lines must be redrawn.* We should opt neither for liberalism nor for socialism; we should struggle for truth and against deception in both ideologies. We should opt for the wellbeing of human beings against dehumanising power structures in any social system - whether liberal or socialist. We should opt for the wellbeing of the natural world and the rights of coming generations against greed and carelessness.

Such a stance is *subversive.* It will undermine the foundations of any prevailing ideological and social system. However, our task is not to foster outdated loyalties, but to strive for the good of all creatures on the planet. Deception should be exposed! Power concentrations, which are not derived from a popular mandate and subject to its control, *should* be subverted! The goal of a balance of power and control of its abuse is in line not only with ethical demands, but also with the professed aims of a liberal democracy and the socialist vision of a classless society.

Let us locate our level of discourse

The debate on economic systems and ideologies is often bedevilled by irrational reactions rather than guided by sober analysis. This is symptomatic of the inability to cope with complexity. The argument may be conducted at the level of fact and logic, while the adoption of a given stance may be located at the level of emotions. To obviate this problem let us distinguish the various levels at which people may be operating when dealing with these questions:

The *emotional* level. There are gut-level predilections in all strata of society which cause people to be disposed favourably towards either the capitalist or the socialist system. These feelings are rooted partly in internalised traditions, partly in collective interests. There seems to be a clear correlation between lower incomes and socialist leanings, and between higher incomes and free enterprise leanings.[1] Such predilections are rationalised in fully blown ideologies and it is very difficult to convince people who have identified with a particular stance that their assumptions may be questionable.

The level of *economic research*. Can we not establish the facts? Yes, we can — at least to a certain extent. Gut level predilections strongly determine perceptions even in ostensibly "objective" research.[2] Nevertheless we can fall back on considerable empirical observation concerning the actual performances and consequences of the capitalist and the socialist systems. There are three basic questions on this level:

- What is the economic performance of the system in terms of the *overall prosperity* of the nation? Here capitalism has proved to be superior to Marxism-Leninism.

- How does the system affect the *economic position of different groups* in society, particularly the wealthy and the destitute, and how does this in turn affect the relation between these groups? Here capitalism has largely failed because it allows vast discrepancies to emerge between rich and poor. Marxist socialism, by contrast, has succeeded in alleviating poverty and narrowing the gap considerably, although corruption and oppression have undone much of the gain.

- What is the system's track record in terms of protecting or harming the *biosphere*? If economic success happens at the expense of the natural environment, future generations are the losers in the game. Here both capitalism and socialism have failed, although capitalism has recently invested more in cleaning up the environment than socialism has.

The level of *values*. In ethics we ask questions such as the following about the two systems:

- Which values inform the system in each case?

- Are these values incompatible with those of the alternative system, or do they complement each other?

- To which particular groups in society do these values belong — and why do those groups foster these values?

- Does the system which claims to stand for these values actually embody them in practice?

- Are the values valid in each case - and if so, according to which system of meaning?

Finally we come to the level of *policy*. Neither capitalism nor socialism exists in pure form in the real world. Both are mixed systems to a greater or lesser extent. All systems also undergo change. This is where policy comes in. Policy is determined by all the previous levels: gut feelings, collective interests, empirical evidence, and value judgments. A policy, however, is meaningless without the *power* to implement it. Here two questions have to be asked:

- Which groups wield power and how much power do they wield? In other words, what is the spread of power in the population?
- Are there checks and balances in the system against the abuse of power?

Section I - Common values embedded in alternative ideologies

We have sketched the overall task. In this chapter we focus on the value assumptions implied in the two systems and ideologies. It would seem that the prime value in capitalist liberalism is *achievement*. Achievement again implies individual freedom to develop your initiative and potential. We have to concede that capitalism has no intrinsic interest in freedom, only in profit,[3] but to make profits you need freedom. In Marxist socialism the prime value is *equality* of power and prosperity. Equality demands state intervention to bring it about.[4]

Both freedom and equality are *positive values* embedded in the Western Jewish-Christian tradition and its secular-humanist counterparts which have since become universal.[5] Let us trace this history briefly:

- The Ancient Near Eastern tradition of justice, refined in the Jewish concept of the covenant law of Yahweh, was superseded by the *New Testament* concept of unconditional (thus universally accessible) acceptance into the fellowship of God. This implied freedom,[6] equal dignity[7] and concern for the other.
- The failure of the church to understand its own gospel, let alone to give structural expression to it, gave rise, through the centuries, to radical demands, culminating in the secular creed of the *French revolution*: liberty, equality, and fraternity.
- *Marxism* again was a response to the failure of liberals to live up to their creed during the industrial revolution. Capitalists had stressed liberty, but dropped equality and fraternity from the agenda.
- The *ecological movement* was a response to the failure of Christianity, capitalism and Marxism alike to extend concern for the other to the non-human world, thus creating havoc within nature at the expense of future generations.
- Not all other cultures have shared these values. However, during and

after the colonial age they have been disseminated all over the globe.[8] Westernised sections of the population in Third World countries, in particular, demand them as forcefully today as their counterparts in the West. Freedom and equal dignity have become *universal demands*. In all cases, however, respect for nature still lags behind.

If we are to sort out the value commitments underlying modern ideologies, we have to go back to their roots in the Jewish-Christian and humanist cultural constellation and retrieve their intended universality and comprehensiveness. Under modern conditions this can only be done appropriately, however, by seeing this cultural constellation in the context of current perceptions of reality. According to the *natural sciences* two overriding principles seem to govern all processes in this world:

- The second thermodynamic law says that because the universe expands, energy moves from infinite concentration (just before the "big bang") to infinite dissolution (i.e. disorder, or "entropy"). Thus, for the system as a whole, any construction implies a greater degree of *deconstruction* somewhere in the system. Technological advance represents an acceleration of deconstruction elsewhere in the natural and social environment. While we are building grandiose skyscrapers, highways and factories, slums grow, rain forests are chopped down and carbon dioxide levels in the atmosphere increase.

- The theory of *evolution* says that the concentrations of energy, which make up our material world, develop into ever more complex entities. Each higher level of complexity, however, depends on the capacity of the respective lower level to yield sufficient material to be deconstructed for the new construct to survive, and to absorb the impact of the waste produced. If human development goes beyond this threshold, it uses up its "natural capital" and the economy is heading towards a crisis, whether creeping or sudden.[9] For these reasons sensitivity towards the social and ecological consequences of our economic system has become a matter of life and death for humanity as a whole.[10]

Ironically the ultimate anarchy of a classless society envisaged by Marxism is akin to the extreme ideal of the liberal creed: *total freedom and unlimited prosperity based on technological advance*. The conflict between the two is essentially concerned with the means to approach that goal. Ecological concerns have not appeared on the horizons of either ideology until very recently. Because our present task is to sort out value alternatives between liberalism and socialism we shall focus on the two values of freedom and equality.

What is our stance concerning these values? Freedom in capitalism has been associated with profit maximisation and socially irresponsible behaviour. Equality in socialism has been associated with bureaucratic inefficiency, corruption and totalitarian repression. An ethicist may ask: *must we accept these packages?* Surely not! As a positive value, freedom is intrinsically linked with *social responsibility*. True freedom can never be a do-as-you-like sort of freedom. It is not only a freedom from fetters, but also a freedom for constructive action. Similarly, social equality as a positive value is intrinsically linked with *personal dignity*. The equality of slaves is not compatable with human dignity. Personal dignity is upheld by social responsibility and social responsibility is based on personal dignity.

I would argue, therefore, that we do not have alternative sets of values between which we have to choose, but rather an irreducible dialectic. It is because the two systems fail to integrate freedom with equality that they end up in opposite extremes. And if responsibility and dignity are extended to include future generations and the non-human world, we will also not destroy our environment.

Motivations

The real alternatives lie between the pursuit of *self-interest* at the expense of others, which is asocial and unacceptable behaviour, and the full development of our potential to *serve the community*. In this connection we have to correct a common misunderstanding. It is a fallacy to think that the freedom espoused by liberalism stands for egoism (selfishness) and the communalism espoused by socialism stands for altruism (self-denial). A closer look reveals that narrow self-interest and responsible service can and do occur in both systems, though in different forms.

A social *self-interest* occurs:

- *in liberalism* in the form of the pursuit of economic power, as well as in the form of profit and utility maximisation;
- *in socialism* in the form of the pursuit of bureaucratic power, as well as in carelessness and corruption. Where asocial motivations, such as ambition and greed, are not overcome from within, the outward change of systems only diverts them from the channels available in one system to the channels available in the other.[11] "When the state becomes supreme, there is ultimately only one prize, the control of state power."[12]

Service to the community occurs:

- in a *liberal system* in the form of a wide range of public initiatives, charities and democratic institutions for which the system provides free space;
- in a *regulated (socialist) system* in the form of conscientiousness and a sense of duty in public offices.

Looking at what happens on the ground, you get the impression that the liberal system is more successful in educating its people for politeness, mutual service and concern. While in communist countries vast resources are invested in educating people for socialist solidarity, in the West those who treat their fellow human beings with contempt simply harm their careers and their profits - and this seems to have a greater impact on their behaviour. On visits to Budapest and Prague, for instance, my wife and have found the customer service of shop attendants and the attitude of bus drivers appalling compared to their Western counterparts. We had the sense that we owed them an apology for entering the shop and disturbing their peace! The West has also developed a much higher ecological awareness than the East.

Similarly there are *victims* of asocial behaviour in both systems. There are dropouts in the liberal system and disempowered people in the regulated system. The difference is that in the first you may starve, while in the second you may become frustrated.

The question of selfishness is closely connected with another pair of concepts. Liberals often stress *realism*, socialists often stress vision. From this we might gather that liberals stress pragmatism, while socialists stress morality. Activists then believe they should be on the side of the stronger moral argument. But this too is a wrong set of alternatives. On the one hand realism and pragmatism without vision lack direction and fail to motivate. On the other hand an unrealistic vision and an impractical norm are fairly useless. The real problem is that selfishness can hide behind both realism **and** vision. The question is not whether or not we should have a vision, but what kind of vision it should be — personal aggrandisement, power and wealth, or mutual enrichment and service to the community? Similarly the question is not whether we should be pragmatic, but what we want to achieve with our pragmatism.

Social structures

Motivations are not enough. The dialectic found in the Jewish-Christian and humanist value systems, which combine freedom with responsibility and equality with dignity, must be given *structural expression*. Appropriate structures do not automatically follow from right motivations. Nor can we postpone structural policies until everybody has acquired right motivations.

Given the continued presence of human selfishness, a good social structure subjects the motivation of *self-interest* to controls and gives the motivation of *service* a chance to develop. Systems cannot make better people, but they can restrain social evil caused by negative motivations; they can also facilitate the impact of positive motivations. For this reason we need a careful balance between freedom and control. Just as a healthy state employs a police force to restrain public crime and makes the freedom of movement on its streets possible, it should take measures to ensure that people are not victimised by their fellow-citizens in the economic realm.

The state also has the positive role of social construction for the benefit of all its citizens. Such a role presupposes, of course, that those entrusted with authority have the *interests of the public* at heart. Unfortunately this cannot be taken for granted. It is obvious that not all state intervention is good. State officials are also less than perfect human beings. Discriminatory laws, fascist arbitrariness and misguided economic policies are cases in point. The state must intervene in a direction which is profitable for the society as a whole. Moreover, it must facilitate, not take over, the activities of individuals, groups and communities.

Given the fallibility and corruptibility of human nature this can only be approximated in a *democratic system*. True, there are also benign dictatorships. But who can guarantee that a dictatorship will be benign? It is sobering to witness how corruption thrived more in Marxist systems than in liberal-capitalist systems, although the former shouted public solidarity and responsibility from the roof tops. Similarly, ecological disasters have been more rampant in the East than in the West.

The reason for this is not that people living in a liberal capitalist system are morally superior to those living in a Marxist system, but that Marxism, as a system, grants uncontrolled power and secrecy to its leaders, who are as corruptible and fallible as everybody else. By contrast, liberal democracy as a system subjects its leaders to public controls. Moreover, in a democratic state all population groups are able to present their legitimate interests to relevant decision-making bodies. The selfishness of the ruled is checked by the rulers and the selfishness of the rulers is checked by the ruled. There is division of power, public accountability, the rule of law and human rights. *Therefore democracy is a goal as well as a means of social transformation* - even in the economic sphere of life.

On the other hand, democracy is not always effective in giving the poor their due. Galbraith, for instance, castigates the hypocrisy of satisfied voters who emphasise the harmful effects of state intervention when it benefits the poor, but clamour for it when it benefits corporate raiders, property speculators and ailing banks. Because their vote does not seem to make any difference, the poor do not bother to vote, so they have no real voice.[13]

State intervention

How much state control and direction do we need? According to the liberal creed the role of the state should be minimal. Ideally it should intervene only to keep order, that is, to protect the freedom of individuals and groups against the encroachment of others. The rest is left to the voluntary interaction of individuals and groups on the open market. The modern slogan is: as little government as possible, as much government as necessary. According to the Marxian creed, by contrast, the role of the state should be maximal - at least until a classless society is firmly established. Ideally it should regulate not only the entire economy but determine all other dimensions of life as well.[14]

At first sight it would appear that minimal state intervention means maximal freedom and minimal equality. Maximal state intervention of a socialist kind, by contrast, seems to imply minimal freedom and maximal equality. If this were the case there would be a clear trade-off between freedom and equality. The more you go in the socialist direction, the more equality you get; the more you follow the liberal line, the more freedom you obtain. This trade-off can be depicted in the following graph:

The graph suggests that we have the best mix of freedom and equality where the two curves intersect. This is correct as far as the trade-off holds true. But the argument becomes even stronger when we discover that, when taken to extremes, both freedom and equality are self-destructive. Let us see why.

- In laissez faire capitalism total freedom leads to cut-throat competition and to rapidly growing discrepancies between those who manage to get to the top and those who are left behind on lower rungs of the social power structure. This is due both to structural mechanisms (such as the accumulation of productively invested capital and technological sophistication), and to the abuse of power. The result is a rapid *deterioration of freedom* in the system. Equality of opportunity, which is an indispensable part of the liberal creed, is destroyed by radical capitalism. "Winners tend to grow and losers disappear. Over time many firms become few firms, competition is eroded, and monopoly power increases. To the extent that competition is self-eliminating we must constantly reestablish it by trustbusting."[15]

- The Marxist ideal of total equality is utopian. Because of the inherent differences in the potentials of individuals and groups, equality can only be achieved in the real world if it is rigorously enforced. Wherever Marxist states have relaxed their controls, discrepancies have emerged all over again. In the real world, therefore, not the classless society but rather the dictatorship of the Communist Party has proved to be the last stage in the evolution of orthodox Marxism-Leninism. Obviously the enforcers of equality cannot be equal with those on whom they impose equality. Think of the cynical adage: "All are equal, but some are more equal than others." As control by the elite over the society increases, *equality deteriorates*.

We arrive at the conclusion, therefore, that there is no gain in freedom when we abandon equality altogether, and no gain in equality when we abandon freedom altogether. Freedom reaches its optimum where equality reaches its optimum, and vice versa. "The arguments concern not the principles of liberal society, but the precise point at which the proper trade-off between liberty and equality should come."[16]

Threshold theory

Threshold theory throws light on the problem of finding this "precise point". In simple terms, threshold theory says the following: in most situations calling for decisions, there is one overriding concern (or group of concerns) which demands to be given priority over all others. As this concern is being met, it gradually loses its urgency, while other concerns gain in importance. At some stage a threshold is reached where other concerns gain prominence over the original concern and demand to be given priority.

So the alternatives underlying economic policy options need to be restated as follows: a system which combines an optimal degree of freedom with an optimal degree of equality, and which serves the real interests of the entire population, must be posited against the dehumanising domination of power concentrations, whether capitalist or communist. Both big business and big government are detrimental to both freedom and equality in society. Social democracy and democratic socialism approach this ideal from opposite sides of the spectrum without having reached it yet. Perhaps it can never be reached, because to do justice to both concerns, social life may have to oscillate between them. Nevertheless the general direction in which we should be moving seems to be clear.[17]

Security vs incentive

There are a number of seemingly contradictory values which are closely related to the values of freedom and equality and which we shall briefly mention here. The first is security vs incentive. Should we expect people to be responsible for their lives or should they be looked after?

The free market system aims at offering *incentives* to the individual; socialism aims at offering *social securities*.[18] Both are important for human development. When people are motivated to do their best, they develop their potential to the full. Too much security lulls. On the other hand, when their survival, security or prosperity are constantly threatened, people become enslaved to their circumstances, lack the freedom to develop their gifts, and become diffident. Again we cannot choose between the two; we can only try to reach the optimal combination. And again it is the threshold theory which can help us to achieve this.

We should never forget that *values are embedded in convictions*. It is interesting to see how one of the convictions which have been seed beds of these values, namely the Christian faith, has dealt with these two values.

- The Christian faith entails both a *demand* (law) and a *gift* (grace). This dialectic cannot be reduced to a single and simple statement. It would seem that the free enterprise system is based on a merciless demand: you have to achieve or go under. Socialism, by contrast, seems to approximate grace: those who cannot fulfil the demand are not abandoned but cared for "by grace". In theology we know that mercy without the law leads to false security — or to "cheap grace" as Bonhoeffer has put it — while the law without grace leads to work-righteousness in those who seem to succeed, and to hopelessness in those who do not.

- Translated into socio-economic terms, social securities may lead to carelessness while the rat race of competition leads to arrogance among achievers, and feelings of anxiety and inferiority among those who remain behind. Only when we see the dialectic between law and grace can grace do its redemptive work. There is no question that this also applies in the economic field.

- The decisive theological insight is, however, that the gift of grace forms the presupposition of the demand while the demand forms the consequence of the gift. People are first accepted and then empowered to make their contribution to healthy communal life. Translated into socio-economic terms this means that rights should be primary and not linked to achievements. Nobody should be allowed to fall into misery because he/she cannot compete; there should be an overall safety-net which does not impede the achievers but which saves people who are vulnerable to marginalisation. On the other hand obligations and responsibilities indeed follow from these rights. The system should not allow loafers to live at the expense of others and get away with it.

Unfolding vs manipulation

Liberals maintain that social systems must evolve and grow if they are to be viable; socialists maintain that humanity is meant to construct its own world. Again, these are wrong alternatives. What we term creativity in technology and growth in economics are, in fact, processes of *deconstruction* and *reconstruction*. We do not create anything; we take reality apart and put it together in a form which satisfies our needs. This inevitably leads to redundancy. To make a few pieces of furniture we have to chop down an entire tree. The organic entity of the living tree is destroyed and much unused material simply goes to waste. That is the basis of the ecological problem.

Let us apply this insight to social processes. Even the *most radical revolutionaries* cannot construct a society from scratch, and have never done so. They take what is there, deconstruct it to a certain extent and then reconstruct it. In the process they inevitably destroy a great deal of what has grown over the centuries. It is also simply not true that *liberals* allow things to grow. As Marx has keenly observed, the bourgeoisie is the most radically revolutionary movement the globe has ever seen. It applies technology to every dimension of reality, including the social order, and ceaselessly continues to deconstruct and reconstruct. The glittering sky-scrapers in capitalist city centres have all been built on the sites of demolished traditional buildings. Probably we cannot do without deconstruction and reconstruction. The relevant questions are, rather, to what end, by which means, at what cost, and costs to whom? Is it done for the private gain of those who wield the power of reconstruction, or is it done in the interests of the society as a whole?

Both liberals and socialists believe in technological "progress". This progress orientation is also applied to the social dimensions of life. Today we have to become aware of the extreme dangers of deconstruction and reconstruction - whether by liberals or by socialists. The ecological concern for balance must also be applied to the social sphere. In the future, progress must be directed towards a *healthy balance* in reality, otherwise it is nothing but deterioration in disguise. We have to regain respect for the world in which we live, whether in nature or society, otherwise humankind may soon be left with nothing to deconstruct.

Competition vs allocation

In a socialist command system resources are deliberately allocated according to rational criteria. A market system allows for free competition in the belief that the interplay of supply and demand will automatically lead to the optimal allocation of resources. But what about allocation and competition as human values? The answer is that competition and allocation are not values but procedures or mechanisms. In themselves they are neither right nor wrong in terms of a deontological ethics.[19] They are also neither good nor bad in terms of a teleological ethics. They are both ethically ambiguous.

Allocation is ambiguous because whether it has positive or negative results depends not only on the efficiency with which allocation can be effected, but also on the criteria according to which you allocate. Its results are positive when resources are allocated to necessary public concerns which private enterprise would not bother to take up. But artificial allocation can also have bad consequences. Eastern European regimes have often invested in products that nobody wanted and failed to allocate funds to items which the population needed. They have also not allocated sufficient funds to cleaning up industrial operations and the result has been widespread ecological disaster. They have further allocated insufficient funds to the maintenance and renewal of buildings, factories and other assets. Moreover, experience has shown that individual or collective selfishness can enter into the equation. An allocation to the benefit of your own collective interests at the expense of others is wrong.

Competition is just as ambiguous. It can be constructive, but it can also be destructive. It is constructive insofar as it cuts out passengers or parasites and forces every member of the community to make a contribution. It also motivates. It prompts creativity and excellence. Freedom and competition are corollaries and without freedom people do not develop their gifts to the full. Freedom and competition are the secret of excellence. Competition also does not have to be asocial. Competition in sport can build social relationships. There can also be competition to serve the community as best you can. Discrimination, privileges, the Marxist command system and capitalist power concentrations all destroy freedom, competition and excellence. In Boulding's words, "I must defend competition as on the whole healthy and necessary."[20]

But competition can also be *destructive*. Those who are outcompeted are stranded. It leads to feelings of inferiority and frustration among some, and to feelings of superiority and glee among others. It can negate public responsibility, destroy social relationships and "degenerate into pathological conflict and malevolence ..."[21] Therefore competition must be conducted within the parameters of structures which secure social justice. These structures must be underpinned by a collective mentality of social concern. Where there is freedom you must have responsibility, otherwise it becomes counterproductive. And responsibility, like freedom, must find both structural and motivational expression. The state must see to it that all people have more or less the same opportunities to compete, which brings us back to the realm of allocation. Again the imperative is to reach the optimum of both in a dynamic dialectic.

Questions

Revision: Explain the complex relation between freedom and equality and its derivatives.

Application: On which of the two basic values do (a) the business community, (b) the unions, (c) the unemployed in your country place the emphasis? Can you explain this difference?

Critique: (a) "You seem to forget that without a vibrantly growing economy, which only free enterprise capitalism can provide, equality can only mean that we share our poverty."

(b) "Competition is always linked with selfishness and never far from conflict, even in sport. What we need in the economy is cooperation." Comment.

Section II - Property and power

Private ownership of the means of production by a tiny financial elite lies at the centre of the Marxist attack against the capitalist system. Liberals, on the other hand, maintain that few aspects in Marxism are more dehumanising than large scale expropriation and collectivisation. But are private property and collectivisation the real alternatives?

The discussion of social philosophers usually gets bogged down on the *right of persons to own what they have worked for.*[22] This right can hardly be disputed. But when liberals use this argument to defend private property we have to ask whether the great capital accumulations which continue to accrue to financial elites can really be defended on these grounds. Productively invested capital snowballs, whether you work for it or not. Marxists, by contrast, have argued that capitalists exploit workers by appropriating the surplus value produced by the workers. But then it does not make sense to take that surplus from the capitalists and give it to state officials rather than to the workers.

We shall follow a different approach to the problem underlying the dispute between liberalism and Marxism. Careful analysis reveals that the problem in capitalist societies does not lie with property as such but with the *abuse of power* which is made possible by an imbalance in property rights. But abuse of power is also made possible by uncontrolled public offices which abound in socialist societies. Both the right to property and the institution of public office are accepted as legitimate in most religious and secular traditions. The ethical objection is directed, rather, against idolatry and injustice in both cases. Let us pursue this observation further.

Property and public office

Property and public office possess a *common characteristic*, namely power. Property means exclusive and lawful control over a given part of reality. Control is power. As Heilbroner puts it, "the drive to amass wealth is inextricable from power, and incomprehensible except as a form of power."[23] So property is a public institution which grants power. Economic power also implies political influence, though this is often denied by liberals.[24]

Public office is a parallel to property in the sense that it also grants power. The difference is that, ideally, public office operates on behalf of the community while property operates in the private interest of the owner. Similarly, public office can be withdrawn by the community, at least in a democratic society, while property is protected against such interference. In other words, ideally, public office is subject to democratic controls; property is not.

In cases where there is a reasonable degree of equity in the distribution of property this should present no problem. Each person can be master over his/her own realm and these masters can cooperate freely in common ventures. This is the *liberal ideal.* If it was applied, it would conform to one of the norms of democracy, namely equal access to power. Alas, this is not the capitalist reality! Liberalism stands for property rights in the name of freedom, but it does not grant property rights on an equitable basis. In practice it favours a wealthy minority.

On the strength of its wealth, this minority obtains a more than proportionate influence in the sphere of political power. The case against capitalism is, therefore, that its control of economic resources is *unequal and undemocratic.* Property can only be defended as a democratic value if it is equally accessible to all and subject to democratic checks and balances. This would demand at least a clear commitment to the principle of equality of opportunity - which again implies a certain degree of affirmative action.

Referring to the power of private enterprises a leading American expert on management goes further and argues that power must be controlled. It should be *geared to function and protected against abuse*: "no organization must be allowed power unless absolutely necessary to the discharge of its function. Anything beyond this is usurpation ... There must be clear and public rules for its exercise, and there must be review and appeal to some one or some tribunal that is impartial and not part of the problem."[25] What this writer does not say is that if this is true for power it is true for property. In fact he discounts the importance of property in the modern economy, which is hardly justified.[26]

Marxism-Leninism, in contrast, demands that all property rights — at least of ·the means of production — be transferred to the state. But this is no solution either. When the state owns a factory or a farm, it is not the workers, or "the people", who are in control but the bureaucrats. This means that power and control are removed from the population and handed to public offices.

These public offices are *not persons* as such, but institutions manned by "mercenaries" who do not necessarily have the interests of the people at heart. On the contrary; ambition is channelled from private money making to control of state power.[27] The incumbents are granted powers which entitle them to shunt around, not only the assets, but also the disinherited population - much more so than the bosses in liberal societies. Because they are protected from public scrutiny and democratic controls they can do a lot of harm — either by design or default.

Moreover, it has often been observed that bureaucracies develop *a life of their own* which is able to escape control even by the top leadership of the state.[28] Secretly the incumbents may then abuse these public assets for private gain. Witness the widespread occurrence of corruption in such states! Moreover, because the bureaucrats do not own the property, they do not necessarily feel the urge to maintain and develop it. As a result society loses valuable assets and opportunities.

It is not property as such that is the problem, therefore, but the *distribution of power and its control*. Just as with public office, property is a problem only because it guarantees control. And control is only a problem if it is excessive, unchecked and more accesible to some people than to others — thus undemocratic. Power must be geared to function and matched with responsibility.[29] Neither the one nor the other ideology reaches the goal of equitable distribution of control.[30]

The significance of property

Our discussion so far could give the impression that property was a neutral institution with no particular value, which we could tolerate under certain conditions. But property belongs, I believe, to the very foundations of a fulfilled human life. It is interesting to note that human property rights have *parallells in nature*. Certain trees, for instance, only grow at particular distances from each other. Many birds demarcate their hunting grounds by means of their morning songs. The right to such an open space, to such a hunting ground, to such a resource base, is respected by all potential competitors. It makes the unfolding of life possible and prevents potential conflict over resources — which would not be in the interest of the species as a whole. We note in passing that public office also has its parallells in nature. Female elephant herds, for instance, are led by a matriarch, while male herds display a hierarchical pecking order.

Freedom and self-determination

Let us pursue the functions of property at some depth. First, property grants a psychologically indispensable amount of freedom. Freedom means self-determination. Self-determination is one of the most fundamental prerequisites of human dignity. Self-determination means *mastery over your life and your world*. So it is intimately connected with power or control. Property includes everything over which the owner is exclusively entitled to take decisions.

The absolute minimum of freedom needed for a healthy life is control over your *own body*. Slaves have no dignity. This is the deepest source of their suffering. In addition to control over your body, property grants exclusive rights over a certain portion of your immediate environment — your own clothes, your own bed, some money to buy food, some space of your own.

In all cultures particular areas are demarcated, protected and respected for exclusive use by the family and, within the family, the individual. A child must have the right to possess her own toy and an old man must have the right to possess his own walking stick. The home — whether in the form of a tent, a shack, or a mansion — is one of the most fundamental mainsprings of human culture. In short, for the sake of freedom and dignity there must be a minimum of ownership in human life.

Of course, there is also *communal* property or control, especially where the society is organised in small groups. Ideally everybody should have a say in communal decision making; in practice most communities are organised hierarchically. Communal control can be widened to encompass more comprehensive areas like the territorial state. But even in this case the control of common property is restricted to those authorised by the society concerned. That is the principle underlying the territorial integrity of a sovereign state.

Let us have a brief look at the way the Jewish -Christian tradition deals with the issue of property and self-determination.

- According to the biblical witness property represents participation of the human being in *God's creative authority* in a limited and specific sphere. The idea that human beings were created in "the image of God", found in Genesis 1:27-28, is directly linked to participation in God's mastery over the world. The "image of God" was a royal title in antiquity. The king was perceived to be the representative and plenipotentiary of God on earth. This title is here applied to every human being, male and female. All human beings are meant to be kings and queens, proprietors and rulers, representatives and plenipotentiaries of God, the true Owner of the universe.

- This again is the presupposition of human participation in *God's redemptive love*. According to 1 Cor 8:9 Christ, *being rich*, became poor to make us rich, so that we could join him in enriching others. There is no virtue in poverty as such. We can only make ourselves available to others as those who we are; we can only make a contribution with the gifts we have; we can only give what we possess. A powerless person cannot serve. A penniless person has nothing to share. Impotence impairs one's dignity. It also jeopardises the sense of acceptance and belonging. Those who have nothing at all to contribute feel useless. For their social environment they are a nuisance, not a valued member.

So both property and power are intimately linked with freedom, self-determination and service. To act freely you need both the power to act and the protection against others, who may abuse their power to interfere. In other words, freedom presupposes an open space protected by a legal structure within which the individuals or the groups concerned can move freely and develop their potentials. That is the deeper meaning of property.

Property grants protection

The second function of property is that it grants protected access to scarce resources. Any organism, any human being, any community needs a protected realm filled with resources to survive and develop its potential. Protection is the mirror image of freedom and control. Again there are parallels between property and public office. Virtually all historic societies have *protected both property and public office* by means of legally entrenched rights against interference by others.

Contrary to widespread beliefs, both property and office have been normal institutions in *African traditional communalism.* Homesteads were strictly private. Cattle was owned. Fields were allocated by chiefs, but such an allocation gave the sole right of utilisation, and this right was normally inherited. Grazing and hunting grounds were free for all members of the community concerned, because they were not in short supply, but they were not supposed to be used by outsiders.

The Marxist utopian idea of abolishing property and public office belongs to the outgrowths of the technological civilisation with its claim to human autonomy. But Marxism too, after initial experiments with the complete socialisation of all aspects of life had failed, respected at least the private possession of consumer goods: a home, furniture, clothes, and so on. It even allowed small gardens and private workshops. Marxism only demanded the socialisation of crucial *means of production above a certain size,* especially capital and land. Even here the motive of socialisation was to protect the equal access of all people to the resource base of the society, though it did not work that way in practice.

The positive function of property has a negative corollary: others are excluded from utilising the space reserved for the owner. This is unfortunate but unavoidable. Because everybody has an equal right to survive and prosper, however, property will be beneficial only as long as, and as far as, all members of a community are given a protected space *sufficient for their survival and prosperity.* Moreover, no member should be unduly privileged. This was the ideal in ancient Israel where every family possessed its own "lot" or "inheritance" in perpetuity. If the property was lost through fate or fault, it had to be returned to the family in the Jubilee year.[31]

Competition vs monopoly

What then must be said about unequal distribution of property which is so rampant in capitalist societies? The concentration of power in a single social location is called *monopoly.* If there are only a few locations it is called oligopoly. In the real world there are not many monopolies, but there are many oligopolies and that is only slightly better. Monopoly is the great curse word of *Marxists* against capitalist concentrations of economic power - and rightly so. Monopoly can lead to domination and abuse of power at the expense of the powerless.

Liberal economic theory is also opposed to monopoly and oligopoly because they restrict competition, distort the market, lead to inefficiency, prevent the rational allocation of resources and the satisfaction of consumer needs. They also cause inflationary pressure. In most democratic states there are public institutions which are meant to control concentrations of economic power and ensure fair competition. But in most cases they do not go far enough. Liberals often attempt to rationalise away the problem of the existence of big companies. They say, for instance, that as long as Ford, General Motors and Chrysler still compete with one another all is well. Of course, these automobile manufacturers are now under enormous pressure from Japanese and European competitors, which adds a complication to the argument.

However, there is a *sliding scale* from monopoly to oligopoly and further to various stages of less conspicuous concentrations of power. Imbalances of economic potential come in various degrees with monopoly only being the worst case. Therefore liberals should stick to their guns and demand true freedom, true equality of opportunity, true competition. This means the greater the spread of economic potential and power in the society the better. Of course, there are sectors of the economy which demand large scale operations to be viable and competitive on world markets, for instance in the microchip and airliner industries. But then their shareholdings could be spread more widely.

Marxists on the other hand have no right to complain about "monopolies" if they strive to put up an all-inclusive monopoly, the *monopoly of the state*. A monopoly does not become more acceptable just because it is a state monopoly. It may even become worse. The state also consists of people with interests, ambitions, need for incentives, temptations to abuse their power — or simply to be careless and irresponsible. Socialist power concentrations can be used to dismantle extreme income discrepancies but then the acquired power must again be distributed and democratised, otherwise inefficiency and oppression are the result.

Big business and big government

The upshot of these comparisons is that neither capitalist liberalism nor Marxism-Leninism provides optimal solutions to the problems of economic organisation. Big government is no better than big business; collectivist power concentrations are as bad as oligopolistic power concentrations. Both make the ideals of freedom and equality illusory. Big business and big government have *exactly the same effect*: to destroy freedom, dignity and motivation. They are both legitimated by ideology. The Marxist critique that capitalist monopolies use the state for their own ends is correct, but this critique should also be applied to the abuse of power by Marxist regimes. The worst case emerges if big government combines with big business to form fascism.

The original liberal idea was absolutely right: the state should not take over control of the economy but *keep public order*. A just order implies that the strong are not allowed to take advantage of the weak. The legal system, the courts and the police limit freedom so as to make freedom possible. Deliberate abuse of power is curtailed. The state should ensure that people can live their lives without fear of victimisation and assault. What is accepted in interhuman relationships must also be applied to the economic realm. If the state does not allow gangs to mug pedestrians it should not allow corporate raiders to oust their competitors!

Moreover, countervailing measures must be taken to *neutralise the asymmetrical interaction* between the powerful and the weak. We must get used to the idea that even in economics power must be subject to a public mandate. The aim should be to balance out both productive potential (which underlies market supply) and purchasing power (which underlies market demand). The question is not whether we should have state intervention or not, but what it should try to achieve. The state should not take over the economy, but make *free enterprise accessible to all*. It should not stifle initiative and productivity, but facilitate them. It should not follow rigid orthodoxies but be pragmatic enough to adapt to changing needs in unfolding situations.

Above all, the state must be efficient, lean and clean. "For markets to work better, government must also work better."[32] A social order is legitimate if it is mandated by the population. There must be *democracy* in economics just as there must be democracy in politics. This thoroughly liberal demand should not be confused with the Marxist approach, which is based on expropriation and state planning. Democracy implies individual freedom, equality of rights, equality of dignity, division of power, a mandate which can be withdrawn and public accountability.

Capital and other factors of production

There is another dimension to the problem of power, namely its shifting location. In traditional subsistence agriculture each family was virtually self-sufficient. Families cooperated during the ploughing and harvesting seasons but all families had essentially the same productive outfit. In modern commercial and industrial systems this is not the case. There is a high degree of *specialisation*. Factors of production consist of large numbers of minute elements which are integrated into huge systems. Each contributor controls only a tiny function within the whole process. To some degree the question of ownership has receded into the background because control is much more complex and much more important.

Historically speaking, the power base which allows overall control *has shifted from one factor of production to another:* from land to capital, then to managerial organisation, then to communications, then to computer control of the automated production process, finally to control over the international flow of financial capital. The Marxist attack focused on the ownership of capital because that is where power was mainly concentrated in Marx's time. Factory workers represented the underdog majority. Capital and organised labour became the great opponents at the time.

But the industrial mode of production has developed dramatically since then, leading to great shifts in the distribution of power.[33] In present-day capitalism the ownership of capital has lost its overriding importance to another factor, namely *managerial organisation.* Actual power is not wielded by the large body of shareholders, including millions of members of pension funds,[34] but by a small and self-perpetuating managerial elite. This elite has again become increasingly dependent on "high tech" computer scientists. The economy is increasingly built on knowledge and communication. *Information* has become the key factor of production.[35]

On the other hand the working class has become *highly differentiated* between experts, skilled labour and unskilled labour. Experts belong to a highly paid elite. In the specialised, information-based organisation, superiors do not necessarily know the job of their subordinates. Superiors and subordinates are partners like the conductor and the players of various instruments in an orchestra. They depend on each other's loyalty. The whole organisation depends on responsibility and conscientiousness.[36]

Skilled labour has moved up the ladder and formed a privileged "worker aristocracy". Unskilled labour has largely become redundant. How to reintegrate the marginalised into the economic process by allowing them to make a contribution of their own has become a central concern of responsible policy makers.[37] But the industrial process as a whole has assumed global dimensions. The marginalised masses are generally not located in highly industrialised centres but in less developed regions. Under these circumstances even trade unions and socialist parties have lost much of their power.

This drift of the power base demands *great flexibility*, both in ideology and social organisation. The Marxist system proved to be too rigid for this dynamic. After the revolution, managerial organisation, controlled by the state, became the most important source of power in Marxist societies. In feudalism and early capitalism power was located in property rights; in Marxism it was located in the state. But who "owns" the state in the Marxist system? Surely not the workers! Trade unions were simply transformed into instruments to control the working class.

With accelerating technological development a more ominous question arose on the horizon, namely whether the clumsy organs of the state were able to ride the storm of innovation. As it turned out, Marxist societies were not able to keep pace with the rapid advances in computer technology and lost their competitiveness.

These developments radically changed the focus of the debate. The problem that a few people can use their power to further their own interest at the expense of others is as acute as ever, but in modern times it is *no longer so easy to come to grips with this power*. Individuals or groups that have developed a rare kind of expertise, "own" this factor of production to such an extent that it is part of their very personalities. Unless they are physically enslaved, it cannot be expropriated and nationalised. A "worker aristocracy" will not necessarily act in the best interest of marginalised unskilled workers. Nor is it easy to "democratise" the process because non-experts may simply not be in a position to take the right decisions. We have not even begun to tackle this kind of issue.

At the *local level* this means, once again, that industrial democracy should be applied. The different contributors to the economic process should participate fully in the running of the process. Those who are in control should act on the basis of a mandate which can be withdrawn. Shareholders, experts and workers should be fully informed and represented on the boards of their enterprises. Managers should be appointed by, and accountable to, the entire producing community. There is also no economic reason why management should not be as loyal to its work force as it is to its shareholders. We shall come back to the principles of industrial democracy in the next chapter.

But what about those who are also affected, but who are not part of the particular enterprise or sector? What about the consumers, for instance, who may be spread all over the world? Inevitably *the state and the international community* will have to assume a greater and much more sophisticated role under these circumstances. But this again does not mean that the state or a group of states should run, own, or control the economy! On the contrary; they should facilitate participation in decision-making within the economy.

Power and collective consciousness

No social system can function without stability. In part stability depends on power to maintain a given structure. The structure is maintained through the use of force. But the social structure has a counterpart in the form of a collective mental structure. This is internalised by the members of a society and consists of assumptions, beliefs, values, norms, cultural traits, technical procedures and so on.

The greater the homogeneity of the internalised mental structure within the population, the lesser the external force needs to be, and vice versa. This fact accounts for the necessity of the dictatorship of the proletariat in the

Marxist scheme of things: if you want to reconstruct collective mental structures you have to use force. The assumption is that once this has been done, the classless society will emerge and the state will wither away. But as long as collective mental structures are divergent, force — massive, oppressive force — is necessary if the system is to maintain its stability. For us, this is an unacceptable proposition.

In *the West* political structures allow pluralism in the realm of collective consciousness. Why does the system not disintegrate? Because of three forms of power, all of which have both social-structural and collective mental manifestations:

(a) There are *deliberately constructed mechanisms* which make it possible that divergent views and goals can be accommodated in society: human rights, the rule of law, and the procedures of a democratic order. But these mechanisms need to be internalised by the population if the system is to function properly. People must be willing to tolerate other points of view; an opposition party must be granted a place in the sun; a party which has lost an election must concede defeat with dignity, relinquish power voluntarily and not declare a state of emergency.

(b) Social-structural cohesion is also achieved through *economic competition*. You have to do your best or drop out. This necessity limits freedom and binds people into the structure. People have to work and cooperate if they want to survive and prosper. The assumption is that nobody owes you a living. This necessity is internalised and taken for granted by the population.

(c) But you also have *economic power concentrations* in the form of giant corporations and other interest groups. They constitute a new form of limited but effective "dictatorship". Their existence is also accepted by the population otherwise they would not be able to operate.

There is nothing wrong with the first structure-giving mechanism. The second is problematic but, as we have seen, the alternative of state planning is even more problematic. To counteract the negative aspects of competition, we need to balance out achievement with equity and security. The third is not just problematic but unacceptable. It is not the hierarchical order which is unacceptable (no society can function without that) but rather the fact that power is *too concentrated and uncontrolled*. It is true that the competition between companies, as well as trade union action, keep some balance. But that is not yet democracy.

In a situation where big power blocs exist, freedom can only survive if these power blocs limit each other. The *greater the number* of such blocs the better, because each would be less able to determine events on their own — until a threshold is reached where the system is in danger of disintegrating because there is no social cohesion left. If that is the case the Marxist alternative is precisely the wrong recipe. Liberalism *must return to its creed*. It has allowed its principles of freedom, equal dignity and fraternity to be corrupted and abused. It now legitimates the opposite of freedom, namely power concentration. Of course, productivity is also a consideration: in terms of productivity a firm can be too big, but it can also be too small to compete. Firms must be allowed to develop to their optimum size, and subject to control.

The limits to growth

In our discussion of the alternatives between liberalism and socialism we have, so far, not sufficiently taken into account the *ecological problem*, which we have characterised, in chapter 1, as an integral part of the economic syndrome as a whole. To avoid addressing this issue would constitute a serious omission.

Liberalism and socialism have both failed in this regard. *Capitalist liberalism* has always believed that progress will lead to ever greater prosperity for all. Its overriding concern was economic growth. For too long it has not even been aware of the ecological problem. Only when the symptoms of an approaching breakdown of the natural environment became too ghastly to be overlooked, did some people wake up. But even then capitalist enterprises and their supporters have tried to play down the problem, to shift the blame, to shirk their responsibility, to ridicule "ecological romanticism", to warn against "leftists" and "anarchists", to build up false optimism by maintaining that "science and technology will solve the problem when it comes!" Of course, all these antics will not make the problem go away.

Marxist-Leninist socialism was only a more radical version of Western scientific-technological optimism. It believed in human progress even more fervently than liberalism did. According to Marx the development of the technological means of production would lead to a stage when "necessity" would be superseded by "freedom". The industrial economy would produce so abundantly that the needs of all people would be met. His vision of the classless society was inextricably bound to this expectation of superabundance.

To prove the superiority of socialism, and to make a dash towards the classless society, the Soviets tried to overtake the West economically, even as recently as the 1960s and 1970s. Ecological problems, like all social evils, were branded either as the outgrowth of capitalism or as Western propaganda. In densely populated and highly industrialised areas, for instance in East Germany and Czechoslovakia, the results have been catastrophic. Air and water pollution are rampant. Forests are dying. In the Ukraine and in China there are nuclear-infested no-go areas. It will take billions to clean up production processes and to rescue what is left of the natural environment.

So we have to insist that both ideologies have to reconsider not only their practice but, more fundamentally, *their basic presuppositions.* In the end there is no alternative to change from quantitative growth to growth in quality - both in terms of industrial production and population.

Questions

Revision: Assuming a common denominator, what are the positive functions and the dangers of property and public office respectively?

Application: Is there conflict or collaboration between the private sector and the public sector in your country? Can you explain this relation in terms of the underlying power struggle?

Critique: (a) "Your attempt to whitewash the atrocious selfishness of private property in capitalism by pointing fingers at a completely different sort of problem in socialism is too clever to be convincing."
(b) "The fact that you question the biblical principle and established human right of private property shows that you stand with one foot in the atheist ideology of communism." How would you respond to these accusations?

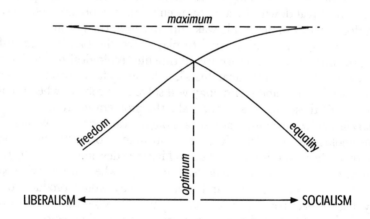

Let us summarise

How can we tackle ideological alternatives? First we *must redraw the battle lines.* The front should not be liberalism vs socialism, but truth vs deception in both ideologies, and structures which enhance human wellbeing vs structures which dehumanise people in both systems. We must also distinguish between the emotional, the empirical, the ethical and the political levels of discourse. Our task in this chapter was located on the *ethical* level.

Coming to basic value alternatives we argued that both *freedom and equality* form part of the Jewish-Christian heritage. To become positive values, however, freedom must be linked with responsibility and equality must be linked with dignity. The motives of selfishness on the one hand and social responsibility on the other manifest themselves in various forms in both systems.

Concerning social structures it would seem that there exists a *trade-off* between freedom and equality. A compromise must then be reached halfway between extreme freedom and extreme equality. Closer investigation revealed, however, that both extremes are self-destructive and that an optimal amount of freedom will probably coincide with an optimal amount of equality. We then discussed related pairs of values: security vs incentive, unfolding vs manipulation, and competition vs allocation, all of which follow the same dialectic.

The second set of problems revolved around the concepts of *property and power*. Property is a form of power because it grants exclusive control over resources. Economic power can be used in your own interest at the expense of others. The liberal capitalist system fails to distribute economic power equitably and to subject its use to democratic controls. But nationalisation does not solve the problem because it only shifts exclusive control to another group of people. In Marxism-Leninism all power is located in the small elite which controls the state.

An analysis of the *deeper functions of property* brought us to the conclusion that property, like power, is a prerequisite of human development. Economic democracy, rather than an abolition of property, appeared to be the way forward. We also saw that the debate has shifted in modern times since capital ownership has been superseded as a source of power by other factors of production, especially *electronic communication.*

We closed the discussion with a reminder that *ecological responsibility* has been neglected in both systems and ideologies. With that we are ready to put together a few directives for policy making in the economic field.

Notes

1   For detail see Nürnberger 1988 207ff.

2   Nürnberger 1988 241ff.

3   Heilbroner 1985:128.

4   See Heilbroner 1985:125ff on the relation between capitalism and freedom, socialism and authoritarianism.

5   Compare the analysis of this dual principle in Fukuyama 1992:291ff. "There will be a continuing tension between the twin principles of liberty and equality, upon which such (liberal) societies are based." (1992:292).

6   In the Pauline tradition this freedom is first and foremost freedom from sin and from the law of God (Gal 3:23-4:11), but it also includes freedom from people and their religious demands, as well as from the "principles governing the universe" (stoicheia tou kosmou - Gal 3:9; Col 2:8ff), ultimately from all "rule, authority, power and dominion ... in this age and the age to come" (Eph

1:20f; applied to believers in 2:6; cf Rev 22:5). It is, therefore, not just a spiritual, but a comprehensive freedom that is envisaged.

7   Gal 3:23-4:7 shows that there is a direct link between liberating grace and universal acceptance of men and women, Jews and gentiles, slave and free. The connection between unconditional acceptance into the fellowship of God and the unconditional acceptance of each other in the Christian community is beautifully spelt out in the two sections of Eph 2, vv 1-10 and 11-21.

8   Fukuyama (1992) has been the most recent and the most ardent advocate of the idea that cultures merge into the liberal democratic mold in a linear flow of history.

9   For nature as "capital" see Schumacher, E F 1973: *Small is beautiful: Economics as if people mattered.* New York: Harper & Row.

10 For a detailed discussion of these greater contexts see my book *Prosperity, poverty and pollution*, chapter 7.

11 Deng Xiaoping has a court which accumulated wealth unprecedented since the Manchu dynasty (C Field in Mail and Guardian, Nov 3, 1995, p 22). When the hard line Marxist-Leninist regime of Honecker in East Germany collapsed, for instance, the population was infuriated by the exposure of rampant corruption in the communist leadership: the transfer of millions to Swiss bank accounts, posh villas, special shops offering Western luxuries, and the like. On the other hand they were embittered by the attitudes of West German capitalists who wasted no time in exploiting the current weakness of the Eastern German economy to enlarge their empires after reunification. Positively one can mention that it is commonly accepted that West German tax payers have to sacrifice for the reconstruction of the economy in Eastern Germany.

12 Korten 1990:51.

13 Galbraith 1992.

14 Cf Lindblom 1977. For a defence of state planning see Bottomore 1990.

15 Daly & Cobb 1989:49.

16 Fukuyama 1992:293.

17 Suggested reading: Lindblom 1977:162ff.

18 Wogaman 1986 41,43; Preston 1983 118ff.

19 For explanations of these terms see the index.

20 Quoted in Lutz & Lux 1979 19 vif.

21 Boulding ibid.]

22 For an overview of the discussion see Ryan 1984; Reeve 1986.

23 Heilbroner 1985:52.

24 Drucker 1993:94ff. However, the point is not whether businessmen who enter politics make a mess of it but that any state depends on financially powerful sections of the population.

25 Drucker 1993:95.

26 p 4ff and passim.

27 Korten 1990:50ff.

28 "... bureaucracies have a life, and death, separate from, and independent of, their constituents. Each bureaucracy is the collective owner of the organization's physical and institutional assets; it also has its own rationale (or rationalization), its own rites, status symbols, rewards, and punishments. Almost all bureaucracies, too, have a prime interest in their own survival and expansion - an interest that cannot easily be challenged or attacked by outsiders ... " Amuzegar 1981:104.

29 Drucker 1993:88ff.

30 Suggested reading: Moll 1991:99ff (on nationalization).

31 Suggested reading: Reeve 1986

32 Klitgaard 1992:16 (Executive Summary).

33 For the following cf Drucker 1993:4ff

34 "In the United States (pension funds) owned in 1992 half of the share capital of the country's large businesses ..." (Drucker 1993:5).

35 Drucker 1993:96ff.

36 Drucker 1993:97.

37 Drucker 1993:99.

CHAPTER 8

Directions for the future

What is the task of this chapter?

Chapter 1 contained a brief sketch of the broad structural problem which economic systems are supposed to address. In chapters 2 to 6 we have analysed the history, rationale and performance of some of the most important systems which have been in operation during our century. In chapter 7 we have tried to sort out the value assumptions underlying these systems on their own terms.

We are now ready to bring the argument to its conclusion. Having scrutinised what has been proposed and tried out in the past, and explored the underlying value systems, we should now be able to formulate the policies which may lead us towards an equitable and sustainable economic system in the future.

It is quite likely that our proposals will not be in line with prevailing sentiments. This is in order, because critical reflection is supposed to question current wisdom, otherwise it would be a waste of time. It is also more than likely that these suggestions do not provide ultimate solutions. There are no ultimate solutions; there is only the common task of finding a feasible and responsible way into the future.[1] We shall try to indicate the direction in which we ought to go by setting up a set of sign posts. They are not meant to provide ready-made recipies; they are meant to provoke ongoing analysis, thought and action.

In the first section of this chapter we account for the *approach* which we think we should follow when designing policy guidelines. In section II we remind ourselves of the *agenda* of academic research and practical policy making, as suggested in chapter 1. In section III we offer a reflection on the optimal distribution of power in the society. In section IV we draw out a few implications for *policy.* In section V we deal with the area of industrial relations as an example of *democratisation* in a free economy.

Section I - The basic approach

Policies should be guided by pragmatism, not by ideology

Before we set out to construct or reconstruct a system, we need to realise what systems can achieve and what they cannot achieve. Systems *give shape to the realm of human freedom,* nothing more. Think of a house. It restricts freedom, but it also protects freedom. The shape of a house can hamper or enhance the unfolding of human life. It is in this sense that systems can be good or bad.

Good systems grant space to breathe, to develop gifts and creative initiatives. There is a clear correlation, for instance, between civil liberties and educational attainment, as well as between female education, a reduction in infant mortality, and a decline in fertility.[2] However, no system is so perfect that it does not also obstruct the flow of life, and few systems are so bad that they suppress all human potential.

Good systems also subject any initiative, which they allow, to the criterion of the *common good*. Good systems cannot make better people, but they can limit the harm caused by ill-intentioned people, and give room for the development of the good caused by well-inentioned people. The implication of these observations is that it is not the system alone which makes the difference; more fundamental are the countless decisions and actions of people within the system. Few people can choose their systems, but all people can act responsibly within them.

Politics is about maintaining, directing, or changing a social system. Such an activity is based on assumptions, values and norms and these need to be made explicit.[3] But for sound politics we do not need a blue print for an ostensibly perfect order which is then to be cast in concrete.[4] History has shown that such ideologies and systems - whether fascism, apartheid, communism, or capitalism - enslave human minds, distort human communities and crush human lives. What we need is a kind of pragmatism which knows what it wants to achieve, is flexible enough to adjust to changing circumstances,[5] exploits the potentials of an unfolding situation, and overcomes obstacles and hazards in the way.[6] Ideologies may not readily make way for pragmatism.[7] But at least we can utilise our human capacity to *analyse factually and reason constructively* in the face of ideological irrationalities.

Pragmatism should be directed by a comprehensive vision

Pragmatism is not an attitude which tries to fulfil laws or to achieve goals; rather it seeks to do what seems to be "fitting" under constantly changing circumstances.[8] But pragmatism cannot simply blunder from case to case without any sense of direction. In practice the direction of decision making is determined by individual desires and collective interests. Capitalist liberalism gives these forces free reign. But they are not very trustworthy guides when it comes to the needs of society as a whole. To avoid selfishness, short-sightedness and narrow horizons, we need an overall vision.

A vision is not a blueprint, a worked-out system, or an ideological construct. A vision is an anticipation of the future which gives direction to the present. Visions are like horizons. They retreat as you move forward, constantly luring you on to new discoveries. But visions must have a content which can be defined. This content may not be destructive or deformative in its implications; it should be supportive of life in all its forms; it should be guided by a basic respect for the reality in which we live, whether human or non-human, and it should include all dimensions of reality.[9]

A vision should place the needs of particular parts of reality into the context of the needs of the greater whole of reality:

- The right of humanity to prosper should be placed in the context of the prerequisites of nature as a whole. For instance, we may not exploit the fish resources of the oceans to the point of extinction.

- Specific, short term and individual needs should be seen in the context of overall, long term and communal needs. The cost-benefit analysis of a nuclear power station versus a coal-fired alternative, for instance, should take account of the costs and benefits to nature, to all people who might be affected, and to future generations.

- Any particular need of the human being should again be placed in the context of the whole package of human needs. It is not appropriate, for instance, to emphasise economic needs, such as profit or utility maximisation, at the expense of communal, cultural and spiritual needs.

Policy directions should be based on interdisciplinary insights

A comprehensive vision aims at a picture of reality as a whole. But reality as a whole extends far beyond human investigation and comprehension. The whole as such is not an empirical category; it cannot become the object of scientific investigation or technological manipulation. It has always been the *realm of intuition*, philosophy and religion.

But a vision, which is supposed to provide a sense of direction, cannot remain abstract. It must be translated into specific directives. Directives are neither laws to be fulfilled, nor goals to be reached. They are *sign posts* which guide concrete designs and actions towards the envisioned future.

It is not easy to define these directives. The human incapacity to perceive the whole has not diminished, but increased through modern science and technology. Because insight into the complexity and vastness of reality is growing faster and faster, science and technology have no choice but to engage in *ever increasing specialisation*. No single scientist can claim to have a grasp of his/her entire field, let alone all other fields. Specialists have sometimes been called "professional idiots". This is not a very kind description but there is some truth in it.

Specialisation leads to smaller and smaller units of knowledge which tend to become *increasingly isolated* from their greater contexts. Such blinkers lead to distorted perceptions, errors of judgment and misguided action. Tackling symptoms rather than systems has led to incredible harm in fields such as medicine, development theory and strategic planning.[10] You treat a patient with cortisone and impair her adrenal functions; you sink boreholes to gain access to water in arid regions and exhaust volatile pastures; you utilise credit facilities for development and land the economy in a debt trap.

Yet the complexity of reality does not imply that the attempt to gain a vision of the whole is a waste of time. In fact, specialisation has made it more urgent. With the enormous power unleashed by modern technology truncated perceptions of reality have become too dangerous for comfort. Human beings have the gift of intuition. Intuition is the capacity to integrate bits and pieces of information from various sources into an overall picture. Intuition has always tried to approximate the whole. To generate a vision of the whole we must process as much information as possible. For that we need to pool the resources of complementary human sciences. *Interdisciplinary consultation* between academics and practitioners in different fields should be formally institutionalised and funded on a wide scale.

Policies should be democratically legitimate

Consultation on the level of academic expertise is insufficient. The *people on the ground* have their own experiences and approaches, which should be clarified, critically examined and utilised. Ordinary citizens are immediately affected by the consequences of any course of action. So they should have a say, perhaps even a veto. "If democracy is justified in governing the state, then it must *also* be justified in governing economic enterprises; and to say that it is *not* justified in governing economic enterprises is to imply that it is not justified in governing the state."[11]

This does not imply that professionals are foolish, or that ordinary people have all the answers. Myths, superstitions, prejudices, delusions and ideological rationalisations abound among the "poor and oppressed" or the "masses". Elevating them to the status of saints and sages, as some left wing traditions did, just adds to the problem. The point is, however, that experts and politicians, who have no experience of grass roots situations, do not have the answers either. The different levels should *interact* in such a way that experts listen, inform and enable; ordinary people evaluate and decide; politicians put into effect. All this should happen not in theory but in real life processes. To use a modern slogan, development is "interactive learning through action".[12]

The demand for grass roots participation is not only based on the intricacies of concrete situations, which may elude the expert, but also on respect for human nature. Human beings are self-directed creatures. They have an intellect which tries to make sense of their world; they have a will which is directed towards particular goals; they have emotions which can be supportive or obstructive; they have the capacity to be creative, which is their most valuable asset, or to be lethargic which is their most devastating handicap. The dignity of human beings demands that they be *in control of their lives*, that they not be pushed around by others or by circumstances, that they be given the space to become creative and responsible.

But human beings are also social beings. The human being can only thrive and prosper in community.[13] A healthy community does not deny its members their freedom but gives a home to freedom within a common sphere of responsibility. Responsibility without freedom enslaves; freedom without responsibility is reckless. Both enslavement and recklessness lead to the rise in conflict potential. Only the dialectic between *freedom and responsibility* makes a liberating and empowering community possible.

Where the convictions, values and norms of particular groups militate against the freedom and responsibility of other such groups, they should be either transformed or dismantled. Religious tolerance is no licence for asocial and destructive behaviour. Truth cannot be relativised to such an extent that deception becomes acceptable. But there is no impartial judge. Groups must become willing to subject themselves to *mutual critique.* To become truly liberating and serving, we need each other. Most convictions have conducive potentials, which can be reinforced, as well as obstructive potentials, which must be neutralised.

The interaction between convictions in a pluralistic society is a complex theme of its own which we cannot take up here.[14] The upshot of these considerations is, however, that economic policies should be based on community serving assumptions and have democratic legitimacy. They should make sense to those most affected, carry *their mandate* and serve their legitimate interests. Mature collective judgment and decision making presuppose basic education, ongoing information, networks of communication, institutionalised consultation and a culture of negotiation and compromise. Democratic legitimacy is a prerequisite for a successful policy and the best way of reducing conflict potential in the population.

This also means that *persuasion has priority over pressure and pressure has priority over force.* This is true for all social players, whether government, opposition, non-governmental organisations, lobbies, minority organisations, or liberation movements. Pressure cannot always be avoided where people do not want to listen, because it militates against their self-interest; force cannot always be avoided where even pressure makes no impact on entrenched positions or on the dead weight of popular lethargy. But political players should never give in to shortcuts, because people should not be treated as things and destructive behaviour is counterproductive in terms of our agenda.

Questions

Revision: What is the relation between pragmatism and vision?

Application: Which political actors in your country are pragmatists and which are visionaries? Are their views incompatible with each other?

Critique: (a) "Pragmatism is a euphemism which covers up the pursuit of self-interest." (b) "If you long for visions and such nonsense, join a charismatic church, but leave the economy alone." How would you respond to these two statements?

Section II - Five priorities on the agenda

1. The preservation of the natural world

Before we continue, we have to remind ourselves of the five priorities on the agenda of a responsible economics and a responsible political economy which we mentioned in the first chapter.

The first and most basic of these is ecological stability.[15] For much of its history humanity has taken for granted that the natural world and its resources are unlimited. In Western thought it has also been assumed that nature exists solely for humankind and could be utilised and manipulated at will.

There has also been a widespread perception that the authentic person is a spiritual being, belonging to another and superior world, while its bodily existence and its earthly habitat are both transitory and without particular significance. Some of these assumptions were derived from the Graeco-Christian heritage. This is not the place to investigate their merits; suffice it to say that *none of these assumptions can still be upheld today.*

The sobering facts of the situation are that the earth's resources are limited; that non-renewable resources are rapidly being depleted; that renewable resources are over-exploited; that the pollution of the environment has assumed dangerous proportions; that the abuse of nature will seriously and irreparably *backfire on human existence*, and that this existence is an indivisible physical, communal, cultural and spiritual whole. "The biosphere is now recognised to be a single, living system or, rather, an organism like the human body itself. Therefore if we continue to inflict grievous injury on the body biospheric, we can only imperil our own existence."[16] By destroying nature, humanity progressively undermines its own chances of survival and prosperity.

The preservation of the natural world must, therefore, be accorded top priority. Putting humanity into the centre of the universe is a type of arrogance which humanity can no longer afford. Rather, we must assign to humanity its *proper and limited place* within the context of the natural world. The slow awakening of some "green" groups and nature lovers to the idea that factory emissions should be filtered, or that dolphins should be saved from dragnets, is better than nothing. But the assumption that we should "do something for" our natural environment is not sufficient as a basis for the revolution in priorities that has now become imperative.

In practical terms, the criterion for establishing the difference between responsible use and wanton destruction or depletion should be the ability of the natural world to *absorb the impact* of such use and regenerate itself, as well as the ability of humanity to *find alternatives* to non-renewable resources. While there can be no objections against the judicious felling of older trees in a forest, for instance, blanket deforestation should be banned.

2. Material sufficiency for all

The second priority for economics and the political economy should be material sufficiency for all. A well developed society needs highways, telecommunications and museums. But a society — including the international community — which cannot meet the *basic needs* of its members must revisit its priorities. "No task should command a higher priority for the world's policy makers than that of reducing global poverty."[17] When children suffer brain damage because of malnutrition, contract crippling diseases because of sanitary deficiencies, or have no opportunity to enjoy basic education, the society should think of redirecting financial resources from luxuries to necessities.

Of course, very few people are satisfied with what they have. So the concept of needs can seemingly be stretched indefinitely.[18] It can also be debunked as an invention of the modern ideology of progress and growth.[19] But avarice is not what we have in mind; needs are not wants. Basic needs do not include items of consumption which people can do without and still be healthy and happy. The concept of basic needs describes the *absolute minimum* needed by a family without suffering material hardship in a particular set of circumstances. And this can be calculated with relative precision.[20]

Article 25 of the Universal Declaration of Human Rights stipulates that "everyone has the right to a standard of living adequate for the health and well-being of himself and of his family ..."[21] This demand is a result of the liberal revolution. Countless generations have accepted that suffering material want is an inescapable fact of life for the majority of humankind. The spectacular advances of scientific insight, technological know-how and productive capacity make it reasonable to believe that, given the collective will, *poverty can be overcome.*[22] But the real revolution is the assumption that it *should* be overcome.

To speak of a right to basic material sufficiency may be problematic. A right against whom? On which grounds? Who owes whom a living? Why should the diligent provide for the indolent? To make the eradication of poverty a policy priority is far less problematic. What is indeed most difficult to achieve is *general acceptance* of this priority against pressure groups which tend to crowd it out in the corridors of power. Of course, there is also the fatalism of convenience which loves to misquote the word of Jesus that "the poor will always be with you". Surely this word did not want to legitimate a lack of concern. Let us consider some moral and political arguments in favour of basic sufficiency for all:

- *A common humanity.* All human beings are vulnerable and mortal. They are subject to sudden whims of fate and turns of fortune. They can be afflicted by misery, impotence and frustration. They are at all times dependent on the goodwill of others. It stands to reason, therefore, that all humans should be committed to securing the basic prerequisites for the survival and healthy life of all other human beings. Nobody should be subject to the indignity and misery of absolute poverty or outright starvation. Inhuman conditions suffered by some *impair the humanity of all others.* In spiritual terms the existence of large scale misery questions the integrity and legitimacy of the affluent — which again impairs their quality of life. The goal of overcoming poverty should indeed be given such weight and urgency that all other human achievements appear as a bonus.

- The needs of the economy. There are *sound structural reasons* for prioritising basic need satisfaction. Poverty leads to population growth, which again feeds back into poverty. As a result the social infrastructure — education, medical facilities, housing, transport, employment — is overburdened. To enlarge its capacity, higher taxes have to be imposed. Poverty side by side with affluence causes resentment. If nothing is done, the breakdown of respect for property forces the rich to invest in defence and security — which again devours valuable resources. When social turmoil ensues, even the privileged lose more than they gain from being unconcerned about the misery of others. Apart from that, the natural environment suffers and the costs of negligence accumulate for future generations to shoulder.

Basic need fulfilment does not imply a cumbersome and expensive welfare state. On the contrary; experience shows that such a system may become counterproductive. In principle a society *should not share consumption but production.* Every person between maturity and old age should be in a position to make a positive and reward-earning contribution to the national product. If this could be achieved, income and consumption would look after themselves. It does not matter which factor of production people contribute - raw materials, energy, capital, labour, entrepreneurship, management, organisation, administration, skills, expertise, training, transport, communications, services, whatever! What matter is that it is a *genuine* contribution to the generation of the national product, not an unproductive entitlement or a token job.

The priority accorded to basic need fulfilment should, therefore, be translated into *human resource development and employment generation* among the least privileged sections of the population. Making space for small business ventures; establishing training facilities; opening up channels of communication, transport links and markets; providing affordable credit facilities, and a host of other possible measures could contribute to this aim. But the overriding task is to balance out the structural discrepancies in economic potency between centre and periphery and to curtail the abuse of power. Obviously the goal of securing sufficiency must also be seen in the wider context of attaining an ecologically optimal level of production and a stable population, to which we shall return below.[23]

3. Equity in the distribution of inputs and benefits

Equity is the third priority for economics and the political economy. Even where absolute poverty has been eradicated, vast discrepancies in wealth and income can still occur. It is also possible that some sections of the population have to bear a *disproportionate part of the sacrifices*, while others enjoy a disproportionate share of the benefits of overall production. Again this causes resentment and raises the conflict potential in a society, with all its unacceptable consequences.

Wrong allocation of resources is largely caused by *differences in bargaining power* between interest groups. There are lobbies close to the levers of power and there are population groups which are virtually forgotten. Democratic principles deliberately grant the same decision making power to the disadvantaged as to the privileged. Each person, whether rich or poor, educated or uneducated, esteemed or despised, employed or unemployed, has the same single vote. By virtue of their greater numbers, the poor could have an advantage over the rich. This is only fair because in all other respects the influence of the rich is so much greater. In line with this principle, decision makers should give priority to the interests of the least privileged, not to those who have the means to fend for themselves.

It is necessary to be sensitive to *two concepts of justice* which vie for recognition at this level.

- On the one hand it could be argued that all people should be given a share of the common product in proportion to their *needs*. As mentioned above, Marxists hoped to reach a situation where all would give according to their capability and all would receive according to their need.

- Liberals may be inclined to consider such a goal as unrealistic; they would probably also consider it to be blatantly unjust. Why should loafers be allowed to prey on the fruits of the labours of hard working people? Justice, according to this school of thought, is that you get what you *deserve*.

This moral impasse can be resolved. As stated above, the explicit aim should be to achieve equity in the distribution of *both* inputs *and* rewards.[24] Again this presupposes that a society aims not at sharing consumption but at sharing production. With this goal in place, no rewards would be allocated without inputs and, ideally, the rewards would be commensurate with the inputs.[25]

Because some people are more fortunate or more capable than others, however, equity demands that population groups with low productive capacities are empowered, while more productive groups are expected to invest at least part of their capacity in such empowerment - whether by private initiatives or via the state. The principles of *equality of opportunity and equal access to resources* should not only be internalised by the members of the society, but also entrenched in the constitution and made an integral part of any public policy package.

But is there not a *trade-off* between the goals of covering basic needs and achieving equity in distribution on the one hand, and growth of the national product, which has to supply the means to do so on the other?[26] No, not if the former are based on empowerment to produce rather than on handouts![27] That much we have learnt from the Taiwanese model.[28] A few big enterprises do not necessarily yield more per unit of capital input than many small ones. On the contrary; often small, intensive family undertakings are more efficient than larger ones because their commitment to succeed is a condition of their survival.[29]

Moreover, equality of opportunity opens up access to resources and training, thus bringing more people into the range where potential entrepreneurial initiative and technological competence can translate into effective intitiative and competence.

Obviously this priority implies that all forms of *discrimination* are taboo: against the poor, the powerless, the uneducated, women, racial, ethnic and religious groups, and so on. Discrimination is not only unjust but also economically wasteful because it does not utilise the human resources of the nation to the full. Where discriminatory practices have been internalised and entrenched for a long time, *affirmative action* has to be practised to restore the balance.

Of course, affirmative action is meant to empower the disadvantaged to develop their gifts as fully as possible and to play their rightful role, *not to grant the unproductive and inefficient a competitive edge* against the productive and efficient. The last thing we can afford is to grant entitlements to people who have no intention of pulling their weight, or who are incompetent in their jobs, while not utilising the most important asset a nation has, the capability and initiative of its most gifted citizens.

195

4. Concern for the weak and vulnerable

Equity based on equality of opportunity and access does not yet cater for those who are, for some reason or another, *not able to make a contribution* commensurate to their needs, especially the young, the old, the sick and the incompetent. This leads us to the fourth point on the economic agenda. Because every human being is, at least at some stages of life, helpless, vulnerable and dependent on others, the human race cannot survive without solidarity.

This has always been recognised in *smaller communities*, particularly in the extended family. Here patterns of mutual obligation and supportive institutions have existed for times immemorial. The principle of granting special status to those who are incapable of meeting their needs is as old as humankind, and it is as valid as ever. One problem is that most communities have very narrow horizons. They tend to perceive, and experience, other communities as threats to their own wellbeing. The first task is, therefore, to generate a more inclusive loyalty.

Another problem is created by the trend towards individualism in urban-industrial societies. Small scale communities have increasingly exploded into *large scale societies*, leaving scattered individuals to fend for themselves. Once isolated, such individuals are at the mercy of their particular fortunes and capabilities, being tossed about, as it were, like grains of beach sand. In many modern societies masses of people are stranded in situations of outright misery, while others hoard masses of resources. Under such circumstances the task of community building and social awareness cannot be overemphasised.

Some richer societies have been able to respond to this collective need by bringing about a greater balance of power through democratic institutions, by institutionalising welfare and founding voluntary associations which support the weak. But richer societies exist side by side with poorer societies in the "global village". Societies tend to function like communities in perceiving outsiders either as irrelevant, or as a threat, particularly if they demand a share in their wealth. The *globalisation* of attitudes and policies expressing human solidarity is part of the unfinished business on the political agenda.

5. Balance in the satisfaction of various kinds of need

In comparison with earlier cultures our civilisation has become incredibly materialistic. Cultural achievements, family and community cohesion, human values and spiritual aspirations have all been crowded out by thinly disguised greed. Superficiality, narrow horizons, short term attitudes and selfishness have become acceptable, fashionable, even expected attitudes. A ruthless entertainment industry, and increasingly sophisticated advertising and marketing techniques, programmatically dismantle natural inhibitions by their constant bombardment of collective consciousness with enticing material channeled through ever more powerful mass media.

Humankind has not become better off as a result. Human time and energy are limited. An oversupply in one dimension of life inevitably *creates shortages in others*. You can be materially rich and yet feel the pangs of loneliness and meaninglessness. If economics is to become true to its proper calling as a facilitator of human wellbeing, it must begin to see material needs in the context of the prerequisites for the fulfilment of human life as a whole.

Questions

Revision: Explain the logic underlying the sequence of the five priorities on the economic agenda.

Application: How would (a) economics as a science and (b) economic policies have to change if this order of priorities was to be implemented?

Critique: (a) "You again come up with this crazy idea, which only affluent Westerners can afford, that plants and animals are more important than starving human beings."
(b) Your dreams get us nowhere. If we want to secure reasonable standards of living in the Third World, industrial growth, built on free enterprise is our only hope." What do these two statements have in common? How would you respond?

Section III - On the distribution of power in society[30]

Human life is embedded in a social system, and any social system is embedded in a natural environment. For human life to survive and prosper both the natural and the social order must be healthy. But what is a healthy social system? We have seen in chapter / that the optimum degree of *freedom* corresponds with the optimum degree of *equality*. But a system must also be stable to survive. Stability depends either on *consensus* or on *force*. A system is stable when the rulers have the power to impose order should consensus break down. The more consensus in a population, the less power is needed to make a system stable, and vice versa.

To clarify the relation between these four variables - freedom, equality, power and consensus - let us depict three ideal cases, namely dictatorship, hierarchy and anarchy:

Type A: Dictatorship

In this system all power is concentrated in one person or a tiny elite. The rest of the population is powerless. There is neither freedom nor equality. Even a dictator is not free because s/he is forced to keep the population subdued. Because power is concentrated at one point, the governability of this system is absolute, and consensus is unnecessary for the system to survive.

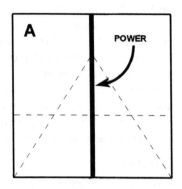

Type B: Hierarchy

In this system power is distributed more widely in the population but in such a way that each higher rank possesses roughly the same amount of power as the combined lower ranks. While there is more freedom and more equality in this system than in a dictatorship, both are also limited by the hierarchical order. The system will function best when there is consensus, but when consensus breaks down, the system is still stable because it is governable.

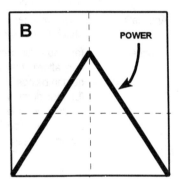

Type C: Anarchy

In this case power is equally distributed among all members of the population. There is "no rule of humans over humans" as Marxists would express it. Both freedom and equality are maximised. But the system is not governable. So its stability depends on total consensus. Any disagreement would lead to disintegration. Because total consensus cannot (and should not) be achieved in this world, it

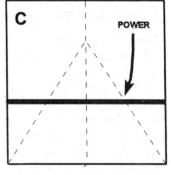

could only be imposed. But once anything is imposed on people we are back at type A (dictatorship).

We see that the alternatives move from a complete absence of freedom and equality to absolute freedom and equality, from absolute governability to absolute ungovernability, from a total lack of the need for consensus to a total dependence on consensus. The former extreme is unacceptable because it is repressive, the latter because it is anarchic. Somewhere between these extremes lies the *optimal combination* of freedom and equality on the one hand and viability on the other, whether based on consensus or power.

In the ideal case, *the power of each higher rank corresponds exactly with the combined power of the respective lower ranks.* Where this is the case, the higher rank cannot impose its decision on the lower ranks unless the latter agree and vice versa. The two levels must convince each other or negotiate a compromise. If one party would use its power to impose its will, the parties would harm each other and achieve nothing. To achieve stability, therefore, there would have to be vertical consensus.

But such a balance also presupposes horizontal consensus, that is, agreement among the respective lower ranks. Once the lower ranks would disagree, the higher rank would have more power and could keep the bunch from falling apart. The well-known tactic of "divide and rule" takes advantage of this fact.

In practice such an ideal situation is not very likely to materialise. Usually there is either a surplus of power in the higher rank or a surplus of power in the lower ranks. The first alternative is *authoritarian*, the second *democratic*. Even in the authoritarian system it is in the best interest of the higher rank to enlist the support of the lower rank, but if it is not forthcoming, power can still be brought to bear to make the system work. In the democratic system it is the lower rank which calls the tune and the higher rank can be replaced if it does not cooperate.

Both these systems can be relatively stable. Even in a democracy the higher rank has more operative power, although this power is *based upon a mandate* from the lower ranks, a mandate which can be withdrawn. The higher rank then exercises power on behalf of the lower rank and in its interest. We can see that such a system depends both on consensus (yet not absolute consensus, as in anarchy) **and** on power (but not absolute power as in a dictatorship). It is, in all respects, the best system available.

None of these ideal types exists in the real world but they provide us with a grid which we can use to explain the character of existing systems. So let us look at the four systems which we have discussed in this book and see how they fit into this grid.

Type D: Dictatorial capitalism

This type lies between type A and type B. There is a great deal of centralised power and little consensus. Both freedom and equality are very limited. This situation is typical of fascism; it also occurs in many Third World countries, and in the relation between industrialised and developing countries.

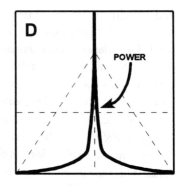

Type E: Democratising capitalism

In this case class struggles have led to the partial empowerment of a section of the peripheral population, especially through trade unions, socialist parties and a bureaucracy which begins to develop its own agenda. The outer periphery is still powerless because it is marginalised.

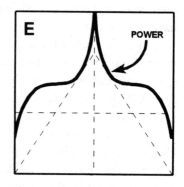

Type F: Social democracy

This system lies between type B and type C. There is still a concentration of power in the centre, but the welfare policies of a democratic government and other forces in society working for the upliftment of the poor have flattened the curve considerably in favour of the broad masses. Due to this institutionalised kind of upliftment the marginalised outer periphery is no longer destitute.

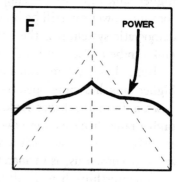

So far we have sketched the line from capitalism to social democracy. Obviously the system improves as it unfolds in the egalitarian direction, but beyond a certain threshold socialist policies become counterproductive. Now let us look at the opposite line, from Marxism-Leninism to democratic socialism:

Type G: Dictatorial socialism

This system also lies between type A and type B but it strives to reach type C with the means of type A. As we have seen, Marxism-Leninism attempted to reach consensus by imposition. Ideally there is a measure of equality (excluding the imposers), but at the expense of freedom.

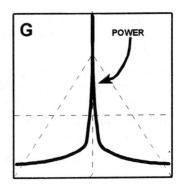

Type H: Democratic socialism

In this system a strong power concentration in the centre guarantees governability. A measure of freedom is granted to the lower ranks, but at the expense of equality.

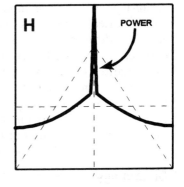

What do we make of the latter two types? Ostensibly *Type G* aims at consensus, freedom and equality. The question is, however, whether genuine consensus can be reached through imposition; whether freedom can be reached through oppression; whether equality can be reached by an elite which is not (and cannot be) equal to the rest of the population. Historical evidence suggests that this is not the case.

Type H compromises the lofty ideals of type G in favour of limited freedom at the expense of equality. The question here is whether there are any advantages in this system over that of type F. This does not seem to be the case. The latter thus again proves to be the best solution we have encountered: the *social democratic* order seems to yield the optimum mediation between power and consensus, as it yields the optimum measure of freedom and equality. The proviso we have mentioned is that it should base equality on equal access to production, not on welfare.

The following prerequisites of a healthy system have crystallised out in this exercise:

- A social system cannot function without a *hierarchy of power*.
- There must be a dynamic *balance of power* between subsequent layers of the hierarchy.
- This does not imply equality of power but rather a situation in which the

surplus of power exercised by the higher rank is exercised in the interest and with the *mandate of the lower ranks*, a mandate which can be withdrawn.

- Ranks must, in principle, be *open to all members* of the society. Those with greater gifts should be able to move up freely, while the less competent have to be content with lower ranks.

- Those who are not in a position to compete successfully are empowered as far as possible.

- Those who cannot make a meaningful contribution are not abandoned to their fate but caught in a *social safety net*.

The unsolved question is how such a system can be applied on the international scene. At the moment social democracy applied within highly industrialised countries exacerbates the discrepancies between industrialised and less developed countries. The same phenomenon can be observed between a developed enclave and a marginalised periphery within semi-industrialised countries, such as Brazil or South Africa.[31]

Another problem is that, in practice, any seemingly balanced power structure leaves *pockets of powerlessness* which are not catered for. A balance between employers organisations and trade unions, for instance, does not cater for the unemployed or the pensioners. A democratic system has to be particularly sensitive to the weak, vulnerable, voiceless and unrepresented.

On strategy

To achieve a balanced power structure, obstructive power structures *have to be dismantled*. Under normal circumstances they will not give way on their own — not only because they represent entrenched collective interests, but also because existing structures are networks of power relationships which have their own logic, dynamic and resilience.

Again the answer lies in the democratic principle which gives disadvantaged majorities *institutionalised power advantages* over entrenched minority interests. But again we need to heed the fact that even a liberal multiparty democracy leaves *pockets of powerlessness* between established parties. We should also not forget the greatest sphere of powerlessness, namely the natural environment.

Seemingly this problem cannot be solved adequately at the structural level alone. The answer lies, rather, in a *social contract* among all political players in which they agree that, whatever power struggles they might wage, they will not abandon any section of the population in a disadvantaged position. There must also be mutual commitment to safeguarding the natural environment, and thus the interests of future generations.

This readiness demands a high degree of social responsibility and an internalised sensitivity to the needs of the powerless and vulnerable. This can only be created by leaders and educators who possess vision, character and stature. Again, a responsible set of motivations is not enough; it must be complemented by a corresponding structural arrangement. Once a general consensus has been reached, therefore, it should also be entrenched in the constitution.

The use of force

But how can a democracy be achieved on the structural level if entrenched elites do not possess the wisdom and the will to abdicate their positions in favour of a leadership carrying a popular mandate? Historically speaking, most democracies have come into being through *social pressure or revolutionary force* exerted by disadvantaged population groups who have become bold enough to demand their rights.

Concerning the use of force we need to be aware of two facts. The first is that a power struggle is a kind of "war". Every war is *destructive*. Whatever the weapons used, they are meant to hurt and harm. So we must heed the costs. The second fact is that those who fight for their rights are at the bottom, while those who wish to maintain the status quo are at the top of the social pyramid. The system which is to be overcome, *protects the elites* and leaves the underdogs in vulnerable positions. To harm the elite at all, the underdogs must harm the system as a whole, which will retaliate on behalf of the elite.

This fact has grave repercussions for the disadvantaged. In the first place, the violence used by the underdogs normally harm the underdog population more than the elite. In a strike or boycott the elite may lose some of its profits, but the strikers may lose their jobs, and the families of the strikers may lose their means of subsistence. In the second place even the leadership of the underdogs always suffers less and gains more than the rank and file of the underdogs. This means that leaders and followers of both parties have to become sensitive to those *who really have to pay the price*. And again we should not forget that ultimately it may be the natural environment (thus future generations) which will bear the greatest burden.

The upshot of both these considerations is that the contesting parties should try to do without destructive power struggles in the first place. Where they cannot be avoided, they should strive to use the *minimum force necessary* to achieve socially acceptable goals. In each stage of history we must draw up a balance sheet which weighs the harm done by enforcing change (revolution), against the harm done by allowing the status quo to continue (evolution).

Obviously, harm is minimised by achieving consensus on the basis of an acceptable system of meaning, values and norms. Historically the exertion of power has been only one of two factors; the other has been *persuasion*. Where

203

there is no democratic philosophy to legitimate a new system, the struggle may continue in endless attrition until one of the parties is exhausted or ousted.

This means that reconstruction at the level of collective consciousness is at least as important as reconstruction on the level of social structures. Political parties, non-governmental organisations, education systems, mass media, grassroots communities and, especially, churches and religious communities have a great role to play in this respect.

Questions

Revision: Describe both the reasons and the criteria for a hierarchical distribution of power in the society.

Application: Find out from a high ranking public servant how the decision-making process works in his/her department, then do the same with the executive of a large firm, then compare the two and check which one meets our criteria best.

Critique: (a) "What a clever way of legitimating authoritarian structures by a member of the privileged elite!"

(b) "Your simplifications conceal rather than reveal the real situation. The Marxist-Leninist system, for example, is a typical hierarchy, yet there is no democracy; the social democratic system sports complete equality before the law, yet there is no anarchy." Is there some truth in these statements?

Section IV - Some policy implications

In section III of chapter 6 we have summarised the basic facets of a successful development strategy for Third World countries. We do not need to repeat them here. We only enumerate a few general principles which can be adapted to various situations.

Commitment to mutual responsibility

Value commitments are indispensable. They should be democratically agreed upon and institutionalised in the form of a social contract. This contract should be written into the constitution, whether of a state or an enterprise, and be subject to the courts. A society should have not only a bill of human rights but also a *bill of social goals*. Ethical demands that are simply channelled into moral appeals are useless by themselves. They should be constitutionally entrenched and translated into policy decisions.

Our goal should be that all individuals and groups have the freedom to develop their potentials in such a way that they complement each other in serving the overall prosperity of the society within ecologically sustainable limits. This presupposes a spirit of mutuality and solidarity. As the Marxist-Leninist experience has shown, collectivism is not the answer. What we need is *voluntary and complementary linkages* between individual and communal initiatives under the umbrella of a common purpose.

In the Western democratic tradition it is accepted that political parties represent the interests of particular sections of the population and that such interest groups lobby in the corridors of power. But if a national government does not have the interests of the *society as a whole* at heart, including its future, this should be considered as treason. Those who strive for the highest offices must also have the highest vantage point - above particularist wrangles and short-sighted benefits to themselves and their constituents.

Striving for generational equity

Our agenda placed ecological sustainability on top of the list of policy priorities. Perhaps a more compelling word for sustainability is "generational equity".[32] We have seen again and again that powerful groups are in a position to exploit and abuse natural and social resources to their own advantage and at the expense of those who cannot defend themselves. *Those least able to push for their own interests are those not yet born.* They will all depend on the earth's resources. Striving only for sufficiency and equity among our contemporaries, even the poorest, is still an option for the relatively powerful against the completely powerless, and this is morally unacceptable.

In the introduction to this book we have mentioned that there are two basic problems which need to be addressed in this regard, namely the *growth of the industrial economy* and the *growth of the population.* Both growth processes lead to pollution of the environment, accelerating depletion of non-renewable resources and overexploitation of renewable resources

Neither of these problems is easy to solve. Is there, for instance, a *trade-off* between economic growth, upon which sufficiency for the present generation depends, and environmental conservation, upon which the sufficiency of future generations depends? Yes there is - at least if the current mode of production and distribution, as well as the population explosion, continue unabated.

But current trends do not have to continue! We could turn *from quantity to quality*; from throughput to basic needs fulfilment; from depletion of resources to recycling; from heavily polluting to less polluting industries; from wastage and luxury consumption to more cultured means of satisfaction; from large to small families. We must create incentives to clean up the production process, or disincentives against pollution by taxing pollution and waste. Industries must be forced to "internalise external costs", that is to pay for public damage caused by private production. The revenue gained must be ploughed back into the economy to stabilise the financial, demographic and ecological situation.[33] We cannot go into detail here; it must suffice to place these concerns firmly on the agenda of economists and policy makers.

A tamed market

As the negative experiences of Marxist socialism have shown the operation of the market mechanism, which balances out supply and demand, is indispensable. But neither crippling atrophy nor cancer-like growth are unavoidable aspects of that necessity. Markets should be "tamed". For that to happen economists and policy makers must look *beyond demand to need, and beyond supply to need fulfilment.*

Supply and demand as statistical quantities conceal rather than reveal the genuine goal of the economy, namely to fulfil the needs of the population. *Demand* is not generated by need alone, but by purchasing power combined with any sort of motivation to acquire, including need, greed and vanity. The demand for staple foods can be at rock bottom though large sections of the population are starving because they have no purchasing power. Neither does *supply* indicate the capacity of the economy to fulfil the needs of the population, because supply can be geared to luxuries for which a market demand has been generated.

An economy which allows purchasing power to accumulate within an elite tends to spiral upwards, serving an ever decreasing minority, while leaving behind a marginalised majority. Vast and growing discrepancies in income and wealth are the result. Another result, often overlooked by the short-sighted self-interest of the affluent, is *economic stagnation.* It is not in the best interest of producers if their markets are whittled down to an affluent elite with saturated primary needs, whose wants have to be inflated artificially to create market demand.[34]

A responsible state has to follow policies which *free up the money* which is sunk into luxury consumption, and build up mass purchasing power. As we have seen, this cannot be achieved through handouts to the poor; it is the capacity to make productive contributions to the economy which should be spread among the population.

The best way to spread productive capacity is to *restore balance* to a distorted factor market. In many countries labour is taxed and capital is subsidised through tax concessions for capital investments. By taxing energy, capital, pollution and waste production, capital-intensive modes of production would become more expensive, labour-intensive modes of production would become more competitive and the impact on the environment would be reduced. Obviously this necessitates international agreements, otherwise the competitiveness of some countries is undermined to the benefit of others.[35]

Participation in the productive process

One of the most devastating critiques of capitalism is that the business cycle of boom and recession periodically leads to high levels of unemployment. But unemployment is not only created by the business cycle. Technological advance and capital-intensive production in the centre demand a *smaller and more sophisticated work force* at the expense of unskilled labour. At the same time, they help produce a surplus of productive capacity over market demand. This surplus seeks markets in the periphery. By offering better, cheaper and "smarter" products, industrial production in the centre *outcompetes* production in the periphery and destroys the markets of the latter.

As a result, peripheral producers are thrown out of business and have no choice but to offer their labour to the centre. However, mechanised centre industries have little use for the unskilled labour which is flocking into industrial core areas. People simply find no employment. Without employment they have no income. Without income they do not constitute market demand. The result is that they no longer constitute "cheap labour", as in earlier phases of the industrial revolution, but *marginalised labour*. People drop out of the formal economy altogether. This again depresses market demand for the centre, and the surplus of productive capacity becomes worse.

For quite some time the labour surplus could be absorbed by a *growing service sector*, including the bureaucracy. But the resources to keep such a sector afloat are mainly derived from the industrial sector. The productivity of both knowledge and service workers is declining — even in developed countries.[36] The lowest productivity is found in the bureaucracy where service workers get salaries and social guarantees irrespective of their achievements. This mechanism is available only to affluent societies, and even there only within limits. In poor countries a growing service sector leads to inflation and economic stagnation because the demand is not backed up by production. Adding the effects of population growth in peripheral regions, it is obvious that a trend towards ever greater unemployment develops in the system as a whole.

When the emphasis shifts from service work to *knowledge work*[37] the problem becomes worse. Whether for genetic, cultural or historical reasons, it may simply go beyond the capacity of most potentially marginalised people to become high-tech knowledge workers. And even if individual potential was not a constraint, the system imposes its own constraints: the number of knowledge workers needed to control computer-driven and mechanised processes is strictly limited.[38]

The result is a new class structure between knowledge and service workers.[39] Moreover, computer driven technology takes over services to an increasing extent. Unemployment among teachers is growing and may continue to do so, partly because the school of the future will be capital-, rather than labour-intensive.[40]

This does not mean, of course, that an *entire economy* cannot vastly improve its international competitiveness, for instance by investing in the production of knowledge, spreading education and training widely across the population and applying creative retraining systems. The production and spread of knowledge was one of the keys to East Asian economic miracles. And in all industrialised countries knowledge formation and dissemination has outpaced capital as the largest investment.[41] There are economists who believe that Japan no longer needs labour because the Japanese population as a whole could simply constitute the economic elite of the entire region.[42]

We can be certain, however, that large scale marginalisation will occur somewhere in the wider environment as a result of such excellence. So the *tango of progress and marginalisation* poses a tricky problem.[43] Research has shown that where governments have made employment creation a deliberate policy priority, unemployment could be reduced considerably. But if this happens at the expense of some other population groups in the international system, the problem is not solved but only shifted elsewhere. This impasse still seeks a long term and global solution.

What can be said, however, is that a solution will probably be found only *if the distorted factor market is balanced out*. As mentioned above, modes of production based on energy, capital and technological sophistication simply has to become more expensive than labour-intensive and energy-saving modes of production. The assumption that "progress" is tantamount to the development of more and more labour saving technology and a greater use of fossil energy is more than questionable in an age of mass unemployment and ecological deterioration. Why should subsidised research continue to be geared to the quest for labour saving technology? Why should governments still grant tax concessions for capital investment, rather than employment creation? Surely the achievements of a civilisation which cast millions of people into redundancy, dependency and meaninglessness constitute anything but "progress".

Giving the grassroots a chance

Contributions to the economy do not have to be in the form of employment. There is also the possibility of self-employment. The principle of "subsidiarity", advocated by Catholic moral philosophy, comes in useful here. It says that tasks *which can be fulfilled by local bodies* should not be taken over by regional bodies, and tasks which can be fulfilled by regional bodies should not be taken over by national bodies. Subsidiarity helps to avoid power concentration and enhances grassroots initiatives. This principle is in line with the general demand that weaker members of the society, rather than stronger ones, should receive support.

This can and should be applied in the economic realm as well. In the first place *small enterprises*, rather than large and powerful ones, should be protected and supported by the state. In the second place concentrations of power in great enterprises through take-overs should be controlled, if not dismantled. Large concentrations can only be justified where a particular sector demands large scale operations, for instance in the jet liner industry. In the third place large enterprises can make their contribution to grass roots empowerment by giving out contracts to smaller manufacturers, service companies, artisans, salespersons or street hawkers. This procedure, called "outsourcing", has definite advantages not only for those who get the outcontracted jobs but for the outcontracting firms as well. Outsourcing may also enhance the efficiency of a bloated public administration.[44]

Economics of scale can be achieved through the exploiting of niche markets both at the national and the international levels. Comparative advantages in niche markets are constantly changing; therefore the exploitation of these markets requires alertness, motivation, information and innovation. Governments can assist upcoming entrepreneurs to utilise potential comparative advantages by providing training, market research, cheap and accessible channels of communication, credit facilities and backup insurance in case of product failure.

A lean and clean administration

Corruption among politicians and bureaucrats is a scourge in many developing countries. But even Western democracies have, to a large extent, become "pork-barrel states", where politicians dish out favours to potential voters which are then financed through budget deficits.[45] This is not only morally outrageous, it is economically counterproductive. Obviously somebody some time has to pay for this selfish extravagance.

The bureaucracy, especially, has always been in danger of harbouring unproductive types of employment. In a country with an industrial base too small to accommodate a growing labour force, this danger is particularly acute because the government service provides the main access to employment. To *create jobs by inflating the bureaucracy* is a temptation especially for regimes which feel constrained to defuse the time bomb of growing unemployment, to enhance their popularity by granting favours, even to accommodate their "home boys". But the bureaucracy can always only live off the productive sectors of the economy; therefore such employment does not create wealth for the nation, but bleeds the wealth creating sectors dry.

Creating more jobs in the bureaucracy is one way of *redistributing income and wealth*, but not necessarily in the right direction. One possibility is that the rich and successful are taxed and the money is used to pay for the salaries of "passengers", another that the poor are taxed to pay for the salaries of comparatively rich bureaucrats.

The policy directive to be derived from these considerations is a "lean and clean" administration. That is what a flourishing national economy needs. Obviously public administration is indispensable, but to be profitable it should be *limited to the absolutely essential*. Budgeting should not begin with a list of needs, which are endless, but with available income. Expenditure should then be prioritised to remain within these limits. Budget deficits and international debts have become a modern economic scourge in both rich and poor countries.

The bureaucracy should also be *held accountable*, subject to public scrutiny and put in place by a democratic mandate - a mandate which the public should be able to withdraw in case of inefficiency, abuse of power or corruption. To subject politicians to democratic controls, but exempt bureaucrats, makes no sense, because the bureaucracy wields at least as much decision making power, and is at least as prone to corruption. A mechanism must be found through which citizens can express their appreciation or dissatisfaction with the bureaucracy. Anti-corruption drives from within an organisation are often ineffectual, especially when top echelons, who are supposed to clean up the place, are themselves not immune to temptation and when there are no lucrative alternatives to the abuse of public office around.[46]

Making state enterprises profitable

This does not mean though that the state should never embark on job creating enterprises when the private sector fails to do so. Where the private sector does not provide essential services, such as education, ecological protection or infrastructure, this is self-evident.[47] But the Keynesian approach — state investment in times of economic recession — should also not simply be written off, though its long term dangers must be heeded.[48] In theory the question is really not whether the state or the private sector makes an investment; the problem is whether such an investment is *productive, profitable and employment generating* or not. The state is running vast administrative operations anyway and we must insist that these become efficient. Often governments do not dare to demand accountability and to clean up or close down unprofitable enterprises, because they do not want to antagonise particular supporters and powerful lobbies. This is where the problem is located.

Finally a reminder

No human being is an island - but neither is a country. Whatever we have said in this chapter has a local, a regional, a national, an international and a global dimension. Often you solve a problem in one locality only *to exacerbate it in another*. Rich countries, especially, are in a position to find internal solutions to these problems, because they can afford to do so. They can clean up their industrial emissions; raise their productivity levels and become more competitive on world markets; pick up their marginalised population groups through retraining and employment schemes; subsidise their agricultural sectors; spend vast resources on basic need satisfaction; locate their polluting industries elsewhere, and dump their waste outside their borders. But what about the effects of such policies on poorer countries? In modern times wide horizons and long term visions have become an absolute necessity for responsible policy makers the world over.

Questions

Revision: Mention a few policy directives which seem to fit our economic vision and agenda.

Application: Which of these policy directives are already being acted upon in your country and which are not?

Critique: (a) "What you have come up with after so much ado is a series of platitudes which are either too vague, or too impractical to be of any use."
(b) "You cannot clamour for growth in productivity and for ecological self-restraint at the same time. To save humankind from self-destruction something much more radical is needed than the few adjustments which you propose to the present system." Comment.

Section V - Industrial relations

Sharing control over a productive operation

Let us apply our theoretical considerations concerning participation to a concrete case, namely industrial relations. As we have seen, a social structure cannot do without a hierarchy of power. But there should be institutional arrangements which prevent the abuse of power at the expense of the powerless. The guiding principle, which has found general acceptance in Western societies, is a *democratic mandate with public accountability*.[49]

In an unmitigated capitalist society this principle is not applied to the economy. The assumptions are, first, that those who own an enterprise are also entitled to control it; second, that *it is the shareholders who own the firm*; and third, that they are entitled to the profit.[50] Thus it is the shareholders who appoint the directors. Because they receive their mandate only from the shareholders, the directors are only accountable to the latter. Workers are not deemed to be owners, whether of the firm or its profits, so they are also not entitled to a say in the running of the firm. The work force is hired like any other piece of equipment, and receives compensation in the form of wages. In cases of financial distress or greater expediency, workers are dismissed and that is the end of the matter. Trade union action and socialist policies have led to various adjustments in Western countries, but the basic assumptions are still in place.[51]

Reflecting on the principles involved, we venture the opinion that this is a distorted concept of property which damages social relationships. If we take into consideration that property means control over resources, as we have argued in chapter 7, we can speak of at least two kinds of ownership: control over the productive capacity of capital and control over the productive capacity of labour. Since classical economics treats capital and labour as impersonal factors of production, which can substitute each other to a considerable extent, *it does not make sense to give one of them priority* over the other within a common enterprise. Both workers and capital owners have a stake in its success; both get hurt if it fails. While capital owners can lose their savings, workers can lose their jobs, which is at least as devastating in its effects.

The perception should be, therefore, that both types of owners — capital owners and owners of labour — pool their resources in a common venture, and that *both are entitled to a share in the control* over this venture. Of course, capital and labour are not the only partners in an industrial enterprise; there are also those who contribute raw materials, professional expertise, administrative skills, management, access to markets, and so on. There is no reason why they should not all be involved in the decision making process at various levels and to various degrees.[52]

Industrial democracy

Research has shown that, in the case of an underdeveloped industrial system, ordinary workers have the *wildest misconceptions* of the financial realities of an enterprise.[53] When they are also ignorant about the product they are helping to produce, it is not logical to expect responsibility on their side. Being interested in nothing but their weekly pay, they cannot be concerned about the viability and profitability of the firm. How can we overcome this undesirable state of affairs?

Perhaps centralised, professional management is indispensable for an enterprise to be viable under competitive circumstances. We have argued above that a command structure is perfectly legitimate but only if it operates *in the interests of the lower ranks* and on the basis of their mandate.

Decision makers should consult with, and be accountability to those affected by their decisions. Lower ranks should be fully informed and allowed to participate as far as this is practically feasible.[54] Ideally lower ranks include all who depend directly on the operation of the firm for their incomes, that is, ordinary shareholders, large investors such as pension funds, loan creditors, experts, workers, customers, suppliers - even competitors.

In recent times the limitations of a purely economic orientation of the enterprise have been recognised and "corporate social responsibility" has become a buzz word.[55] Especially the decisions taken by managers of large firms have a substantial impact on the wider community; public accountability is, therefore, a social necessity. As far as stakeholders cannot be directly involved in decision making processes, it is important to guarantee public accountability through social and ecological audits.[56]

Industrial democracy can also greatly enhance performance. It may also greatly enhance the general level of social responsibility.[57] When we talk of social responsibility and public accountability we do not refer only to management. In the past, some unions have been extremely self-centred and short-sighted — to their own detriment as well as to the detriment of their firms and of society as a whole.[58] Historical evidence shows that *cooperation and participation in decision making* among all contributors, on the basis of full information, mutual trust and absolute fairness, yields the best results in terms of prosperity and social harmony. Mutual loyalty pushes up productivity and benefits the society.

The reluctance of industrial partners to withdraw their contributions is one of the secrets which made the *Japanese system* so successful.[59] Relatively peaceful industrial relations, based on a "social contract" between state, employers and labour, were also co-responsible for the German economic miracle after World War II.[60] By contrast, industrial antagonisms caused the decline of the British economy during the same period. These systems have also been adapted to South African conditions with considerable success by various enterprises, so that the argument of cultural and educational discrepancies is no longer convincing. It should be clear by now that participatory management makes economic sense; dictatorial management and an incessant "class struggle" do not. Therefore, enterprises should be proactive in this regard, rather than reluctantly reacting to union pressure.

There seem to be a number of *alternative routes* towards economic democracy in practice:

- Workers are free to organise trade unions which then negotiate on equal terms with employer organisations. This is the liberal-capitalist version.
- Workers are represented on the decision making boards of the enterpris-

es in which they work, together with the suppliers of other factors of production. This is the social-democratic version. In Germany, for instance, employees are entitled to no less than half the seats on the supervisory boards of larger corporations.[61]

- The operation is democratised in the sense of "participatory democracy" at all levels. Work teams decide how best to organise their work on the shop floor, and link up with other such work teams in evaluation and planning sessions. They "own" their equipment in the sense that they can acquire, control and dispose of it within the framework of the organisation. Workers are even free to start a "free intraprise" within the organisation if they can find the necessary customers, capital and expertise to do so.[62]

- The employees both own and run the enterprise.[63]

- Workers do not own, but control the enterprises and appoint the directors under the tutelage of the state. This is the Yugoslav democratic-socialist version.

- All enterprises are owned by the state and run by a bureaucracy. The workers are employed by the state. This is the Marxist-Leninist version.

Once again, the intermediate versions seem to be more democratic in practice than the two extreme versions, and the social democratic version is the most balanced and feasible. In practical terms industrial democracy implies, at the very least, that all those who depend on the enterprise for their incomes *should be represented* on the boards of directors. If these representatives are to take part in responsible decision making, however, they have to be fully informed and adequately trained.[64] The representatives in turn should be accountable to their respective constituencies.

Is a loaded franchise acceptable?

In the political realm democracy assumes that, at least in principle, all members of society are equal in dignity. To avoid the domination of more powerful partners over less powerful ones, *political democracy rejects a "loaded franchise"* (meaning that some citizens have more votes than others depending on their status, wealth or education) and demands the principle of "one person one vote" (meaning that each citizen has an equal say in the decision making process).

In the capitalist industrial system this principle is not even applied to the body of shareholders, let alone the employees. Shareholders possess voting rights according to the size of their respective holdings. On the one hand this seems to be quite reasonable: why should somebody who has invested R 100.00 have the same say as somebody who has invested a million Rand! On the other hand it is obvious that smaller shareholders are at the mercy of the bigger ones. And smaller shareholders, or workers for that matter, are much more dependent on their income than big shareholders. This is precisely why a loaded franchise is rejected in the political realm.

If we included all stakeholders in the decision making process, but on the basis of a loaded franchise, we would have to establish the *exact size of the contribution* each stakeholder makes to the productive process as a whole. In some cases labour may turn out to contribute 50% of value added and capital only 30%. Marginal productivity calculations provide us with the economic tools for establishing the relative contributions made by various participants in the productive process. The problem is that professionals, for instance, though fewer in number, could outvote workers, cleaners and messengers because of their high marginal productivity. And, as mentioned above, workers, cleaners and messengers are at least as dependent on employment as professionals for their survival.

Perhaps a "one person one vote" principle would not be practically feasible in the industrial world. The answer might be to have *collective representation* of different kinds of stakeholders on the board of directors and grant these representatives an equal, rather than a loaded franchise. Then the interests of a particular section of the work force, for instance, can be upheld with as much power as the interests of any other body of stakeholders. It is also important to note that institutionalised joint decision making by representative bodies can be built either on the adversarial or the consensus model, just as in the case of its political counterpart. In principle the consensus model is preferable.

Paradoxically, representative democracy can still become authoritarian and bureaucratic, and thus stifle initiative.[65] The ideal of "participatory democracy" goes further than representative democracy: employees should "own" their firm; they should apply their experience to its improvement; they should have a say in the actual running of the operation at their particular places in the system. *Shop floor democracy* activates creativity, prompts ingenuity, calls for responsibility, makes employees identify with the firm, and raises their dedication.[66]

In a situation where masses of potential workers are marginalised, where management and unions can strike a deal at the expense of the unemployed, where national interests and international competitiveness are at stake, the *wider society* should also be represented on the boards of large enterprises through political representatives. This is particularly important in situations where labour and management regularly come to terms with each other at the expense of the unemployed and marginalised.

The right to withhold your contribution

We have spoken about industrial democracy. The second, seemingly contradictory principle is that those who have less bargaining power should not be tyrannised by those who have more. To ensure fairness, all participants should have the *right to withhold* their contributions.

In practice this principle gives more leverage to more powerful than to less powerful contributors. In most cases workers are less powerful than shareholders because they have only their labour to sell; by contrast, large capital owners have vast resources at their disposal. However, there have also been cases in history where trade unions have acquired sufficient power to hold enterprises, sectors, even whole states to ransom and cause considerable damage not only to the profitability and competitiveness of their firms but also to the public good.[67]

At the personal level the problem of withdrawal is not serious. Individual capital owners can sell their shares and invest their capital elsewhere, while individual workers can give notice and seek other jobs. The problem arises when either of the industrial partners *embarks on collective action*. In modern capitalism workers are entitled to withhold their labour collectively in a strike, while capital owners can lock out workers from their work places.

These measures are not very satisfactory because they lead to great losses on both sides. Of course, strikes are an important means for workers to reach parity of power with capital owners. However, they also cut deeply into the flesh of the strikers themselves and harm the industry on which the workers depend. Moreover, unions may achieve higher wages and better working conditions *at the expense of the employment opportunities of others*. Management responds to higher labour costs by rationalisation, professionalisation of the work force and capital-intensive production. This means that relatively privileged workers are able to better their lot, but at the expense of their (contemporary and future) fellow workers. The result is a new class division between a small, skilled "worker aristocracy" and masses of unskilled workers whose chances of finding employment are progressively diminishing. High labour costs also impair the international competitiveness of enterprises.

Social tensions can be creative, but they can also create great disruption, distortion and failure. So industrial action of this kind should be avoided as far as possible. It is better for all parties to *negotiate a compromise*. Most social democratic states have institutionalised negotiation and arbitration processes. If an enterprise is controlled by representatives of both capital owners and workers and if these representatives have full information concerning the assets and liabilities of the enterprise, strikes and lock-outs can largely be avoided.

More serious, however, is the case of *mass retrenchment* of workers in times when an enterprise is in financial distress. Its counterpart capital owners is the massive loss incurred by capital owners when the enterprise is no longer profitable. Again a jointly controlled enterprise would be better able to tackle the problem in a way which minimises hurt on both sides. Retrenchments will then only take place as a last resort, and with as many safeguards for the retrenched as possible, while the capital stock of the firm is also protected as far as possible. We should also not forget that it is the task of governments and the international community to minimise recessions and their effects.

The upshot of these considerations is that the "struggle" of the workers, which Marxists have been talking about, should be redirected at efforts to *democratise* not only the political economy as a whole, but also particular industries, and to raise the stakes of the workers in the wellbeing of the enterprises on which they depend. Apart from representation on the boards, workers should also become shareholders. At least some examples seem to suggest that the highest motivations are reached when workers are the principal shareholders of the companies in which they work.[68]

To maintain a healthy balance within the enterprise the following additional safeguards could be taken:

- In *structural* terms the greater the diversity of contributions made, and the more indispensable the linkages between these contributions, the greater the stability of the system. Computers (capital) cannot work without computer scientists (expertise), computer operators (labour), and electrical power (infrastructure). The one normally would not dare to antagonise the other.

- In *motivational* terms there is no substitute for a climate of loyalty, reliability and dedication to the common venture. Such attitudes should be fostered very deliberately. Initiatives and innovations coming from the workers should be taken seriously. People should "own" their enterprises and develop a sense of pride in them. A sense of belonging, pride and mutual faithfulness among the partners is especially important in times of economic downturn.

Before we close, we need to remind ourselves that industrial relations should not be seen in isolation. The population of a country does not consist only of managers and workers. Management and labour can easily agree on a deal which *serves their combined interests at the expense of others*. This can happen on a large scale when through trade union action workers obtain higher skills, better wages and better working conditions and when, as a result, labour as a factor of production becomes more expensive and is replaced by capital. Mechanisation leads to a reduction of employment. We should not forget that the interests of the unemployed are not represented at wage negotiations. Similarly, doctors, nurses or teachers can go on strike to improve their positions, but it is the patients and the pupils who suffer, rather than the bureaucracy against which the strike is directed.

It is *the state* which should look after the wellbeing of the society as a whole. It should provide institutional controls that safeguard against some groups becoming the victims of the greed and ruthlessness of others, and apply them rigorously. If they cannot represent themselves for lack of information and organisation, the affected third parties should be represented on decision making bodies through ombudsmen and other statutory institutions. Obviously this role of the state can also be taken over by umbrella bodies, such as professional organisations, the stock exchange, bodies appointed to lay down standards, and so on.

Questions

Revision: How could an equitable balance of power be achieved in industrial relations?

Application: Imagine that the proposed approach would be applied to a major sector in your country, say agriculture or mining. Do you think that this would be feasible? Which preconditions would have to be fulfilled?

Critique: (a) "The industrial power play just does not work this way, my friend. Capital is a multinational force which has successfully shrugged off every attempt undertaken to make it democratically accountable."
(b) "Your argument is built on a basic error of judgment: capital is something you have, while labour is something you are, namely your own body. It is typical of capitalist inhumanity that it bestows the same dignity on things as it does on persons."
(c) "If you allowed the endless palaver of ill-informed and irresponsible people to determine the running of a private enterprise the economy would grind to a halt." Do you agree with any of these statements?

Let us summarise

In section I we reflected on the *basic approach* which underlie our suggestions. We called for pragmatism, guided by a vision which aims at the wellbeing of the entire fabric of society within its natural environment. The task of deriving concrete directives from this overall vision should be undertaken by an *interdisciplinary team*, including representatives of various human sciences as well as practitioners in various fields. It should be democratically legitimate, accountable and participatory.

In section II we spelt out five priorities on the agenda of economics and practical policy making. The first is to secure the *natural resource base* and habitat for the present and all future generations. We saw that this can only be achieved if humanity no longer behaves as a selfish and reckless tyrant over creation but serves the greater whole of which it forms a part. The second priority is *basic need sufficiency* for all people. The third is equity in the distribution of the inputs and the benefits of production. The fourth is concern for those who are incapable of making a contribution. The fifth is *bal-*

ance in the satisfaction of needs.

In section III we engaged in a reflection on the *optimal distribution of power* in society. This optimum lies between the extremes of dictatorship and anarchy at a point where the power of each higher rank is balanced out by the combined power of the respective lower rank. In practice the higher rank must have more power, but this power must be mandated by the lower ranks and exercised in the interest of the latter. We then applied these models to the various economic systems discussed in this book.

In section IV we suggested a few *directives* which seem to follow from our deliberations. The first is an institutionalised commitment to mutual responsibility. Then follow: a "tamed" market, that is a market which serves the fulfilment of needs and not the proliferation of luxury wants; participation of all economically active people in the productive process; a lean and clean administration; subjection of state enterprises to profitability criteria; grass roots empowerment, and "generational equity" - which means that the interests of the not yet born must be protected. These principles also have to be applied to the international scene, which is a difficult but not impossible task for the future.

In section V we discussed *industrial relations* as an example of democratic power play in the economic realm. We argued that, in principle, all contributors of factors of production, not only shareholders, should be represented on the decision making bodies of an enterprise. Third party stakeholders should be represented by the state. On this basis, conflicts of collective interest can be articulated and negotiated; the costly practice of withholding your contribution through strikes and lockouts can be avoided; retrenchments will be relegated to the status of a last resort and, if unavoidable, cushioned as far as possible. At the same time it is the task of governments to overcome recessions as far as possible.

Notes

1   To get an impression of the immensity and complexity of the task, see the two contributions by Terrence Moll 1991.

2   World Bank 1991:50,55.

3   "We assume that the principal purpose of government is to secure the conditions for public well-being. This public well-being includes the paramount values of prosperity, welfare, equality, freedom, stability, and security." Chang 1992:1.

4   Chang 1992:8.

5   Klitgaard 1992. World Bank 1991:49.

6   Chang 1992; Petr 1990; cf also R E Hiebert in *Public Relations Review*, 18/1992, 117-126.

7   Eatwell 1993:12ff; Shtromas 1993. That ideologies do not always address the realities of a situation has been demonstrated, for instance, by Klitgaard 1993.

8 I owe this term to H R Niebuhr in his book, *The responsible self.*

9 We widen Albert Schweitzer's philosophical concept of "respect for life" to include the non-organic world as far as human understanding and imagination can embrace it.

10 Due to specialisation and isolation of the sciences, "the physical body of world society has outgrown its intelligence. Any organism whose body is out of proportion with its brain capacity will not be able to maintain its integrity." (Prof Wasi Prawase, Bangkok, at the 1995 ICEA conference in Jomtien, Thailand). For the systems approach see Senge 1990.

11 (Dahl 1985, quoted by Narveson p 29).

12 Wasi Prawase ibid.

13 Cf the popular adage found in African cultures: "Umuntu ngumuntu ngabantu" (a person is a person through other people).

14 See Nürnberger 1988, parts II and III.

15 See Turner et al 1994.

16 Nardindar Singh in Glaeser 1987:248.

17 World Bank 1990:5.

18 See chapter 3 of the companion volume, *Prosperity, poverty and pollution*, for a precise description of the concept of human needs.

19 See Illich, Ivan in: Sachs 1992:88ff.

20 See Copp in Paul et al 1992:250ff. It is interesting to see that he connects the concept of human autonomy with basic need satisfaction.

21 For an appraisal of the basic human right to an adequate standard of living see Copp in Paul et al 1992:231ff. According to Copp this right "is best viewed as a conditional right against the state, a right to be enabled to meet one's basic needs, provided that one's society is in favorable circumstances."

22 In the companion volume, *Prosperity, poverty and pollution*, we have sketched the measures that we think would have to be taken if the goal was to be achieved.

23 Suggested reading: Moll 1991:75ff.

24 Cf Arneson in Paul et al 1992:203ff.

25 "I am proposing a right to be enabled to meet one's basic needs; I am not proposing a right to be provided with what one needs." Copp in Paul et al 1992:252.

26 See Fields, G: Assessing progress towards greater equality of income distribution; and Hicks, N: Is there a trade-off between growth and basic needs? In: Seligson, Mitchell A 1984: The gap between rich and poor: *Contending perspectives on the political economy of development.* Boulder / London: Westview, pp 292ff and 338ff.

27 See Fields 1980:122f

28 "The notion of a trade-off between growth and equity, which helped to entrench antigrowth policies in socialist economies and antiequity policies in conservative ones, has been further discredited by the many economies that consistently outperform the rest on both counts: Costa Rica, Indonesia, Japan, Korea, Malaysia ... and the Scandinavian economies." World Bank 1992:137.

29 See Kuo S W Y et al: Rapid growth with improved income distribution: The Taiwan success story. In: Seligson op cit. pp 379ff.

30 Compare the following with Tinbergen in Basu 1993:205ff.

31 We deal with these issues in the companion volume, *Prosperity, poverty and pollution*.

32 See Brown Weiss, Edith: Intergenerational equity: A legal framework for global environmental change. In: Brown Weiss, Edith (ed) 1992: *Environmental change and international law: New challenges and dimensions.* Tokyo: United Nations University Press, 385ff.

33 Turner et al 1994:141ff.; von Weizsaecker & Jesinghaus 1992.

34 These mechanisms are described fully in the companion volume on *Prosperity, poverty and pollution.*

35 For detail see Von WeizsÑcker, Ernst U & Jesinghaus, Jochen 1992: *Ecological tax reform: A policy proposal for sustainable development.* Antlantic Highlands NJ: Humanities International/London: Zed Pr (UK). UNISA 336.205 WEIZ.

36 Drucker 1993:75ff.

37 Drucker 1993.

38 Drucker's whole argument concerning the shift to knowledge work underlines the problem: Japan only needs to produce knowledge workers because "the supply of young people in the developing countries qualified for nothing but manual work in manufacturing is so large ... that worrying about the 'industrial base' is nonsense" (1993:62ff). The first assumption is that the Triad will remain the economic elite; the second, that the expansion of industrial production is limitless; the third, that computers and machines do not render those peripheral industrial workers uncompetitive as well, at the latest when they begin to clamour for a living wage.

39 Drucker 1993:78.

40 Drucker 1993:181.

41 Drucker 1993:169f.

42 Drucker 1993:62ff. See also pp 178f for the historical background of this achievement.

43 It is analysed in greater detail in the companion volume on *Prosperity, poverty and pollution.*

44 "The case for outsourcing" (Drucker 1993:84ff).

45 Drucker 1993:121ff.

46 For detail see Klitgaard, Robert 1988: *Controlling corruption.* Berkeley et al: University of California Press and Klitgaard, Robert 1991: *Tropical gangsters.* London/New York: Tauris.

47 World Bank 1991:5.

48 For a defense of Keynes against Monetarism see Vicarelli 1985.

49 The field is covered by the journal *Economic and Industrial Democracy.*

50 Cf Heilbroner 1985:67.

51 "The capacity of the market to secure acquiescence in a provisioning process in whcih the surplus automatically accrues to the property of only one class obviously makes the market mechanism an executive instrument for a particular social order ... this is to say no more than that capitalisms, like tribal societies, imperial kingdoms, feudalisms, or socialist states, are at bottom regimes of power and privilege, built on the granite of family ties, community norms, and above all, on a deeply inculcated 'habit of subordination'." Heilbroner 1988:31.

52 As Drucker points out, the idea that management should be a trustee which is accountable to all the stakeholders of an enterprise has been around since the 1950s (1993:71ff), but the "business audit", which Drucker has to offer, neatly circumvents the need for accountability to all stakeholder constituencies.

53 A South African study revealed that the lowest paid workers did not know of the existence of shareholder capital and believed that 85% of company profits were paid to management and 1% to workers. NÅrnberger 1988:251.

54 For a discussion of the task of management see Drucker 1993:71ff. The suggestion that management should be "bevevolent despot" led to all sorts of "frantic financial manipulations", scandals and the "bubble economy" of the 1970s and 1980s. In response there was a reversion to the idea that management should maximise shareholders' value, which again led to shortterm strategising with devastating longterm effects.

55 Carroll A B 1991: The pyramid of corporate social responsibility: Towards the moral management of organizational stakeholders. *Business Horizons,* July-August 1991, pp 39-48.

56 Drucker 1993:73.

57 See the instructive comparison and summary of experiences made in Western countries so far by Sisson 1987.

58 For examples and for the concept of social responsibility see Drucker 1993:89ff.

59 The Japanese system includes, among others, (a) "quality circles", that is, groups who reflect jointly on quality, cost reduction, safety, maintenance and workplace improvements; (b) "green areas" where supervisors discuss the previous and the current day's work with their teams; (c) in general a joint commitment to the whole person, to shared values and to consensus building. Some Amercian firms, for instance General Motors, have tried to emulate and improve on the Japanese system with great success.

60 The German system is built on the concept of "co-determination". The Co-determination Acts of 1952 and 1976 provide for worker directors on the (policy forming) supervisory boards of firms employing more than 2000 persons. The Works Constitution Acts of 1952 and 1972 provide for elected Works Councils.

61 Ordelheide & Pfaff 1994:45ff.

62 Pinchot 1993:114,283ff.

63 Polaroid and Mondragon are examples.

64 Cf Glautier, M W E & Underdown 1991: *Accounting theory and practice.* London: Pitman, p 7.

65 Pinchot 1993.

66 "The nineteenth century believed in the expert knowing the answers. By now we have learned that those who do a job know more about it than anybody else" (Drucker 1993:82).

67 For two example from the US (Lewis) and Britan (Scargill) see Drucker 1993:89 and 94.

68 See for instance the description of "Genentech" by Kehrer 1989:130ff as an example of a firm with high incentives and motivations caused by the fact that the workers were also the share holders. Shares could not be sold unless the firm reached set goals.

EPILOGUE -
Faith and economics

Our aim in this epilogue

I have endeavoured to offer an analysis and an argument in this book that *can make sense to anybody with a critical mind*, irrespective of his/her particular convictions. However, as a professional theologian I should not pretend as if collective predispositions, attitudes, decisions and actions were not *ultimately based on convictions*. Nor should I hide the fact that I would not have written this book if I were not motivated by my own faith as a Christian.

That convictions can be ignored with impunity is one of the more serious fallacies of the modernist world-view. It has come to be rejected in recent times not only by cultural anthropology and religious studies, but also by the theory of science, systems theory, ecology, and the whole post-modern movement in philosophy. Obviously it is also rejected by theology. Without going to the *transcendent foundations* of convictions our discussion of economic ideologies and systems will remain truncated and superficial.

In this epilogue we offer a critical reflection on the religious quality of economic ideologies and the economic impact of religious convictions. We begin by pointing out the pervasive *impact of convictions* on human behaviour. Then we *evaluate* economic ideologies on the basis of biblical criteria. Then we deal with the indispensability of *critical dialogue* between different convictions in a pluralist society. Finally we construct an argument designed to show that the struggle for an appropriate economic system is not only in line with, but actually demanded by the *Christian tradition.*

Why focus on Christianity? Part of my job description as a Christian theologian is to clarify the *basic thrust of the biblical faith* and subject its various manifestations to critique — whether in relation to economics or to any other dimension of life. This is not meant to exclude anybody. Representatives of other religions and world-views have to do the same for their own convictions. I cannot presume to speak on their behalf.

However, the focus on the biblical faith is also entirely appropriate in historical terms, because the ideologies we have discussed in the book have all emerged in the Western cultural context. At least to some extent, they can be considered to be *secular offshoots* of the Jewish-Christian heritage. Without an understanding of their historical derivation, our grasp of these ideologies will remain superficial and our evaluation will lack a definite set of criteria. There is no such generative link between Western economic ideologies and other religions, such as African traditional religion or Buddhism.

Section I - The foundational character of convictions

It should be clear by now that human behaviour is based on assumptions. Assumptions are derived from *systems of meaning* — however fleeting and flimsy they may have become in a pluralist and direction-less society. A system of meaning includes a set of values, norms and procedures which form the criteria of legitimacy, justification, acceptability and belonging - in short, the *right of existence*. These criteria are largely linked to particular statuses and roles in society. Legitimacy again is the prerequisite of one's *authority* to take decisions and actions in accordance with ascribed roles and statuses in society. It is the function of convictions, whether secular or religious, to provide access to the "depth dimension" reality, namely meaning, right of existence and authority.

Systems of meaning have, by definition, some kind of transcendent foundation. They *express* themselves in terms of fact and reason, but they are not *based* on fact and reason. They are based on vision, intuition, inspiration, and aspiration. The economic ideologies which we have discussed in this book are themselves "secular religions" in this sense, otherwise they would not have developed such compelling power over masses of people, nor would there be such fundamental disagreements concerning the validity of their perceptions and aspirations.

The modernist world view, whether liberal or Marxist, feels justified in ignoring convictions because it believes that attitudes, decisions and actions are *motivated by self-interest*. This can hardly be disputed. But interests themselves are undergirded by convictions. Human beings are not simply guided by instincts which urge organisms towards the fulfilment of raw material needs. Human beings never regard need fulfilment as a simple, factual and mechanical necessity, as animals do. Human beings have the capacity to define, interpret and prioritise their needs.

These interpretations and prioritisations are *based on convictions*. Even the most basic needs, such as food, clothing, shelter, or sexuality, are subject to the search for meaning, right of existence and authority. The result is that their fulfilment produces the most sophisticated and diverse cultural forms. The need for food or sexual gratification, for instance, is subject to endless taboos, directives and sanctions. Changes or breakdowns in these cultural definitions can have most far-reaching consequences, for instance, when the strict sexual taboos of traditional African communities make way for licentiousness and promiscuity in the course of urbanisation.

This also means that convictions *must be subject to critique*. Not all convictions are concerned about avoiding the deterioration of the biosphere. Not all cultural forms support human life in all its fullness. Not all convictions are committed to social justice. Not all convictions generate a conscience about the weak and vulnerable. Not all convictions strive for a balance in the whole range of human needs. Convictions need to be confronted with these priorities. Their theoretical basis and their actual performance need to be evaluated and challenged. If we want to build a responsible society we cannot afford to ignore deceptive and detrimental convictions.

Section II - A critique of economic ideologies on the basis of the biblical faith

Against this background we can venture an evaluation of the economic ideologies we have discussed in this book. In a short appendix like this our critique can only consist of a few pointers; obviously the subject matter merits a far more profound and extensive treatment. The criteria will be taken from the Christian faith. We shall use *four such criteria:*

1. The quality of the transcendent dimension of a conviction.
2. The comprehensiveness of its redemptive vision.
3. The dialectic between gift and demand, or empowerment and expectation.
4. The dignity of the human being as a moral agent.

Marxism

It has been argued rather persuasively by Ernst Bloch, himself a Marxist, that Marxism, with its passion for social justice and its determination to reconstruct society, is a secular development of the biblical heritage. In Bloch's estimation Marxism is, in fact, the *legitimate heir of the biblical faith.*[1] Similar sentiments were expressed by Joe Slovo, the celebrated South African communist leader.[2] A liberal analyst has this to say: "The religious promise of Marxism, far more than its convoluted ideology and its increasingly unrealistic economics constituted its tremendous appeal, especially to intellectuals ... For them... the most powerful appeal ... was Marxism's promise of an earthly paradise, that is, Marxism as a secular religion."[3]

Stated more precisely, Marxism is a secular version of *apocalyptic messianism* as found in late Judaism and early Christianity. This is from where its compulsive fervour is derived. Every genuine Marxist is a missionary! Elsewhere I have highlighted the *intriguing parallells* between the two mindsets.[4] They share uncompromising commitment to social justice; priority accorded to the poor and oppressed at the expense of the rich and powerful, and the demand for unquestionable dedication to the cause. The Marxist "avantgarde" is a parallel to the biblical "suffering servant";[5] the utopian "classless society" to the eschatological "kingdom of God"; the agonies of the "dictatorship of the proletariat" to the "birth pains" which mark the transition between the "present age" and the "age to come"; the "proletariat" to "the elect people of God"; "ideological legitimation" to "idolatry"; the "historical dialectic" to God's "providence" in history. As in the biblical faith, there can be only one truth for Marxism; heresy is called false consciousness and syncretism is called revisionism. Both are eradicated — often with violent means.[6]

It is precisely this *religious quality* of Marxism — its fiery appeal to selfless dedication, its rigorous social ethic, its down-to-earth soteriology, and its tantalising eschatology, rather than its indigestible metaphysics, that accounts for the fascination it was able to evoke among intellectuals and ordinary masses alike. On the other hand, there are critics who maintain that the religious trappings of Marxism have led to mass delusions and neurosis.[7]

The parallells between the two mindsets are striking — but so are the distortions, if compared with the original. And it is at this level that the critique of Marxism by Christianity is indispensable:

a) *The quality of transcendence.* Transcendence in Marxism is located in the historical dialectic which inexorably leads the historical process towards the classless society. For Christians transcendence is located in the mastery and benevolence of a personal God who is committed to bring his creation to ultimate fulfilment. The difference between mechanical and personal transcendence is fundamental for an understanding of the world and the human being. Humans can only reach their freedom and dignity if they are able to transcend the mechanisms of the world in which they are embedded.

b) *Comprehensiveness of redemption.* Marxism envisages the redemption of society on a global scale through the transformation of the social circumstances of production. A transformation of the superstructure (collective mindsets and institutional arrangements) will follow automatically. Nature will be finally and totally subdued. The Christian faith locates the need for transformation in the field of human attitudes and personal relationships — towards God, the source and criterion of reality as a whole, towards fellow human beings and towards the rest of creation. A change of institutions and renewed attitudes towards nature must be motivated and underpinned by personal transformation.

c) *The dialectic between gift and demand.* Marxism is based on absolute demand. Only those who commit themselves totally to the struggle are acceptable. Those who obstruct the revolution have to be liquidated. The Christian faith is defined by a dialectic between demand and gift. While God has definite expectations, humans are not deemed able to fulfil them on their own accord. Commitment follows from God's unconditional, as opposed to conditional, acceptance into his fellowship. Here the Christian faith differs fundamentally from other members of the Western cluster of religions and worldviews.

d) *Human dignity.* At least in its orthodox version, Marxism-Leninism has a fairly mechanical view of human nature. Human consciousness must be deconstructed and reconstructed, whether by means of force, propaganda, social pressure, or brain washing techniques. Christianity believes that humans are called to share God's creative authority, God's redemptive concern and God's comprehensive vision for the world. It is through spiritual empowerment that the dialectic between freedom and responsibility materialises.

Fascism

Fascism does not fall within the scope of this book. It is mentioned here only because it is the worldview most viciously attacked by Marxists. This is no accident! It offers precisely the opposite reading of a common biblical and humanist heritage.

In fascism, *transcendence* is located in a mysterious "fate" which endows a charismatic leader with absolute power. *Redemption* is strictly limited to the glory of an ethnic group and its "fatherland". "Germany must live, even if we have to die" (Adolf Hitler). *Acceptance* is conditional on belonging to the elect nation or the "master race" and on total submission to the dictates of the "leader". Personal *dignity* is defined as "honour", which again is bound up with the readiness to sacrifice oneself for the "greater cause".

It is clear that the Christian faith has to reject these propositions across the board. While chauvinism has often been legitimated with notions of an elect nation found in the Old Testament, for Christians *ethnic exclusiveness* has been overcome precisely on the grounds of God's unconditional, suffering acceptance of the unacceptable, which makes it impossible to posit human conditions of acceptance based on race or ethnicity.[8] It needs to be recorded with shame that Christians have not lived up to their faith in this regard for most of their history.

Capitalist liberalism

At first sight the derivation of *capitalist liberalism* from the biblical heritage seems to be as far-fetched as that of Marxism. It has been argued rather convincingly, however, that the demystification, demythologisation and secularisation of reality in modern *science* have their origins in the fervour with which the biblical tradition rejects the ascription of divine qualities to earthly entities.[9] It was the biblical faith which located transcendence beyond the world and it was secular humanism which scrapped it altogether. Since then transcendence has simply been denied or ignored.

The biblical tradition has also been accused by ecologists and social critics of instigating and legitimating the ruthlessness, with which modern *technology* exercises mastery over nature, by granting humanity the divine mandate to subject reality to its control.[10] Obviously this is a misunderstanding, because according to Gen1:26ff, humanity, defined as the "image of God", is meant to share God's concern for his creation. However that may be, in the liberal capitalist worldview the notion of *redemption* has been reduced to immediate personal gratification of the most primitive kind. The interests of others, the preconditions for a healthy society, and the necessity to maintain ecological viability are simply of no consequence. Profit, utility and pleasure maximisation are all that is left of the once lofty goals of reaching universal and comprehensive wellbeing.

Acceptance in capitalist liberalism is again based on the fulfilment of absolute demands. The key words are productivity, efficiency, performance, achievement. Those who fulfil these demands are rewarded, those who don't are abandoned. It is true that charities flourish in liberal societies. However, this is not due to the liberal capitalist creed, but to the fact that the system leaves room for private initiatives, which can be geared to humanitarian motivations as much as to greed and ruthlessness.

Human dignity is inextricably linked to emancipation. The crusade against authority has been characteristic of modernity since the Enlightenment. Paradoxically this crusade has been instigated and fed by the biblical promise of freedom. However, the biblical tradition derives freedom from participation in God's creative authority, and links it to participation in God's redemptive concern and God's comprehensive vision. Human autonomy, licentiousness, avarice and self-aggrandisement — the bread and butter of capitalist profit, utility and pleasure maximisation — are rejected. Freedom without responsibility is not only fraudulent but also deceptive, because those tyrannised by their own cravings cannot claim to be free.

It is important to note at this juncture that capitalist liberalism indeed represents a creed, though it poses as hard-nosed realism and pragmatism. Remember that Marxism-Leninism too believed that it was "scientific", while in fact it was nothing but metaphysics of a rather questionable kind! The much invoked *homo oeconomicus* in liberal economics — meaning the human being defined as a profit, utility and pleasure maximiser — is a metaphysical construct whose validity is simply taken for granted. It cannot be challenged by evidence or argument; it is an article of faith.[11] Any behaviour which does not conform to the characterisation of "economic man" is considered to be "irrational". In fact, nothing can be more irrational than rampant selfishness and greed!

The conflict is for real

We have formulated some of the incongruencies between the biblical faith and modern economic ideologies. Nobody should suspect that these are irrelevant and harmless niceties! Nowhere are enmities more acute than between orthodoxy and heresy. Marxism has sensed the conflict very profoundly and has persecuted its rivals wherever these threatened to make a social impact. The church in turn rejected Marxism and provided havens for the few remaining pockets of resistance against Marxist regimes. It was from churches that the bloodless revolution against the Berlin Wall was conducted!

The conflict between the biblical faith and capitalist liberalism is much more subtle. The incessant drive of the advertising and entertainment industries to *undermine traditional inhibitions* against covetousness, promiscuity, violence and indulgence is located in the assumption that the pursuit of self-interest and pleasure is not only legitimate, but constitutes the ultimate goal of human life. Obviously this clashes with the biblical assumption that human authenticity is defined by a sacrificial life in service of a transcendent God and a needy community. Therefore faith is either banned to the private realm and spiritualised, or it is ridiculed, or it is — commercialised! It is at this level that the impact of alternatives in metaphysical assumptions on economic processes makes itself felt most keenly. And it is here, again, that the critique of capitalist liberalism by the Christian faith has become quite indispensable. It has a historical-cultural mandate to do so.

Section III - Critique of religious convictions

The impact of religion on economics is not restricted to economic ideologies. The different versions of the Christian faith also have economic repercussions, some of which are quite unacceptable. This necessitates a critique also of the Christian faith — whether by Christians themselves or by others.

We begin with the belaboured thesis of Max Weber[12] and R H Tawney[13] that the frugality and diligence demanded by the Puritan version of Calvinism (the socalled *Protestant Ethic*) gave rise to capitalism in Europe.[14] If the theory is correct, it is a classical example for the distortions which occur when motivations geared to the transcendent realm become secularised. It has also been observed that the emphasis on individual integrity, frugality and diligence among Pentecostal groups has led to rapid upward mobility. On these and other grounds, capitalist liberalism has found staunch defenders and legitimisers among Christian theologians.[15]

On the other hand the spiritualisation of the Christian concept of salvation by *Evangelical groups* has provoked the accusation that religion detracts from the task of social reconstruction by offering a "pie in the sky when you die". *Liberation theology*, by contrast, has vehemently attacked capitalist liberalism and added considerable fervour to the emancipatory and developmental drive of revolutionary movements, impoverished communities, ethnic minorities and feminists.[16] Not surprisingly it as been criticised for selling out the transcendent dimension of the biblical faith to Marxist assumptions. Christian theology needs to sort out this conflict within its ranks and I shall try to do so below.

Obviously *other religions* also have an economic impact of their own. African traditional religion, for example, is geared to ancestor veneration. It derives its system of values and norms from a sacred past, perpetuates a pre-scientific (magical and mythological) view of reality, and legitimates a patriarchal structure of society. The effects of Hinduism on upward mobility (the caste system in India), or on animal husbandry (prohibition to kill animals), are well-known. Muslim fundamentalists again reject the emancipation of women and other facets of modernity.

We cannot go into further detail. All we are saying is that *convictions are fundamental* to economic behaviour and must be subjected to critique. The tendency of economics and other social sciences to ignore the role of religion in social processes is *naive* at best and dangerous at worst. It is naive insofar as the motive for the exclusion of religion from the public realm is itself rooted in a particular conviction, namely the modern combination of secular humanism with empiricism and hedonism. That secular humanism represents what is normal and common to all human beings, while religious convictions are crazy fancies which should not be allowed to surface in public discourse, is nothing but the imperialist assumption of a dominant creed.

It is *dangerous* because, when conviction is relegated to the private spirituality of the individual, it is removed from public scrutiny, academic analysis and penetrating critique. A hidden, irrational and uncontrolled dimension of life can do incredible harm to human life, whether through long term clandestine influences, or through sudden violent eruptions. We must bring it into the open, take its pervasive influence seriously, and subject it to critique!

Critical dialogue in a pluralist society

Against which criteria can convictions be scrutinised? The problem is that there are no such criteria which are not embedded in convictions. There is also *no overarching spiritual authority*. If one conviction is measured against the criteria of another, it will obviously be found wanting. It will also not easily accept the criteria applied. It will justify itself on the basis of its own criteria. That is the price we have to pay for living in a pluralist society.

How do we deal with this problem? The *attempt to impose* the beliefs, values and norms of a particular religion or world view onto a pluralist society can only be undertaken by a state which is willing and able to use totalitarian means. This has often been attempted in history, including states supported by the Christian church. In our century fascism and communism are cases in point. Humankind has witnessed the immense human costs of totalitarian regimes and will want to steer clear of any such attempt. The sophisticated and incessant use of *mass media* by capitalist entrepreneurs to deconstruct conscience and arouse desire is much more subtle in its methods and far more effective in its results. We are far from having learnt to reject this kind of tyranny as well.

Whether in the form of totalitarian terror, or in the form of psychological seduction, impositions *destroy the dignity, the freedom and the responsibility of the human person.* Slaves cannot devise feasible and beneficial social systems. Nor can slaves effectively critique and challenge the social systems under which they labour. And systems which must be imposed prove that they are neither feasible nor beneficial — by the simple fact that they need to be imposed.

If we do not want impositions, we have to live with our differences. This does not imply, however, that convictions, values and norms have become meaningless, irrelevant or dispensable in a pluralist society. *Human life is not possible* without the three transcendent dimensions underlying all religious convictions: an overarching system of meaning, the assurance of one's right of existence, and the authority to take one's life into one's hands.

Nor can the truth claims of different convictions be relativised with impunity. While we should respect each other's convictions, we are in this boat together. Detrimental pursuits sanctioned by one conviction have consequences for people with other convictions. We cannot afford to ignore life-reducing convictions. There must be both *self-critique* within each conviction and *mutual critique* between different convictions. Critical dialogue between convictions can only take place in an atmosphere of transparency and trust. Participants must be willing to reveal their most fundamental assumptions and intentions to each other, and expose themselves to each other's critique.

In genuine pluralism, every group has the external, constitutional *right*, and the internal, religious *obligation* to witness to its convictions. If there are convictions which contradict one another, this simply means that they have to *enter into constructive dialogue and confrontation* with each other. Most of the time this happens implicitly — simply by interacting with each other. But it should also happen consciously and explicitly.

In such a dialogue the validity of a truth claim has to *establish itself* against the validity of a rival truth claim in the consciousness of both dialogue partners. There is no other way. A truth which cannot assert itself in human consciousness, without the help of social or psychological fortifications and pressures, is not the truth. It is in this spirit that the present appendix has been written.

Religious conviction and popular wisdom

So much for the religious discourse, a discourse which is of crucial importance in its own right, even for economics. It is highly unlikely, however, that even the most open, profound and frequent dialogue will ever bring about consensus at the level of religious conviction. That again does not imply, however, that a pluralist society is unable to function. In fact pluralist societies function remarkably well. This is possible because there is another layer of assumptions, values and norms, which is seemingly independent of particular religions and world views and which most members of the society *hold in common*.

This layer of assumptions is based on "popular wisdom". Popular wisdom is the outcome of the unceasing stream of *common experience and social interaction*. It is strongly determined by ongoing power struggles between collective interests and their ideological legitimations. The urge to conform to this driftsand of public opinion constitutes a soft kind of imposition. People subject themselves to fashions, fads, prejudices and superstitions because they want to be acceptable to their peers and have no better answers for the present. Therefore the designation of "civil religion" for this phenomenon is not without justification.

Popular wisdom provides support and direction in everyday life without demanding much reflection. To be convincing, however, popular wisdom *appeals to evidence, common sense and basic values*, which are simply taken for granted within a society. But it also exploits religious convictions to legitimate collective self-interest. It even lends respectability to irrational cravings, prejudices and superstitions of both communities and individuals.

Therefore popular wisdom is *unlikely to be very profound, consistent, or indeed valid*. It can be thoroughly misleading if based on error, indulgence and emotion. It can cause intolerance and violent conflict. Racism, ethnic nationalism, imperialism, revolutionary fervour, fundamentalist fanaticism, and the acquisitive mentality of our times are all examples of misguided sets of ideas which have grabbed particular population groups with devastating consequences.

Such aberrations *must not remain unchallenged*. It is the constant tasks of leaders, academics, journalists and educators to clean out factual errors by means of empirical evidence; to spell out the unacceptable consequences of a line of thought; to call for responsibility; to penetrate wayward sets of arguments with the light of reason, and to keep social processes on track. That is the secular level of discourse.

Ultimately it is impossible, however, to deal adequately with assumptions, values and norms on the level of observation and reason. As mentioned above, convictions are not grounded in fact and argument, but in aspiration, inspiration, intuition, and vision. It is the task of representatives of religious convictions to transcend the superficial levels of popular wisdom towards its more profound foundations.

It is on the *secular level* that our discourse in the first 8 chapters of this book has been conducted. We tried to unearth the facts, subject them to critical analysis, and come up with suggestions based on reasonable argument. It is now our task to go to the *transcendent foundations* of human life — at least in a very rudimentary form — because the secular discourse is ultimately grounded in the transcendent dimension of life. We shall now attempt to do that in terms of the Christian faith. As mentioned above, this does not preclude non-Christians to do the same in terms of their own convictions.

Section IV - Economics and the thrust of the biblical faith

Mission in general is a process in which people are activated by the *irresistible urge of a vision.* That is also true for other powerful convictions such as Islam, secular humanism and Marxism. The word "irresistible" is not meant to conjure up images of enslavement and tyranny. It only points to an authority which transcends our fears and desires and enlists our commitment and dedication. In any kind of mission there is something to be achieved, or a goal to be reached.

The biblical faith believes in a personal God. This God has disclosed himself as a God with a vision. According to the biblical witness the ultimate goal of God is the *comprehensive wellbeing* of all human beings within the context of the comprehensive wellbeing of their entire social and natural contexts. The Old Testament calls this vision shalom, the New Testament calls it the "kingdom of God", or "the age to come".

These ancient concepts express the discrepancy between what is and what ought to be in cosmic, communal and personal terms. Even a cursory look at the biblical witness reveals the pervasive contention that God's goal has not been achieved. It can be argued that the yawning discrepancy between what is and what ought to be primarily refers to our personal relationship with God. But who is this God? God is conceptualised by the biblical faith as the Master and Redeemer of the universe as a whole. It is his intention to reconcile *all things* to him in Christ.[17]

The biblical faith has *three ways* of expressing what ought to be. In terms of space it speaks of "heaven above", where "God's will is done".[18] In terms of time it speaks of "the beginning", when reality "was very good",[19] and "the end" when there will be "a new heaven and a new earth in which righteousness dwells".[20] In each case what ought to be is beyond what is — and in conflict with what is.

The important consideration here is that what ought to be is not something entirely different from what is, but *represents the authentic version* of what is - the design into which current reality is supposed to be transformed. God, the creator and master of reality, is not at peace with the world until this transformation has taken place. Mission is the expression of God's restlessness, which translates into the restlessness of his people. Their "peace with God", achieved by the cross and resurrection of Christ, can only mean that they share this redemptive restlessness of God. It is the anticipation of God's future which forms the basis of their hope and their action.

Due to historical circumstances, which cannot be spelt out here, the biblical future orientation has become *ever more comprehensive and radical* in its historical evolution. In its earliest stages limited and down-to-earth concerns drew the biblical faith into the future. Examples are Abraham's need for male progeny; the people of Israel's need for freedom from Egyptian slavery; the need of roaming nomads for a country of their own, and the need of dispersed Israelite tribes for a centralised authority (a king) to defend themselves against Philistine raids.

Towards the end of this history, however, concerns had become *universal*. Apocalyptic speculations proclaimed the demolition and reconstruction of the entire universe to be close at hand, while its hellenistic counterpart maintained that we could leave this world behind for a better, spiritual world.

Both these versions *radicalised* the biblical hope for a world become whole. The biblical concept of redemption is comprehensive by definition. It includes body and psyche; reason and emotion; identity and integrity; communal, social, political, economic and ecological concerns. A reduction of God's salvation to an imaginary peace of disembodied souls, taken out of their social and natural contexts, a peace concluded with a purely spiritual God and in a timeless heaven, ostensibly located somewhere above the struggles and agonies of this world — such a reduction is an aberration of the biblical faith, which deprives it of its missionary power and its situational relevance.

Human needs as targets of God's redemptive concern

If it is true that the ultimate goal of God is the comprehensive wellbeing of his creation as a whole, then the specific targets of God's redemptive action are *particular deficiencies in comprehensive wellbeing*. According to the biblical witness these deficiencies can occur in any dimension of life: disease, famine, barrenness, broken families, ostracism, defeat on the battle field, drought, social chaos, unjust rulers, a guilty conscience — whatever.

To understand God's mission in its total context, therefore, we have to analyse the structure of human needs. For our purposes the distinction between immanent and transcendent needs is of particular interest:

- *Immanent needs* belong to the sphere which is, in principle, accessible to human understanding and under human control. They include physical, psychological, intellectual, communal, social, economic, political and ecological needs. When the Israelites were liberated from Egyptian slavery, and when Jesus healed the sick and fed the hungry, God was seen as acting redemptively at this level.

- *Transcendent needs* go beyond human accessibility and control. They include a valid system of meaning, assurance of one's right of existence, and the authority to use one's powers to achieve one's goals. When Christians speak of the forgiveness of sins, or of justification by faith, this refers to God's affirmation of our right to exist in spite of our failures. In all cultures, world views and religions, meaning, assurance and authority are ultimately derived from a source beyond human control, on which life is perceived to depend.

Transcendent needs do not occur on their own but form the *depth dimension of immanent needs*. For Abraham, for instance, the question whether God would allow his family to die out or whether he would give him a son was an expression of the deeper question whether God was for him, and with him, and not against him. That is a decisive insight, because it prevents us from spiritualising the Christian message. Experiences of deprivation, misery, rejection, disease, inexplicable fate, vulnerability and mortality are the mainspring of the human quest for meaning, reassurance and authority.

At the root of the biblical faith lies the conviction that *God responds redemptively to this whole range of human needs*, whether immanent or transcendent. God's "justification of the sinner", for instance, is a response to the transcendent need for one's right of existence. The latter can be questioned, not only by personal guilt and failure, but also by a fateful accident or by grinding poverty. The presuppositions are that God has the *power* to redeem and that God has the *will* to redeem. God's mastery and God's benevolence are the most fundamental assumptions of the biblical faith.

Without doubt the problem of the *right of existence* — expressed in terms such as acceptability, belonging, legitimation, and justification — has become the pivot of faith in God in New Testament times. The rabbinic tradition insisted on the validity of God's demand that the torah, which is the law found in the Old Testament, be kept. Those who kept the law were blessed, and saved eternally, those who failed to keep the law, were cursed, and condemned eternally.[21]

The apostle Paul, especially, realised that, if this were the case, we would all be condemned. No human being is not a sinner! In Christ, however, *God accepts the unacceptable* into his fellowship, suffering their unacceptability. He does this not to condone, but to overcome their frailty and failure, by granting them participation in his creative authority, his redemptive concern and his comprehensive vision. This is the basis of their participation in God's mission, thus the basis of Christian ethics.[22]

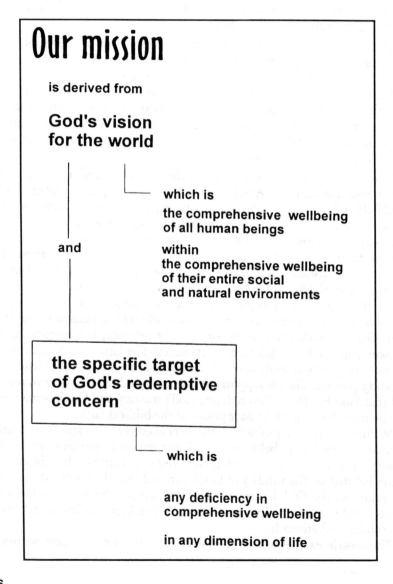

Our mission

is derived from

God's vision for the world

which is
the comprehensive wellbeing
of all human beings

and

within
the comprehensive wellbeing
of their entire social
and natural environments

**the specific target
of God's redemptive
concern**

which is

any deficiency in
comprehensive wellbeing

in any dimension of life

Participation in God's mission

The biblical witness maintains that God's redemptive intention, just as his creative mastery, is *mediated by inner-worldly events and human actions*. According to the biblical witness God uses his creatures to intervene as Judge and Redeemer within the realm of his creation. The highest manifestation of this is God's redemptive act in Christ.

Those who belong to Christ are *privileged to participate* in the life and service of Christ. Pauline theology speaks of the Christian community as the "Body of Christ". A body is the concrete manifestation of a person, the material basis of his/her action and communication in this world. By sharing the new life of Christ in the fellowship of God, the Christian community participates in God's creative authority, God's redemptive concern and God's comprehensive vision.

It is this participation which makes the pull of the Christian vision and the urge of the Christian mission "irresistible". Where we do not experience this dynamic, we are not involved in God's mission. We simply theorise and moralise. For mission to get off the ground we need a *spiritual awakening* which involves us in God's response to the entire spectrum of human needs.

There are two complementary ways of meeting transcendent needs:

- The first is to *fulfil* the immanent needs which gave rise to the transcendent needs in the first place. To regain meaning, assurance and authority, outcasts must be accepted into communities, famine victims must be fed, warring factions must be reconciled. When feeding the hungry, we affirm their dignity — that is, their right to exist — and restore their authority over their own lives.

- But our capacity to put things right is limited. The second way of meeting transcendent needs, therefore, is to *go beyond* the limitations placed upon our own abilities and the possibilities of this world. This happens through prayer, proclamation and symbolic enactment. A cancer patient is reassured of God's redemptive purposes (meaning), God's personal concern (assurance) and God's calling (authority). The capacity of humans to transcend the limitations imposed upon their lives in this world makes it possible for them *not to accept* the proposition that experienced reality as such is ultimate. Our limits and the limits of our world are not the limits of God. That is the basis of human freedom.

Under no circumstances may the second act, the act of transcending our limits, bypass the first. Transcendence is legitimate only at the point where we have reached our limitations, *not before*. To tell a sick person that her disease is of no consequence because her soul has been healed in Christ, or to tell an oppressed person that slavery is of no consequence because we are all set free in Christ, is fraudulent.

Mission and the economic discourse

Needs are always *historically and contextually specific*. To be relevant, Christian mission has to ask where the needs of actual people are located in actual situations. As mentioned above, these can be war, oppression, famine, disease, cultural anomie, spiritual enslavement, pangs of guilt and remorse, or whatever. Mission also has to seek for the most effective means available and utilise them courageously and judiciously to get out of the predicament.

For that purpose Christians, like other humans, have been given their healthy powers of *observation, reason and determination.* Christians believe that they are not slaves but mature "sons and daughters of God".[23] They share in God's redemptive purposes and they share in God's creative power. They do not need to be led by the hand, nor do they have to look up rules for their conduct in the Bible. The biblical witness is only a prototypical series of narratives which depict God's specific action in particular situations.

In this book we have been dealing with *a particular complex of problems* with which contemporary humanity has to struggle: industrialisation; marginalistion; population growth; destruction of nature; depletion of scarce resources; armed conflict with ever more devastating weaponry, and so on. What is the way out of these predicaments? Liberals and socialists have come up with models and supporting arguments. Some of these models have been in operation for some time and we are in a position to sort out their merits and their flaws. That is what we have been doing in this book.

All this is completely in line with the mission of God in this world - as long as it is *guided by the redemptive concern of God.* The God in whom we believe is not merely interested in personal peace of mind or harmonious family relationships, as most Sunday sermons seem to suggest. Our God is interested in any instance where the welfare of his people is hampered by any kind of suffering. And he wants us to get at the roots of this suffering.

Christian directives are meant to be flexible, relevant and *universally valid.* They must be able to make sense to any unbiased and reasonable human being, irrespective of culture or creed, simply because they are built on a redemptive motivation, profound analysis, and sober judgment. If they are not, they are also not valid, whether for Christians or for anybody else.

The world under God

Two paradigmatic texts, one from the Old Testament and one from the New Testament, may serve to illustrate the way in which the biblical witness perceives God's concern for the world as a whole.

* In the Ancient Near East, collective mindsets which determined the lives of people were conceptualised in the form of divinities. In Psalm 82 one

finds the depiction of a heavenly court case. The "gods", who had been mandated to rule over the nations, are called to give account of their actions. They are found wanting, condemned and demoted — not because, metaphysically speaking, there can be only one God, but because they have failed to *uphold God's justice* among the nations. It is an ethical, not a speculative criterion that is being applied. To Israel it does not really matter what non-Israelite rulers believe in, as long as their conviction is in line with God's justice — here defined as upholding the rights of the poor and powerless.

- We find a similar model in Eph 1:20ff. The risen Christ, representing authentic humanity, is enthroned above all authorities and powers that rule over this world. The rule of God, represented by Christ, is universal. But the kingdom of Christ is distinguished from its instrument, the "Body of Christ". The body of Christ is the community of believers composed of Jews and Gentiles: it is representative of humankind as a whole (Eph 2). According to Eph 3:10 the special task of this community is to *inform the cosmic powers* of God's ultimate purposes. They are to execute their rule according to the norm of redemptive concern, as revealed in Christ's self-giving love. They also have to fall in line with the vision of God to unite the entire universe under this norm. Once again, their existence, identity and authority as such are not questioned, but they are subjected to the criteria of God's redemptive concern and God's comprehensive vision.

One could also refer to the Protestant teaching of the *two kingdoms of God*.[24] According to Luther, God rules both internally and externally: through his Word in our hearts, and through public offices and institutions in society. Both of these realms are under God's authority and subject to the criterion of God's redemptive love. Public leaders do not have to be Christians, but they are expected to serve the interests of the people entrusted to their care to the best of their ability. Under no circumstance may they utilise their power for personal or collective self-interest at the expense of their subjects.

Calvin has taken over this model from Luther, though in a modified form which does not concern us here. Catholic social thought has operated with the concept of a *natural law*. This set of norms can only be established by detecting the rationale behind particular aspects of experienced reality. Thus sexuality is meant to serve procreation. In sum, the Christian tradition not only allows Christians to participate in "secular" attempts to find workable and just solutions; they are actually *called upon* to do so.

To summarise

To ignore the assumptions, values and norms which underpin human attitudes, decisions and actions leads to a truncated picture of reality in the social sciences. Convictions and interests need to be *exposed, critiqued and led into dialogue* with each other. This is particularly important in this case because the ideologies we discussed in this book are secular offshoots from the Western Jewish-Christian heritage.

The mission of God, as Christians understand it, *encompasses secular responsibility.* God wants us to carry his redemptive concern into all corners of the world in which we live and on which we depend. Our God has no favourites. "He makes his sun rise on the evil and the good, and sends rain on the righteous and the unrighteous."[25]

When confronted with people who hold another conviction, Christians have to witness to their faith in a dialogue between equals. When confronted with economic problems, they have to enter the economic discourse on the basis of *observation and reason* and act redemptively in this context. But they should do so *in responsibility to God*, and in solidarity with all affected members of the human family. We have a common problem, we speak a common language, and we seek a common solution.

Notes

1   Ernst Bloch 1970: *Atheismus im Christentum: Zur Religion des Exodus und des Reichs.* Reinbek: Rowohlt.

2   "To be Christian is to be socialist": Summer School lecture at the Univ of Cape Town in Jan 1994.

3   Drucker 1993:10.

4   Nürnberger 1987.

5   Is 52-53.

6   Deut 7.

7   H J Maaz 1995: *Behind the Wall: The inner life of communist Germany.* W W Norton.

8   Refer to Gal 3 or Eph 2.

9   Friedrich Gogarten 1953: *Verhängnis und Hoffnung der Neuzeit: Die Säkularisierung als theologisches Problem.* Stuttgart: Friedrich Vorwerk.

10 Gen 1:28ff. The ideas was first mooted by Carl Amery 1972: *Das Ende der Vorsehung: Die gnadenlosen Folgen des Christentums.* Reinbeck: Rowohlt.

11 See my article: Is the human being a profit and pleasure maximiser? The concept of the homo oeconomicus in economic theory as a deceptive norm and its theological demythologisation. *Religion & Theology*, Vol 3, No 3, 1996.

12 Max Weber 1969 (1905): *Die Protestantische Ethik.* Hamburg: Siebenstern.

13 FN R H Tawney 1969 (1926): *Religion and the rise of capitalism.* Harmondsworth: Penguin.

14 For a new assessment see Budde 1992.

15 E.g. Novak 1982.

16 E.g. Hinkelammert 1986.

17 Col 1:19f; Eph 1:20-23; Heb 1:2; Mat 28:18f.

18 Cf the Lord's prayer.

19 Gn 1.

20 FN 2 Pet 3:13.

21 Superbly formulated in Deuteronomy, e.g. Deut 30:15ff.

22 Refer to Romans 3, or Eph 2.

23 Gal 3:23ff. "Son of God" is a royal title in Ancient Near Eastern cultures which expresses the status of the king as God's representative and plenipotentiary. Cf Ps 2.

24 For detail see my essay: Martin Luther's political ethics against the background of his theological approach. *Theologia Evangelica* XVIII/1985 44-65.

25 Mt 5:45.

ANNOTATED BIBLIOGRAPHY

{Note: The literature on topics discussed in this book is unfathomable. The following items are those that I have used or jotted down over the years. I have concentrated on recent literature and added some classics. To assist the student to gain entry I have arranged them under headings, added a short annotation to some of them in brackets, and indicated the shelf numbers in the UNISA and UNP libraries if I happened to have them ready.}

A. Aspects of capitalism, socialism, and Marxism-Leninism in general

Amuzegar J 1981: *Comparative economics: National priorities, policies, and performance.* Cambridge Mass: Winthrop. [Very instructive comparisons.]

Armstrong, Ph et al 1991: *Capitalism since 1945.* Oxford: Basil Blackwell.

Arnold, N Scott 1990: *Marx's radical critique of capitalist society.* London et al: Oxford Univ Press.

Bahro, Rudolf 1978: *The alternative in Eastern Europe.* New York: Routledge, Chapman & Hall. [A critical stance against the system in East Germany which cost him his carreer.]

Bardhan, Pranab & Roemer, John E 1992: Market Socialism: A case for rejuvenation. *Journal of Economic Perspectives*, 6/1992 101-116.

Barratt Brown, Michael 1984: *Models in political economy: A guide to the arguments.* London: Penguin. [An overview of the main models designed to explain capitalist and socialist systems from a left-wing perspective.] UNISA 338.9 BARR.

Basu, K, Majumdar, M & Mitra, T (eds): *Capital, investment and development.* Oxford: Blackwell. UNISA 330 CAPI. [Essays in honour of prominent Indian economist S Chakravarty highlighting development and the capitalism-socialism debate.]

Becker, David G et al 1987: *Postimperialism: Capitalism and development in the late 20th Century.* Boulder: Lynne Rienner.

Berger P L 1986: *The capitalist revolution: Fifty propositions about prosperity, equality, and liberty.* New York: Basic Books. UNP 330.122 BER. [An apology for capitalism; the emphasis lies on empirical tests of certain hypotheses.]

Berger, P L 1987: *Equality in America: Modern Capitalism*, vol I. Lanham: Univ Press of America.

Berger, P L 1987: *Equality in the Third World: Modern Capitalism*, vol II. Lanham: Univ Press of America.

Berger, Peter (no date): *The structure of freedom.* Grand Rapids: Eerdmans. UNP 323.01 BER

Bertramsen, R B, Thomsen J P F & Torfing, J 1991: *State, economy and society.* London: Unwin Hyman. [A modern Neo-Marxist analysis of the problems of state intervention.]

Bleaney, Michael 1988: *Do socialist economies work? The Soviet and East European experience.* Oxford: Oxford Univ Press. UNP 338.947 BLE

Blumberg, Paul 1989: *The predatory society: Deception in the American marketplace.* Oxford: Oxf Univ Press.

Boote, Anthony R & Somogyi, Janos 1991:

For missing items, refer to other sections of the bibliography

Economic reform in Hungary since 1968.
Occas. Paper No 83. Washington DC:
IMF.

Bottomore, Tom B 1985: *Theories of modern
capitalism.* London: Allen & Unwin.
UNP 330.122 BOT [Analyses the positions of Marx, Weber, Schumpeter and
Hayek.]

Bottomore, Tom B 1990: *The socialist economy: Theory and practice.* New York:
Guilford Pr. [Defends economic planning in spite of the failures of the
regimes in Eastern Europe.]

Buhle, Paul 1987: *Marxism in the United
States: Remapping the history of the
American Left.* London: Verso. UNISA
335.409 73 BUHL [A history of
Marxist thought, action and influence
in the country most antagonistic to its
philosophy.]

Chappell, D J 1980: *An economic history of
England: From 1066 to the present day.*
Plymouth: Macdonald and Evans.
UNISA 330.942 CHA. [Invaluable
overview of the entire economic history
of England from the Middle Ages, the
country where the agricultural revolution, the industrial revolution and the
seminal thoughts of Karl Marx have
originated.]

Clegg, S R & Redding, S G 1990:
Capitalism in contrasting cultures. New
York: de Gruyter.

Crone, Patricia 1989: *Pre-industrial societies.*
Oxford: Basil Blackwell. [Argues that,
in contrast to stable economic and
political systems such as those found in
India, China and Islamic countries, feudal society in medieval Europe was frac-
tured and conflict ridden, providing
space for independent cities, democratic institutions and a dynamic bour-
geoisioe to develop, which were the driving forces behind early capitalism.]

Dahl, Robert A. 1985: *A preface to economic
democracy.* Berkeley: Univ of Calif. Press.
["If democracy is justified in governing
the state, then it must also be justified in
governing economic enterprises"]

Davies, C 1992: The Protestant ethic and
the comic spirit of capitalism. *Brit
Journ of Sociol.* 43/1992 421-42. [Good
description of Weber's thesis that the
development of capitalism was legitimated and encouraged by Puritanism;
evidence of the "spirit of capitalism" in
popular jokes.]

Davis, H & Scase, R 1985: *Western capitalism and state socialism: Comparative perspectives.* Oxford: Basil Blackwell. UNP
330.122 DAV.

Dembinski, Pawel H 1991: *The logic of the
planned economy: The seeds of collapse.*
Oxford: Clarendon. UNP 330.124 DEM

Derber, Charles et al 1990: *Power in the
highest degree: Professionals, capitalism and
the rise of a new Mandarine order.* Oxford:
Oxf Univ Press.

Drucker, P F 1992: The post-capitalism
world. *Public Interest* 109/1992, 89-100.
[Believes that we are entering a new age
beyond socialism and capitalism.]

Drucker, P F 1993: *Post-capitalist society.*
London et al: Butterworth- Heinemann.

Dumenil, G & Levy, D 1993: *The economics
of the profit rate: Competition, crises and
historical tendencies in capitalism.*
Aldershot Hants: Edward Elgar.
UNISA 338.516 DUME [Focus on the
profit rate as determinant of fluctuations in the capitalist system.]

Dyker, David A 1990: *Yugoslavia: Socialism,
development and debt.* London:
Routledge. UNISA 338.949 7 DYKE.

Eatwell, R & Wright A (eds) 1993:
Contemporary political ideologies. London:
Pinter. UNISA 320.5 MODE
[Descriptive overview of modern ideolo-
gies including liberalism, conservatism,
social democracy and democratic social-

ism, communism, anarchism, nationalism, fascism and ecologism.]

Feinberg, R E, Echeverri-Gent, J & Müller, F (eds) 1990: *Economic reform in three giants.* New Brunswick (USA) / Oxford (UK): Transaction Books. UNISA 338.9 ECON [Describes economic reforms in the Soviet Union, China and India after the failure of socialism, as well as its geopolitical consequences.]

Friedman, Milton 1962: *Capitalism and freedom.* Chicago: Univ of Chic Press. [Leading thinker of the neo-liberal approach].

Fields, Gary S 1980: *Poverty, inequality, and development.* Cambridge: Cambridge Univ Press. UNISA 338.567 09 FIE [Shows that there is no trade-off between equality and development.]

Fukuyama, Francis 1992: *The end of history and the last man.* New York: Free Press (London: Hamish Hamilton). [Influential contemporary thinker who believes in the final victory of capitalist liberalism.]

Funderburk, C & Thobaben, R G 1989: *Political ideologies: left, center, right.* New York: Harper Collins. UNISA 320.5 FUND [A simple overview over ideologies, including communism, democratic socialism, liberalism, conservatism, authoritarianism, fascism.]

Galbraith, John Kenneth 1958: *The affluent society.* Boston: Houghton Mifflin. [Classical Western critique of capitalism].

Galbraith John Kenneth 1967: *The new industrial state.* Harmondsworth: Penguin. [Describes the post World War II economy in Western countries and dispels economic myths.]

Galbraith, John Kenneth 1992: *The culture of contentment.* London: Penguin. [Criticises the hypocrisy of satisfied voters who emphasise the harmful effects of state intervention when it benefits the poor, but clamour for it when it benefits the rich]

Gerrard, Bill 1989: *Theory of the capitalist economy: Towards a post-classical synthesis.* Oxford et al: Basil Blackwell. UNP 330.122 GER. [Shows that classical economic theory offers no solution to the problem of unemployment.]

Gilbert, Neil 1985: *Capitalism and the welfare state: Dilemmas of social benevolence.* New Haven: Yale Univ Press.

Gross, Bertram 1985: *Friendly Fascism : The new face of power in America.* Montreal: Black Rose. [Radical critique of power concentration and abuse of power in the US].

Grundmann, Reiner 1991: *Marxism and ecology.* Oxford: Oxford Univ Press.

Haas, Michael 1991: *Cambodia, Pol Pot and the United States: The Faustian pact.* New York et al: Praeger. UNISA 327.730 596 HAAS. [Describes the problematic role of the US in the conflict in Indo-China, claiming that the brutal communist regime of the Khmer Rouge was a product of US diplomacy.]

Hain, Peter 1996: *Ayes to the left: A future for socialism.* Lawrence & Wishart. [An attempt to formulate a winning left-wing agenda of "libertarian socialism" for the Labour Party in the UK.]

Hampe P 1986: Imperialism. *World Encyclopedia of Peace*, Vol 1. Oxford: Pergamon, pp 429-437.

Hartmann, C & Vilanova, P (eds) 1992: Paradigms lost: The post Cold War era. London et al: Pluto Press.

Harvey, David 1982: *The limits to capital.* Oxford: Basil Blackwell. [A modern analysis and critique of the capitalist system from a Marxian perspective.]

Hay D A & Vickers J (eds) 1987: *The economics of market dominance.* Oxford: Blackwell.

Hayek, F A von 1976: *Law, legislation and liberty*, vol 2: The mirage of social justice. London: Routledge & Kegan Paul.

        For missing items, refer to other sections of the bibliography

Hayek, F A von 1983: *Knowledge, evolution and society*. London: Adam Smith Inst. [Leading thinker of the new right wing.]

Hayek, F A von 1988: *The fatal conceit*. Chicago: Univ of Chicago Press. [Powerful attack on Marxism by the "father of neo-conservatism". See also his early attack against Marxism "The road to serfdom" 1944.]

Heilbroner, Robert L 1985: *The nature and logic of capitalism*. New York / London: Norton. UNISA 330.122 HEIL [Very instructive and easy introduction by a prominent economist informed by classical and Marxist analysis. Consult chapters 2 - 6.]

Heilbroner, Robert L 1988: *Behind the veil of economics: Essays in the worldly philosophy*. New York / London: Norton. UNISA 330.122 HEIL [Assails the ideological assumption of capitalist economics.]

Henry, John E 1990: *The making of neoclassical economics*. London: Unwin Hyman.

Hillinger, Claude (ed) 1992: *Cyclical growth in market and planned economies*. Oxford: Clarendon Press. UNISA 338.542 CYCL. [German and Hungarian research which seems to show that fluctuations are the result of adjustment lags in investment and production, or accelerator-based investment cycles.]

Hirschman A O 1977: *The passions and the interests: political arguments for capitalism before its triumph*. Princeton NJ: University Press.

Hoover, K & Plant, R 1989: *Conservative capitalism in Britain and the United States: A critical appraisal*. London / New York: Routledge. UNISA 320.520 941 HOOV [A description and critique of the economic policies of Thatcher and Reagan from a modern leftist point of view]

Hunt E K 1986: *Property and prophets: The evolution of economic institutions and ideologies*. London et al: Harper and Row. [Offers a broad historical overview of the development of major economic institutions and contemporary schools of thought. Easy to understand.]

Hunt E K & Sherman H J 1981: *Economics: An introduction to traditional and radical views*. London et al: Harper and Row, fourth or later edition. [A useful text book on economics, taking account of capitalist and Marxist views.]

Hunt, R N Carew 1950: *The theory and practice of communism*. Harmondsworth: Penguin. [Though outdated, it is still a useful introduction.]

Ingersol D E & Matthews R K 1991 (1986): *The philosophical roots of modern ideologies: Liberalism, communism, fascism*. NY et al: Prentice Hall. UNP 320.5 ING

Kenworthy, Lane 1990: What kind of economic system? A leftist guide. *Socialist Review*, 20/1990, pp 102-124. [Useful but much more complex overview of economic policy options.]

King, Desmond S 1987: *The New Right: Politics, markets and citizenship*. London: Macmillan. UNISA 320.52 KING. [Description of the history, the arguments and the applications of New Right policies under Thatcher and Reagan.]

Klitgaard, Robert 1993: *Adjusting to reality: beyond "state vs market" in economic development*. UNP INR/LS 338.90091724KLI [Shows that Third World countries are faced with a set of problems different from the alternative between capitalist and socialist approaches.]

Kolakowski L 1978: *Main currents of Marxism: Its rise, growth and dissolution*. 3 volumes. Oxford: Clarendon. UNP 335.409 KOL.

Korten, David C 1990: *Getting to the 21st Century: Voluntary action and the global agenda.* West Hartford, Conn: Kumarian Press.

Leatt J 1987: Neither Adam Smith nor Karl Marx. In: Fischer, A & Abeldas, M (eds) 1987: *A question of survival: Conversations with key South Africans.* Johannesburg: Jonathan Ball. [A good introduction, following the same line as this book.]

Lehman, Howard P 1993: *Indebted development: Strategic bargaining and economic adjustment in the Third World.* London: Macmillan. UNISA 338.900 917 24. [Provides background to the debt problem in the Third World.]

Levitas, Ruth (ed) 1986: *The ideology of the New Right.* Cambridge: Polity Press. UNISA 320.52 IDEO.

Lichtheim G 1975: *A short history of socialism.* London: Fontana. UNP 335.009 LIC. [Good historical overview.]

Lichtheim G 1982 (1969): *Marxism: an historical and critical study.* London: Allen Lane.

Lindblom C E 1977: *Politics and markets: The world's political-economic systems.* New York: Basic Books. UNP 330 LIN [A thorough analysis of the relation between state control and the market mechanism.]

Lux, Kenneth 1990: *Adam Smith's mistake: How a moral philosopher invented economics and ended morality.* Boston: Shambala.

Lydall H 1984: *Yugoslav socialism: Theory and practice.* Oxford: Clarendon Press. [Good text on principles, history and performance.]

Marx, Karl 1948 (1848): *The Communist Manifesto: Centenary edition.* London: Lawrence & Wishart. UNISA 335.4 MARX. [Use any edition. Absolutely critical for an understanding of Marxism. For other writings of Marx

see the great issue of the works of Marx and Engels published by Lawrence and Wishart in 1976.]

Millar, James R 1981: *The ABCs of Soviet socialism.* Urbana IL: Univ of Illinois Press. UNISA 330.947 MIL

Millar, James R 1990: *The Soviet economic experiment.* Urbana IL: Univ of Illinois Press.

Mises, Ludwig von 1979: *Economic policy: Thoughts for today and tomorrow.* South Bend Ind: Rennery/Gateway. UNISA 330.157 VONM [A spirited advocacy of capitalist liberalism versus its socialist counterpart by a classical proponent.]

Mises, Ludwig von 1985 (1962): *Liberalism in the classical tradition.* San Francisco: Cobden. [Seminal thinker of modern economic and political liberalism, defending the free market and limited government.]

Moll, Peter G 1991: *The great economic debate.* Johannesburg: Skotaville. [The reader will detect that the word "radical" has changed from Marxist-Leninist to social democratic connotations.]

Newman, K S 1988: *Falling from grace: The experience of downward mobility in the American Middle Class.* London: Collier MacMillan. [Analyses the effects of "downward mobility" of higher level executives due to recession in a capitalist economy.]

Nkrumah, Kwame 1965: *Neo-colonialism: The last stage of imperialism.* London: Panaf. [Applies Lenin's thesis that imperialism was necessitated by the capitalism to post-independent Africa.]

Nozick, R 1974: *Anarchy, state and utopia.* Oxford: Basil Blackwell. [Neo-classical liberal defense of the free market.]

Offe Claus 1985: *Disorganized capitalism : Contemporary transformations of work and politics.* Cambridge: Polity Press.

For missing items, refer to other sections of the bibliography

[Discusses, inter alia, unemployment in modeern capitalist societies.]

Ordelheide, D & Pfaff, D 1994: *European Financial Reporting - Germany.* London / New York: Routledge.

Pack, Spencer J 1991: *Capitalism as a moral system: Adam Smith's critique of the free market economy.* Aldershot, Hants: Edward Elgar. UNP 330.122 PAC. [Shows that Adam Smith was a moralist who had a social and liberal conscience.]

Paul, E F, Miller F D, Paul, J & Ahrens, J (eds): *Marxism and liberalism.* Oxford: Basil Blackwell. UNISA 320.51 MARX. [Tries to explore the compatibility between Marxism and liberalism.]

Phelps Brown, Henry 1988: *Egalitarianism and the generation of inequality.* New York: Oxford Univ Press. [Summarises the literature on inequality. Indicates the religious-psychological roots of the drive for equality. A reviewer comments that egalitarianism is often more rhetoric than practice among upper class Western egalitarians and revolutionaries alike, and where pracised, it has led to greater problems for the poor.]

Pinchot, G & Pinchot, E 1993: *The end of bureaucracy and the rise of the intelligent organization.* San Francisco: Berrett-Koehler. [An inspiring book advocating not only industrial democracy, but participatory democracy at the work place, with a strong emphasis on moral accountability.]

Popper, Karl 1966: *The open society and its enemies.* London: Routledge and Kegan Paul. [A classic defense of liberal democracy against totalitarianism, including Marxism.] UNP 320.5 POP

Prout, Christopher 1985: *Market Socialism in Yugoslavia.* London: Oxford Univ Press. UNISA 338.949 7 PROU. [Good overview of the original system.]

Reeve, Andrew 1986: *Property.* London: Macmillan. UNISA 330.17 REEV

Robinson: Herbert W 1991: *The challenge to government: Management of a capitalist economy.* Fountain Hills AZ: IMS Press. [Argues that government is, in fact, managing the economy in a capitalist country and should do so more consciously and purposefully.]

Robinson, Joan 1990: *An essay on Marxian economics.* Philadelphia: Porcupine Press, 2nd ed.

Roemer, John E 1988: *Free to loose: An introduction to Marxist economic philosophy.* Cambridge: Harvard Univ Press.

Rostow, W W 1990 (1960): *The stages of economic growth: A non-communist manifesto.* Cambridge: Cambridge Univ Press, 3rd edition. UNISA 339.5 ROST. [A classical statement of liberal development theory; see the critique of Marxism in chapter 10.]

Rothschild, K W (ed) 1971: *Power in economics: Selected readings.* Harmonds-worth: Penguin. [Though outdated, it gives an impression on the leftist debate in the sicties.]

Rubinstein, W.D.1993: *Capitalism, Culture and Decline in Britain 1750-1990.* New York: Routledge.

Ryan, Allan 1984: *Property and political theory.* Oxford: Basil Blackwell. UNISA 330.17 RYAN

Sachs, Wolfgang (ed) 1992: *The development dictionary: A guide to knowledge as power.* London: Zed Books, second ed. [A collection of essays on relevant themes from an unconventional and critical point of view. Consult e.g. the essays on "Market" by G Berthoud pp 70ff and on "Socialism" by H Cleaver pp 233.]

Schmidt, Manfred G 1987: West Germany: The policy of the Middle Way. *Journ Publ Pol,* vol 7/1987 135-177. [German state intervention has been based on a unique combination of conservative-reformist, liberal and social democratic policies, thus bridging pure forms of welfare capitalism and market capitalism, after lessons learnt from historical catastrophes. Indispensable for an understanding of the German success story.]

Schumpeter, Joseph A 1943: *Capitalism, socialism and democracy*. London: Allen & Unwin. [Classical author of the "Austrian school".]

Seligson, Mitchell A 1984: *The gap between rich and poor: Contending perspectives on the political economy of development*. Boulder / London: Westview.

Senge, Peter 1990: *The fifth discipline: The art and practice of the learning organisation*. New York et al: Doubleday. [Instructive introduction to systems thinking in the enterprise.]

Shtromas, Alexsandras (ed) 1993: The end of "Isms"? *Political Studies*, vol XLI, Special Issue. [Various views on whether economic ideologies, particularly socialism, have come to their end.]

Sik Ota 1985: *For a human economic democracy*. New York: Praeger. (*Ein Wirtschaftssystem der Zukunft*. Berlin: Springer). UNISA 330 SIK/SPRING. [Influential Eastern European thinker from the time of the Prague Spring. No English version available.]

Sisson, Keith 1987: *The management of collective bargaining: An international comparison*. Oxford / New York: Blackwell. [Very instructive book on experiences made so far in the field of employer-union-state relations in Western countries.]

Slovo, J 1990: *Has socialism failed?* London: Inkukuleko Publ. UNP 3354.4 SLO

Smith, Adam 1976 (1776/1802): *An inquiry into the nature and causes of the wealth of nations*. Oxford: Clarendon. UNISA 330.15 SMI [Fundamental for the argument of capitalist liberalism.]

Streeten, P 1992: What's left of what's left?

Or: what does it mean to be a socialist today? *The Review of Black Political Economy* 21/1992, 5-18. [The left groping for directions.]

Tawney, R H 1948: *The acquisitive society*. New York: Harcourt, Brace & Co. [Classic Western critique of capitalism.]

Tawney, R H 1969 (1926): *Religion and the rise of capitalism*. Harmondsworth: Penguin. [A parallel to Weber's famous 'Protestant Ethic' thesis.]

Turner, R K, Pearce, D & Bateman, I 1994: *Environmental economics: An elementary introduction*. New York et al: Harvester Wheatsheaf.

Vicarelli, Fausto (ed) 1985: *Keynes's relevance today*. London: Macmillan, sec ed. UNISA 330.156 KEYN. [Defense of the type of state intervention proposed by Keynes against the upcoming monetarist school.]

Von Weizsäcker, Ernst U & Jesinghaus, Jochen 1992: *Ecological tax reform: A policy proposal for sustainable development*. Antlantic Highlands NJ: Humanities International/London: Zed Books. [Important for the concept of ecological control through the manipulation of market forces.]

Wallerstein, Immanuel 1980 (1974): *The modern world system*. New York: Academic Press. [Important theory concerning the evolution of the capitalist system.]

Weber, Max 1976: *The Protestant Ethic*. London: Allen & Unwin. [Famous thesis which links capitalism with Puritan religious motivations.]

Williamson, Jeffrey G 1985: *Did British capitalism breed inequality?* Boston: Allen & Unwin. UNP 339.220941 WIL. [He questions the relationship between growth and inequality].

Williamson, Jeffrey G & Lindert, Peter H 1980: *American inequality: A macroeconomic history*. New York: Academic

   For missing items, refer to other sections of the bibliography

Press. [UNP 339.220973 WIL. [They question the relationship between growth and inequality].

World Bank 1990: *World Development Report 1990: Poverty.* Washington: World Bank.

World Bank 1992: *World Development Report*

1991: The challenge of development. Washington: World Bank.

World Bank 1996: *World Development Report 1996: From plan to market. Oxford: Oxford University Press for the World Bank.* Unisa Ref 330.91704 WORL

B. On change in the former Soviet Union and Eastern Europe

{Note that developments in these countries are so rapid that books tend to be obsolete by the time they have been acquired by libraries. The following publications document the crucial phase in which Marxism-Leninism was abandoned in favour of liberal and democratic approaches.}

Alcamo, Joseph (ed) 1992: *Fair wind, foul wind: Coping with crisis in Eastern Europe's environment.* Laxenburg (Austria): IIASA.

Baranovsky, V & Spanger, E 1992: *In from the cold: Germany, Russia and the future of Europe.* Boulder: Westview Press. UNISA 327.404 7 INFR. [Essays analysing the new roles of Germany and Russia in Europe.]

Bergson, A 1987: Comparative productivity: the USSR, Eastern Europe, and the West. *American Economic Review*, 77/1987, 342-57. [The finding, conceded by Gorbachev, that productivity of labour was 25 - 34 % lower than in the US.]

Bialer, Seweryn 1992: The death of Soviet communism. *Foreign Affairs,* 70/1991-1992, 166-181. [Discusses the significance of the dramatic events surrounding the coup de etat against Gorbachev.]

Bird, Graham (ed) 1992: *Economic reform in Eastern Europe.* Aldershot Hants: Elgar. UNP 338.947 BIR

Blanchard, Olivier Jean 1991: *Reform in Eastern Europe.* Cambridge Mass: MIT. UNP 338.947 BLA.

Brand, H 1992: Why the Soviet economy failed: consequences of dictatorship and dogma. *Dissent 39/*1992 232-44.

Clague, Ch & Rausser, G C (eds): *The emergence of market economies in Eastern Europe.*

Cambridge: Blackwell. UNP 330.947 CLA [Essays on the transition of Eastern European to the market system.]

Clark, Bruce 1995: *An empire's new clothes: The end of Russia's liberal dream.* London: Vintage. [Argues that post-communist Russia is far from becoming a liberal democratic state and has the capacity to continue with its imperial tradition.]

Cook, Linda J 1994: *The Soviet social contract and why it failed: Welfare policy and workers' politics from Brezhnev to Yeltsin.* Cambridge: Harvard Univ Press.

Csaba, Laszlo 1990: *Eastern Europe in the world economy.* Cambridge: Cambridge Univ Press. UNISA 337.147 CSAB. [An account of the financial system of the CMEA in the context of the world economy in the 1980s, that is just before the great transition.]

Dyker, David A 1992: *Restructuring the Soviet economy.* London: Routledge. UNP 338.947 DYK

Easterly, W & Fischer, S 1994: The Soviet Economic decline: Historical and republican data. Washington: World Bank. UNISA 330.947 085 EAST. ["Planned economies are apparently less successful at replacing labor effort with capital" (cover).]

Ellman, M & Kontorovich, V (eds) 1992:

The disintegration of the Soviet economic system. UNP 330.947 ELL

Feige, E 1990: Perestroika and socialist privatization: What is to be done? And how? *Comparative Economic Studies,* 32/1990, 1ff. [Argues that private enterprise and the free market should be embedded in the socialist value system by distributing the state's assets to the population on an equal basis. Note the following comments.]

Feinberg, R E, Echeverri-Gent, J & Müller, F (eds) 1990: *Economic reform in three giants.* New Brunswick (USA) / Oxford (UK): Transaction Books. [Describes economic reforms in the Soviet Union, China and India after the failure of socialism, as well as its geopolitical consequences.] UNISA 338.9 ECON

Fitzpatrick, Sheila 1994: *Stalin's peasants: Resistance and survival in the Russian village after collectivization.* Oxford et al: Oxford Univ Press.

Flaherty, Diane (Center for Popular Economics, Amherst, MA): *Can markets work in Eastern Europe?* [Very instructive, but undated and unpublished paper.]

Gorbachev M 1987: *Perestroika: New thinking for our country and the world.* London: Collins. [Indispensible for an understanding of democratic reform in the USSR before its collapse.]

Gregory, Paul R 1990: Restructuring the Societ economic bureaucracy. Cambridge: Camb Univ Press. UNP 330.947 GRE

Hart, Gary 1991: Russia shakes the world: The second Russian revolution and its impact on the West. New York: Harper Collins. UNP 947.0855 GOR

Jeffries, I (ed) 1992: *Industrial reform in socialist countries: from restructuring to revolution.* UNP 338.947 JEF

Kagarlitsky, Boris 1990: *Farewell Perestroika: A Soviet chronicle.* London: Verso. UNP 947.0855 KAG

Kagarlitsky, Boris 1990: *The dialectics of change.* London: Verso. UNP 947.084 KAG.

Kaiser, R 1988: The USSR in decline. *Foreign Affairs,* 67/1988/9 97-113. [Argues that reform is difficult even in farming because initiative and responsibility have been smothered in rural areas by a repressive system.]

Keithly, David M 1992: *The collapse of East German communism.* Westport & London: Praeger. [An extensive account of the transition.]

Korbonksi, Andrzej 1987: *The Soviet Union and the Third World: The last three decades.* Ithaca: Cornell Univ Press. UNISA 327.4701724 SOVI [

Kotz, D 1992: The direction of Soviet economic reform: From socialist reform to capitalist transition. *Monthly Review* 44/1992 14-34.

Lenches, E T 1992: Can Perestroika still be reformed? *International Journ of Social Economics,* 19/1992, 3-26. [Argues that Perestroika failed because the reform movement compromised with the old system.]

Milanovic, Branko 1993: *Social costs of the transition to capitalism: Poland 1990-91.* (A Policy Research Working Paper). Washington: World Bank. UNISA 338.943 8 MILA

Moskoff, W & Nazmi, Nader 1992: Economic stabilization in the former Soviet Union: Lessons from Argentina and Brazil. *Comparative Economic Studies,* 34/1992, 67-81. [Argues that Eastern Europe has similar problems to those encountered in Latin America and could learn from the experience gained there.]

Nwankwo, Arthur 1990: *Perestroika and Glasnost: Their implications for Africa.* Enugu (Nigeria): Fourth Dimension.

UNP 327.4706 NWA

Petr, J L 1990: Economic reforms in socialist economies: An evolutionary perspective. *Journal of Economic Issues*, 24/1990 1-
15. [Argues that reforms should be
geared to the needs of the situation and
not to pre-formulated ideologies.]

Pipes, Richard 1995 (1974): *Russia under
the old regime*. London: Penguin, second
edition. [Very instructive history of
Russia before the revolution.]

Piyasheva, L 1991: Economic reform: A
great bubble or a faint chance to survive? *Cato Journal*, 11/1991, 293-298.
[Depicts the power struggle between
conservative Marxists, market socialists
and proponents of radical free enterprise, which hampers reform.]

Raico, Ralph 1992: Liberalism, Marxism
and the state. *Cato Journal*, 11/1992,
391-404. [In spite of reforms the old
clumsy bureaucracy continues to determine the economy.]

Symposium on economic transition in the
Soviet Union and Eastern Europe. *The
Journal of Economic Perspectives*, 5/1991,
the whole of number 4.

Tanzi, Vito 1993: *Transition to market: studies
in fiscal reform*. Washington DC: IMF.

Tsypko, A 1991: Revitalization of socialism
or restoration of capitalism? *Cato Journal*,
11/1991, 285-292. [Argues that reform
from the top, which tries to maintain the
old power structure, cannot work.]

Walker, Martin 1992: The old and the
new: How the former USSR has
changed: Or has it? *Europe*, 315/1992 p
10f. [Highlights the rural-urban
divide in the reform process.]

White, S (ed) 1991: *Handbook of reconstruction in Eastern Europe and the Soviet
Union*. UNP 330.947 WHI

World Bank 1996: *World Development Report
1996: From plan to market*. Oxford: Oxford
University Press for the World Bank. Unisa
Ref 330.91704 WORL

Yemelyanov, A 1991: Economic and political Perestroika. *Cato Journal*, 11/1991,
269-276. [The relation between economic and political reform.]

Young, C 1992: The strategy of political
liberalization: a comparative view of
Gorbachev's reforms. *World Politics*
45/1992 47-65.

C. On developments in China

Blejer, Mario; Burton, David; Dunaway,
Steven & Szapary, Gyorgy 1991: *China:
Economic reform and macroeconomic manage-
ment*. Washington DC: IMF.

Bulletin of Concerned Asian Scholars
1983: *China from Mao to Deng: The politics and economics of socialist development*.
London: Zed Press. [Instructive but
difficult to read.]

Chang, David W 1988: *China under Deng
Xiaoping: Political and economic reform*.
New York: St. Martin's.UNISA
338.951 CHAN. [A short, revealing
overview of the new situation.]

Cheung S N S: 1982: *Will China go capi-

talist? An economic analysis of property
rights and institutional change*. London:
Inst. of Econ. Affairs.

Derbyshire, Ian 1987: *Politics in China from
Mao to Deng*. Cambridge: Chambers.
UNISA 320.951 DERB [A concise
overview with a wealth of facts.]

Dreyer, June T 1993: *China's political system: Modernization and tradition*.
London: Macmillan. UNISA 320.951
DREY. [Concentrates on political,
rather than economic dimensions.]

Feinberg, R E, Echeverri-Gent, J & Müller,
F (eds) 1990: *Economic reform in three
giants*. New Brunswick (USA)/Oxford

(UK): Transaction Books. [Describes economic reforms in the Soviet Union, China and India after the failure of socialism, as well as its geopolitical consequences.] UNISA 338.9 ECON

Gelb, A, Jefferson, G & Singh, I 1993: *Can communist economies transform incrementally? China's experience* (A Policy Research Working Paper). Washington: World Bank. UNISA 338.951 GELB.

Glaeser, Berhard 1987: *Learning from China? Development and environment in Third World countries.* London: Allen & Unwin. UNISA 338.951 LEAR.

Hamrin, Carol L 1990: *China and the challenge of the future: Changing political patterns.* Boulder: Westview. UNISA 338.951 HAMR. [Alternative visions for the future of China after Mao.]

Hartzell, Richard W 1988: *Harmony in conflict: Active adaptation to life in present-day Chinese society.* Taipei (Taiwan): Caves Books. [Handbook on understanding the Chinese culture and mentality].

King-yuh Chang (ed) 1990: *Mainland China after the 13th Party Congress.* Boulder: Westview. UNISA 320.951 MAIN [Interesting studies, for instance 404ff on the ownership system; or 408ff about a share system.]

Ogden, Suzanne 1989: *China's unresolved issues: Politics, development and culture.* Englewood Cliffs NJ: Prentice-Hall. UNISA 320.951 OGDE [Revealing book on China's internal workings.]

Reynolds, Bruce L (ed) 1988: *Chinese economic policy: Economic reform at midstream.* New York: Paragon House. UNISA 338.951 CHIN [See Vogel's contribution pp 1ff on the model of the "young tigers" and whether it could be applied to China.]

Riskin, Carl 1987: *China's political economy: The quest for development since 1949.* Oxford: Oxford Univ Press. UNISA 338.951 RISK. [Highly instructive historical analysis.]

Roberts, J A G 1996: *A history of China.* Phoenix Mill, Gloucestershire: Alan Sutton. UNISA 951 ROBE.

D. Tanzania and Africa in general

Albright, D E (ed) 1980: *Africa and international communism.* London: Macmillan. [Essays on the relation between international communism - USSR, China, Cuba - and Africa]

Berg-Schlosser, Dirk & Siegler, Rainer 1990: *Political stability and development: A comparative analysis of Kenya, Tanzania and Uganda.* London: Lynne Rienner. UNP 320.9676BER [Very revealing comparisons.]

Bundy C 1988 (1979): *The rise and fall of the South African peasantry.* Cape Town: David Philip. [Shows that African subsistence peasants have produced for markets when attractive opportunities arose].

Campbell, H & Stein, H (eds) 1992: *Tanzania and the IMF: The dynamics of liberalization.* Boulder: Westview. UNISA 338.967 8 TANZ [In the introduction a good summary of the history and the problem, including ideological legitimations of the switch in policy.]

Cohen John M 1987: *Integrated rural development: The Ethiopian experience and the debate.* Uppsala: Scandinavian Institute of African Studies.

Duggan, W R and Civille, J R 1976: *Tanzania and Nyerere: A study of Ujamaa and nationalism.* New York: Orbis.

Falloux, F & Talbot, L M 1993 (1992): *Crisis and opportunity: Environment and development in Africa.* London: Earthscan. UNISA 338.96 FALL [Describes African

For missing items, refer to other sections of the bibliography

National Environmental Action Plans with some enthusiasm.]

Fimbo G M 1992: *Essays in rural land law in Tanzania.* Dar es Salam: Univ of Dar es Salam: Faculty of law. [Describes the intricacies of land rights under Ujamaa on grass roots level.]

Fontaine, Jean-Marc (ed) 1992: *Foreign trade reforms and development strategy.* London/ NY: Routledge. [See the contribution of Paul Mosley pp 27ff for a critical analysis of the Structural Adjustment Programmes of the World Bank.]

Helmsing, A H J & Kolstee, Th (eds) 1993: *Small enterprises and changing policies: Structural adjustment, financial policy and assistance programmes in Africa.* London: Intermeditate Technology Publications. UNISA 338.642 096 SMAL.

Herbst, Jeffrey 1990: *State and politics in Zimbabwe.* Harare: Univ of Zimbabwe Publications. [See chapter 5 for Zimbabwe's agricultural producer price policy which led to grain surpluses]

Hughes, Arnold (ed) 1993: *Marxism's retreat from Africa.* Portland OR: Cass.

Jeffries Richard 1993: The state, structural adjustment and good government in Africa. *The Journal of Commonwealth and Comparative Politics.* XXXI/1993 20-35. [Discusses bad government and the resultant failure of the Structural Adjustment Programme].

Kasfir, Nelson 1986: Are African peasants self-sufficient? *Development and change* 17/1986 335-357. [Critical review of two books by Goran Hyden, viz 1980: "Beyond Ujamaa in Tanzania: Underdevelopment and an uncaptured peasantry", and 1983: "No shortcuts to progress: African development management in perspective." Hyden argues that subsistence peasants were too independent from the state for reform to succeed.]

Lappe F M & Beccar-Varela A 1980: *Mozambique and Tanzania: Asking the big questions.* Birmingham: Third World Publishers. Note the date.

Leatt J, Kneifel T & Nürnberger K (eds) 1986: *Contending ideologies in South Africa.* Cape Town: David Philip. [A description of conflicting ideologies - political and economic - under apartheid.]

Lensink, Robert 1996: *Structural adjustment in sub-Saharan Africa.* London/New York: Longman. [Analysis of the reasons for economic failure in Africa and the prescriptions of the IMF and the World Bank.]

Maliyamkono T L & Begachwa M S D 1990: *The second economy in Tanzania.* London: James Currey/Athens Ohio: Ohio Univ Press. [Discusses the informal sector in Tanzania.]

Moll, Peter G 1991: *The great economic debate: A radical's guide to the South African economy.* Johannesburg: Skotaville. [Tries to draw conclusions from recent socialist experiences for the new South Africa.]

Moll, Terence 1991: Macroeconomic redistributive packages in developing countries. In: Moll, Peter, Nattrass, Nicoli & Loots, Lieb (eds) 1991: *Redistribution: How can it work in South Africa?* Cape Town: David Philip, pp 25ff. [Together with the next item this essay gives a vivid impression of the difficulties encountered in the attempt to achieve greater distributive justice in a situation of great economic discrepancies.]

Moll, Terence 1991: Microeconomic redistributive strategies in developing countries. In: Moll, Peter, Nattrass, Nicoli & Loots, Lieb (eds) 1991: *Redistribution: How can it work in South Africa?* Cape Town: David Philip, pp 1ff.

Munslo, Barry 1986: *Africa: problems in the transition to socialism.* London: Zed Press. [Note the date!]

Nwankwo, Arthur 1990: *Perestroika and Glasnost: Their implications for Africa.*

Enugu (Nigeria): Fourth Dimension. UNP 327.4706 NWA

Nürnberger K 1988: *Power and beliefs in South Africa: Economic potency structures in SA and their interaction with patterns of conviction in the light of a Christian ethic.* Pretoria: Unisa.

Nyerere, Julius K 1968: *Freedom and socialism: Uhuru na Ujamaa.* Dar es Salam: Oxford Univ Press.

O'Neill, Norman & Mustafa, Kemal (ed) 1990: *Capitalism, socialism and the development crisis in Tanzania.* Aldershot Hants / Brookfield Vermont: Avebury - Gower Publ Co. UNP 338.9678 ONE; UNISA 338.967 8 CAPI. [Revealing essays on the Tanzanian transition after Ujamaa].

Omari C K 1989: *Persistent principles amidst crisis.* Arusha: ELCT (Box 3033 Arusha; Uziika Press Box 48127, Nairobi). [Reflections by a prominent Tanzanian sociologist.]

Otim JJ 1992: *The tap root of environmental and development crisis in Africa.* Nairobi: ACLCA (Association of Christian Lay Centres in Africa). [Sharp and informative critique.]

Ottaway, David & Ottaway Marina 1981: *Afrocommunism.* New York: Africana.

Przeworski Adam 1991: Could we feed everyone? The irrationality of capitalism and the infeasibility of socialism. *Politics & Society* 19/1991 1-38. [Reviews various critiques of capitalism and socialism.]

Rahmato Dessalegn 1993: Agrarian change and agrarian crisis: state and peasantry in post-revolution Ethiopia. *Africa* 63/ 1993. [Argues that Marxist policies were successful in redistributing land and defusing ethnic tensions, but committed a grace mistake by transferring the land to the state which the peasants resisted. An example of a principled ideology removed from practical reality.]

Roberg C G & Callaghy Th M 1979: *Socialism in Sub-Saharan Africa: A new assessment.* Berkeley: Instit. of Intern. Studies. [Note the date!]

Robinson, Peter B & Somsak Tambunlertchai 1995: *Africa and Asia: Can high rate of growth be replicated?* San Francisco Cal: CS Press.

Rugumisa, Savator 1990?: *A review of Tanzania's economic recovery programme 1986-89.* Dar es Salam: TADREC (Box 14126 Nairobi). [Spells out both the achievements and the problems caused by the recovery programme.]

Rwelamira, J B 1988: *Tanzanian socialism: Ujamaa and Gaudium et Spes.* Rome: Pontificia Universitas Lateranensis, Acad. Alfonsiana.

Semboja, J & Therkildsen, O (eds) 1995: *Service provision under stress in East Africa: The state, NGOs and People's Organizations in Kenya, Tanzania and Uganda.* Copenhagen: Centre for Development Research.

Sender John 1990: *Poverty, class and gender in rural Africa: A Tanzanian case study.* London: Routledge. UNISA 305.509678 SEND

Shipton, Parker & Goheen, Mitzi 1992: Understanding African land-holding: Power, wealth, and meaning. *Africa* 62/1992 307-325. [Shows how the political, economic, cultural and ecological dimensions of land policies are intertwined.]

TURP (Trade Union Research Project) 1994: *A user's guide to the South African economy.* Durban: Y-Press.

Van Binsbergen, Wim M J 1985: *Old modes of production and capitalist encroachment: Anthropological explorations in Africa.* London: KP UNISA 306.3 OLDH.

Van Buren, Linda (ed) 1993: *New African Yearbook 1993.* London: IC Publications.

Yeager, R 1982: *Ujamaa: An African experiment.* Boulder COL: Westview.

For missing items, refer to other sections of the bibliography

E. Taiwan and the newly industrialising countries in general

Caporaso, James A (ed) 1987: *A changing international division of labour.* Boulder: Lynne Rienner. 382.104 2 CHAN [The authors deal with the shifts in industrial production to the South and their impact on international labour. Many theoretical considerations.]

Chan, Steve & Clark, Cal 1992: *Flexibility, foresight, and Fortuna in Taiwan's development: Navigation between Scylla and Charybdis.* London/New York: Routledge. UNISA 338.951249 CHAN [Instructive overview of different development models and the "puzzle" of development in Taiwan: it is not geared to any orthodoxy but to pragmatic eclecticism.]

Galenson, Walter (ed) 1979: *Economic growth and structural change in Taiwan: The postwar experience of the Republic of China.* Ithaca/London: Cornell Univ Press. [Comprehensive overview of developments up to 1970s.]

Gates, H 1987: *Chinese working-class lives: Getting by in Taiwan.* Ithaca NY: Cornell Univ Press.

Gregor, A James 1981: *Ideology and development: Sun Yat-sen and the economic history of Taiwan.* China Research Monograph, Inst of East Asian Studies, Univ of California. 330.951249 GREG

Ho, S P S 1980: *Small-scale enterprises in Korea and Taiwan.* Washington DC: World Bank. 338.709519 HO [Describes the change from family workshops to factories]

Hodder, Rupert 1992: *The West Pacific Rim: An introduction.* London: Belhaven. UNISA 330.951 HOD [Very useful overview of policies in South East Asia as a whole.]

Keesing, Donald B 1988: *The four successful exceptions: Official export promotion and support for export marketing in Korea, Hong Kong, Singapore, and Taiwan.* Washingtom: World Bank, Policy Trade Division, Occasional Paper No 2.

Kim, Wheegook 1990: *A comparative study of export-led growth: Case study of South Korea and Taiwan.* UMI Dissertation Information Service. Ann Arbor MICH: Univ Microfilms International. [Mentions key factors: export orientation, free trade, efficiency, flexibility].

Lindenberg, M & Ramitez, N 1989: *Managing adjustment in developing countries.* San Francisco: ICS Press. UNISA 338.90091724 LIND

Little, Ian M D 1979: An economic reconnaissance. In: Galenson, Walter (ed) 1979: *Economic growth and structural change in Taiwan: The postwar experience of the Republic of China.* Ithaca/London: Cornell Univ Press, pp 448ff.

Maddison, Angus et al 1992: *The political economy of poverty, equity and growth: Brazil and Mexico.* New York: Oxford Univ Press (for World Bank). UNISA 338.972 MADD [This book describes the Latin American type of industrialising country.]

Müller, A L 1996: Export-oriented industrialisation in Korea. *South African Journal of Economics*, vol 64/1996, 75-99.

Ogle, George E 1990: *South Korea: Dissent within the economic miracle.* London: Zed Books. UNISA 339.509 519 5 OGLE. [The author highlights the cost of industrialisation to the internal working class in Korea. The economy maximises productivity while holding down labour costs. The workers rebel against severe repression by state and management.]

Purcell, Randall B (ed) 1989: *The newly industrializing countries in the world econ-*

omy: *Challenges for US policy.* Boulder/London: Lynne Rienner. UNISA 382.097 301 724 NEWL [Developments in industrialising countries, including Latin America. Global division of labour and liberalisation of trade are positive phenomena, but poor countries will find it difficult to gain entry.]

Ranis, Gustav 1979: Industrial development. In: In: Galenson, Walter (ed) 1979: *Economic growth and structural change in Taiwan: The postwar experience of the Republic of China.* Ithaca/London: Cornell Univ Press, pp 206ff.

Schive, C 1996: Implications of Taiwan's economic development experience. *South African Journal of Economic and Management Sciences,* vol 18/1996, pp 25-46.

Storey, Robert 1994: *Taiwan - a travel survival kit.* Hawthorne, Australia: Lonely Planet Publications.

Thorbeke, Erik 1979: Agicultural development. In: Galenson, Walter (ed) 1979: *Economic growth and structural change in*

Taiwan: The postwar experience of the Republic of China. Ithaca/London: Cornell Univ Press, pp 132ff.

Uwechue, Raph (ed) 1991: *Africa today.* London: Africa Books. [Excellent introduction to Tanzania on pp 1815ff.]

Vestal, James E 1993: Planning for change: Industrial policy and Japanese economic development, 1945-1990. Oxford: Clarendon. UNISA 338.952 VEST. [Very illuminating book, especially concerning successful state intervention in the economy and the merits of equalisation policies.]

Wade, R 1990: *Governing the market: economic theory and the role of government in East Asian industrialisation.* Princeton: Princeton Univ Press. [Shows that liberalism-Marxism dichotomy is misleading].

Wu, Yuan-li 1985: *Becoming an industrialized nation: ROC's development on Taiwan.* New York et al: Praeger Scientific. [Simple answer: export orientation making use of inexpensive labour force].

F. Ethical and theological assessments

{You are also advised to consult the great library of liberation theology and related movements, which are critical of capitalism, including works by Gutierrez, Miguez Bonino, Boff, Sobrino, Miranda, Dussel, Camara, Shaul, Cone, and many others.}

Antoncich R 1987: *Christians in the face of injustice: A Latin American reading of Catholic social teaching.* Maryknoll, NY: Orbis. [A subdued advocacy of liberation theology in terms of main line Catholic teaching.]

Baird, J Arthur 1989: *The greed syndrome: An ethical sickness in American capitalism.* Akron OH: Hampshire.

Baum, Gregory 1982: *The priority of labour: A commentary on Laborem exercens - encyclical letter of Pope John Paul II.* New York: Paulist Press.

Baumann, Fred E 1986: *Democratic capital-*

ism? Essay in search of a concept. Charlottesville: Univ Press of Virginia. [The clash between freedom and democracy in economics.]

Benne R 1981: *The ethic of democratic capitalism: a moral reassessment.* Philadelphia: Fortress.

Berger P L 1974: *Pyramids of sacrifice : Political ethics and social change.* New York: Basic Books (paperback available). [In this book Berger offers an even-handed critique of both capitalism and socialism in the Third World, using Brazil and China as examples. In

 For missing items, refer to other sections of the bibliography

later books he opts for capitalism.]

Block, Peter 1993: *Stewardship: Choosing service over self-interest.* San Francisco CA: Berrett-Koehler. [A revealing (secular and rational) application of the options for service, redistribution of power and wealth, and hope over experience, for a successful liberal-capitalist enterprise.]

Boff, Leonardo 1995: Ecology and liberation: a new paradigm. Maryknoll, NY: Orbis. [See part 2 for a deep reflection on the relation between liberation theology and socialism after the collapse of the latter.]

Budde, Michael L 1992: *The two churches: Catholicism and capitalism in the world system.* Durham and London: Duke Univ Press. [Argues that there is a correlation between religion and economic system in the West and that the church has to come to terms with the fact that capitalism leads to the centre-periphery structure of the world economy.]

Catholic Bishops of the USA 1984: *Pastoral letter on Catholic social teaching and the US economy.* Washington DC: Catholic Conference. UNP 261.85 GAN.

Chmielewski, P J 1993: *Bettering our condition: Work, workers and ethics in British and German economic thought.* Bern/New York: Peter Lang. [The German version of social democracy is well worth a deeper study because it combines basic concerns and approaches which tend to fall apart elsewhere.]

Cosmao V 1984: *Changing the world: An agenda for the churches.* Maryknoll: Orbis.

Dahl, Robert A. 1985: *A preface to economic democracy.* Berkeley: Univ of Calif. Press.

Daly, Herman E & Cobb, John B 1991: *For the common good: Redirecting the economy toward community, the environment and a sustainable future.* Boston MA: Beacon Press. [Daly is one of the most prominent

critics of destructive economic growth.]

Dorrien, Gary J 1990: *Reconstructing the common good: Theology and the social order.* NY: Orbis. 335.7 DORR.

Duchrow, Ulrich 1987: *Global economy: A confessional issue for the churches?* Geneva: World Council of Churches. UNP 261.85.

Duchrow, Ulrich 1992: *Europe in the World System 1492-1992.* Geneva: World Council of Churches.

Duchrow, Ulrich 1995: *Alternatives to the global economy: Drawn from biblical history for political action.* Utrecht: International Books.

Freeman John R 1989: *Democracy and markets: The politics of mixed economies.* Ithaca: Cornell Univ Press.

Friedman M and Friedman R 1980: *Free to choose: A personal statement.* New York: Avon Books. [Friedman is a prominent exponent of neo-orthodox liberalism in economics.]

Gorringe, Timothy J 1995: *Captial and the Kingdom: Theological Ethics and economic order.* Maryknoll NY: Orbis / London: SPCK.

Gray, Craig M 1993: *With liberty and justice for whom? The recent Evangelical debate on capitalism.* Grand Rapids: Eerdmans. [Discusses left and right positions, current realignments, points out semantic manipulations, etc.]

Harries R (ed) 1986: *Reinhold Niebuhr and the issues of our time.* London: Mowbray. [One of the leading theological ethicists and social philosophers of the 20th Century. See the index for Niebuhr's critique of capitalism and Marxism]

Haslett, David 1991: *Ethics and economic systems.* Oxford: Oxford Univ Press.

Hay D A 1975: *A Christian critique of capitalism.* Nottingham: Grove Books.

Hay D A 1989: *Economics today: A Christian*

critique. Grand Rapids: Eerdmans. [Offers a set of Christian principles for economic life. More conservative than Preston.]

Hinkelammert F J 1986: *The ideological weapons of death: A theological critique of capitalism.* Maryknoll: Orbis. [A radical anti-capitalist theologian.]

Holland, Stuart 1987: *The market economy: From micro to mesoeconomics.* New York: St Martin's Press. [Argues that multinational corporations have formed a new power between private enterprise and the state.]

Holland, Stuart 1987: *The global economy: From meso to macroeconomics.* New York: St Martin's Press. [See above].

Jones, Arthur 1992: *Capitalism and Christians.* Mahwah: Paulist. [Critical of capitalism].

Kee, Alistair 1990: *Marx and the failure of Liberation Theology.* London: SCM/ Philadelphia: Trinity Press. UNISA 230.046 KEE [Argues that Liberation Theology is inconsistent with Marx's ideas.]

Klay, R K 1986: *Counting the cost: The economics of Christian stewardship.* Grand Rapids, Mich: Eerdmans. UNISA 261.85 KLAY [discusses the market versus the command system in a Christian ethical perspective.]

Lochman J M 1988: *Christ and Prometheus? a quest for theological identity.* Geneva: WCC. [Prometheus, a rebel against the gods in Greek mythology, taken as a symbol of Marxism.]

Lukes, Steven 1987: *Marxism and morality.* Oxford: Oxf Univ Press.

Machan, Tibor R 1990: *Capitalism and freedom: Reframing the argument for a free society.* New York: Harvester Wheatsheaf. UNISA 320.51 MACH. [Strong defense of personal freedom in capitalist societies on moral grounds,

against Marxist critique.]

McGovern A F 1981: *Marxism: an American Christian perspective.* Maryknoll NY: Orbis.

Meeks, M Douglas 1989: *God the Economist: The doctrine of God and Political Economy.* Minneapolis: Fortress. [review by Gottwald 1993 281ff]

Miguez Bonino J 1976: *Christians and Marxists. The mutual challenge to revolution.* London: Hodder & Stroughton. UNISA 522890. [Note the date: the heyday of Marxist-Christian dialogue on social justice and revolution.]

Mulholland C (ed) 1988: *Ecumenical reflections on political economy.* Geneva: WCC.

Myers, Max A 1987: The contemporary crisis of Marxism and our responsibility. *Thought* 62/1987 96-109. [Argues that crises occur when ideological systems, which emerged in one situation, are not flexible enough to retain relevance in another. The basic problem is the incapacity to transcend, which leads to the idolatrous absolutisation of a system.]

Nielsen, Kai 1988: *Marxism and the moral point of view: Morality, ideology, and historical materialism.* Boulder: Westview.

Novak M 1981: *Toward a theology of the corporation.* Washington DC: American Enterprise Institute. [The corporation is depicted as the "suffering servant".]

Novak M 1982: *The spirit of democratic capitalism.* New York: Simon & Schuster. [Novak is the most prominent theological advocate of capitalism.]

Novak M (ed) 1979: *The denigration of capitalism.* American Enterprise Institute.

Novak, Michael 1993 (?): *The Catholic ethic and the spirit of Capitalism.* Free Press. [Highlights the creative subjectivity of the human person and compares it with Pope John Paul's Centesimus Annus. Denies the accusation that capitalist suc-

          For missing items, refer to other sections of the bibliography

cess is due to ruthless individualism and cold calculation.]

Nürnberger, K 1987: The eschatology of Marxism. *Missionalia* 15/1987 105-109.

Nürnberger, K 1998: *Prosperity, poverty and pollution.* Pietermaritzburg: Cluster Publications. [An interdisciplinary analysis of economic-ecological imbalances, their structural and ideological causes, the transformation of collective consciousness, and directions to be followed.]

Paul, Ellen F, Miller, Fred D & Paul, Jeffrey (eds) 1992: *Economic rights.* New York et al: Cambridge Univ Press.

Peffer, R G 1990: *Marxism, morality and social justice.* Princeton NJ: Princeton Univ Press.

Preston R H 1979: *Religion and the persistence of capitalism.* London: SCM.

Preston R H 1983: *Church and society in the late Twentieth Century: The economic and political task.* London: SCM.

Preston R H 1991: *Religion and the ambiguities of capitalism.* London: SCM Press. UNP 261.85 PRE. [Calling for a more pertinent interaction between theology and economic analysis concerning the economic issues of our time. Offers a general overview and critique of economic systems from a theological standpoint; similar to the present book. Strongly recommended reading.]

Rasmussen L L 1981: *Economic anxiety and Christian faith.* Minneapolis: Augsburg.

Rawls, John 1971: *A theory of justice.* Cambridge: Harvard Univ Press. [A classic on social ethical issues.]

Rwelamira, J B 1988: *Tanzanian socialism:*

Ujamaa and Gaudium et Spes. Rome: Pontificia Universitas Lateranensis, Acad. Alfonsiana.

Sahlins, Marshal 1977: *The use and abuse of biology: An anthropological critique of sociobiology.* London: Travistock Publications. [Shows how evolution theory and laissez faire capitalism go hand in hand.]

Segundo, J L 1974: Capitalism - Socialism: A theological crux. *Concilium* 6/1974 105-123.

Simons, Robert G 1995: *Competing gospels: Public theology and economic theory.* Alexandria (Australia): Dwyer. Unisa 261.85 SIMO. [Competent theological critique of capitalist economy].

Sherman, Amy L 1993: *Preferential option: A Christian and neoliberal strategy for Latin America's poor.* Grand Rapids: Eerdmans. [A defence of the development and free market model on Christian and empirical grounds.]

Thomas, J M & V Visick 1991. *God and capitalism: A prophetic critique of market economy.* Madison WI: A-R Editions Inc.

Thrower, James 1992: *Marxism-Leninism as the civil religion of Soviet society.* Lewiston NY: Mellen.

Wells, Harold 1995: *A future for socialism? Political theology and the 'triumph of capitalism'.* Valley Forge PA: Prinity Press International.

Wogaman J P 1977: *Christians and the great economic debate.* London: SCM. [Good overview of the systems before the crisis of Marxism.] UNP 241.6426 WOG

Wogaman J P 1986: *Economics and ethics: A Christian inquiry.* Philadelphia: Fortress.

INDEX AND GLOSSARY

Absolute poverty [a situation where the income does not cover basic needs for a healthy life] 59 82 193 194

Accountability [demand that those entrusted with a public office fully expose what they are doing to public scrutiny] 165 177 210 211 213

Accumulation of capital - see capital accumulation

Achievements of democratic socialism 117f

Achievements of Marxism-Leninism 84f 87 99

Achievements of social democracy 111f

Achievements of Taiwan 144f

Achievements of African Socialism 134f 138

Advantages of capitalism 20 37ff 49 65

Advantages of socialism 59ff 65f

Affirmative action [a policy which gives disadvantaged population groups a temporary advantage over their competitors to enable them to become fully competitive] 172 195

Affluence gap [the amount with which the means of a family surpass all their reasonable needs] 11 42

African socialism [a version of socialism which attempts to build a new social order on African traditional values and social structures] 3 20 22 56 131 - see also Ujamaa.

African traditions [customs, beliefs, legends handed down from generation to generation in African social groups] 20 22 136 138 150 154

Age to come [a future perfect condition of the universe as expected by Jewish Apocalyptics and early Christianity] 226 233 - see also Kingdom of God

Agenda for economics 161 186 191-197 200 205f

Agriculture [the production of food for sale or exchange, using technological methods and machinery] 19 80f 96 120 134f 138 140 144 154 177

Alienation [impairment of a relationship in Marxist philosophy] 64 66 72 104 136

Allende, Salvador (1908-1973) [Chilian president who attempted to introduce democratic socialism] 54 115

Allocation of resources [the act of applying factors of production in particular ratios to productive processes to achieve particular ends] 34f 37 49 58 61 63 65f 98 108 110 138 169f 175f 183 194

Ambition [to aspire to succeed in some ideal or goal] 37 46 86 153 163 172 176

Amin, Idi [Ugandan dictator] 135 154

Analysis [systematic and critical investigation] 1ff 6 9 29 68 78 90 95 158f 171 183 186 188 223 230 233 238

Anarchy [a situation where nobody rules over anybody else] 13 162 198f 204 219

Angola 56 83 94 96

Anomie [the breakdown or confusion of values and norms in a group or society] 238

Anthropology [an understanding of the nature of the human being] - see anthropology of liberalism / Marxism

Anthropology of liberalism 30-36 37-39 39-45

Anthropology of Marxism 70-72 72-78 84-94 102f

Anticipation [an active imagination of a desired future leading to attitudes and actions in line with this future] 187 234

Apocalyptics [Movement in late ancient Judaism which believed in the imminence of a divine reconstruction of the universe] 78 225 234

Armaments / arms race [intense competition between countries or political groups for military superiority] 10 15 41 43 96 99 120 142 153

Asian tigers [four newly industrialising South East Asian countries: Taiwan, Hong Kong, Singapore, South Korea] 97 125 143 - see also Taiwan.

Arusha Declaration 132f 138

Atheism [the belief that God does not exist] 88f 90 182

Austerity measures 67

Authoritarianism [a political system where individual freedom is completely subordinate to the power of the state, controlled by one person or an elite group] 24 92 103 118f 122f 125 142 144 145 149 153 155

Avant garde [bourgeois leaders of the revolutionary movement] 68 76 225

Balance of payments / balance of trade [record of

a nation's sales to, and purchases from, all other nations] 32 110 135 151 154

Balance of power [situation where a group, a nation, or a group of nations has sufficient military, political, and economic resources to restrain the potential threat of another equally powerful group, nation, or group of nations] 159 196 201 218

Bargaining power [the ability to effectively press for one's demands] 140 194 215

Base [Marxist concept indicating the economic conditions which allegedly give rise to institutional and spiritual phenomena called the "superstructure"] 74 - see Materialism

Basic needs [what is absolutely necessary for a healthy life] 57 59 192 195 205 224

Bernstein, Edouard (1850-1932) 54 74

Big business [great, often multinational, corporations with a tendency to have monopolistic or oligopolistic power in the market] 167 176f

Big government [a government which assumes vast powers to control the economy] 167 176

Bill of social goals [proposed companion to a national bill of rights which would embody the values inherent in a vision of social justice and equity as well as realistic developmental goals] 2 04

Biosphere [the thin layer of the Earth, including land, sea and atmosphere, in which life is able to flourish] 4 10 158 160 191 224

Body of Christ [expression for the community of believers in Paul's theology] 237 239

Boom [a time of rapid growth in production and prosperity] 29 32f 42f 112 147 154 207

Bourgeoisie [term used for the class of capital owners in Marxist social philosophy; synonymous with the "Middle Class"] 20 69 75 76f 79 82 104 108 169

Breshnev, [Soviet leader before Perestroika] 119

Budget deficit [the access of expenditure over income in the planning stage of national accounts] 34 57 112 152 209f

Bureaucracy [the collective power exercised by public offices] 20 61ff 65 80 82 101 108 112 114 122 137 142f 155 200 207 209f 214 217

Bureaucratic drag [a phenomenon where the economy is stifled by the inefficiency of state organs on which it depends] 67

C factors [causes of inequality located in economic centres] 12

C/P factors [causes of inequality located in the interaction between economic centres and economic peripheries] 12

Cadre [Marxist term for party officials] 83 119 136f 140

Capital accumulation [the process in which the surplus of production over consumption is used to enhance productive capacity] 63 67 137 146 171

Capital formation - see capital accumulation

Capital [all non-human assets which can be expressed in financial terms and which are capable of enhancing the productivity of economic enterprises, such as machines, warehouses, etc.] 13 17 31 34 38ff 43f 47 58 61 63f 66f 76 80f 91 111 116f 137 142f 145ff 150ff 166 171 175 178 183 195 206 208 212 214- 218

Capitalism [a system geared to the accumulation of capital in private hands] 1-8 13 17 19 20- 24 28-50 53ff 56f 58ff 60 63-67 69 71 73 75ff 79f 84 86f 91f 94f 97 101ff 104f 108- 115 117f 121 125ff 131 134 137f 141-148 149f 154 158-161 165f 167 169-172 175f 178 180ff 183 187 200 207 211 213f 216 218 227-231

Capitalist liberalism [see capitalism, liberalism]

Cash crop [agricultural products sold on the market] 131 135

CCM (= Chama Cha Mapinduzi) [name of the ruling party in Tanzania (TANU) after 1977.] 133

Central planning [a process in which the state organises the entire economy] 98 122

Centre and periphery [the centre is a concentration of economic power and the periphery is its relatively powerless and remote surrounding] 10-17 23f 29f 40f 47 79 102 113f 118 169 178 194 200ff 207

Chartists 54

Chile 54 115 119

China 4 6 53f 66 81-83 85 88 92f 97 101f 104 109 115 124 125 138 142 144 149f 181

Christianity 54 68 74 84 87 89 93f 102 104 133 161f 164 168 174 182 191 223 225-240

Civilisation, modern [culture based on science, technology and utilitarianism which became dominant in the West after the Enlightenment and spread among the universal elites through colonialism, international trade and politics] 13 17 19f 24 28 32 36 39 47ff 56f 60 64 74f 98 101f 114f 138 144 153 155 162 166 172 177 179 183 188f 192 196 210 211 216 223f 227-230

Civilisation - traditional 13 17 19 28 40 48 52 56 66 72 82 101 114 121 131-141 144f 150 155 158 169 175 177 223f 229f - see also traditionalism

Class struggle [the conflict between the rich and powerful on the one hand and the poor and powerless on the other which underlies all historical processes according to Marxist philosophy] 182 202f 232

Classless society [the last stage in history according to Marxist philosophy where all economic and political inequalities have been overcome] 20 57f 75 77 86 87 104 108 132 159 162 166 180 181 225 226

Cold War [intense political and economic rivalry between nations just short of military conflict, especially between the West and the USSR following World War II] 2 6 8 23 137 150

Collective consciousness [a set of assumptions, values and norms shared by large groups of people] 12 14 77 82 91 118 158 179 180 196 204

Collectivisation [a policy which aims at collective and state controlled, rather than individual and private, organisation of economic processes] 80 120 133 145 149 171

Colonialism [the policy of establishing subservient outposts in foreign countries] 11 19 29 44

Comecon [Council for Mutual Economic Assistance - East European economic bloc under Soviet leadership] 81

Comintern [Communist International - an organisation designed to integrate all communist parties and movements] 79 80

Command system [an economic system planned and directed by the state] 20 38 67 100 108 123 169 170

Commodification [a trend where all things are treated as tradable commodities] 43

Communalism [a system based on the economic cooperation and joint ownership of small communities] 19 28 48 66 75 150 163 175

Communism [the word has two meanings: in Marxism it means the classless society; in colloquial terms it means the same as Marxism-Leninism] 2 8 58f 68 75 77 79 80 83 86 92-95 103f 122 124 145 182 187 231

Communist Manifesto [the basic "creed" of Marxism-Leninism, drawn up by Marx and Engels in 1848] 39 71f

Comparative advantage [the advantage one nation has over a trading partner in the production of a particular commodity or service which is due to the ability of that nation to produce the latter at a lower cost] 16 35 146 150f 155 209

Competition [the attempt of various parties to outdo each other] 1 13 30 34 40 43 49 57 63 65 73 77 91 99 101 110 138 140 149 166 168ff 175f 180 183

Comprehensive wellbeing [a situation in which all living organisms or species are able to unfold their inherent potential optimally without endangering the opportunity of other such organisms or species to do the same] 228 233f

Compromises between capitalism and Marxism-Leninism 24 108-130 138 158 183 190 199 201 216

Concern [a sense of responsibility for the wellbeing of others or the appropriateness of a situation] 17 39 43 46 48 52 89 90 112 117 132 158 161f 164 167 169f 178 181 193 196 206 212 218 224 227f 234 236-240

Confucianism [the system of ethics, education, and statesmanship taught by Confucius] 147

Consensus [general agreement or accord within a group] 133 147 197-203 215 232

Consumption [the use of goods and services having exchange value] 4 9 13f 16 23f 28f 33 41f 49 52 57f 65 108 113 153 192f 195 205f

Contextuality [dependence on the changing nature of a situation] 238

Contradiction [the clash of propositions, goals, phenomena, etc which seek a resolution - see dialectics] 2 20 64 69 72-75 104 139 143

Convictions [deeply held beliefs of a fundamental nature] 8 30 39 56 66 71 89 93f 97 102 123 147 167f 190 223ff 229-235 239f

Core-periphery paradigm [see centre and periphery]

Corporate [acting as a social group or body] 32 41

165 177 213

Corporations [private economic institutions in which many investors participate] 12 32 40f 47 63 65 114 137 146 148 151 153 180 214

Corruption [the use of public power for self-interested ends] 46 61f 65 67 88 100 109 114 121 122 124 138f 144 151 154 160 163 165 172 209f

Counter-revolution [the attempt to obstruct or undo revolutionary change] 119 121 123 128

Coup d'etat [bloodless take-over of the government by unconstitutional means] 119

Creative / creativity [original thought leading to productive initiatives] 7 37 45 53 61f 81 103f 121 168 170 174 187 190 208 215

Credibility [ability to enlist confidence and belief] 55 87 119 124

Critique of capitalism 39-48 161 182 197-201 206 209 212-218 227-229

Critique of democratic socialism 117-118 123f

Critique of social democracy 111-115

Critique of socialism 59 266 (see also: Critique of Marxism-Leninism, of Democratic Socialism, of Social Democracy)

Critique of Taiwan 143-150

Critique of Ujamaa 134-139 140f 148-150

Cultural Revolution [revolt of the youth against established communist leaders instigated by Mao in China] 81

Czechoslovakia 55 94 101f 115 118f 126 164 181

Debt, international [the accumulation of funds and their interests borrowed on the international money market] 15f 34 43 65 99 137 139 141 147 151 189 210

Decolonisation [withdrawal of foreign control from a previously occupied nation] 56 141

Deconstruction [taking something apart] 162 168f

Deficiencies in comprehensive wellbeing 234

Deficit [shortfall of income against expenditure] 34 57 115 138 153 209f

Demand, market [the amount of particular goods and services which buyers are collectively prepared to acquire at certain prices - see market] 14 33 35f 42ff 49 60 95 108 122 146 169 177 206f

Democracy [a form of government in which power is exercised by the people through their freely elected representatives] 8 13 29 38 41 46 53-56 60 65ff 72 79 83 86 88 90-94 101 104 109 112 115f 118 120 123ff 132 143 154 159 163 165 171ff 176f 179f 183 186 189f 194 196 199-205 209-219

Democratic socialism [a Marxist system which has been modified in the direction of a market economy and democratic institutions] 20f 24 68 81 108f 115-126 158 167 200f

Deng Xiaoping [Chinese leader after Mao] 83 115

Dependency / dependency theory [theory which attributes Third World misery to domination by rich countries] 40 47 60 84 134 137f 143 150 208

Depletion of resources [using up limited resources which cannot be replenished] 1 4 42 192 205 238

Devolution of power [delegation of the tasks of the state to subordinate or regional bodies] 116

Dialectic [two seemingly contradictory statements which have to be combined to express the full truth; two sides of the same coin / philosophical principle in Marxism, taken from the philosophy of Hegel, which says that a proposition (thesis) produces its opposite (antithesis) and the conflict between the two is resolved in a higher proposition (synthesis)] 12 22 70 72 74-78 86 89 93 159 163f 168 170 183 190 225ff

Dialogue between religions 223 230ff 240

Diamat [dialectical materialism - the Marxist philosophy which believes (a) that economic conditions and processes determine social structures and collective consciousness rather than the other way round and (b) that such processes evolve in a dialectical fashion in history] 74

Dictatorship [the institutional capacity to exercise absolute authority] 54 80 86f 165f 180 198f 202 219

Dictatorship of the proletariat [second last stage of history in Marxist philosophy in which the Communist Party exercises absolute authority on behalf of the worker class to prepare for the classless society] 20 76 79f 86f 91f 104 108 166 179 226

Dignity 6 37 44 48f 55 57 60 65f 84 86f 161-164 174 176f 180f 183 190 193 214 225 226ff 231 237

Discrepancies between rich and poor 3f 7f 10 13f

Fascism [an ideology which combines nationalistic ambitions with totalitarian powers of the state] 2 55 68 91f 177 187 200 227 231

Fetishism [fetish = a magical charm; term used by Marxists for attaching transcendent qualities to material things] 40 73

Feudalism [a social system with an aristocracy at the top, followed by successive social classes] 5 19 28 48 75 178

Feuerbach, Ludwig (1804-72) [radical thinker who believed that religion was an abstraction from experience and a projection of unattainable wishes] 70f

Fiscal [pertaining to state finance] 112

Flexibility [a quality making an entity able to adapt to changing situations] 8 46 49 69 72 90 98 102 113 123 141 144 145 150 151 155 158 178 187 238

Force [use of strength or power] 3f 15 28 36f 41 46 52 61 64 76f 80ff 87f 93 97 99 101 119 123 133 136 149 155 164 179 180 190 197 202f 205 227

Free enterprise [a system in which individuals and groups are free to develop their gifts and initiatives for private benefit = market economy] 3 20f 24 32 36 37 40 45-48 55f 63 64 83 97 101 108 109 115 121 124 126 145 148 151 160 168 197

Free trade [trade uninhibited by government regulations and interventions] 34 83 139 148f 151 - see also liberalisation

Freedom [autonomy, self-determination; the power to make one's own choices] 1 7 15 20 22 2430 33 36f 38-41 44 46-49 55ff 61f 65 67 86 87f 90f 100f 108-112 115-120 123 125 132 154 161-183 186 190 197-204 226-231 234 237

French Revolution [1789-1799; overthrow of the Bourbon monarchy and the establishment of a republic in France] 53 69 161

Future orientation [gearing one's thoughts and activities towards goals and expectations] 1ff 5f 19 22f 31 36 74 82 84 90 93 114 121 150 158 16-163 169 186ff 193 203 205 218 234

Friedman, Milton [liberal (neo-classical) economist particularly influential in the Reagan-Thatcher era] 2 33

Gang of Four [leadership elite in China after Mao] 83

GATT [General Agreement on Tariffs and Trade] 33

Generational equity [fairness to those who are still to be born] 205 219

Germany 3 53ff 66 71f 80 94 96f 99 102 111 114f 119 140 144 181 214 227

Glasnost ["openness" - the principle during Gorbachev's reforms in the USSR which demanded freedom of speech, public accountability and access to information] 112

Global economy 1 18 33 41-44 79 97 102 104 113f 121 150f 153178 192 196 208 211 226

Globalisation [a process which draws the entire international community into one economic system] 1 151 196

Glossary [a list of concepts with their explanations] 2

Gorbachev, Mikhail (1931-) [Soviet leader who tried to reform Marxism-Leninism] 61 81 88 100 120-125 127

Governability [the condition of a social system where rulers are able to control and direct the situation] 198-202

Great economic debate [the discussion on alternative economic systems and ideologies] 1ff 8 17 19 22ff 33 46 65 85 159 179 183

Gross domestic product per capita (GDP pc) [total output of a country within its borders divided by the number of its citizens] 44 112 117

Growth of population [increase in the numbers of people within a given geographic area] 1 9 10 238

Growth of the economy [increase in the production of goods and services within a country as a whole] - see Economic growth

Hedonism [philosophy which ascribes ultimate value to human pleasure] 31 230

Hegel, Georg Friedrich (1770-1831) [German idealist philosopher, teacher of Marx] 70 74 86 104 226

Hegemony [leadership of a state within a group] 83 104

Hellenism [late ancient Greek philosophy which believed the spirit to be distinct from, and superior to matter] 234

Hierarchy [a social system constructed in the form of a pyramid with an elite at the top followed by dependent layers of status and com-

16 20 23f 35 40-44 46 52f 55ff 60 66f 77 82f 85 102 104 108 112 126 160 166 176 194 202 206 213

Distribution [allocation of available resources, income, or products] 9 21 23 40 44 49 52 58f 100 110 117 125 136f 171 173 175 178 186 194f 197 204f 218f

Dogma [system of inflexible doctrines] 46 71 102 121 123 150 151 156

Dubcek [Czechoslovakian leader during the "Prague Spring"] 94 118f 120 125

Eastern Bloc [the cooperative network linking the Soviet Union with its satellites] 96 99 101

Ecology / environment [considerations concerning the health of the natural environment] 1 4f 9f 15ff 30 108 111 160 162f 173f 181 191ff 197 202f 205f 208 218 223

Economic growth [a steady increase in the production of goods and services in an economy] 1 3f 9-13 16 22 24 30 34 42 44 47 49 52 63 80 83 92 101f 110 112 114f 117 122 125 132 142 144 146f 149 151 153 156 168 181f 192 195 205f

Education [acquiring general or specific knowledge by instruction, training, or study] 13 16 30 34 43 46 59 66 69 82 90f 98 110 113f 134 138f 142 145ff 151 154 187 190 192f 204 208 210 213f

Efficiency [the quality of a productive process operating in the best possible way to achieve the desired results] 6 8 12 31 34 38 45 49 57 61ff 67 75 88f 95 99 109 111 114 133 137 143 149 154 163 169 176 209f 228

Egalitarian [description of a policy aimed at achieving equality in dignity and income] 21 52f 56 62 77 109 110 113 118 200

Elite [a group in society which is highly privileged in terms of influence, wealth or education] 8 10 13f 20 40 45f 74ff 81 83ff 88 91 105 108 112 114 134 138f 144f 155 166 171 178 183 198 201 203f 206 208 234f

Emotions [experience of the affective nature (as opposed to cognitive) such as joy, sorrow, hate, fear, love, etc.] 5 159 182 189 232 234

Empiricism (empirical) [the assumption that reality is restricted to what can be registered by sense perception or experiment] 5 31 47 78 160f 188 226 230 232

Engels, Friedrich (1820-1895) [friend of Marx and co-author of the Communist Manifesto]

39 53f 68 70ff 76 78ff 90 104

England 53 71 104

Entropy [disorder or "chaos" due to the universal process in which energy concentrations are dissipated] 162

Entrepreneur [person or group taking business initiatives for profit] 21 30ff 37f 47 83 109 137 139 142 144 150 153 193 195 209 231

Environment [the natural context on which human life depends] - see ecology, pollution

Equalisation policy [policy aimed at ensuring equality of dignity, income, or opportunity for all people] 17 110 117 122 145 153 155

Equality of opportunity 7 15 21 29 58f 64 101 109 110 153 166 172 176 192 195 196

Equality [a situation where all people have the same power and opportunity in society] 20 22 24 28 47 52f 57f 66f 77 86 102 108f 111 117f 125 133 151 153 161-170 172 176f 182 183 195-204 - see also equity

Equity [something that is fair and just] 3f 7 22 23 52 56 84 86 102 113f 126 142 145 149 151 154 156 158 171 180 194ff 205 218f - see also equality

Ethiopia 56 83 96f

Ethnic tensions [state of hostility between two or more cultural groups] 21 43f 49 79 92f 97 118 195 227 230 232

Euro-Communism [mild form of Marxist socialism operating in the context of European multi-party democracies] 68 83

Evolution [the process in which simple forms develop into more complex forms] 16 28 48 54 59 66 70 90 104 132 166 234

Export-orientation [focus of production on goods for sale outside the country] 3f 22 24 131 139 140ff 146f 150f 155

Extraction [making natural resources available] 9 23

Fabian Society 54

Factors of production [elements needed in the productive process, such as natural resources, labour, capital, etc] 14f 23 31f 34 49 58 91 95 113 122 177 183 212 214 219

Family values [see also Ujamaa] 42 61 132-136 139 141 145-150 153 156 173 175 177 192 195f 235

Fanaticism [an attitude which pursues its goals blindly irrespective of the costs] 85 90 104 154 232

petence] 28 61 98 173f 180 198 201 204 211

Histomat [Historical materialism - the Marxist philosophy which maintains that historical developments in the economic structure of society determine institutions and collective thinking] 74

History in Marxist philosophy 71-77 84-87 89 104 226

History of capitalism 28-30 44 48f 55 73 75f 84f

History of Marxism 69-72 78-83 93f 96 103 115-125

History of socialism 52-57 - see also History of Marxism

History of Taiwan 22 24 45 142ff

History of Tanzania 131f 134 141

History [the sequence of past events as interpreted by humans]

Human autonomy [ability of the individual to act independent of higher authorities] 86 89 104 175 228

Human nature 37 39 46 61 70 73 88 165 189 227 - see also anthropology

Human resources [human abilities which enhance the productive process] 195 - see also Labour, Entrepreneur, Education, Training

Humanism [a school of thought with a strong concern for human dignity] 57 78 86f 89 103 161f 164 223 227 230 233

Humanitarian [pertaining to the attempt of alleviating human suffering] 31 228

Hungary 55 101f 105 125

Idealism [philosophical school which believes in the primacy of human thought over social structures] 70 84 103f 124

Ideology [a system of assumptions and arguments, often designed to direct, legitimise or conceal the pursuit of collective interests] 1ff 5f 8 17ff 23 28 38 40f 44 48 56 65 68 74f 79ff 83ff 90-95 96ff 101 105 113l 120f 123-126 136 141 143 147 149 151 153 155 158-162 173 176 178 181ff 186f 189 192f 223-227 220 232 240

IMF [International Monetary Fund; international financial organisation established to help member countries finance balance-of-payments deficits by granting temporary loans] 3 16 33f 97 132 137 139

Immanent needs [needs in the realms of life which are accessible to human understanding and control; compare with transcendent needs] 235 237

Immanentist [one whose belief system is confined to things which are accessible to human understanding and control] 78

Imperialism [a policy designed to extend the sphere of influence or dominance of a nation] 6 11 28f 43f 56 75 79f 93f 105 230 232

Import substitution [a policy of industrialisation which emphasises manufacturing of those articles locally which were previously imported] 140 146f 150f 155

Incentive [a reward which motivates people to take initiatives or work harder] 13 16 31 48 61 136 154 167 176 183 205

Individualism [an attitude which assumes that the interests of the individual are more important than communal or social concerns] 31 196

Industrial capitalism [stage in the history of economic development in which manufacturing with machines became the primary means to generate wealth] 19 29 48 75

Industrial democracy [a system in which the workers participate in the decision making processes of a firm] 177 207-209 211 218

Industrial relations [the relation between workers and management] 74 186 211-218

Industrial revolution [transformation of the British economy to the factory system of production] 19 29 53 69 76 104 161 207

Inequality, causes and effects - see Discrepancies between rich and poor

Inflation [significant increase in prices] 29 33 43 92 110 113 118 137 139 143 151 176 207

Information as factor in development 19 30 42 98 111 119 178 189f 209 213 216 218

Infrastructure [the external requisits of a productive process, such as energy, water, transport, credit facilities, communication networks, etc.] 16 32 98 110 136 151 193 210 217

Initiative [the courage of beginning something new in spite of the risks involved] 7 13 15ff 20f 30 32 37f 45 47ff 52 57f 61f 64 67 76 81 85 87f 95 98 100 104 108f 116 122 124 137 139 140f 148 153-156 158 161ff 177 187 195 205 209 215 217 228

Innovation [the design and implementation of better tools and procedures] 111f 179 209 217

Interactive learning [gaining skills and experiences through participation in co-operative projects] 13 16 189

Interests [benefits which individuals or groups strive for] 1 5f 8 13 17 23 31-34 36 41 44f 49 56ff 60f 73 75f 80 84 86 88 90ff 94f 97 101 105 108 111 114 118 122f 131 143 145f 149 151 160f 163ff 167 169-173 176 179 180 183 187 190 194 199 201ff 205f 212 215 217 219 224 226 228f 232 235 238 239 240

Internalisation [the psychological process in which assumptions or values are made one's own to such an extent that they become "second nature"] 12 101 160 1791 180 195 203 205

International Monetary Fund - see IMF

Intervention - see state intervention

Invisible hand [Adam Smith's expression for the mechanism by which individual selfishness works for the common good] 31

Japan 4 33 35 55 99 142 144f 147ff 153 155 176 208 213

Jubilee [Jewish institution according to which freedom and inheritance had to be restored after 49 years] 175

Justice [conforming to generally accepted standards of right and wrong and their expression in law] 5f 15 30 46 53 55 69f 72f 84f 89f 92 102 104f 114 127 161 170f 194f 225 239

Kenya 57 131 134 138 148

Keynes, John Maynard (1883-1946) [a British economist who advocated state intervention to regularise a wildly oscillating capitalist economy in the 1930s] 29 33 210

Kingdom of God - see Age to come 225 233 239

Khrushchev, Nikita [Soviet leader] 81 88 119

Kuomintang [ruling party on the Chinese mainland which was defeated by the Communists and fled to Taiwan in 1949] 142 144

Labour theory of value [Marxist perception that the value of a product is determined by the amount of human work invested in its production] 95 105

Labour value [value of effort invested to produce a commodity, as opposed to utility value] - see Labour theory of value

Labour [a factor of production constituted by the investment of human energy] 14 16 28 30 32 34f 38 40 42 43 47 58 63-66 73 76ff 80f 95 105 112 125 143 145f 150 153 155 178 193 195 206-209 212f 215ff 229 231

Labour-intensive production [a mode of production in which labour is dominant in relation to capital] 29 81 145f 153 206 208

Laissez faire [literally, "let (them) do"; liberal slogan demanding that the state keep its hands off the economy] 29 166

Land reform [equitable redistribution of land] 145 153

Lean and clean administration 151 177 209f 219

Left-wing [leaning towards socialism] 4 138 189

Legitimacy / legitimate [the quality of a regime, system or policy which is accepted by the people affected by it] 6 17 69 80 111 124 145 149 151 153f 165 171 177 189ff 193 212 218 224f 229 237

Legitimation [the attempt to make interests, institutions, regimes, systems or policies seem metaphysically or morally valid] 6 10 23 29f 44 71 74f 78 84 87 91 94 120 123 147 153f 176 181 193 204 226ff 229f 232 235

Lenin, Wladimir Iljitch (1870-1924) [founder of Marxism-Leninism and first leader of the communist state in the Soviet Union] 53 68 79ff 91 104 120 123

Liberalism / liberal / liberalise [a philosophy which believes in the freedom of individuals and groups from interference by the state or other external authorities] 2f 6f 13f 20 28-48 52-55 57 64f 69 83 86ff 94 96 101f 115 121 122 124f 139 143 148f 151 158f 161-182 187 192 194 202 213 224f 227-230 238

Liberation [to be set free, as from bondage or oppression] 15 30 54 56 84 86f 89 92 131 154f 190 235

Limits to growth [the perception that the industrial economy and the population cannot grow indefinitely on a limited planet without destroying the natural resources on which they depend] 42 150 181f 204 - see also Growth of population, Economic growth

Linkages 205 217

Little Red Book [booklet containing sayings of Mao recited daily by Chinese in a ritual manner during the time of Mao] 82

Loaded franchise [an election process in which people with a higher status possess greater voting powers] 214f

Luxuries [goods and services enjoyed over and above the ordinary necessities and comforts of life]

Management [the decision making body that organises an enterprise] 9 16 40ff 57 65 81 100 114 140 192 205f 219

Mandate [the authority to act on behalf of somebody] 60 123 159 177 179 190 199 201 203 210 211f 219 228 229 239 - see democracy

Mao Zedong (or Mao Tse-tung) [communist leader who founded, and ruled over, Red China] 54 66 68f 81-83 88

Maoism [Chinese version of Marxism-Leninism designed by Mao Zedong] 54 68 81 83 104

Marginal productivity [the additional output gained from an additional unit of input] 34f 95 215

Marginalisation [the process by which certain groups are pushed out of the formal economy] 1 4f 9 13f 30 42 95 102 141 145 153 168 178f 200 202 206ff 211 215

Marginal utility [the additional use derived from the last unit invested or spent] 2 104 115 125 142

Market / marketing [the economic realm in which the interaction between supply and demand determines prices and quantities] 1ff 13f 16f 20 22 33-36 42 46 75f 79 91 96 99ff 111f 114 116 135ff 140 141-151 153ff 166 176 194 196 206-209 211f see also Demand

Market economy 2f 13f 20ff 32 35f 39ff 43f 49 59 60f 63 65 83 91 97f 101 108ff 115ff 122 124ff 139f 149 167 169 176f 206f - see also Capitalism, Liberalism, Free trade

Market demand - see Demand

Market mechanism [the mechanism which determines prices and quantities of commodities and services traded at the point where supply meets demand in a particular situation] 35 44 63 108 110 139 206 - see also Supply, Demand, Market, Market Economy

Marshall Plan [the plan for aiding European nations to recover economically after World War II, proposed by US Secretary of State George Marshall] 80

Marx, Karl (1818-83) [founder of Marxist philosophy and the Marxist movement] 29 39f 53f 63 68-71 72f 76 79 83f 86 90 94 102 104 169 181

Marxism / Marxist [an ideology based on the philosophy of Marx which believes that a classless society can and will be achieved through a revolution of the worker class] 3f 20f 24 28 38 41 49 53ff 60 68-71 73-78 78-8 84-95 96-103 104f 115 117 125 127 132 160ff 165f 170f 175-179 181 206 225f 229f

Marxism-Leninism [the official ideology of the Soviet Union and its satellites in communist times, built on the works of Marx and Engels and consolidated by Lenin] 1ff 4f 8 19-24 30 38 46 53-56 58 66 68-107 108f 115-120 121ff 125f 149 158 160 166 172 176 181 183 200 204f 214 227f

Mastery [control of one's life and one's world] 37 61 86 173f 226 228 235 237

Materialism [philosophy which ascribes ultimate reality to matter or to material interests] 71 74 79 120 147 196

Maximisation of profit / utility / pleasure [gaining the most material benefit or satisfaction from the least input or cost] 13 16 88 112 151 162f 188 228

Means [anything used to achieve an objective] 9 11 29 31f 41 44 47 54 57 59f 64f 69 73f 77f 85-89 94 96 109f 113 121 127 137 176 151 158 162 165 169 171ff 175 181 194f 200 203 205 216 226f 231f 238

Means and ends [the ethical question whether a good goal justifies evil ways of attaining it, or whether the means must correspond with the good end pursued] 5 14 86-89 176

Means of production - see Factors of production

Mercantilism [a system in which the state sets up barriers against imports and furthers exports to bolster the wealth of the nation] 5 29 48

Metaphysics [a set of assumptions and deductions which underlies a particular view of reality but which cannot be empirically verified] 68 83 89f 103 132 226 228f 239

Middle class [the capitalist elite which originally took the place between the aristocracy and the lower classes in the feudal system] 29 - see also bourgeoisie

Mission [the perceived urge or calling to reach a goal which is beneficial to others] 42 225 233-240

Mixed economy [an economy which includes both a strong private, and a strong public sector] 4 7 59 161

Mobility [the movement of people from a lower social status to a higher one and vice versa] 30 147 229f

Modest [being frugal] 7 85 141 144 151

Modernity [world-view based on emancipation, utility, science, and technology] 13 17 101 223f 228 230

Monetarism [an economic theory and policy designed to overcome stagnation and inflation by regulating the supply of money in the economy and determining interest rates] 33

Monetary policy [guidelines concerning control of the flow of money in society] 32 98 144 - see also monetarism

Money [a circulating medium of exchange] 33 36 40f 43 45 61 73 113f 137 139f 144f 172f 206 210

Monopoly [the capacity of a single supplier to dominate the market] 40 94 166 175f

Morale [a mood of courage and hope] 100

Motivation [the inner urge to achieve certain goals] 8 12f 37 46 49 61 63 67 82 85 89 103 120 154 163f 170 176 203 206 209 217 228f 238

Mozambique 56 83 94 96f

Multinational corporations [large enterprises with interlinked components located in various countries] 12 40 65 114 146 151

Mwalimu ["teacher", title of President Nyerere of Tanzania] 132

Nationalisation [the transfer of the productive assets of an enterprise to the ownership and control of the state] 58f 133 137 140 145 149 155 179 183

Nationalism [an ideology which attaches ultimate value to the existence, prosperity and status of a national state] 44 70 92 97 118 232

Necessities 42 94 192 - see also basic needs

Needs [the requirements of an organism to survive and prosper] 6 7 9f 14 17 23 28 42 47 56-59 63 65f 73 77 84 86 100 113 117 132 134f 158 168 174 176f 181 187f 192-197 203 205f 208 210 218ff 224f 227 230 234f 237f

Neo-liberal economics [the school of thought proposing a return to minimal state intervention in the economy after the Keynesian school had advocated greater involvement of the state] 2 33

Neo-Marxism [also called Revisionism: a group of social philosophers who take the basic insights of Karl Marx as their point of departure without being straight-jacketed into Marxist orthodoxy] 14 55 68 83 94 102f

Newly Industrialising Countries [countries, mainly in South East Asia, which recently began to transform themselves successfully into industrial economies] 4 146 153 - see also Asian Tigers

Non-governmental organisation (NGO) [voluntary organisation engaged in welfare and development work] 48 114 190 204

North Atlantic Treaty Organisation (NATO) [Western defence pact initially directed against the Soviet bloc] 99

Nyerere, Julius [Tanzanian leader and father of Ujamaa African Socialism] 131-137

Oil crisis [shortage of petroleum products in the 1970s due to Arab oil embargo in 1973 and consequent pricing policies of OPEC] 135 155

Oligopoly [a group of suppliers small enough to dominate the market] 175f

One-party state [socialist effort to unite hostile factions and ethnic groups by limiting political activity to the governing party] 19 132f 149 202

Ontology [a reflection on reality which considers what things essentially are, not how they evolve or develop in time] 74

Oppression [an unjust and crippling exercise of authority or power] 30 44 46 49 55 71 77 82 84 86ff 92ff 103 108 115 154 164 176 180 189 201 225 237f

Optimal / Optimum [not the maximum of any entity but the most desirable or productive combination of different entities considering all costs and all benefits] 22 32 77 95 167 169 170 176 181 183 186 194 197 199 201 219

Optimism [a mood which expects a good future] 31 39 69 73f 149 181

Output [the quantity of a product emanating from an economic enterprise] 4 9 34 38f 101 113f 148

P factors [causes of inequality located in the economic peripheries] 12ff

Paradigm [a drastically simplified depiction of reality] 10 238

Parameters [a framework of factors deemed to be

constant within which variations of other factors may occur] 110 116 125 170

Parliamentary democracy [a system of government in which the legislature is composed of chosen representatives of various political parties and in which the executive is appointed by, and accountable to, these representatives] 72 93

Parasites [people who benefit from the efforts of others] 170

Participation [sharing in any collective activity] 21 86 88 109 111 116 120f 153 174 179 189 207 211 213ff 218f 228 236f 239

Participatory democracy [a system in which people participate in the actual decision making processes which affect their lives] 116 213ff 218

Paul [an author of New Testament documents] 235 237

Perestroika ["restructuring" - the reform process in the Soviet Union under Gorbachev] 88 115 118 120 124 127

Periphery - see centre and periphery

Personality cult [the elevation of a political leader to superhuman status] 91

Persuasion [making people change their minds]

Petit bourgeoisie [owners of small private enterprises in Marxist thought] 56 87 190 204 225

Pietism [a spiritualised form of the Christian faith characterised by strong personal attachments to Christ and an other-worldly concept of salvation] 71

Pluralism [a situation in which various convictions coexist peacefully in society] 121 180 190 223f 230 231 232

Policy [a formulated programme of political action] 22 29 32f 53 55 85 95 108 117 131ff 136 139 144f 147 149f 155 204-211

Polit-Buro [executive body of the Communist Party] 80 92

Pollution [the introduction of foreign substances into an ecological system which are detrimental to its natural condition] 1 4 42 47 143 181 191 205f

Popular wisdom [a set of common beliefs and values based on tradition and experience] 81 143 147 158 186 232f

Population growth - see Growth of population

Poverty [a situation where needs are higher than income] 3f 8-10 14 23 38ff 42f 52 56f 59 63

67 70 82 124 133 160 174 192 193f 235

Power abuse [misuse of the ability to control and determine one's social and natural environment] 9 13 15 24 41 87 94 119 151 159 161 166 171f 174-177 181 194 210f

Power concentration 20 30 36 40 46f 49 76 91 108 110f 159 167 170 175 180f 200f 209 - see also Centre

Power distribution 173 178 186 197-202 204 219

Powerlessness 85 174f 195 198 200 202f 205 211 239 - see also Periphery

Pragmatism [an attitude geared to practical ways of achieving goals rather than to theoretical principles] 6 8 37 98 103 121 132 135 143 147 150 154 158 164 177 186-188 218 228

Prague Spring [an attempt to reform Marxism-Leninism in Czechoslovakia] 94 119f

Praxis [the expression of a conviction or commitment in the practical conduct of life] 78f 81 87 89 90 120

Price control 16 93 110 136 139 149

Price [the amount of money exchanged for a unit of a commodity] 16 29 35 50 49 98 117 122 135 139f 143 154 - see also Price control and Market mechanism

Private sector [the part of the national economy which is in private hands, as opposed to the public sector] 33f 62f 210

Private enterprise [a system in which individuals and groups are allowed to develop initiatives for their own benefit] - see Free enterprise

Private ownership [a system in which factors of production are owned by individuals or groups rather than collectives or the state] 12 30ff 37 39f 49 53 59 110f 152 171 173ff 177f 183 212 216

Production [the generation of goods and services] 7 11f 14-17 24 28f 32 34ff 38 40-43 46 49 52 57f 73 77 95 90 111 134f137 139 143 146ff 151f 154 178 181f 193ff 201 205-208 216 218 226

Productivity / productive [the relation between output and input which expresses the access of the former over the latter] 7 20 23f 31 34f 38 45f 48f 52 62 66 95 109 111- 114 117f 125 177 181 207 211 213 215 228

Productive capacity [the existing potential to

produce] 1 11 23f 29 30 38 43 63 75 134 192 195 206f 212

Profit / profitability [the surplus of output over cost] 13 16 31 34 36 39 42ff 49 57 60 63f 66 73 88 108 112 117 122 132 151 161-165 188 203 210ff 216 219 228

Profit maximisation - see Maximisation of profit

Profit motive - see Maximisation

Progress [development toward a goal or toward a higher level] 11 13 16f 19 28f 31 39 57 69 84 87 99 109 114 135f 138f 140f 146f 150-153 169 181 192 208

Proletariat [the worker class in Marxist philosophy] 20 69 72 75f 79 86 87 92 97 104 108 136 179 226

Property [the realm over which a person or group has exclusive rights] 20 37 86 122 145 165 171-178 183 193 212 - see also Private ownership

Property and public office 171-178

Protection [safeguard against harm or interference] 7 31 62 80 110f 145 150 152 160 165 171-175 186 203 209f 215 219

Protestant Ethic [the norms of frugality and hard work found in Puritanism which, according to Max Weber, were instrumental in the rise of capital accumulation in early capitalism] 29 229

Psalm 82 238

Public necessities [goods and services necessary for the proper functioning of society as a whole] 14 38 42 192 211 213 228

Public services - see Social services

Radical [going to the roots; extreme]

Ranks 197ff

Rank and file [ordinary members or citizens] 92 203

Rationalism [philosophical approach which subjects reality to human reason] 31

Rational [following the demands of reason; in economics: behaviour which leads to profit or utility maximisation] 17 39 47 49 60 72f 78 89 143 151 159 169 176 187 228 230 232

Rationale [the reasoning behind an action or institution] 12 28 42 81 111 186 239

Rationalisation [ideological: the concealment or justification of true motives by means of ostensibly good arguments] - see also Ideology 52 160 176 189; [technical: cutting

down an unwieldy organisation to necessary constituents and functions] 216

Re-education 82

Reaganomics [the neo-liberal economic policy applied by President Reagan in the US] 2 23f

Recession [a situation in which production and consumption are involved in a downward spiral] 32 42f 96 112 135 140 207 210 217 219

Reconstruction 2 33 84 87 90 96 152 168 169 180 204 227 229 234

Recycling [the repeated use of scarce materials] 16 205

Red Guards [youth formations used by Mao during the "cultural revolution" in China] 81

Religion 40 52 70f 73f 82 118 188 223-239

Retrenchment [the laying off of workers] 32 62 216 219 - see also Unemployment

Revisionism [revised and adapted forms of Marxist philosophy and social analysis] - see Neo-Marxism 54f 68 72 83 90 94 102 226

Revolution from above [radical change brought about by those in power] 119 121 123 132

Revolutionary [person or group actively engaged in a revolutionary struggle] 64 97 104 168f 203 230

Revolution [radical change of social and mental structures and processes] 13 19 20 29 53ff 64 104 109 112 119 132 192 203 226 229 232

Ricardo, David (1772-1832) [classical pre-Marxian economist] 71

Russia 38 53 64 78f 93 101 124f - see also Soviet Union

Sandinista [left-wing party in Nicaragua] 54 97

Satellites [states dependent on a dominant state] 55 81 88 102 104

Scientific socialism [the self-appraisal of Marxism-Leninism claiming to be entirely scientific] 71 78 132

Secularism [world-view which rejects a transcendent or religious dimension of reality] 31 71 86f 89 161 171 223ff 227 229f 239f

Self-determination [being in charge of one's life] 30 60 87f 121 173f

Self-interest 17 31 44f 61 86 143 163f 190 206 224 226 229 232 239 - see also Interest

self-reliance [the ability to depend upon one's own powers and resources] 22 37 47 82 131 133ff 137 141 150

Selfishness [concerned only with one's own individual or collective interests] 31 37 39 42 44 46 49 61 64f 88 108 114 132 163ff 170 183 187 196 209 218 228

Service to community 33 39 57 73 82 86f 117 132 134 150 163f 170 190 229

Services sector [group of agencies engaged in carrying out necessary tasks, rather than producing material goods] 9 35ff 46 48f 57 61 95 100 110 113f 116 133 139 164 193 207 209f

Shalom [Hebrew for "peace", that is, the state of comprehensive wellbeing in peace with God, community and nature] 233

Sharing production rather than consumption 195 211

Shining Path [revolutionary movement in Peru] 21 97

Siberia [remote Eastern part of the Soviet Union] 93

Sinfulness [the discrepancy between what humanity is and what it ought to be] 235f.

Sisal [a fibrous plant used for making rope, rugs, etc.] 131 135 140 154

Smith, Adam (1723-90) [the classical economist of the liberal school] 29 31 33 71

Social benefits 98 100 113 - see also welfare

Social contract [a written or unwritten agreement between various social partners to their mutual benefit] 153 202 204 213

Social democracy [a capitalist system which has been modified in the direction of social concerns] 3 19 20f 24 29 54 64 66 102 108-115 117 125 126 149 158 157 200 202

Social engineering [the organisation of a society with technical means] 5 85 87 104 162

Social justice - see justice] 55 69f 84f 102 104f 170 225

Social market economy 21 109 - see social democracy

Social securities [institutional rights to health services, unemployment benefits and pensions in cases of need] 19 21 29 34 47 53 57 59 62 109-114 121 126 167f

Social services [tasks the fulfilment of which is necessary to achieve the well-being of society] 48 110f 113f 116 133 139 210

Socialisation [in sociology: the integration of individuals into social processes] 13; in economics: transfer of productive assets from private owners to a collective] 58 175 - see also Nationalisation

Socialism with a human face [an abortive attempt to reform Marxism-Leninism in Czeckoslovakia] - see Prague Spring

Socialism [a system in which the economic process it geared to the welfare of the society as a whole rather than that of private individuals] 1-8 17 20ff 24 28ff 38 41 45-49 52-67 68-106 108-128 131 141 148 150 158-183 200f 206 212 214 226 238

South Africa 44 94 96f 117 132 141 145 202 213 225

South East Asia 3f 47 53 141ff - see also Asian tigers

Sovereignty [full control over one's own affairs] 31 36f 49 86 174

Soviet Union / USSR 21 23 37f 53-56 62 64 68 79-83 85 88 91-94 96f 99-105 115 117ff 120-124 125 127 181

Soviets [local decision making councils in the former Soviet Union, already established before the communist take over] / leadership of the Soviet Union

Specialisation [concentration of activity on particular fields of expertise and experience] 177 188f

Stagflation [the combination of inflation and stagnation (or recession) of the economy] 33 43

Stagnation [a process which is coming to a halt] 13 33 139 206f

Stalin [Soviet dictator] / Stalinism [a dictatorial form of government in Marxist-Leninist states] 54f 68f 80f 89ff 104 119f

State capitalism [a system in which the accumulation of capital is conducted by the state, rather than the private sector] 38 64 80

State enterprise [a system in which economic activities are undertaken by the state, rather than the private sector] 33 98 210 - see also Nationalisation

State intervention [a policy where the state attempts to control the economy, rather than leaving it to its own devices] 29 32f 49 58 110 145 149 158 161 165f 177

State ownership 116 122 - see also Nationalisation, Socialism

Status quo [the condition obtaining at present] 72 76 78 84 203

Strike [the decision of employees to lay down their tools to press their demands] 32 61 146 203 215-218 219

Structural Adjustment Programme [a set of economic policies promulgated by the IMF and the World Bank to overcome economic stagnation and deterioration in Third World countries] 3 16 34 132 137 139

Structural mechanisms [once organised in a certain way, social institutions tend to operate according to their own inherent principles, for instance the accumulation of invested capital or technological advance] 12f 16 24 41 108 166

Subsidiarity [ethical norm according to which higher bodies should not do what can be done by lower bodies] 122 208f

Subsistence economy [an economy in which people produce what they need for their own consumption rather than for an outside market] 19 28 52 75 131 135f 138 140 177

Sufficiency [a situation where one's income covers one's needs] 7 16 23 86 89 139f 147 169 17 177 192f 205 218

Superstructure [a Marxist term denoting social structures and collective consciousness which are derived from the "base" of economic processes] 74 - see Materialism

Supply [the amount of particular goods and services which people are collectively prepared to sell for particular prices - see market] 14 28 32f 35 44 46f 49 60 63 100 108 122 147 149 169 175 177 195 197 206 - see also Demand

Surplus [the excess of production over consumption] 32 43 63f 100 117 136 171

Surplus capacity 38 135 143 207

Surplus value [difference between what workers produce and their wages] 76

Sweden 3 21 33 66 109 111f 152

Taiwan 2 22 24 45 131 141-153 158 195

Talent [a specific capacity to do something well] 62 67

Tamed market [a market in which distorted interactions of supply and demand are restored to greater balance] 206 219

TANU [Tanganyika African National Union - ruling party in Tanzania under Nyerere] 133 138

Tanzania 2 20 22 24 56 131-141 148-153 155

Taxation 16 36 45f 62 110 112 143 149 193 205f 208 210

Technocratic [dominated or determined by technicians and technology] 144

Technology [a set of human made tools to enhance production] 6 9 14 16 19 29-32 38 47f 73ff 77 81 84 96 98f 101 122 143 150 168f 179 181 188f 207f 228

Teleological ethics [an ethics which is based on goals or outcomes of an action, rather than rules or laws] 77 169

Thatcherism [the neo-liberal economic policy applied by Prime Minister Margaret Thatcher in the United Kingdom] 2 23 34

Theology [the academic study of faith in God] 8 68 70 89 168 223 227 229 233-2398

Third World [the group of less developed countries as opposed to the industrialised countries in the West and in the East; also called the "South" as opposed to the "North"] 2ff 10 15 19-22 24 28 33f 47 56 66 68 83 85 92 96f 99 102 114 127 131 138 141 148f 154f 158 162 200 204 - see also Periphery

Threshold theory [at the point where a priority need is being satisfied other needs gain in prominence] 167

Threshold 143 151 162 167 180 200

Throughput [the flow of material and energy from the resource base over production and consumption to waste] 42 66 205

Tiananman Square [square in Peking where a student led revolt was crushed in 1989] 83 115

Tito, Marshall (1892-1980) [Yugoslavian leader who developed democratic socialism in this country] 21 115 118

Totalitarianism [a regime which attempts to control and determine all dimensions of life, including the cultural and spiritual] 2 20 54f 68f 78 80 87-91 102 104 108f 123 163 231

Trade-off [more of one implies less of another] 109 127 151 166 183 195 205

Tradition [a set of symbolic narratives, assumptions, values, norms and procedures handed over from one generation to another] 5 17 30 40 56 72 93 103 120f 145 147f 158 160f 169 171 174 189 205 223 227f 229 235 239

Traditionalism [world-view based on historical, social and religious authorities] 13 17 19f 22 28 30 48 52 56 66 82 101 114 132f 136 138 141 144f 150 154 175 177 223f 230

Training 13 30 38 46 58f 110f 114 134 145f 151f 193ff 208f 211

Transcendent [going beyond specified certain

limits, especially going beyond the boundaries of empirical experience] 70 86 223-231 233 235 237

Transcendent needs [spiritual needs arising in the context of immanent needs, that is, the needs for meaning, right of existence and authority] 235 237

Trotzky Leon 1879-1940 revisionist Marxist theorist who fell into disfavour with the Soviet Communist Party

Truth [validity of a proposition] 2 5f 39 41 49 64 94 119 122 159 12 188 190 226 231

Truth claims [propositions which are believed to be valid and which demand commitment] 230-233

Ujamaa ["familihood" - name for the type of African Socialism applied in Tanzania under President Nyerere] 56 131 134- 141 149 154

Underdevelopment 9 56 64 149 212

United States / US 2 4 33f 41 65 96f 99 115 121 147 150

USSR - see Soviet Union

Utilitarianism [philosophy which focuses on the utility of objects and acts as means to achieve material ends] 31

Utility value [the value a product has for the consumer as opposed to labour value] 31 36 73 108 112 163 188 228

Utopia [a vision of reality which motivates transformative action] 17 53 58 93 126 166 175 225

Value added [increase in the worth of a resource or commodity through economic activity] 149 215

Value, economic [worth of commodity as measured against some specified standard such as money or labour] 73 76 95 105 142 149 171 215

Values and norms [values are cultural traits which people believe to be worth upholding; norms are rules believed to be binding] 2 5-8 12 17 22ff 30 39 48 57 117 124 133f 141 158-183 186f 190 196 204 224 230ff 233 239

Villagisation [policy to move rural peoples into villages so as to provide services and collectivise agricultural production in Tanzania] 133 135f 140 154

Vision [the intuitive imagination of reality as it ought to be (and could become in the future) which gives direction to one's attitudes and actions] 57f 71 77 84 90 103 123 125 132 159 164 181 187ff 203 211 218 224f 227f 233 236f 239

Von Hayek, Friedrich [liberal economist] 2 33

Warsaw Pact [the defence agreement between the Soviet Union and its East European satellites] 81 99 117 119

Wealth of Nations [title of a classic book on economics by Adam Smith] 29

Weber, Max [sociologist who proposed the theory of the "Protestant Ethic"] 29 229

Welfare [policies to achieve the satisfaction of basic needs, especially by the state, for instance medical aid, unemployment benefits and pensions] 2ff 57 62f 65 67 98 101 111ff 117 139 145 152 155 193 196 200f

Welfare capitalism [capitalist system in which the needs of marginalised sections of the population are addressed] 21 109-115

Work / worker / work force 4 17 28-32 34 36-43 46f 53f 57 60ff 64-67 69 71 73 75ff 79 81f 88 91 95 97 100 110 116ff 122f 125 133f 142 146f 150ff 171f 175 178ff 195 207 212-217 - see also labour

Worker aristocracy [part of the work force which attained greater privileges than others such as stable jobs and high incomes] 178f 216

Worker self-management [the management of a firm by workers or their representatives] 116

World Bank [International Bank for Reconstruction and Development, established in 1944 by the United Nations] 3 33f 132 135 137 139

Yeltsin, Boris [Russian reformer, later president, who attempted to liberalise the former socialist economy] 124

Young tigers - see Asian tigers

Yugoslavia 21 92ff 109 115-118 126

Zanzibar 35 131

Zimbabwe 56 97 136 138 141